CW00828078

The Martial Arts Teacher 2

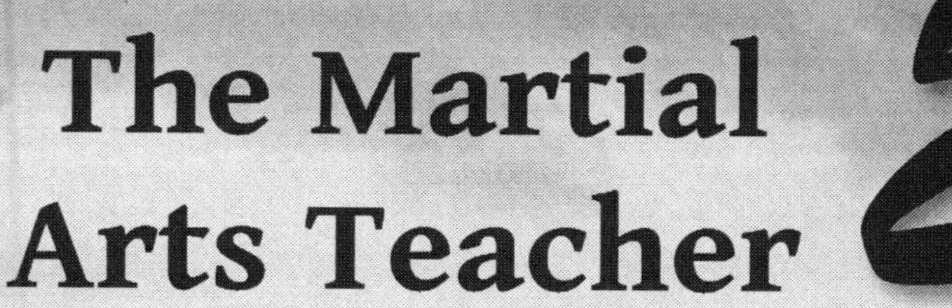

A Practical Guide to a Noble Way

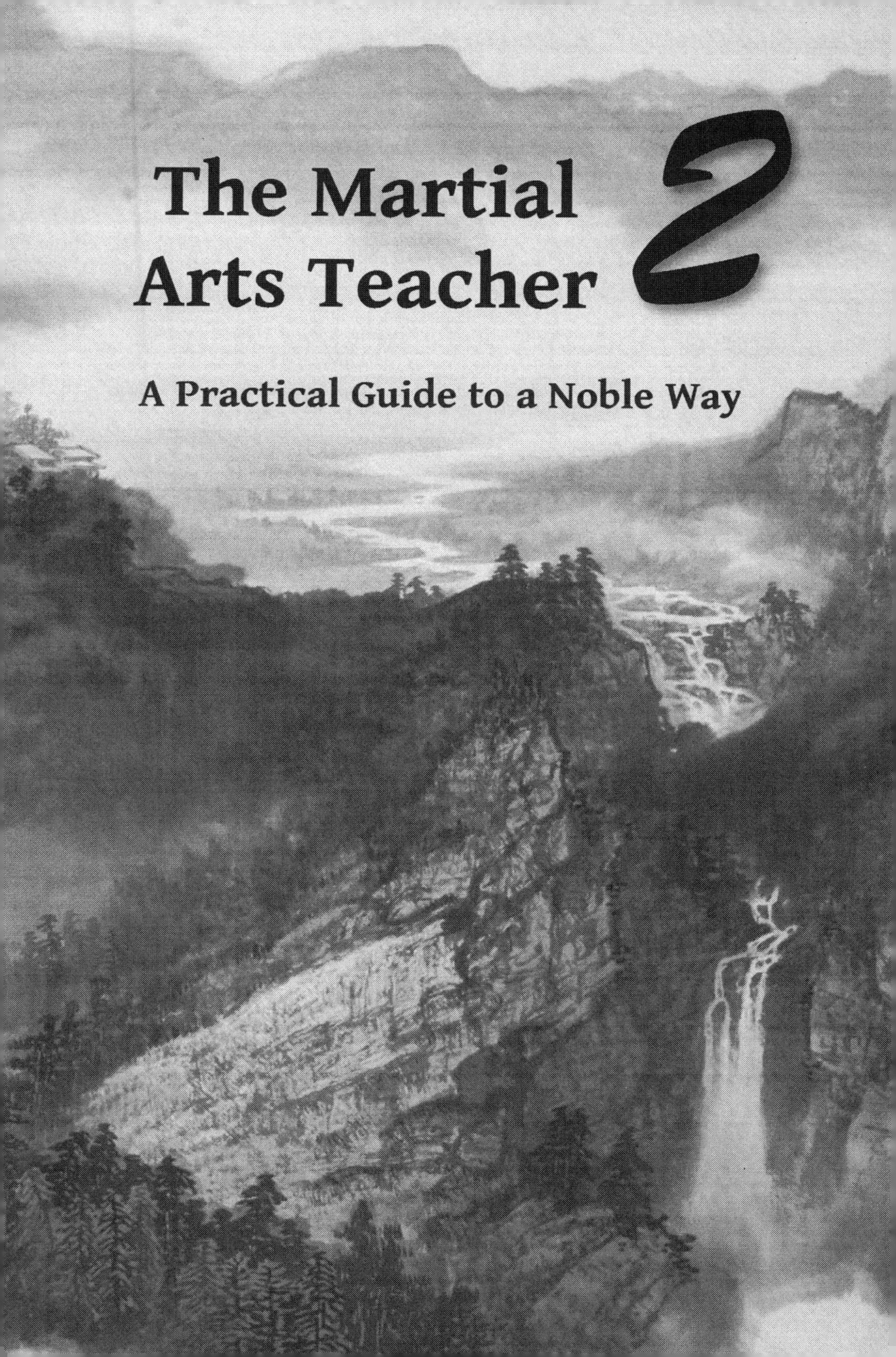

"One repays a teacher badly,
if one always remains
nothing but a pupil."

— Friedrich Nietzsche

Acknowledgements

Firstly, I would like to thank my Shifu **Nitzan Oren** and his teacher, my Shigong, late master **Zhou Jingxuan**. My first book was dedicated to these two gentlemen. My technical and philosophical understanding of the martial arts as a whole is entirely due to their sincere efforts and kind teachings. My cherished friend and former teacher too, **Itzik Cohen** Sensei, has been and still is to me a true mentor in the art of teaching. His positive influence upon me has been long-lasting.

I would also like to thank five individuals, friends who are dear to my heart, for aiding me by reviewing the manuscript of this work before it was published. These people are Shifu **James Tan**, Shifu **Ken Gullette**, Shifu **Gary Stier**, grand-master **Keith R. Kernspecht** and **Rick Matz**. The five abovementioned gentlemen, all experienced and veteran martial arts teachers and practitioners, helped ensure that this book was published in pristine condition.

Lastly, I would like to thank **Buzz Durkin** Sensei, a great man whom I have never met. His wonderful book, '*Success Is Waiting*', inspired me to write this publication which you are now reading. Wherein you have found my book to your liking, please refer to his work as well.

This book was written using the **Gentium** (Book Basic) font. This font is under free open-font license (created by the talented Victor Gaultney), and supported by SIL International.

This book is graciously dedicated to my Jook Lum Southern Mantis teacher, and friend, Sifu Sapir Tal. For many years now he has been of great inspiration to me as both a martial arts teacher and a human being.

Table of Contents

The Heart of the School

The Soul of the Teacher

10

The images above are anonymous illustrations of characters from the famous Chinese novel 'The Water Margin' 水滸傳.

About the Author

Shifu Jonathan Bluestein (LLB) is an accomplished scholar, martial arts teacher and author. He is the head of Blue Jade Martial Arts International. He has lived in several countries, visited dozens, was an infantryman, a police investigator, a translator and even hosted a short television spot in his youth.

Shifu Bluestein has trained extensively and taught the arts of Xing Yi Quan, Pigua Zhang, Jook Lum Southern Mantis and Bagua Zhang. An eclectic researcher and intellectual, he has published 5 books and over 50 articles, on topics ranging from socio-economic theories, Jungian Psychology, Oriental histories and traditional Chinese martial arts. His English-language books include: **'Research of Martial Arts'** (2014CE), **'The Martial Arts Teacher'** (2017CE Edition 1, 2020CE Edition 2), **'Prosperism'** (2020CE), **'Exceptional Ideas About Humanity'** (2021CE) and **'Chinese Medicine Can Heal You'** (2021CE). Several more books shall be published by him in the years 2021-2022CE. Shifu Bluestein's books and articles typically step outside the boundaries of accepted genres and norms, expressing ideas and concepts which other authors are afraid to discuss or even consider.

Striving to better martial arts literature in our time, Shifu Bluestein has been working tirelessly for years to deliver readers unique, useful, practical, and entertaining martial arts books. His works stand out with their novel approaches and exceptional interpretations for the traditional martial heritage of the Orient. Countless practitioners and teachers have thus far enjoyed these books, as is evident from the hundreds of positive reviews they have earned on Amazon-affiliated websites and elsewhere. For more information about Shifu Bluestein, his books and his teachings, please visit: www.bluejadesociety.com

Since the inception of the 21st century, there had been but a few dedicated martial artists who engaged in writing quality works about exceptional skills and unique abilities, as well as the related cultures, philosophies, morals and histories. Shifu Bluestein is one of these people. His mission is to share with the world the tremendous depth of knowledge found in the martial arts in order to benefit humanity. He believes that through sharing we can all grow together, and continue to successfully develop the martial arts for the generations to come. This important mission is perhaps even more crucial and meaningful in this generation, as knowledge handed down from our martial ancestors has been rapidly disintegrating, and people have been shaping their arts into forms of cheap entertainment and light amusement, forgetting their roots.

After the enormous success of his previous works, especially the international best-seller **Research of Martial Arts**, Shifu Bluestein opted to write a different type of book, intended for martial arts teachers. In this work he hopes to share advice and insights from his experiences in teaching the arts with those who have also chosen to carry forth such a monumental and important task.

Foreword

My name is Keith R. Kernspecht. I have been a student of the martial arts since the age of 5, and a teacher of them since my late teenage years.

A series of events had led me to the writing of this foreword. In the year 2000CE, I was honoured with the 10th master-grade title in Wing Tsun Kung Fu from the last disciple of late grand-master Yip Man. Following this event, I felt a need to investigate the internal Chinese styles, to become more complete in my training and teaching. Since the beginning of this century therefore, I have met, practiced and studied with nine of the most important internal masters of our time. All of these martial arts I researched were great, and of them I was especially fond of the Yi Quan of my friend, grand-master Yang Lin Sheng from Mongolia.
The grand-master whose style I liked most and ended up staying with was my dear friend Sam Chin. His Zhong Xin Dao (I Liq Chuan) system, based on Zen Buddhism and grounded in science and convincing logic, is exceptional.

My journey into the internal arts also included much scholarship, of course. In 2015CE I purchased Jonathan Bluestein's book, **'Research of Martial Arts'**, and was delighted to see that both my great friend Yang Lin Sheng and my internal arts mentor Sam Chin were listed in it.

Intrigued by many of the things that Jonathan wrote concerning internal styles, I reached out to him via e-mail. This was the beginning of a two-year correspondence, on the theory and practice of the internal arts, that led to him interviewing me for his forthcoming 2nd edition of that book, and culminated with my inviting Jonathan to join me in for a week in Pisa (Italy) together in August of 2017CE.

I felt honored when Jonathan asked me to be interviewed for his book, because while I had some experience in the external arts, the internal arts were a new research field and challenge for me. Here I followed the old maxime: Once you have attained mastership in one style, become a beginner again in another style.

From the first moment of our encounter in Pisa, Jonathan proved to be an authentic, engaged and dedicated individual and researcher. For several hours a day we conversed, shared, and touched hands; with Jonathan expounding his understanding and insights gleaned from the theory and practice of Xing Yi Quan, Jook Lum Southern Praying Mantis, and Pigua Zhang. Jonathan's openness and enthusiasm were undeniable.

Perhaps Jonathan chose me to write this foreword because I have been a teacher nearly as long as I have been a martial artist. The reason why I love teaching so much is because it is my way of learning: Pretending to teach martial arts to my students, I teach it to myself, while they listen to me and ask me questions that help me understand. Beside teaching martial arts I have always been a teacher of sorts: I taught languages and sports as a high-school teacher, in the University of Kiel I was a lecturer in the philosophical department, and since the late 1990s I have been a Professor for Sports Education for the State University of Plovdiv, Bulgaria.

The martial arts, I began teaching first with Oyama Karate, in 1963, to the German riot police. At the time I was a policeman myself. From 1967 I taught Karate, Ju Jutsu and Kobudo at my own Budo Club. In 1970 I began studying Wing Chun under Sifu Joseph Cheng in London, and later I was the first to introduce Yip Man's style to Germany. Since 1976CE our EWTO, the European Organization of WingTsun, has mainly been teaching the style of grand-master Leung Ting, and also grand-master Bill Newman's Escrima. The

EWTO proudly counts some 60,000 members among its ranks in Germany and most other countries in Europe. The only purely internal art we teach is Sam Chin's Way, Zhong Xin Dao, for which we now serve as the European umbrella organization.

Reading his latest book, **'The Martial Arts Teacher'**, I am impressed with what Jonathan is bringing to the table. He could even surprise a veritable Professor of Education with his ideas on teaching. Jonathan offers up real, definite opinions and advice, based upon his many years of training and teaching. He has walked the walk, and now he is sharing his experience with his readers.

This book is unique in that it covers a variety of subjects not usually discussed in a guide for teaching the martial arts, such as the delicate balance a teacher must strike between discipline and encouragement, managing personal relationships with students in and out of the classroom, establishing clear boundaries for various student interaction, mitigating contracts and payments, barter, ego, dealing with naysayers, asking for help, happiness, and the teacher's own personal development.
Of course, in his book he also talks of such topics as teaching methodology, curriculum design, cultivating a learning environment, practice time, student retention, teaching adults vs. children, as well as the role of testing and ranking.

He presents his views with passion and conviction, and you are left with the feeling that his experience has been hard-won. This is a forthright exposition of one man's experience and advice, dedicated to fellow teachers of the martial arts.
After reading this book you will feel that you have gotten to know Jonathan personally, that you had conversation with a close friend or mentor on the ins and outs of running

your own school. Not only has he shared his opinions, but he is also open to feedback.

For Jonathan the martial arts are not only a passion, not only a profession, but also a mission. Through his work he is seeking to elevate the current standard of martial arts literature and education. A worthy endeavor indeed! For me, the following quote best sums up Jonathan's approach:

"Be to your students the teacher whom you wish had been there for you."

One could not ask for anything more.

Today at the age of 72, I am able to both look back over at my nearly seven decades of training with a critical eye, and look forward with great excitement at the prospect of further development, for both myself and for martial arts as a whole. Less than half my age, Jonathan is a young and talented martial arts teacher, educator, and innovator with many years of development ahead of him. I look forward to seeing who he, both the person and the teacher, evolves into.

It is therefore with an open heart and great pleasure that I have written this foreword.

Dr. Keith R. Kernspecht

Prof. em. Plovdiv State University Education of Sports
10th Grade Wing Tsun Kung Fu (Leung Ting, Hong Kong)
8th Dan Kyokushin Allround Karate (Jon Bluming, Holland)

Kiel, Germany, October 2017CE.
Originally written for the first edition of The Martial Arts Teacher.

Introduction

Perhaps you have picked up this book so you can make more money from your martial arts teachings. Then it seems you have the wrong book in your hands. Surely, this book can aid in you becoming more financially successful. That is not the main point of it, though. This book is about helping you, a fellow colleague, be a better version of yourself, in both your professional sphere and as a human being. The world of martial arts is big enough for everybody. I want people such as yourself to be better. I want our entire society of martial artists, as a whole, to become better. This is not rooted in financial success, but in education.

Benjamin Franklin, in his excellent essay **'The Way to Wealth',** brought up the issue of people's complaint's over high taxation. He then commented wisely, that aside from that problem of high taxes, we are in fact "*taxed twice as much by our idleness, three times as much by our pride, and four times as much by our folly*". By so saying, Franklin was keenly observant that the greatest obstacles to financial achievements and accomplishments in one's life are usually not found in external causes, but in lack of cultivation of one's Self. Indeed, when our Ego is unruly, and we allow trifle matters and unworthy people to be rulers upon our emotional kingdom, then how can success be spoken of?
In line with this type of thinking, the book which is here before you shall focus on the art of Self-cultivation, the healthy maintenance of human relationships and the requirements for leading a prosperous community of industrious individuals; all of this, in light of the unique challenges and attributes of our distinguished profession, of the martial arts teacher.

Those of you who had already explored another book I have written, **'The Martial Arts Student'** (to be published in 2022CE), may notice that book and this one have a few chapters in common, featuring the same title. I urge you to nonetheless review these chapters once more, as their versions and overall message often differ between these two works of mine.

Unlike my well-known best-seller **Research of Martial Arts**, this book is mostly not heavy on science, history and theory. It is a light and easy read, meant to hone your skills quickly and do so within moments of reading each chapter. Every single part of this book is applicable to nearly all styles of martial arts and their teachings. In it you will find countless novel approaches and ideas which are not commonly discussed or addressed in other works – I guarantee you that.

This book is an honest conversation, from one martial arts teacher to another. Although it may appear like a monologue, I do urge you – talk to me through the text. Ask questions and debate what is written here. After all, much of this can affect your teachings, so you need to be sure that it will work well for you. I trust though that this book will serve you, the martial arts teacher, very well.

In the words of Mahatma Gandhi: Be the change you want to see in the world.

The Heart of the School

All Eyes on You

You are the greatest show in town. Yes, you! How is that possible? Well, do you know a movie people agree to see at the cinema several times a week, for a month? A restaurant someone is willing to attend a few times a month for 5 years? A musician whose performances fans would attend every day for a decade? Such examples hardly exist. Yet here you are, the martial arts teacher, giving the best show in town – the crowd keeps coming, on a regular basis, some of them for years on end – sometimes for as long as they can physically stand.

Here is, then, an idea to transform your outlook on what you and I do. Did you think this profession is about long-standing traditions of heroic warriors? A great service to the community? Maybe a unique and incredible way to move the body or a vehicle for spiritual awakening? Yes, for the both of us it might be so, and more. Eventually, long-term students will come to see these many aspects to the art, too. But through the eyes of most of your students, something else stands out before the rest right from the beginning – the fact that you are on a stage, and they are attending your show. You are a performing artist, and expected to entertain. Accept that reality, and your profession will change forever.

People need an inspiration. You are **it** – the rock star of their martial universe. Otherwise, they would have been studying with someone else. In this context, your presence, and that of your teachers, is what inspires the students to become the best they could be. They want you fresh. They want you at your peak, pushing the limits, yours and theirs. On the floor or atop the mattresses, you are the embodiment of an ideal, despite the students knowing that you are made of flesh and blood [1]. They chose you because they see in you a

[1] I cannot stress enough the importance of keeping students in check about the fact that their teacher is 'human' and not 'perfect' and 'flawless'. Repeating this sentence in front of

model for something they would have liked to become, or qualities they wish to imitate or borrow strength from.

Are you familiar with the situation in which a famous dancer has a headache, and therefore stays at home the day of the show? Or when a great theatre actor chooses to stop his act in the middle because he became emotionally upset about something or someone? The audience tends to get agitated about such behaviours. Even the fans are not always patient. Still, these people (dancers, actors, etc) are 'allowed' by the public to have their little dramas. That is, because for most who come enjoy their entertainment, they are not a personal 'ideal'. The martial arts teacher does not possess such a luxury. The reality of your realm dictates that you will most definitely deliver the goods, and do it so smoothly it would seem impossible. That is what is expected of you.

Being the role model for others, there is no room for poor decision-making in your life and teachings. Your students want strength and stamina – you cannot collapse from exhaustion before some of them because you slacked off in training for two weeks. Your students want happiness – you cannot come to class looking depressed. Your students want a moral compass – you cannot be seen acting immorally. Your students want vibrant health – you need to be so busy training hard, eating the right foods and sleeping well, that you would not even have time to get sick.
My former teacher **Itzik Cohen** Sensei, I never witnessed throwing trash on the street. My teacher Shifu Nitzan Oren, I never saw swearing and cursing in class. My teacher Sifu Sapir Tal gave up smoking because he could not bear little children noticing a person of his stature having this type of vice. None of us are without faults, but at least in front of our students, we should strive for perfection.

---

students often is helpful: "I am only human". As silly as it sounds, without humbling oneself to an extent, cult worship can be easy and quick to develop in martial arts schools.

To the martial arts teacher there are no 'bad days'. Confucius said (and many repeated): "*Find a job you love and you will never have to work another day in your life*". Those among you who feel burdened by 'work', necessarily have the wrong 'job', or need to change the way they do things. But regardless, even if you feel the onset of negativity or distress, your students cannot be allowed to know [2]. Wear that smile until you become it. 'Fake it 'till you make it', as they say. This is not hypocrisy – this is the striving for a completion of a mission more important than yourself.

Being a teacher, you know just as well as I do, that excellence in the martial arts is made of an accumulation of countless small moments of perseverance in time. That same devotion which earned you the right to instruct others needs to be applied to your performance on that teaching stage. There can be very little compromise about such matters. All eyes are on you, even when you think they are not looking. Do not fail those who have put faith in you. Their future is literally in your hands. Your actions will determine a lot in their lives, from their possible success with romantic partners and job interviews, to surviving serious illnesses and the onslaught of violent criminals. When the ground feels like quicksand and the sky weighs down like a mountain, keep this in mind:

You are the supporting pillar of this martial arts school. Those who in you see cracks, will scatter. From your core resonates a pulse and illuminates a light, attracting many from afar. Reach with your hand, touch with your smile. Ask and listen. Your time to ache and moan the troubles will come, later. In the meanwhile, you are the best show

---

[2] Eventually every school ought to develop a group of more dedicated students, some of whom are to be trusted by the teacher with personal issues and troubles. But as a general rule of thumb, the majority of your students should never know the full extent of problems which may exist in your personal life. Some say that "familiarity breeds contempt". While I tend to disagree in the context of martial arts, I do believe a strong familiarity with those who have not 'earned' a close-relationship status will cause issues which would later be hard to mend.

in town. Make them wish they could be there up with you, on that stage. Then point to them and call them by their name, one by one. Raise them to your position and let them feel, each and every one, that they matter – to you and to everyone else in that room. Remember that once upon a time, you too were a man lost in imagination, and then your own fantasy had manifested, with the aid of those who stood where you now stride. Be to your students the man whom you wish was there for you, when you needed a shining light to guide your lost ship at sea. Do this, and they will bring their friends next time. Do this long enough, and you will never have to play in front of an empty hall.

Merit, Equality and Leadership

What is the best philosophy, by which should we govern a martial arts school or organization? The great Goethe once wrote: **"You ask which form of government is the best? Whichever teaches us to govern ourselves"**. In my personal opinion and understanding, there is a surefire and traditional manner of applying this idea in teaching the martial arts. To apply Goethe's advice, a good school ought to be a **Meritocratic Egalitarian Dictatorship**. These big words have simple meanings, which are profoundly important for running a martial arts academy smoothly.

Meritocracy

This means a martial arts school is naturally and rightfully led by a small group of people who are the most knowledgeable and qualified to teach. In the beginning this is only the teacher, but as time progresses and hopefully with success in teaching, veteran students join the 'leading team'. The students need to understand that merit, and especially knowledge and ability to teach (not necessarily fighting ability), are what determines who gets more 'authority'. No one in the school is entitled to lead more than others based on race, gender, ethnicity, rank, amount of time spent training, friendships, politics, being someone's relative, etc. In martial arts, especially the traditional martial arts, Merit is what sets the tone. There are several reasons for making this clear to your students:

1. So those who hold superior or inferior social positions outside the martial arts school would not feel that such positions should affect the manner in which they are perceived inside the school. The martial arts school, by means of a meritocratic approach, encourages everyone to start anew and build themselves from the ground up.

2. So that people understand that those to be respected and listened to are those who worked harder and learned more than their peers.

3. In order for students to know and believe that within the school community anyone can become successful and respectable by his or her peers.

Despite the meritocratic approach, a teacher should instill in his students the sense that you can nonetheless learn from anyone – even a child, regardless of whether that person holds a teaching positions by merit. This is made clear to students when the teacher cares to state out loud when he had just realized something new or had an inspiration based on an interaction with a student. Another way is to note publicly when a student had managed to create and use a new and useful technique, which you have yet to teach him or that perhaps even you did not know. By doing such things the students understand that within each of them is the capacity to excel and become great. The teacher should also tell that to all students regularly, in group and private settings, that with time and effort they can aim high and reach higher.

Egalitarianism

A meritocracy only sets the tone with regard to those who ought to be looked up to and trusted with imparting knowledge. With anything else in the school, the approach is Egalitarian – meaning, in the context of martial arts, that everyone is required to meet the exact same standards of training, according to their level. Also, that all must carry the burden equally [3]. At any stage of training, the demands, challenges and testing procedures (if they exist) should be equal. No one can receive exemptions, unless he or she are physically or mentally challenged in some justifiable way.

In every class I try to make use of all students for demonstration of methods and techniques, so even though I personally have a preference for certain students, all feel I treat them equally [4]. Likewise, all tasks and chores are shared. Everyone cleans from time to time. The teacher cleans with the students. In my school there is a 70 year old multimillionaire who is the CEO of a large company. He sweeps the floor and washes the dishes alongside 18 year old kids. Every week one person is assigned on 'food duty', required to bring a bunch of healthy foods to be placed on a table and shared communally throughout the week. All take part in this duty. When there is a social gathering, I try to give most people some role in that event's organization, and aid them myself of course.

In the course of training and teaching, everything the students are required to physically undergo and suffer, you need to be able to do as well. The only exceptions perhaps are stretching capacity and fighting ability. There are always those who are naturally extremely flexible or who are too big and tough to be challenged even by their

---

[3] The teacher is the only person within the school who should be expected to work harder than everyone else, unless having grown ill or old.

[4] This is also important for the teacher. You need to challenge yourself to be able to demonstrate effectively each technique and method with any type of person and student.

teachers[5]. The teacher may not be the best at these, and that is alright, as long as he is striving and trying as hard or harder than anyone else in the school. With this in mind, do consider that a teacher who wants to have students who will eventually train 3 hours a day, will need to let the students know and demonstrate that he is training at least 3-4 hours a day himself.

When the students understand that they are treated equally and rightfully, then there will not arise any complaints or issues regarding discrimination. You should be aware that a sense of being discriminated against or being treated unfairly by the teacher or a fellow student is a very common reason people leave martial arts schools. Often they do not even bother to share such feelings with anyone, and one day they simply disappear. With a true egalitarian spirit however, that risk is reduced to a minimum and this phenomenon rarely if ever occurs.

Dictatorship

People come at a martial arts school with false notions about the right type of interaction with their teacher. Some mistakenly assume that having paid a person makes that man their servant or equal. Others think that a martial arts school is yet another venue for exercising democratic principles, and that they can take a vote on what they like and dislike. Both notions are misinformed and disastrous.

Wherein you live in a country belonging to 21st century 'Western Civilization', you are used to thinking that a 'leader' is someone who was democratically elected. Such is person is not necessarily a

---

[5] Those who expect a 5'7 (1.7m) teacher in his 70s to be able to fight toe to toe with an athlete student who is 6'5 (1.98m) and in his 20s, are delusional. Though exceptions abound, usually this is not possible. One should not be expected to be able to beat all of his students in a sparring match or a real fight. Neither would I say it is necessarily a must for the teacher to be sparring with his students regularly, or at all. Such things differ from school to school. The important point is that the teacher was capable of real fighting when younger, and that he can impart sincere knowledge of self-defense and combat to his students.

leader – he is in fact usually a follower. The elected representative is a follower of the majority view. He is a charismatic sheep, but alas, one selected from the herd. A true leader takes a stand and creates his own position of leadership, and a good leader does so through displaying virtue and being a model to others [6]. Thus, a good martial arts teacher is a benevolent dictator [7]. Only he can set the tone and determine the rules, while being attentive, empathic and considerate at all times, to the best of his ability under the circumstances.

There cannot arise a situation in which any student seeks to determine for you how to teach or how to operate the school. At best, polite suggestions for such things can be made, but only by trusted and veteran students and solely in private. Some people think that because they are men of knowledge or social standing in the world outside the school, they are entitled to tell you what do to. You need to respectfully put them in their proper place the first time they try this. You need to let them know that while you appreciate their feedback and positive intentions, the school etiquette demands that they behave differently.

There exists a very delicate balance here. On one hand, you want to encourage constructive criticism for the sake of improvement, and on the other hand too much of it, or stating things too bluntly, undermines your authority. You wish to let someone know their boundaries, but by doing so you may also insult them. The solution is to set the right tone for every discussion. For example: at the end of each class I encourage people to ask questions about today's practice. Any questions may be asked, but usually I would not allow them to ask freely. Instead I call them each by name, one by one, and ask: "Noam, any questions?"; "Gil, any questions?". Every student

---

[6] Confucius said: "To rule with virtue is like the North Star in its place, around which all other stars revolve, in homage". The Analects, chapter 2, verse 1.

[7] The martial arts teacher should be so (a dictator) **only** within the premises of the school and while teaching or interacting with students in an official capacity. He should be very careful not to exercise the same approach elsewhere or in different circumstances.

then gets special attention, but they also have to wait for their turn. Commonly as they begin talking, another student may be impatient and begin to speak out of order, commenting on what was said. I will often immediately shut that student and scold him lightly, asking him to wait patiently for his friend to finish. Then when the friend is finished, I do not neglect to eventually return and allow expression for what that student wanted to say, rewarding him for his patience.

The important point here is that you, and only you, are in control. No one may assume higher dominance than yours, or any dominance for that matter, without your explicit permission. Cursing, swearing or overt disrespect towards you or any other student for that matter should be met with immediate scolding and banishment – either to sit aside for a while, go home, or in extreme cases – throw that person out the school for good.

I still bitterly remember a few mistakes I had made when I first began teaching, when I was still too gentle in my role as a dictator. Once I had a male student who was about 18 years of age, quite immature. The class was stretching, and I with them, as that male student took note of another student, a woman a few years older than him. That woman was quite flexible, and the student complimented her politely about her flexibility. Then he asked that woman for permission to "further comment on something which may be a bit more controversial". The woman, flattered by the earlier comment and not sure what to do, told him to go ahead. That young fool then said that "her boyfriend must be a happy man" – obviously making a most inappropriate sexual remark. It was at that moment that I suddenly realized my failure to not stop that discussion from its onset. I scolded that student well in front of everybody, explaining how awful his words were. Later I also had a conversation with the female student and apologized to her for this ugly interaction, assuring her it would not happen again.

On my part, this was not the correct manner of action. I should have actually sent the guy straight home at that moment when he opened his mouth, and later demanded him to write an apology letter to the other student. But at the time as a young and less experienced teacher, I was cautious about making a big fuss and creating social uproar. I had never had to kick someone out of class at that point. I should not have hesitated. Beyond being nasty towards a fellow student and setting a bad example for everyone else, that student in his actions was also undermining my authority.

After that event transpired, I never allowed for similar things to happen ever again. Now I know better. Whenever I hear a student beginning to speak or even think out of line, I stop them right there. Sometimes a student will say: "*Shifu, may I ask something which may be a bit more controversial or not as polite?*". I answer: "*No! You may not!! Think about it several times over, and if you still wish to say it, then talk to me privately after class ends*".

Students who believe they know better than you are also a nuisance and cause social disharmony. On such students and their nature I have written more in this book, in the chapter called '**Martial Arts Students and the Middle Path**'.

While it is important to maintain the position of the undisputable leader of your student community, one also has to cultivate humility and modestly (to a degree), and imbue within the students the sense that outside the school premises you are an ordinary human being, just like them. You may carry a unique set of skills and abilities, and they should still respect you wherever you go and at all times, but they should also recognize your humanity [8].

One of the best ways to ensure this happens is to commonly tell stories of one's teachers and his respect for them, and make sure one continues to have teachers, for as long as possible. In Hebrew we say: "Every man needs a Rabbi"; meaning that each of us needs, for his sake and for that of how others see him, to have a higher authority to continue to guide and teach him. Showing sincere appreciation for others who are more skilled and knowledgeable than oneself, in words and actions, is a good way to demonstrate and prove that you do not consider yourself 'superior to everyone else'. Know that you can expect your students to treat you in the manner that you treat other people, and especially your teachers and superiors.

[8] "Confucius said: To rule with virtue is like the North Star in its place, around which all the other stars revolve, in homage". – The Analects, Chapter 2, Verse 1.

The Benevolent Ruler

The Analects is an ancient book, summarizing the teachings of Confucius[9]. This book – The Analects of Confucius, is very relevant to all leaders, martial arts teachers included. Chapter 2 of The Analects is titled 'To Rule' and is addressed to people who aspire to be benevolent leaders – of families, clans, villages, cities, states, and perhaps – of a martial arts school, too. Verse 20 of that chapter reads as follows:

Ji Kangzi (a student of Confucius) asked: "How can one foster respect and loyalty among the people, by means of encouragement (to be virtuous)? Confucius answered: Preside with dignity, and there is respect. With filial piety (towards parents, superiors and subordinates), and there is loyalty. Elevate those good and virtuous and teach the incapable, there is encouragement.

How fitting, timely and appropriate is this advice for us as well. Although the text is somewhat self-explanatory, I shall elaborate nonetheless to elucidate its meaning for those less familiar with Confucian thinking and Chinese culture.
To be effective leaders and successful teachers of the martial arts, is required of us to have the loyalty and respect of our students. To gain loyalty and respect, we need to use methods of encouragement rather than coercion, even if the end result we aim for, is having the students doing exactly what we want them to do.

Confucius explains that first and foremost, setting a personal example through a dignified bearing to one's character and

---

[9] You can read the entire book of The Analects in a few short hours. It contains 499 brief chapters. These small, bite-sized chapters are usually comprised of single paragraphs or a handful of sentences. The contents are things which Confucius said or taught to his disciples throughout his lifetime, covering broad subjects such as statesmanship, morality, leadership, psychology, sociology, military strategy, etiquette and proper use of language.

leadership, is what sets the tone for gaining the student's respect. [10] This means for instance, that the teacher cannot be observed by students meddling with trifles such as hateful bickering and unnecessary personal conflicts. He ought to show grace of character and consistency in the execution of his positive vision.

Then next in line of importance for effective leadership is maintaining noble and upright relationships between people of differing social status. The teacher should care for his students like father to children, and in being a child to his own parents and teachers, he ought to show that he cares for these people appropriately, also. Once the students see that the teacher caters wholeheartedly to these relationships as both people's superior and subordinate, then they will seek to imitate his good example. Through this, one earns the students' loyalty.

Finally, there is the question of how to encourage students to not stray from the path, and dedicate themselves more to one's teachings. This is always a very difficult thing to attain in this historical era of ours. In ancient times, when a teacher of worth was present and available, then his knowledge would have been far more appreciated. Today, information and instruction are so readily accessible, that the value of traditional teachers have diminished in the eyes of the common folks. Because of this, the teacher finds himself 'competing' for the student's attention and dedication with other social stimuli, often perceived to be more attractive.
Confucius offers a solution, by saying that we essentially ought to do two things: support and make a positive example of our best and most virtuous students, but also invest in teaching and helping those who are the least coordinated and of poorest skill or lowest understanding. When people observe through such behaviour, that we are fair, equitable and impartial, they will be encouraged to not stray from the path.
All of these important provisions and tasks, suggested to us by Confucius, are demanding, and require expertise and careful

---

[10] The ancient Romans had a proverb: "***Qualis rex, talis grex***" – As the King does, so do the people.

attention. This is especially true for the topic of what is called 'Encouragement' – how to elevate the better ones without bringing forth overt dominance and delusions of grandeur, and how to cultivate the needy and weak without damaging their fragility. We ought to follow the advice of Goethe: **"Correction does much, but encouragement does more"**. The many chapters in this book address such challenges and many others, and will no doubt provide you with the appropriate answers and solutions.

The Right Kind of Fear

When we are children, if we were educated properly, our parents held a power over us which had more psychological potency than physical threat. Assuming your parents did not hit you as a child, your reasons for being afraid of them were limited. Nonetheless, good education yields an awe of the parent regardless of the fact that he may not strike down the child. For in the mind of the immature being, the parent holds a position of power, authority, knowledge and skill which are thought of as supreme. Most young children take this for granted, rarely questioning the status of their parents, even when they defy them. They have the tendency to think of their fathers for instance, as 'most powerful' or 'smartest' among men, for it is their father who optimally teaches them all of the crucial physical skills required for understanding the world and surviving in it. Having limited exposure to other adults, they logically conceive that if their father can know so much, as compared to them, he must be extraordinary. Then, once more under optimal conditions, they have an immense awe of their father – the right kind of fear; an emotion driven by respect, which motivates them to aspire for greatness and act, rather than freeze in place and dwell upon their inability. To have students in awe of our position, then, is also appropriate for us as martial arts teachers. Allow me to elaborate.

I remember vividly one Friday afternoon, when I had a conversation with a veteran student of mine. The conversation took place a few years after I opened my first school. The student surprised me by saying, that he feels some of the other students were afraid of me. My initial reaction was a mild shock. Then, I became amused. I thought to myself, that this is silly. Normally I am a pretty amicable person, and the students have not even had the chance to see how terrible I could really be, as I appeared sometimes in my capacity as a police officer years earlier, when dealing with career criminals. But over the next few days I continued to ponder deeply this issue. My veteran student was cautious, suggesting this might not be a positive aspect to the atmosphere at our academy. Yet I came to realize, that what he was speaking of was not truly fear, but awe; and as you can already tell, the distinction between these two makes a world of a difference. Still, a thin line exists between causing the students to be fearful of you, and having respectful awe of you.

In my opinion and experience, these are some of the seemingly contradictory dualities which a martial arts teacher must embody, in order to carefully and successfully tread that thin line:

Everyone is safe, but also unsafe: On one hand, there should be an aura of personal security at the school – both for one's body and status. On the other hand, students should know that sometimes, they might need to take a good hit for the sake of demonstration, or to understand a technique, or to learn how to fight. Such is the physical side to it. As for status – a student should feel confident that he would not be easily lose face, be expelled for whatever reason, or be 'demoted' for any reason. But then, when there are students who cross some moral or behavioural lines, they need to be set straight, sometimes in public, or even let go of. The latter action I have only needed to undertake twice in my career, as I choose my students well. More of this shall be discussed later in the book.
So essentially, although the martial arts school should be a safe place most of the time, it is not a petting zoo. Students ought to be kept vigilant enough, so that they remain alert and in awe. It is good for one's status as a teacher, but also for them as martial artists.

You are predictable, but also unpredictable: It is of vital importance that a martial arts teacher arrives to class on time, every time, and does his best to cancel as few classes as possible. I have had several years during which I cancelled an average of 3 classes a year. Many of your habits, ideas, philosophies, teaching style, the curriculum you teach, etc, should be consistent. Being the pillar of the school, part of your strength from which the students borrow, is your consistency. I know a certain teacher of Wing Chun who taught at the same city where my first school was located. Over the years, dozens (!) of his former students called me, and many came to check out my classes. The reason was, for the most part, as they had told me, that this teacher had been inconsistent in many of his words and actions. Not lacking in skill or ability – only inconsistent in words and actions. That was enough to cause many students to leave and to damage his reputation. You do not wish to be like that man.

But then, an aura of unpredictability is essential as well. When the students cannot fully and completely anticipate your actions, both physical and strategic, then a part of you remains a mystery to them. This is a good thing, for then they yearn to understand that part of you which is 'hidden' and 'exciting'. Creating new plans for the school, both short and long term, but omitting to mention **some** of them until they are already well-developed, is a good thing to do. Also in class, surprising students is a useful skill to cultivate.
Once I was sparring with a student of mine, who was surprised when I gave him a light headbutt. He paused for a second and proclaimed: "Hey, I did not know we had that!". I replied: "There is no limit to what you can do in self-defense". While still in a state of psychological shock, I immediately grabbed him by his nipples and hair and pulled him to the ground (note – this choice of technique, few students can take well emotionally). The student did not expect that. He liked that element of surprise so much, it became a myth at the school. Some years later, he even grabbed me by the nipple once... and subsequently was punched in the face, as he should have continued to fight following this diversion. I did not anticipate his sneaky nipple attack however, and was very proud of him. Little surprises and maintaining the element of unpredictability, can do a lot of positive things for student culture and lore, cementing your status as a teacher.

Approachable, yet not approachable: My students know that they can approach me with any question. I make an effort to be patient, polite and forthcoming with their questions, about 99% of the time. But sometimes, a question may be so dumb, inappropriate or out of context, that a student may be reprimanded for even asking. It makes little sense for example, to ask about a romantic date while I explain something; or to make a false pretense of a question, which is actually a challenge to my authority, like: "Oh, but do you think this will work against such and such? Because I learned differently from my former teacher!"; or hypothetically, if a student were to publicly ask me how much money I was making teaching the martial arts. I do not take kindly to such questions, and they are met with a stricter, harsher and less welcoming tone than usual, putting the student in his place. The students understand therefore, that there exists the possibility to make some statements which would yield an unfavorable, even adverse reaction from me. Then, they have to think twice before they blurt something out. Teachers who fail at being like this, tend to lose control of their classes and student community over time. Their schools develop the free-for-all atmosphere of a fitness club, and can sustain neither tradition nor discipline.

A friend, but not a friend: This subject I have covered thoroughly in a later chapter titled **'From Customer to Friend'** (do not jump there just yet – read this book by the order of its chapters). Although one could only hope to have students who are 'friends', percentage-wise, very few of one's students should ever attain such a status. You should be a friend to your students in the sense that:

- You have a relationship of trust.
- You are not strangers to one-another.
- You genuinely care about their well-being.
- You are willing to listen to most of their problems.
- They can rely on you in times of need, to a degree.

But with those of them who have not proven themselves dramatically in very prominent ways through close relationships spanning many years, they should not be your friend in the sense of, for instance:

- Sharing intimate information about their sex lives.
- Discussing intimate stories about their families.
- Discussing financial investments with you.
- Inviting you to parties with their friends.
- Asking you overly personal questions.
- Etc.

Where and when is the line being crossed? I find that this is very culture-dependent, and changes from country to country. A minor but significant example: In the United States, I know that many people consider it a personal affair to be asking about someone's political inclinations. In Israel, such an inquiry is natural, commonplace and may be made even between complete strangers. Therefore, it would not be wise or accurate to attempt drawing the line for you. The bottom line is, that the great majority of students, especially those who have not proven their character for many years on end, should not feel comfortable in approaching you as a friend of theirs.

One of the main reasons for this, is that people find it exceedingly difficult to learn anything substantial from friends, as they tend to consider them as equals. The same is true in the relationship between parents and children. When highly specialized and elaborate gongfu is concerned, like playing a musical instrument, painting, sculpting, singing, etc – parents usually have more success outsourcing the instruction of their children to someone else, preferably a more distant family member, like a grandfather or an uncle. Then among friends, the situation is even more dire, as they could hardly even start to convince their buddies to begin to engage in that thing which specifically interests them. To make a student into a friend then, too early and not based on a very long and time-proven relationship, guarantees that the teaching will fail, which shall spell disaster for both parties involved.

Going back to the original opening paragraph – think once more of the father and the son. When do most sons stop learning effectively from their fathers, in modern cultures? It is at the time when they begin to lose their awe of them, and think of them as their equals – perhaps even friends. They make the mistake of thinking themselves to be 'safe' because they physically matured, supposedly not needing the protection and support of their father anymore. They fancy themselves to have some intellect and experience, allowing to supposedly anticipate their fathers, bringing about a sense of predictability. They challenge the father's authority and tire him, until he relents and becomes approachable at nearly all times, even when their questions and demands are excessive and inappropriate. In short – when all the rules listed in this chapter are transgressed.

Few are those who can carry forth any teaching under such circumstances (as the father who fails), and indeed, when this happens, a lot of parents are inclined to say that "they have by now given up on trying to discipline and enlighten their children, who are older and therefore should care for their own continuing education". Then, ironically, such parents may send these children to us, the martial arts teachers, to be taught the things which were missing at home. Whether these children be 8, 18 or 55 – be for them the mentor that their parents never could. Strike into them the right kind of fear – the blissful awe of a true and worthy authority figure, and witness as progress and harmony shall arise naturally.

Mencius said [11] :

"When one by force subdues men, they do not submit to him in heart. They submit, because their strength is not adequate to resist.

When one subdues men by virtue, in their hearts' core they are pleased, and sincerely submit, as was the case with the seventy disciples in their submission to Confucius".

[11] The Book of Mencius, Chapter 3, Gong Sun Chou 1, part 3. Mencius was an intellectual descendent of Confucius who extrapolated on the teachings of his forebearer.

Not a Business, But a Community

After I opened my first martial arts school, throughout the first years, I was getting a lot of advice from whoever was willing. It seemed that most people were focused on the business side of things. They were talking of 'leads', 'selling', 'marketing', 'contracts', 'customers', 'going with the market demands', etc. These were also strongly emphasized in articles and books I read at the time about how to operate a martial arts school. But over the years I have come to believe and support the notion that running a proper and upright martial arts school – a serious traditional school, is in fact more about understanding people, than finance. More about a community, than a typical 'business'. Then let me speak of communities.

In the 1990s, British anthropologist and neuroscientist professor Robin Dunbar discovered an old truth about mankind. He realized through his research that humans are best thriving in groups of up to 150 individuals. This number, 150, was henceforth known as **'Dunbar's Number'**. What happens is that most of us find it difficult to maintain over 150 meaningful relationships. In modern times we may have hundreds, at times thousands of so-called friends, family members, acquaintances and colleagues. But normally only a handful of these interactions make for significant relationships. The rest never achieve any noteworthy depth of interaction. There are several reasons for this, among them:

- Humans are programmed to live in modest tribes, which tend to break up into smaller tribes if they become too large.

- We cannot physically handle the personal details of hundreds or thousands of people or to care for them emotionally with sincerity.

☯ On the purely technical level, we do not have enough time for so many serious relationships.

So we are limited to a core group of roughly 150 important individuals in our lives, and most of us will do with less than that (in fact we prefer and tend to thrive with less). Put a bunch of humans in a group larger than about 150, and they begin to require centralized organization and specialized laws to maintain order among them. Our core '150 clique' is also mutually supportive and protective, providing us with communal backing and a sense of security.
Modern society confuses us in that respect. We want and need to have the sense of belonging to a tribe which is small, but which tribe ought we belong to – that of our family? The tribe of our nation state? The tribe of our favourite sports team and its fan club? Perhaps the tribe which is the company we work for? Or the tribe of childhood friends?... Even one's religious congregation often numbers over 150 individuals. Oh, so many tribes to choose from, and altogether too many people to interact with. We find ourselves torn between our obligations to various tribes and intimidated by their mass. This problem causes a lot of stress to modern humans, who desperately seek to belong, but feel tiny and insignificant in the ranks of huge tribes, with too many members to them. Some even go to extreme measures in order to stand out, and use violence to create a personal statement, life-meaning and goals for themselves (as particularly evident among sports fans and even terrorists). Many do such things as means of desperation, in light of their inability to deal with the sense of being 'no one' and having no meaning in this world, as they exist in huge groups without a social role or a purpose assigned to them. This is unlike in small communities of people which are self-sustainable, where there are no idle hands – everyone has a job and a role to play, because then everyone in the tribe are co-dependent.

The martial arts school can be for a person the cure and solution for this social illness of feeling isolated and insignificant in a world made of enormous tribes. Your martial arts school could and should provide people with a proper sense of community which is friendly, welcoming, mutually-supportive and small enough in scale to not threaten the innate limited capacity expressed in Dunbar's Number [12]. The martial arts school is a world in and of its own, with the main agenda hopefully being the personal and communal growth of the people who are its members. Therefore, the martial arts school is a non-political entity, and is not supposed to clash in its objectives with other 'tribes' a person may belong to.

When professor Dunbar came up with his number of 150, he had in mind ancient human tribes who lived in groups of roughly this size, and would split when they grew too large. Dunbar hypothesized that in such tribes, much of the time would have been dedicated to 'social grooming'. In nature, this type of activity involves the animals helping each other stay healthy and maintain a close bond from the actions of grooming, cleaning, petting, massage, hugging and other such positive interactions. The martial arts school is not that different. As long as the general atmosphere within the school is not too competitive, we martial artists do actually engage in something very much akin to social grooming, as we come into close and intimate physical contact for the sake of forming strong bonds and helping each other stay healthy. That is, at least, one of the goals of a worthy martial arts school.

But beyond a community and perhaps through it, the martial arts school delivers a promise perhaps even greater and more important to its members – a sense of personal meaning for each of them. You see, outside the confines of religion, people seldom speak of

---

[12] Even a martial arts school which goes beyond 150 members typically divides into several compartments or sections, usually based on rank, seniority or both. Thus, each part of the school is a miniature community in its own right, within the bigger tribal union. Still, under optimal social conditions, the martial arts school should also not number hundreds of people.

meaning anymore. Instead they speak of money, schooling, politics, television, status, sports and the likes of these empty subjects. But provide a person with meaning and that person has hope for himself and for the world. With meaning and hope, that person can be happy, and make others happy as well. Then the world becomes a better place. Meaning in turn is commonly created through two things: work and direction. One has to do some challenging work. Then this work needs a serious direction – a worthy purpose. Martial Arts fit here quite nicely. They make people work hard, for a purpose. This gives them meaning, which also builds hope, in turn leading to happiness and a better existence for us all.

Some teachers focus too much on the training, and forget to talk with the students at length of the many good reasons for doing all that hard work. You would be surprised – the students forget about the reasons to work hard. They need weekly reminders. Then there are teachers who talk much of the purpose but do not make their students work as hard as they should. This is also not a complete solution. One needs both the hard work and the right direction (purpose and reasons) to get to creating a meaning for oneself. So make sure that in your classes you have both.
Then in conversing with your students, relate these aspects to that community you all share. Because all of that hard work and the many words expressing the purpose of it are not worth a damn if the students cannot act humanely and honorably towards each-other, and in their interaction with other human beings. Do make that connection. Lead your students to realize that improving their moral character is in this school directly related to their ability to develop martial prowess. But do not just say it – do it! Demonstrate to them how those who will not make an effort to improve themselves, you will not offer them the opportunity to grow as martial artists. This would be making the connection for them artificially, of course. But over time, or so one would hope, they would naturally come to see for themselves why the building of character through a belonging to a community is a vital asset in one's life and personal development.

Consider how most modern human 'tribes' all share the same issue, of their members being so different to one-another. What makes a tribe 'work'? That would be a shared sense of culture and history. These exactly are the strengths of your martial arts school. You want your students to be heavily invested in a local culture which is unique to your school or organization, and remember well their shared history. Let me break this down into the two components:

Shared culture: This includes the very type of practice that you do and that is unique to your school; the special language you use for the martial arts taught in the school; things which excite the senses like incense, food, music or tea you drink before class; private jokes among school members; your etiquette as has been developed traditionally in your school and the morals you all believe in; the technical and philosophical discussions which relate to your particular martial arts practice; proverbs and anecdotes commonly spoken by school members; etc. All of these should be encouraged.

Shared history: This pertains to the sense of having been through a lot together through months, years and decades of training. This is expressed by repeating historical stories, tales, allegories and such in written form, but more so in verbal discussion. Oral storytelling of the school's best and most beloved histories should be something you and veteran students do frequently. The value of these for communal well-being is truly priceless. Also important are stories of one's own teachers and those of those teachers who came before him, too. It is good to provide the historical context of the society, country and times these men lived through, to ensure the students could relate.

You should actively pursue the creation of a shared culture and history within the school. Actions as such should take place on a weekly basis. Every week should contain at least several things or elements which strengthen the shared culture, and a few moments of reliving shared history.
Even a person who attends a class at your school for the first time can sense when there are strong foundations in shared culture and history. In fact, such people are more attuned to these because they are outsides and take nothing in the school for granted. Sometimes they can be frightened by the overwhelming amount of new input. However, if you and the students make a sincere effort to share with them that culture and history, and go out of your way to be welcoming and forthcoming, then from a liability in presentation this turns into an advantage. For the newcomer will realize he or she are now invited to be a part of something deep and meaningful, and this is what a lot of people covet and wish they had in their personal lives.

You may have noticed that nothing here in this discussion of the school community has even the slightest connection to money. There are many books about running a martial arts school, and a lot of good information in them concerning the handling of finance, advertising, marketing, accounting, legal issues, and the likes of these. Yet all of these subjects, while **very important** to learn and master, bow in insignificance and are trivial when compared with the need for a vigorous, supporting and unified student community. For a school with a malfunctioning community full of unworthy individuals is like a person sickly and without a soul, and such a man is damned regardless of how much money, lawyers or accountants he has. Therefore, you need to augment your mindset. Your school may be a business, but it is first and foremost a community. Take care of that community as a foremost priority, and watch the school thrive.

Less is More

Let me have a short discussion with you, from one martial arts teacher to another, about the nature of what we do.

I personally am not fond of referring to martial arts as a 'business', even if teaching them is one's means of making a living. But were we to equate the martial arts to some type of business, then what type of business would they be? I say we are in the '**customer preservation business**'. This is true for everyone who teach the martial arts. The goal of the martial arts teacher, whoever he or she are, is to gain a certain amount of students, and then keep them for as long as possible or required. This is the reality even if one does not charge a fee for his teaching, and certainly if one needs to earn money from this dignified profession.

Now, consider this graph I had plotted below. The bottom row counts how many years a student has been studying at a given traditional martial arts school. The left column attempts to assess the odds of that student never leaving the school, based on how many years he or she have been practicing there. Meaning, that this graph presents the assumption, that the longer someone has been our student, the more likely he is to stay with us to the end.

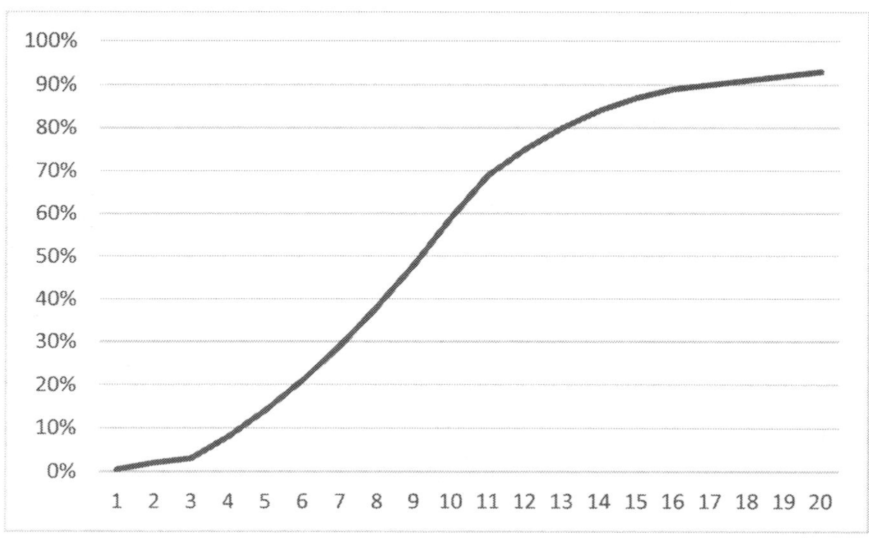

Yes, I know... this is a rough estimate and a broad generalization. But bear with me here for a moment. Some truths are nearly universal.
For instance, a person whose experience at the school is less than 1 year's time, has very little chance of forever remaining a part of the school. Certainly, less than 1%. Why? Because if you operate a 'commercial' school, less than 1 in 100 people who come to their first class, or came by for a month or two , will end up staying with you for a few years. This is quite rare. Such a statistic is a fact.
Then at the other extreme, those with over 20 years' experience under you, are probably over 90% sure to stick around until either the school closes, or one of you can no longer practice or teach. It would take some unusual circumstances, for a 20-25 year veteran to suddenly stop coming to class, or otherwise quit an organization.
The big jump, in my opinion, as can be seen in the graph, typically occurs around the 4-7 year mark, or 5.5 years on average. Please view the graph again, and look at this period, between 4-7 years. It is at roughly around that period, that a dedicated student will become more involved with training, and often rise more sharply in rank also. In my own experience and that of my colleagues, if you can get students past the 4-7 year mark, then retaining them by your side would later be much easier. Such students become more invested in the school and its teachings. The notion of cutting themselves off from such habits and community, is now more difficult to entertain in their minds. They are on a roll, and you – the teacher – can pick up that momentum of theirs and run with it.

Here is another interesting and related anecdote - you need to keep the students more than you need new students. Why? Because martial arts are always a small business venture. With 100 students, a martial arts teacher will likely earn a very good income. With 300 students, you can even become a rich man (not that this should be the goal of teaching martial arts!). Even the largest schools very rarely surpass 300 students, and I dare say that any single school (not an organization) with over 350-400 students is no longer really in the business of 'teaching' – it is in the business of making money, or at the least, that of management (for most schools, that's true even when they cross the 200 student line). But in any case, the number of 'customers' one needs in this 'business' is rather small. Many will even suffice with as little as 10-70 students. A martial arts teacher who can get the number of students he aims for, and can keep them attending classes for years, does not need any new students coming, at least not on a regular basis. Therefore, mastery of the ability to conserve the student population will resolve almost completely the 'business side' of the teaching. A teacher who can keep all or most students, essentially has nothing to worry about but the teaching and the practice – this is what we all want.

There are people 'in our business', who are opposed to that point of view, of student preservation being more important than student intake. These teachers believe, that it is more important to keep new students coming in. One of the arguments they make, is that it is bad to have a school with "too many black belts". What do they mean? Suppose that you have a school with 30 students, but of them, 20 have been practicing your martial art for over ten years. This means you have many more veterans than you do beginners. The typical 'business-savvy advice', is that this is a negative situation, because new students would find it difficult to relate to those who are advanced. Indeed, what happens is that schools with a large percentage of advanced students, seldom go past the 30 student count.

But is the fault here really with the numbers and ranks? The real problem is actually a social one. The teacher is the main instigator of this sort of problem. It is a teacher who allowed the formation of 'cliques' within his school, and snobbish, unfriendly behaviour on part of more advanced students. In a healthy student community, the more advanced students there are, the better! In Japan for instance, where people are culturally taught to persevere more so than in Western nations, we see how this situation can be an advantage. The majority of veteran Judo, Kendo and Aikido schools in Japan have many more veteran students, than they do beginners. Still, the novice newcomers feel welcome, embraced and blessed by the terrific accumulation of experience and skill surrounding them. It is only in an unhealthy student community, with low moral standards, that beginner students feel intimidated, afraid or even threatened, by having many advanced practitioners around them.

All of this is to say, that less is more. You do not need countless students to come in your door. You need less students coming, so you can focus more on those you already have. Then, once their character and skill have been solidified, their experience and merit could be leveraged, to gradually have more. That is because, the graph I showed you before only demonstrates one reality – the likelihood of a student persisting over time. But in fact, this may be strengthened and quickened, if the student can be made to feel, that he or she are a part of something greater than themselves, and have many people to cater for their needs.

Remember!

You are the first teacher of the school – the headmaster. But every student you earn, can be a teacher in his own right. That is especially true, of those who have been by your side for a good number of years. When a person steps into a room full of aspiring tyrants, he flees. But a room packed with benevolent mentors, is something else entirely.

The Secret Flow to Teaching Martial Arts

There is a hidden mechanism in the teaching of martial arts, which pervades everywhere regardless of school and style. This mechanism, I believe, is the key component in achieving success in the teaching of these arts, and retaining students over time. I will now tell you all about it, and how to put it to practice with ease.

As far as student retention goes, there are unfortunately many things we cannot control. Disease, marriage, having children, injuries outside the school, moving far away, army service, major changes in personality and more... all of these will take students away from us over the years, and there is little we can do about it. But there is the one thing we *can* control, and that is **the quality and the nature of our teaching.** Here we can do something, just one single thing, to make a tremendous improvement in our ability to keep the students with us. That one thing is no less an art than the other skills we practice and teach. That thing is the application of **Flow Theory** to the teaching of our martial arts. Bear with me now for a single paragraph, while I explain to you what this theory is, so you can later understand how it may be easily applied to teaching the martial arts.

Flow is a popular concept in modern psychology. It was 'discovered' by Mihaly Csikszentmihalyi, who was the first to make a science out of this common human phenomenon (no, his family name was not typed by my cat walking on the keyboard). Everyone who had ever lived have experienced flow many times in their lives. You know it too. Flow is the state you experience when you do something which is for you, subjectively speaking, the most difficult you can handle with ease, and you also really want to do it. When that thing you are doing is quite difficult but you can still handle it with ease, and you

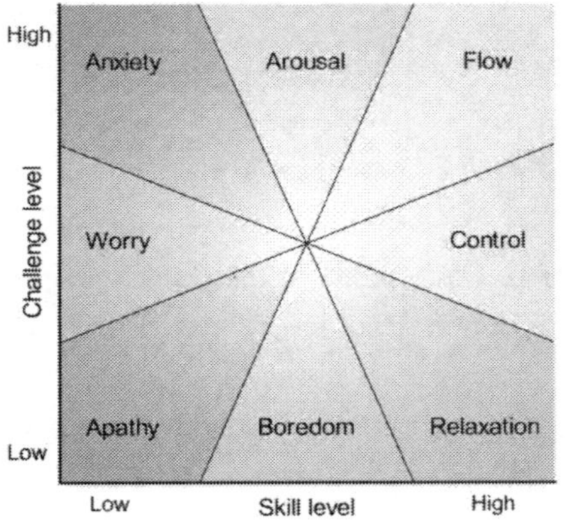

are also motivated to do it, you experience a blissful state of great joy and inner concentration which is detached from time and place. It is this ultimate moment in time when you do something and everything works exceptionally well. You feel uplifted, euphoric, and completely engulfed in the moment.

Although people who write of Flow often use examples from the lives of the very skilled and gifted, Flow can in fact be experienced by anyone – including each of your students, no matter who he or she are. We all experience flow commonly in play, whether it be football, baseball, soccer, box games, card games, sexual activities, handling a musical instrument we have some skill with, etc; Cooking, driving, gardening, singing, dancing, and countless more activities – even negative things like killing and waging wars - whichever things humans can find to be 'fun', they can achieve a state of flow while doing them. Flow can even be achieved by thinking challenging thoughts in your mind, without moving. Computer games especially are built to make flow happen. This is the reason computer games have levels of difficulty, and often many of them. The player, based on their skill, can choose how challenging the computer game is going to be for him. What the player actually does is to draw the line of flow for himself. He chooses a level of difficulty which is, for him, difficult but not too much, and that level of challenge, together with the player's interest in the game, makes the experience the most enjoyable. Likewise, Flow can also be experienced through a wide range of human endeavors, including the martial arts of course, if the person is skilled enough. There is much more to this phenomenon with regard to martial arts practice, and I have written of it more extensively in my international best-seller, **Research of Martial Arts**.

Athletes often refer to flow as 'being in the zone'. When in flow, one performs best with his set of skills. It is also the state in which **we are able to absorb the most and learn best from what we are doing.** It makes sense therefore, that as martial arts teachers we would want our students and ourselves to spend as much time in flow as possible. It would benefit all of humanity if that were the case. But here is the problem we face as martial arts teachers: although our martial arts can manifest flow like any other skill, their training methods were not designed to make flow happen immediately, but rather after a very long time. This all relates to our ability to conserve the student population, and I shall now explain how.

In the martial arts we tend to most commonly have two types of approaches to teaching people. These two approaches, put simply, are "take it hard on them" and "take it easy on them".

The first approach is embodied in the traditional martial arts schools, but also in the sports-oriented schools. In such martial arts schools, students are expected to work very hard to achieve skill. They either suffer through painful training, a type of training which stresses their strength and stamina to the utmost, or both. This could be in the form of holding low stances for prolonged periods of time, placing the body in awkward and difficult positions, suffering a beating from others, exhausting their aerobic or anaerobic limits, etc. This is the Yang end of the scale – too difficult. With this approach, there is the underlying and often unspoken expectation that only the best (most fitting) will survive, and that indeed happens – usually fewer people tend to last and continue over the years than the teacher would have liked.

The second approach takes the opposite route, considering the martial arts as a sort of pastime. The teacher does not believe the intended population has what it takes for more serious martial arts training. Therefore, the teacher keeps the training and curriculum at a low level of physical and mental challenge. This is fantastic for recruiting students. Many people come and within their first class already feel as if they have achieved something. Then this experience is repeated in many classes. But the student also senses quite quickly that the practice is not challenging enough. That is akin to a person who is 'too easy' when going on romantic dates with others, and because of this is eventually shunned by most potential partners. This person becomes the martial arts school teacher, and just as many come at his doorstep, sooner than later most leave. This is the Yin end of the scale – too easy.

As you may remember from earlier, I have asserted that Flow is found in the delicate balance between 'too difficult' and 'too easy'. Bringing the student into a state of flow again and again is, in my opinion, the most reliable way to keep that student interested and pursuing the practice for a lifetime. This is because of the nature of Flow, being experienced as a blissful and joyous state which is self-perpetuating and addictive, all the while providing significant personal growth.

Yet there is a reason most schools do not make the effort to keep students in flow. The Yang schools want a serious student who is hard-working, so they do not wish to compromise their teachings to 'spoil' the students (or, for that matter, to bend over backwards to make a student happy). The Yin schools wish to make money, and fear that pushing their students in class will drive the students away. What then can be done to accommodate for these challenges?

Well, I should start by saying that back in the old days, things were simpler. Just 50 years ago, people were overall far more physically hard-working and willing to take on challenges, and less likely to complain. Martial Arts were very new to the Western world and people did not have expectations of something they did not at all understand. Nowadays we have populations in the Western world which are, on the whole, quite degenerate. In addition to that, the sophisticated brainwashing by the modern media had led people to believe that what they watch on the screen is not only reality, but something they can learn and apply in reality on all walks of life. This led us to this day and age, in which a new student attending our schools usually has two prominent qualities, regardless of age:

1. He knows less than he thinks he knows, especially of the martial arts.

2. He can physically do less than he thinks he can, especially in the martial arts.

Because of problem number 1, the student is often too quick to decide whether a martial art is right or not for him, before truly experiencing it. Because of problem number 2, the student will tend to have a disproportional response to his successes and failures in training. Put in other words – people today lack good body constitution and self-awareness of body and mind. This makes the challenge for martial arts teachers greater than before.

To make Flow work with the students we need to change our mindset. We have to decide and **believe** that the student, albeit being a novice, can genuinely reach flow or near-flow experiences, if we provide him or her the right conditions for it. Also, we have to realize something else which is very important: While it is true that we want only the best and most appropriate people as our students, going to extremes will not necessarily help us get these people. Just look at what I have written in the previous paragraphs. Most people are not ready for real martial arts training when they come at our doorstep. Neither should we expect them to be ready. We should make them so. By learning to accommodate our teachings to many types of people, over time a significant number of students will evolve their body and mind, changing their attitudes and seriousness about training. Were we to go by 'only winners' or 'only losers' approach, then we shall get very few winners (if at all) to remain after 5, 10 or 20 years of teaching, or rather thousands of students who came and went without many or any to carry on what we do at a decent level.

Coming from a background teaching the traditional Chinese martial arts, I would like to address the appropriate solutions for the more

Yang-inclined schools – those in which the teachers tend to expect a hard-working mentality from the get-go.

The most common problem I see today in such schools is that the curriculum is simply not well made for modern society. Often the curriculum itself is excellent, but it begins at too advanced a level, physically and mentally. The curriculum of such arts often assumes a population of students which has been doing tough physical labour, commonly in fields, from early age. This is not where we are at today. This was well understood by pioneers in Okinawan Karate during the 20th century, who were wise to accommodate for the problem by creating many kata to be taught even before the 'beginner' parts of the curriculum. This pre-beginner direction is the way to go. It allows a student to be challenged, but not too challenged, and then when this becomes easy, he or she can begin training the 'real' art. Actually, it is often stated in Okinawan Karate and other arts, that true training begins with the first black belt. This is exactly because, everything before that was simply beginner-friendly material. Sadly, for Okinawan Karate and Japanese Karate, that experiment also failed miserably in many schools in which the beginner-friendly mentality was preserved in the long-run, and people could never get past that stage of training, even when they 'earned' their black belts.

But the undertones of this approach are valid. The teacher needs to create a version of the curriculum that suits the physicality and mentality of the students in his time, and then from it slowly increase the intensity and difficulty until the 'real training' can begin. In this manner, the student can experience Flow or near-flow states, by keeping the practice challenging and difficult, but not too much. But where stands the limit between making it easier, and prostituting one's art to accommodate for a student's needs? From my personal perspective, I believe you can determine the limit by asking several questions about the beginners' curriculum:

1. Does the student actually make progress towards 'real training' by doing this stuff?

2. Will this type of training lead to the 'real training' within a reasonable amount of time?

3. Is this level of training respectful of the student and of his honest wishes?

4. Can this type of training yield any useful skills for either self-defense or health?

5. Am I taking care to add difficulty when the practice becomes too easy?

A person cannot begin to learn until you 'meet them where they are'. Through these questions, you will know whether your attempts to help the student are alright, and adequately access his being. Remember though, that such modifications ought to be made on a student-to-student basis. The changes need to fit the special needs of each student, and what his or her unique challenges are. Can you recall the 'beginner Kata' created by Karate pioneers during the 20th century to help novice students, which I mentioned earlier? One of the reasons that the creation of 'beginner kata' caused problems for Karate in the long-term in many schools, was that these kata were created for the masses, and not optimized for each practitioner. Not that creating new forms is necessarily the way to go, either. Sometimes single movements require changing. Other times the height of steps and stances or their length beg your attention. Rhythm is also an issue. Following a fixed rhythm of practice is not conductive to the individual. As in the teaching of music and language, each person needs to follow a personal rhythm before they can mold themselves unto the rhythm of the group and of the art. Forcing people to blindly follow rhythm before they can execute movements well is in my opinion, albeit a common teaching method, not a very effective one. The alternative of course, in the manner of more personalized teaching, requires more attention, effort and ingenuity on behalf of the teacher, which is why most teachers opt to forgo such an undertaking.

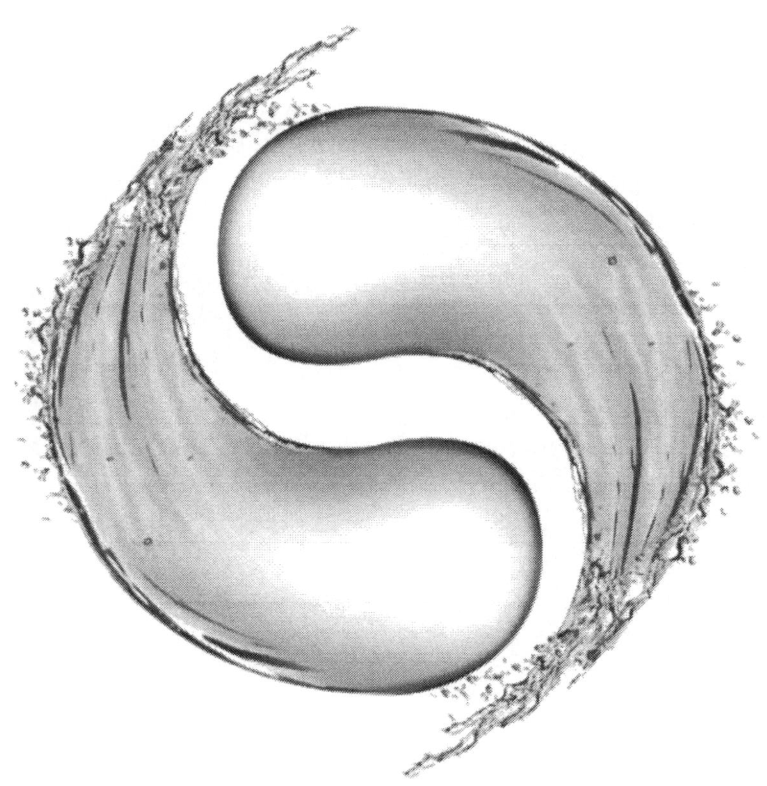

Keeping the student in flow has more to do than just the physical movement themselves. It is also affected by how said movements are perceived by the student. A beginner is strongly affected by his extreme feelings and reactions to the practice. This has to be controlled, through the use of physical and verbal language. A few examples:

Smile to make the student relax when it hurts. Frown and make displeased sighs when the student fails to meet his and your expectations. But most of all – know when to quickly transitions between negative and positive feedback with accordance to the student's actions. Do not forget to include both! Commonly a teacher praises too much or too little; yells too much or too little. Strike a balance in such things. The 'carrot and stick' method never fails. With children I make it even more pronounced. A child whose mind goes wandering too much and too often might get a gentle slap on the cheek and a moderate raising of voice to put him in place. Then 5 minutes later when he makes a sincere effort to concentrate, even if he does not succeed with the technique, I may give him a hug, and then at the end of class applaud his efforts in front of the other students. One must use both the carrot and the stick to help the student locate the right point between 'too easy' and 'too difficult', and this relies on the development of empathy and subtle skills for manipulating people.

Another thing I do is to suit the classes to the level of the people who attend them. I take advantage of the changing attendance for this purpose. When today's class features mostly the less skilled or the more skilled, I will change the teaching content to 'meet them at the flow point'. When the classes have people of varying levels of skill, I will teach one thing, but then as people work on their own or with partners, I will go personally to those more advanced and issue detailed modifications in their ear so they could increase the level of challenge to their flow point.

Then it is important to remember that once a student reaches a certain level, he needs to learn to 'eat bitter'. That is, to practice by your order or through his own initiative exercises, techniques and methods which are not in a 'flow state', but rather challenging to the point of eventual physical near collapse and failure, involving much pain and duress. **Eating Bitter** (Chī Kǔ 吃苦), a Chinese term, refers to that substantial effort one needs to go through and maintain for years, against one's own intuition, to gain higher-level skills. Eating bitter is torturous by nature, and therefore not suitable for beginners. But it is the only path to true skill in the martial arts. Fortunately for those who persevere, eating bitter for years on end eventually leads once more to experiencing the entire art in flow, without any suffering. All of the philosophy embodied in this chapter is meant for a teacher to be able to lead as many students as possible to the gates of bitter training, and have them arriving there ready and mature to accept that sort of challenge. Once there with all of one's being, the way to excellence is almost guaranteed.

The Chinese understood this well centuries ago, which is why their arts have the social model of 'entering the gate'. In the traditional Chinese martial arts, regular students came for pastime classes in which not much was expected of them, and the higher methods, skills and techniques were also kept from them. Then if a student had proven himself in training and as a human being via various means, he may have been accepted into the inner martial arts family and 'enter the gate' of the family compound (a metaphor based on the fact that in the past many Chinese lived in walled compounds with gates, and family affairs would be conducted behind closed doors). This is a good model which helps distinguish those who still require special accommodations and flow-encouragement, and those who are mature enough to suffer of their own volition and accept the pain which will eventually lead them to true flow, in the manifestation of truly advanced practice and application.

Here too however we have a challenge, in that there is a definite line between that regular student and the inner-family student. But people, sadly, are volatile creatures. Many can prove themselves to be worthy for a while, making great progress, and then later through life's circumstances deteriorate and wither into a lower version of their former Self. Then, they may no longer abide by the standards of a student who had entered the gate. This is why traditionally, many Chinese teachers waited a long time, often several years, before admitting a person into the family. This was also a request which had to come from the student, and not the teacher.

Whichever teaching model and paradigm one chooses, Flow is the way to go. Do not be tempted to act upon your Ego, and expect the student to be this or that. As a teacher I take the greater responsibility for my relationship with my students. Although they have to meet me half-way, I can wait forever on the road if I did not provide them with a decent enough map. Therefore, make sure the students walk the right path, and be by your example their compass. Then you will find, that things tend to flow smoothly on their own.

Martial Arts and the Great Learning

Much is said and written of how martial arts, especially the Oriental varieties, have been affected by various philosophies. Yet very little has been written of how we as martial artists can learn from the social philosophy of Confucianism. The purpose of this chapter is therefore to introduce the reader to some of the doctrines of Confucius, and explain in great detail how his thoughts and ideas can be readily applied to the practice and teachings of martial arts, as well as to our everyday lives over 2000 years past Confucius' time. To begin this journey into ancient Chinese thought, first it is important to describe the nature of Confucianism, as it is somewhat different to other 'philosophies' and thinking paradigms. In the course of a human life there are, at the least, three distinct and parallel processes of so called 'Self-Improvement' which relate to the body and mind; that is – ways in which we gradually evolve our human capacity.

The Three Types of Self-Improvement			
	Individuation	**Enlightenment**	**Self-Betterment**
Type of Cognitive Process	**Psychological**	**Philosophical and Spiritual**	**Behavioural**
Description	The process of developing one's Cognitive Functions to the fullest extent possible; thus enabling one to become the 'best of himself'.	The gradual understanding and realization of 'the Way of the world' (the Dao). Some would argue: also the becoming of its embodiment.	The evolution of one's thoughts and actions into an ideal model, which is created by a combination of one's own wishes and society's expectations through the medium of culture and social traditions.
Associated Schools	Freudian and Jungian psychology, and their successors. Humanistic Psychology.	Daoism, Buddhism.	Confucianism.

This is the subject of the chapter you are reading.

It is a common mistake, made by most people, to think of these three types of self-improvement (Individuation, Enlightenment and Self-betterment) are the same thing. Not only are they separate, but moreover – they are often unevenly developed. Nonetheless, they have an intricate relationship between them, and advances made in one open up more potential for developing the others further.

What both Martial Arts and Confucianism have in common is that they focus, more so than other things, on the behavioural process of **Self-Betterment**. This therefore shall be the subject of this chapter.

In all human beings, Self-betterment is process of attaining **balance** between their Nature and their Nurture. It is the process of becoming a 'cultivated person' - what Confucius called Junzi [13]. In his time, Confucius had a rather specific list of traits for his 'superior man', with some of them better suited the feudal society he lived in. However in our time, and under a different cultural context, we are free to utilize his practical notions of self-betterment using broader, more liberal terms and interpretations.

Now then - what is the meaning of this "balance", which supposedly can turn one into "a superior version of himself"? And how can this help with my martial arts? To understand partly what Confucius had thought of as 'balance', and how achieving this balance can help with martial arts, we shall have to first refer to one of the famous texts associated with him, called the **Great Learning**. It is a very short text, and I have included it below in its entirety (translation by A. Charles Muller):

---

[13] Junzi 君子 – a term meaning 'A Gentleman'; a virtuous man; a person with worthy moral virtues and behaviour. Someone who is both educated and humane. Often referred to as 'the superior man'. Becoming such a person is the Confucian ideal.

The way of great learning consists in manifesting one's bright virtue, consists in loving the people, consists in stopping in perfect goodness.

When you know where to stop, you have stability.

When you have stability, you can be tranquil.

When you are tranquil, you can be at ease.

When you are at ease, you can be deliberate.

When you can be deliberate, you can attain your aims.

Things have their roots and branches, affairs have their end and beginning. When you know what comes first and what comes last, then you are near the Way.

The ancients who wanted to manifest their bright virtue to all in the world first governed well their own states.

Wanting to govern well their states, they first harmonized their own clans.

Wanting to harmonize their own clan, they first cultivated themselves.

Wanting to cultivate themselves, they first corrected their minds.

Wanting to correct their minds, they first made their wills sincere.

Wanting to make their wills sincere, they first extended their knowledge.

Extension of knowledge consists of the investigation of things.

When things are investigated, knowledge is extended.

When knowledge is extended, the will becomes sincere.

When the will is sincere, the mind is correct.

When the mind is correct, the self is cultivated.

When the self is cultivated, the clan is harmonized.

When the clan is harmonized, the country is well governed.

When the country is well governed, there will be peace throughout the land.

From the king down to the common people, all must regard the cultivation of the self as the most essential thing.

It is impossible to have a situation wherein the essentials are in disorder, and the externals are well-managed. You simply cannot take the essential things as superficial, and the superficial things as essential. This is called, "Knowing the root." This is called "The extension of knowledge".

So, what was Confucius talking about?

The way of being a superior version of oneself, in martial arts or any other endeavor, depends on several factors and methods. I shall now present these according to their order of appearance in the text of The Great Learning, discussing those I find more relevant to our practice.

Perfect Goodness

In the first part of the text, Confucius spoke about "stopping in perfect goodness". It is about knowing your limits. The concept of "stopping in perfect goodness" is the Golden Rule, also found in Greek Philosophy and Judaism. A great example for it would be that of stopping eating once you are nearly full, but not completely so – to not over-satisfy your hunger, for the prevention of fattening and disease. This also applies to martial arts. One needs to learn when "to stop in perfect goodness" – to not stop training until one has trained enough, but to stop training before one becomes too exhausted, to avoid over-training. Most practitioners suffer from not knowing 'perfect goodness' in that sense, for they do not push their limits to the best of their ability. The majority of competing athletes, on the other hand, overreach their upper limit, and push their body into a state of injury.

Wherein you know the location of 'perfect goodness' (where or when to stop) on your scale of doing things, you can also know your limits. So Confucius tells us one thing leads to the next:

Locating perfect goodness leads to >>> Stability. Both mental and physical. Consider that in movement too, if I can find the perfect stoppage point in the middle of a martial technique, I have stability. This is one reason why in the Internal Martial Arts one is often practicing at very slow speeds – to find the point of perfect goodness and stability.

Stability leads to >>> Tranquility. Because when I am stable, I no longer have to think about gaining balance all the time.

Tranquility leads to >>> Being at ease with one's movements, thoughts and actions.

Being at ease >>> Allows me to be deliberate. This means that both practice and fighting are no longer on 'auto pilot' – I can actually direct what I want to do, because I feel more comfortable.

And when I am **deliberate** >>> I can **attain my aims**.

In the long shot therefore, the point Confucius was making is as follows:

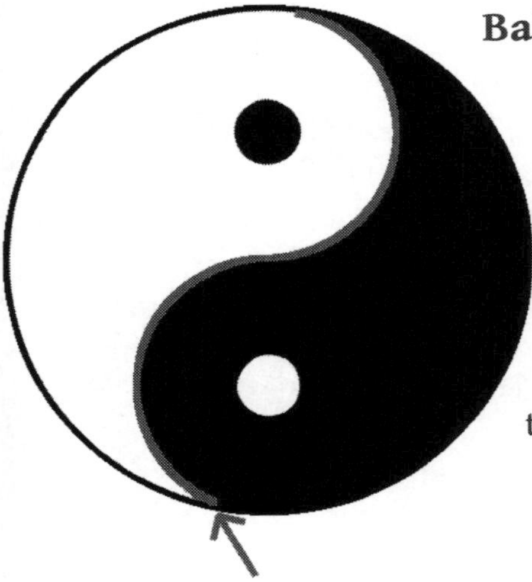

Balance will eventually lead you to attaining your goals.

Therefore to succeed in life and in martial arts, first find your balance, which in turn is located at the point of 'perfect goodness' [14], and so forth. This is the first measure in one's Self-Betterment according to these teachings.

The Middle Path

[14] Another appropriate name for 'Perfect Goodness' is the 'Middle Path'. As seen in the illustration above, the Middle Path is made of those points of balance between Yin and Yang. By recognizing that when Confucius speaks of 'Perfect Goodness' he is referring to the 'Middle Path', we may observe that he taught the same principle as the Greek philosopher Aristotle. For Aristotle said that having virtue is always choosing the Middle Path ('the mean') between two extremes. So both Confucius and Aristotle, two of the greatest thinkers who ever lived, arrived at the same conclusion – that following balance in action, thought and decision-making is the road to both excellence and the cultivation of virtues.

Confucius also said the following in the text quoted before:

"Things have their roots and branches, affairs have their end and beginning. When you know what comes first and what comes last, then you are near the Way."

This stresses further that the root of things must be known. In martial arts, this can relate to the origins of methods and techniques. Why were these techniques and methods I practice and teach created? What is the most basic variation on them, and what can be the most complex? What are the principles which guide them? Answering these questions is also a part of the exploration of Balance, as it relates to what should come first and what should come last in one's training.

The Investigation of Things

Before, Confucius was talking about why it is necessary to find balance, and how balance leads to the attaining of one's goals. In the second part of the text, Confucius deals with a social philosophy that strives to explain how balance affects not just one person, but the entire world. He draws the following line of influence, with one thing leading to another:

Well-governed State >>> Harmonized Clan (or family) >>> A cultivated person >>> A person with a correct mindset >>> A sincere person >>> A person whose knowledge is 'extended' >>> Meaning he or she have 'investigated things'.

And also vice-versa:

The 'investigation of things' >>> An extension of one's knowledge >>> Sincere Will >>> A corrected mindset >>> A cultivated person >>> A harmonized clan (or family) >>> A well governed state.

In between these lines are hidden the following understatements:

1. If all states [15] were well-governed, then all people would have been proficient in the 'investigation of things'.

2. If everyone had put an effort to 'investigate things', then eventually this would have such a huge effect, that even the state would naturally become well-governed and there would be peace everywhere.

The 'investigation of things' is a concept in Confucianism that revolves around avoiding self-delusion in the social context. What is self-delusion? The inability to discern between Nature and Nurture. There are things, habits and tendencies which we are born with – Nature. There are also many more things which we were taught to do, think or believe – Nurture. The investigation of things consists of asking difficult questions about the things we do in daily life, especially those we take for granted, in order to learn to distinguish between Nature vs. Nurture.

Case in point: Why do I sit on a chair? Why do you sit on chairs? Is it because the chair is the natural mode of human sitting? It is not. Observe all small children who can walk – they naturally squat, or sit on the floor. The chair destroys part of your natural flexibility. It often makes you lean forward, causing pain and damage to your back and spine. It costs you money. Over time you have to buy more of these items, and take care of their maintenance. Many chairs force the arms to rest in uncomfortable positions. Most chairs are

---

[15] Feel free to replace the word 'state' with the term 'martial arts school'. The same logic applies.

bad for your back posture. A chair is most commonly fixated and does not adapt to different leg lengths.

There is no reason whatsoever to make chairs the preferred method of sitting or resting, yet we have done so for countless generations. This is because as an ingrained cultural habit, barely anyone bothered to question it. But through the investigation of things, we can discern and know better – about the history of chairs, their shapes, why they were invented and by whom, what are the reasons for which we sit on them and, most importantly – why this is something we ought to do or avoid. This is why Confucius has written that the investigation of things leads to the extension of one's knowledge, which in turn leads to a sincere will (being honest with oneself about things) and having a corrected mindset.

The same notion ought to be applied to martial arts methods and techniques. The vast majority of practitioners never question what they have been taught. They do not make time for the investigation of things, and therefore their knowledge of their art cannot be extended. It can for this reason be said, that by looking deeply into one's habits in the martial arts, one would be able to discern what is the original purpose (Nature), and what is merely habit (Nurture). This provides one with balance, and extends one's knowledge. This requires **deliberate**, thoughtful practice. It is something that should be encouraged in your own training and that of your students.

Another aspect of our training heavily affected by the non-existent investigation of things is habitual physical cues. These are movements or sounds we make out of habit, usually to deal with difficulty or stress. There are many examples I have seen with my own students. One student, while practicing Zhan Zhuang, would blow air evenly through a small hole he made with his lips, and use that action to alleviate the mental pain. Another student would say: "OK, I understand" often after I have explained something. She did not actually understand much, but would repeat the words "I understand" frequently to convince herself that she could deal with what was being told to her. Another silly thing we are all used to doing is making a sound when we are hurt – in the West, the famous 'Ouch' sound and its many variations. In the martial arts, the latter effect signals to opponents that we are vulnerable.

All the above examples are Nurture, not Nature. They are taught mechanisms that we use to deal with difficulty. Instead of taking charge of that difficulty in a conscious manner, we transfer the mental load unto the habit to relieve it. This is very bad. It hinders our self-betterment, and also our progress in the martial arts. To make progress, we ought to investigate such things, and get rid of the bad aspects they manifest. For this reason, Confucius has written that the extension of knowledge depends of "knowing the root" (the causes and reasons for things). Such is the process of learning to avoid self-delusion, and dismantle it from our lives.

Once we investigate things, our knowledge is extended. Once our knowledge is extended, our Will becomes sincere. This means that we can be honest with ourselves about what we do and why we do it. This in turn leads us to correct our mindset – our way of thinking of the world, and gradually evolves us into more cultivated versions of ourselves. Thus we can see, that the wise words of Confucius bear much significance to our time and the practice and teachings of martial arts. Though he had spoken and written of a social and political philosophy, its essence points to the central process of making ourselves better as human beings.

Using Proper Names

"...We are ready to learn the true names of things. These names are the keys to higher knowledge. Initiation (into higher spirituality) is learning to call the things of the world by the names they have in the minds of their divine authors. These names contain the secrets of things. Initiates speak a different language from the uninitiated, because as initiates, they call things by the names through which they were created."

– Rudolph Steiner; How to Know Higher Worlds.

Another doctrine of Confucius, which is very relevant to our previous discussions and the martial arts, is called the **Rectification of Names.** It is not originally from the Great Learning, but is found in The Analects – a compilation of Confucius' teachings, collected and written by his students [16].

The premise of this concept, of the Rectification of Names, is simple. It means: the use of either correct or incorrect language can shape one's reality in very profound ways. So says Confucius in the Analects (chapter 13, verse 3, translation by James Legge):

"A superior man (Junzi), with regard to what he does not know, shows a cautious reserve.

If names be not correct, language is not in accordance with the truth of things.

If language be not in accordance with the truth of things, affairs cannot be carried on to success. [17]

[16] Refer to a previous chapter in this book: **The Benevolent Ruler**.

[17] This is in line with the wisdom of Socrates, who said that "the misuse of language induces evil in the soul".

When affairs cannot be carried on to success, proprieties and music do not flourish.

When proprieties and music do not flourish, punishments will not be properly awarded.

When punishments are not properly awarded, the people do not know how to move hand or foot.

Therefore, a superior man considers it necessary that the names he uses may be spoken appropriately and also that what he speaks may be carried out appropriately.

What the superior man requires is just that in his words there may be nothing incorrect."

These ideas can be broken down as follows:

The superior man does not speak of what he does not know, because then he would not be using the right words (or facts) to describe things. He must be careful about the usage of words and knowledge, or lack thereof.

Incorrect language is not aligned with how things truly are – does not represent well the reality one speaks of. Failing to describe things well hinders the possibility of success in one's endeavors.

Confucius then goes to claim this affects other things too, but these are related to his political philosophy more so than to our discussion here.

The bottom line and most important point he raises is that the precise use of language is vital to the successful implementation of whatever one seeks to achieve. In this we see, that the proper use of names is but another aspect of 'the investigation of things' – it is the investigation of proper use of language. But how can this be applied to the martial arts and the teaching of them? I can propose several examples.

Let us consider first the case of translation of martial arts technical terms. One of the most well-known movements in martial arts worldwide is often called the 'karate sideways block', with either its 'inward blocking' or 'outward blocking' variation. The Japanese terms for these 'blocks' are pronounced as either 'Uchi Uke' or 'Soto Uke'. However the original Japanese word, Uke (受け), does not mean 'to block', but 'to receive'. A comparison of these two meanings, alongside with a similar movement from Xing Yi Quan called 'Heng Quan', reveals interesting things:

Uchi/Soto Uke (meaning #1)	Uchi/Soto Uke (meaning #2)	Héng Quán 横拳
Translation: Inward/Outward **Receiving**	**Translation:** Inward/Outward **Blocking**	**Translation:** **Crossing** Fist
Nature of the term: **Yielding** to incoming force.	**Nature of the term:** **Passive** in the face of an incoming force.	**Nature of the term:** **Aggressive** towards an incoming force (crossing it).
Psychological and verbal connotations: Taking in. Receiving punishment. Absorbing. Not going against. A **Yin** nature to the movement.	**Psychological and verbal connotations:** Stiff. Being like a stone. A metal or concrete object. Clogging something. A road-block.	**Psychological and verbal connotations:** Coming to meet an obstacle. Going through something. Passing across. A **Yang** nature to the movement.

In this we see that the name of a given technique can do a lot to how we perceive it, and how we imagine things to be. Consciously or subconsciously, the names of techniques affect greatly the way we move, and the emphasis we put into movements. To receive something is not the same as to block it, and certainly not identical to the action of crossing it.

The same phenomenon can be noted with many different examples. Another is that of the 'Karate punch', which I would be comparing with the most basic punch of Xing Yi, known as 'Beng Quan':

Tsuki 突き (translation #1)	Tsuki 突き (translation #2)	Bēng Quán 崩拳
Translation: **Thrust** (original Japanese translation)	**Translation:** **Punch** (altered translation used in the West)	**Translation:** **Crushing** Fist
Penetrating into something.	**Blunt** striking.	**Compressing** something until it breaks apart.
Fencing thrust. A stake. Sexual connotations (in terms of dominance; very Yang in nature). Making something forcefully stick into a tight spot and embedding it into that place.	A boxing punch (probably the most well-known cultural reference in the West). Punches seen in movies. Baseball bat hitting something. The distinctive 'punching sounds' used in films and television series.	Pestle (the tool used to crush herbs and spices). Breaking into many small pieces. Overwhelming force. Something that cannot be resisted. Causing deformation.

Here we see the effect of language on the type of power one perceives his strike is ought to have. The three translations carry differing flavours, and arguably these can affect the manifestation of the type of power put behind each technique.

The Chinese were aware of this, perhaps stemming from the influence of Confucianism on their culture, and possibly simply through insight and experience. For this reason, the Chinese martial arts use a lot of creative language tricks to make the practitioner realize a point in practice. Oftentimes, this is done in the form of borrowing metaphors from nature.

In many Chinese martial arts, movements are codified by short cultural descriptions. In Taiji Quan, each movement in the forms uses a matching phrase, such as 'White Crane Spreads its Wings', or 'Parting the Horse's Mane'. Each of them illustrate a different mindset, and a way of doing things physically.

One of the most famous examples, common in many Chinese martial arts, is 'Monkey Steals the Peach', which often refers to technique

wherein the gonads of the opponent are grabbed and pulled (but can mean other things as well). The analogy to a 'stealing monkey' is very useful, since monkeys are abundant in the Orient, and people are familiar with their type of movement from first-hand experience and many folk tales. A stealing monkey is manipulative, cunning, quick, stealthy, surprising in action, agile, grips hard, grabs and pulls towards his body and then changes direction, does not stare at the object about to be stolen, etc. The peach itself is a small round object, which can only mean certain things as far as human fighting goes. In naming a movement 'Monkey Steals the Peach', the creators of it therefore contained a multitude of analogies and distinct hidden meanings.
Similarly, certain movements and movement forms are connected to the name of an animal, so that the practitioner would know which mindset these methods and techniques should assume in physical practice. Even mythical animals like the Chinese Dragon are used, because their movements are described in great detail in Chinese folks tales. The animal itself does not matter – what is important is that the practitioner could understand the cultural context and kinesthetic imagery.

Back in the day, a contemporary of Confucius had been Zhuang Zi (pronounced: Juang Dze) – a famous exponent of Daoism, which had been a competing school of thought with Confucianism. Zhuang Zi criticized Confucius a lot, and famously mocked his obsession with names through this short passage:

"Nets are for catching fish; after one gets the fish, one forgets the net.

Traps are for catching rabbits; after one gets the rabbit, one forgets the trap.

Words are for getting meaning; after one gets the meaning, one forgets the words.

Where can I find people who have forgotten the words, so I can have a word with them?".

In this humorous segment, Zhuang Zi makes the point that words are an inferior way of conveying the essence of things. By so saying, he supposedly dulls Confucius' point about the importance of using correct language. In reality though, both Confucius and Zhuang Zi were right in their thoughts and observations. They were simply discussing these matters with differing goals in mind.

Confucius was interested in teaching (associated with his orientation with his Behavioural Self-Betterment). Zhuang Zi wrote of the process of becoming one with the Dao and realizing intuitively the way things work (related to his Philosophical Enlightenment approach). For the purpose of teaching and the transmission of knowledge, one requires the usage of correct and precise language as Confucius had preached. But then as a person reaches a high level of understanding in a given field of study or practice, that person can transcend words and attain an intuitive understanding. This indeed describes the end result of the transformational process that both schools these schools of thought seek. One talks of the Way, and the other describes its qualities.

The Superior Man
Treading the Middle Path
Looks into the Nature of things
And by the virtue of his sincere will
Finds the Dao

Martial Arts Students and the Middle Path

This chapter is in a way a spiritual sequel to the previous chapter in this book, titled: '**Martial Arts and the Great Learning**'. It is advised to read that previous chapter first, before tackling this one.

Confucius said: "***Men look for happiness in that which is above or below them. But happiness is at the same height as man***". Likewise, the longer I teach the martial arts, the more I observe that most beginners stray from the right path to success (and happiness) – the middle path endorsed by Confucius and many other philosophers through the centuries. This pertains to a major issue in the teaching of martial arts novices, which I shall now explain.

When people approach the study of the martial arts, or any other new endeavor, as mature adults, they come to us teachers already bearing an 'attitude' and a personal 'method' for learning. Most commonly, this method they have adopted and adapted over the years was not of the own invention, but is of the generic kind they were taught either by schools or trends in the popular culture of their time. There is always among all students the struggle to reconcile this personal learning method of theirs with the new learning method presented by the teacher. The fact that the traditional martial arts have their own preferences for how one ought to learn makes the experience more challenging.

The majority of students realize early on, most often without admitting, that their preferred ways of learning are mostly useless in the context of traditional martial arts, and that they have to change. But change rarely comes with ease to anyone – and so, instead of changing, they bargain. There begins a long process which I call 'the struggle to accept the art'. During this period of time, the student attempts to learn, but cannot do so well because much of the learning is still being done 'his way' and not the 'art's way'. Usually what is created is a mixture of attitudes, with the student willing to accept some things as a given, and others he might reject ferociously. This stage of learning is recognizable by the willingness of the student to argue against the teacher or the art. In Western societies where criticism in the face of superiors is deemed acceptable, this arguing is often done in an obvious and overt fashion. The student will utter clearly before the teacher his dismay at a given technique or his wish to avoid doing certain things the way he is told. In more traditional Eastern societies, when a student feels uncomfortable sharing such thoughts out loud, he may nod in acceptance for the teacher or say he understood something, but in reality do something else more to his liking. These are generalizations though, and students in East and West adopt both these passive and aggressive tactics for disagreeing with the teachings of the art.

One is prompted to ask, why is it that most students are prone to act in such a provocative and uncooperative manner, which only hurts their own efforts? After all, they came to study with a certain teacher in order to hopefully gain from his knowledge, insights and skills. Then why come forth, and then reject much of the teachings? The reason is that people fear change, and the beginning stages of traditional martial arts training intimidate and threaten the core of people's values and personality. To change one's way of thinking, learning and physically acting is to convert a person into a new being entirely. A positive process for sure under the tutelage of a good and responsible teacher. Yet, consider that this is not what most people had in mind when they first signed up for classes. They were yearning for feeling better, becoming healthier, being happier. In this cheerful future outlook was not at all included the idea that to achieve all this, they will have to change! Now, as reality slaps them in the face and bitter, painful work begins, they naturally 'rear their legs' and demonstrate argumentative tendencies, attempting to protect themselves from this new 'threat' which they had not anticipated.

Alas, the process of letting go of this defensive stage of learning can be difficult, often lasting several months. Some people can never get over this stage, and such individuals will never reach even a moderate level of proficiency in the study of the traditional martial arts. That being said, I find that with most people, they can resolve their difficulties and raise themselves out of this trench which they had dug, if I simply take care to patiently explain to them why arguing with me over what is right or wrong is not the most brilliant strategy for progress. Once they can understand this intellectually, many people can then slowly but surely give up on their ego-driven fears and become more compliant and open in their learning within a short amount of time.

Among those still stuck in the 'argumentative' stage of learning stand out two very stereotypical characters. I would affectionately refer to them as the '**micro-scientist**' and the '**macro-fantasizer**'. Both types of individuals reflect two very common strategies people use for making sense of the world around them.

The 'micro-scientist' is a person who always reiterates and insists on receiving answers to the smallest questions, in accurate detail. When walking the path of martial arts learning, he is tempted to constantly stop and examine the flowers, insects, pebbles and other little wonders of nature. In Confucian terms, he is looking for "everything which is <u>below</u> him". He will not do with a foot's angular position which **cannot** be attached to geometric logic. A metaphor for how to perform a movement **cannot** be taken as-is, but begs a breakdown to the muscles, tendons and joints involved in it. A strike **cannot** be really learned unless its power-generation method is analyzed in a rational manner with a clear explanation. Furthermore, if something **cannot** be 'proven' right then and there, it is to be rejected or taken with a grain of skepticism. All of this is very characteristic of people with a college-level education and above, especially those classically trained in the sciences. This approach is also correlated with personalities which demonstrate (even slight) inclinations for being either neurotic, anxious, feature an urge to manifest control over people or situations, are resentful of spontaneity and unexpected changes to plan, etc – some or all of these attributes together in the same person. For the 'micro-scientist', insisting on the investigation of the smallest details and being provided with the most 'accurate' answers is the manner by which such people can protect themselves from having to change.

The 'macro-fantasizer' is a person who finds it difficult to take anything for what it is, and insists on discovering correlations between everything taught to him and grander, more majestic themes. When walking the path of martial arts learning, he is tempted to constantly stop and wonder endlessly at the lakes, mountains, stars and similarly inspiring natural monuments. In Confucian terms, he is looking for "everything which is above him". A breathing method **must** be a way to connect with a greater consciousness. A partner practice **must** also suggest a technique for realizing the depth of the other person's psychology. Anything which exudes power **must** be tapping from the vast energy reservoir of the cosmos. Furthermore, the art and its way **must** always feature 'hidden meanings', which often they can discover but even the teacher must have not paid attention to before. All of this is very characteristic of people who have a spiritual vibe going on for them in their lives for this or that reason, who are not often enough told by society that it is high time they stop uttering so much vague gibberish and start focusing on the production of coherent speech and thought for the sake of themselves and everyone around them. Basically, they have been on the loose with their energy talk and hippie new-age silliness for many years, often decades, and were never under circumstances dire enough to force them to even consider becoming more rational and to the point. Like the 'micro-scientists' they are a product of modern society, in which too few people reveal their true thoughts and feelings concerning the actions and beliefs of others. This approach (of the 'macro-fantasizer') is also correlated with personalities which demonstrate (even slight) inclinations for being either delusional, schizoid, schizotypal, bipolar, overly dreamy, detached from reality, hostile to criticism, manipulative, etc – some or all of these attributes together in the same person. For the 'macro-fantasizer', insisting on uniting one's understanding with something bigger than himself is the manner by which such people can protect themselves from having to change.

The irony is that in a way, the approaches of both types [18] I have described are completely valid. There is a truth and legitimacy to all of their strange mannerisms and ideas, and they are all excellent interpretations for how to further explore and explain one's martial art. The problem is not in that they think in the way that they do (as long as it is not excessive), but in that they attempt to force this type of thinking on something which they have yet to fully comprehend.

There is after all a time and a place for everything. An infant cannot be talked to in a complicated language. A toddler is not to be handed tools requiring complex dexterity. A child is not ready to absorb the full meaning of sexual intimacy. A young teenager has no emotional capacity for realizing the complete role of a father. A young adult is seldom ready to lead a nation. So is the beginner student neither adept nor prepared to explore his new martial art of choice to its

---

[18] Obviously, these two types of students are merely stereotypical examples, and life is more complex. Additionally, not all 'argumentative' students fall under such categories – although most of them do. These stereotypical students are not specifically correlated with Jungian personality types, although some personality types do tend to be associated with either this or that type of problem student.

uttermost depths or great heights without having first understood it thoroughly at a basic level.

This is the middle path in learning the martial arts. It requires of the beginner student, during the first few years of his diligent practice, to not stray too far above (macro) or below (micro), but maintain a steady progress on a road laid out by a competent teacher and those who came before him. By following this middle path it is later possible to see the road diverge into many others. But by foolishly wishing to take every twist and turn from the start, one will end up forever walking in circles. To avoid walking in circles, simply aid that student in listening to the person providing directions, rather than arguing with him over which road seems the most correct to him...

Change and Cooperation

"If you do not get what you want, you suffer; if you get what you do not want, you suffer; even when you get exactly what you want, you still suffer because you cannot hold on to it forever. Your mind is your predicament. It wants to be free of change. Free of pain, free of the obligations of life and death. But change is law and no amount of pretending will alter that reality." - Socrates

The more I train in the martial arts and teach them, the more I see that the number 1 obstacle to progress for everyone is their willingness to CHANGE [19]. People who want to change and welcome change are far easier to teach than those who do not. I have seen major progress made by people within a single month, sometimes more progress than they have made in a year, just because they welcomed a certain physical or mental reality which they had rejected before. Once you want to be the art AND accept its dominion over you, great things are possible.

The problem here is that the adult body and mind do not like changes. We have survived thus far by being something. That something we are has proven its ability to sustain a life into maturity, even if that life is unsatisfactory or miserable. Then why should we change?

This, in a nutshell, is the subconscious process going in the mind of every single adult student you will ever teach. Unless you are an enlightened being, you too must experience the same type of subconscious process from time to time. Want some proof? Try to learn something new. Anything would do, really, but try

---

[19] Of this exactly Benjamin Franklin had written: "*They that will not be counseled, cannot be helped*".

studying something related to the martial arts to really hit it on the head. Go and have a class in a martial art very different to yours, which you have never attempted to practice before. You will notice that, unfortunately, you will also be encountering difficulties similar to those of your students, even if you can learn better than them. Indeed, very few adults maintain the fast learning capacity of children, who have less of an Ego and are more willing to accept new realities.

The problem with change is most evident when you observe how a student performs a new technique he had learned from you. Very commonly you will see something strange happening – the student will alter angles, alignments, speed, tempo, height, power and other variables in the technique, whether it be performed solo or with a partner. You may attempt to teach him again, and he will repeat the same changes he made before. He may even keep on insisting doing it that way after months and possibly years. This is in fact the meeting point between his psyche and yours. He wants to learn, but whilst doing so he does not truly absorb your truth, but creates a compromise between what you want him to do and what he feels is comfortable for him, in the context of his personality and physical nature. It is very interesting that usually when questioned why they have altered the technique taught to them, the students will be completely unaware that they have done so. The process which governs the changes they make to what you teach them, is partly or fully unconscious. Their **Persona** – the mask they wear on the surface – the lie they tell themselves – swears to you that they have changed nothing and this is how you taught them. But their true **Ego** has worked out its way behind the scenes, and you can tell.

Because of this, the first thing to remember is that it does not help to scold them badly for changing what they have learned. They will feel you are being mean and unfair, because they do not realize what they have done. Blaming them will only create tensions, and will cause their Ego to become even more vigilant and antagonistic to the learning process. What you should do instead is to employ the power of empathy. You have to try and feel what they feel. You have to get down to the roots of what causes them discomfort with what they try to learn, and how you can convince their Ego to accept that discomfort in order to promote personal growth. Granted, it is difficult to convince an entity (the Ego) when you cannot directly converse with it! But you can whisper the right words and phrases, and when these are well spoken their echoes will reach deep down into that massive cavern which is the student's whole consciousness.

Watch the student's expressions and body language. Is he in pain? If so, realign him to deal better with the pain, and assure him via logical means and explanations that the pain is temporary and not posing a physical risk of injury.
Is he changing the method because of his disbelief in its efficacy? If so, show he how it works, bring forth a more veteran student who can already do it well, and assure him that with time he would be able to do it too, if he trains correctly and accurately.
Is he feeling cocky and altering what he has learned because he thinks he knows a 'better way to do it'? If so, bring another student and prove to him he would not be able to succeed, or otherwise explain and demonstrate to him why it is important to learn a multitude of ways to do similar things. Then assure him and show him why variation does not come at the expense of who he is now, but only adds to him arsenal and enhances his Self.

Above all else, make sure the students breathe. There is no talking with someone's Ego if their breathing is in disorder. Teach them to breathe well, and this will enhance the learning experience in each and every class. I use the brief resting pauses between warmup exercises to work on correct breathing, and also encourage students practice their breathing while they listen to others.

I go a step further by controlling the students' body language as they are listening to my explanations. The Ego seeks to escape a situation and fortify itself by changing bodily postures or behaviours. For this reason I make sure the students' bodies are held in a manner more conductive to learning, when I am explaining something to them. I do not allow them to cross hands in any way, in front or behind the body. The hands hang loosely at their sides. Crossing the legs is forbidden, too. The knees must not collapse. The feet should be at least shoulder width apart. The posture should be erect but relaxed. They should be looking in my general direction and not elsewhere. They should keep their mouths shut unless allowed to speak, and I enforce this latter requirement more harshly when they get into the words of another student and cut him in the middle of speaking. Whenever a student deviates from these alignments and behavioural guidelines, I would immediately comment and make him realign. Within a short time the students get the habit. Once they stand or sit like this, they can listen more genuinely and with less interruptions from their Ego.

You may think of me as a harsh disciplinarian. I plead guilty. But this type of physical control I am not exerting upon students because I admire military discipline. In fact, at my academy students are freer to express themselves than in many other traditional martial arts schools. In terms of uniform, the only item required is a certain type of shirt, because of my belief that it is important to allow students some personal expression through the means of wearing something of their own choice alongside what everyone else are wearing [20]. The students are

---

[20] This follows the notion of balancing between the student's need for individuality and the school's need for conformity – the Middle Path.

also allowed to talk and walk about freely during partner practice – I do not believe in enforcing silence or making students immobile and sticking them at specific points in the room. Overall, I do try to give my students a strong sense of personal freedom within the learning environment, and encourage them to experiment a lot with the curriculum. But that particular aspect of how they manage themselves when receiving explanations, that I certainly tackle with a stricter attitude.

The truth is that unless you do this, the students will drive you mad with their supposed inability to understand your explanations. In the event that you are a good teacher, it is not that they did not understand. Neither that they did not hear. But their minds were not processing, because their Egos were in the way; and they were in the way because one allows their Egos to control their bodies and shut them down.
This is very easy to demonstrate and prove. Open up your computer right now and watch a video from any martial arts seminar. Fast forward to a point in such video from a martial arts seminar, when a teacher is explaining things, and you can see the students standing near him. Now, completely ignore the teacher and what he says, and focus instead only on the students and their body language. There you have it. The crossed arms and legs, either in front or behind the body. The impolite chit-chat in the background while the teacher is speaking. The eyes taking a stroll around the room. Often you would be able to notice all of these things happening at once, sometimes even perpetrated by the same student. Then you will also be able to observe, that this is like an infectious disease. Once a single person does this, and by doing so demonstrates it is possible and acceptable to shut oneself off from the teachings, then others will follow. Teachers are sadly too busy thinking about what to say and how, that they fail to notice that this is happening. Or perhaps they may notice, but at a setting such as a seminar they do not care enough to make the effort to help the students listen, because they do not

have to interact with these people on a daily basis. Either way, this is harmful, and should be dealt with.

In summary, to promote change in your students you need two things: their willingness and their cooperation. Their willingness you create by making them believe what they learn is beneficial for their Ego. They do not need to think that the art is this or that (no need to 'prove' the art) – they need to believe that the art is right for **them**. Their cooperation you achieve by meticulously controlling the teaching stage, so things are conducted like you want, without their Ego getting in the way through their unconscious. They need not know how they are being manipulated into learning more efficiently – you only need to get them to open their minds and bodies so they could help themselves.

Your Vision and Theirs

Wherein you have been teaching for a while, you must have experienced scenarios which are similar to the following:

There is a student who does something quite strange in class. Perhaps they bow to you all the time, but you teach a martial art where bowing is not part of the tradition. Maybe, she feels tired, so she goes and sits at some remote corner when you do not notice, and it takes you two minutes to realize she 'disappeared'. Or a student left you for a silly reason, like having difficulty with the warmup exercises, but you only find out why they left a few years after it happened.
In each of these cases you wonder: "*Why did the student not speak to me about his or her behaviour? I would have expected the bowing student to ask whether it is customary to bow. The tired student to ask whether she can sit down and rest. The student who left, to tell me he was having difficulties*". Well, this is what happens when there is a misalignment between your vision and theirs. Beyond the need for cultivating open communication with the students, sometimes they just do things because they think these actions are acceptable and reasonable. They apply their inner world-view and logic to what happens at the school, and then there are clashes of interest and misunderstandings.

It is important to keep in mind at all times, that what is obvious to us as teachers is not at all clear and well-understood to most students. A teacher should know how to avoid the all-too-common psychological error of considering the other as he considers himself. That is true for knowledge, but also for the unique personality of each individual, his or her learning style, their history and background, the state of their health, etc.

Very important to take note of by the teacher, are the different goals of students, which do not always align with what he has in mind. Myself, I am very much interested in the martial aspects of my arts, but with self-honesty and common sense I must realize that many of my students are not highly enthusiastic about such matters. It is therefore my responsibility to portray a decent amount of liberalism and acceptance, allowing these people with a different mindset to my own to best find what they look for by learning from me, while keeping them in the boundaries of reason and good taste. While they should 'go along with the program', there is a limit to how much one ought to force his own aspirations, vision and ideas upon his students.

This will become a point of contention with many students. Adults usually dislike being subjugated to another man's vision of things, but learning martial arts requires them to submit to the teachings for their own sake. It is therefore wise to allow students to express their own personality, wishes and creativity in various ways, so they do not feel pressured into a mold. In my school, I do several things to encourage such expressions of individuality. Here are some examples:

- The uniform is partial (not complete) – shirt only, so that the students have a choice with regard to any other clothing item. A part of what they wear represents their affinity to the academy, and the rest their own temperament and preferences.

- In class, I care to ask the students of their opinions and not be the only one speaking. I also tell them they can learn a lot by questioning and talking to each other, and not just from me.

- I publicly acknowledge when a student had taught me something or was the inspiration for something new I understood, and give credit to that student.

- Whenever one student is being a smartass and suggests that he has a better way of doing something I taught him in his personal practice, I do not silence him. Usually this pertains to an uncomfortable body alignment which is correct, but that he does not like getting into. I tell him: "Alright then, try it! Your method must be better, so I need not teach you". The wiser ones understand they made a mistake. The sillier ones do try, fail, and then earn more respect towards me. But the important point here was that I did not prevent them from attempting to employ their own vision.

- Often when working with a partner, a student wishes to express himself by asking to perform a technique differently, and you know it is not wise. I let such students try it, often on me (or I will execute it on them), and allow them to learn from their own bitter experience, rather than feel I prevented this self-expression.

Via such measures and others, over time there shall develop a proper balance between the student's own vision and that of the school, and those who cannot change will fade away.

Carrot and Stick

When teaching the martial arts, it is important to use both the carrot and the stick – positive and negative feedback. A lot of teachers are afraid to scold the students too harshly, or alternatively believe that compliments should be scarce. Avoid being one of these teachers.

By not scolding the students when necessary, they become directionless, or otherwise begin to make up their own rules for how to practice, or may develop disrespect and lack of etiquette. By not complimenting students when appropriate, they feel you do not appreciate them, or may have uncertainty as to whether they have performed something well. A balance needs to be struck between the two. Here are examples from my teaching experience, some of which I have used many a time. Pseudonyms are used for the students:

- Johnny is a 19 year old, training six months with you. Lately he has developed a habit of lifting his heel a lot when performing some movements, when it is inappropriate. You notice another student, who is new, beginning to imitate Johnny's mistake. You stop the class and bring Johnny to the center. You praise Johnny for trying hard in training and being a good kid (carrot). Then you add that Johnny has been making a big mistake with his heel and has not changed his habit yet, and now his habit has spread to another student too (stick). You explain why this is bad and how Johnny can change it. You make Johnny do it right in front of everybody by encouraging and helping him (stick when he cannot make it, and carrot once he succeeds). Then later when you see Johnny corrected his flaw you praise him out loud for everyone to hear (carrot). Johnny now has a sense of accomplishment.

- George is a 10 year old kid with what some call ADD or ADHD. He tends to zone out a lot and be lost in the clouds of his imagination. You know better than to drug him with 'medication' for making him compliant – you have your carrot and stick. Every time George makes a trip to a faraway galaxy, you gently slap him on the cheek (stick). The slap does not hurt, but George sure is shocked and rocked back into reality. "Earth to George, over", you say **with a smile**. Then you cheerfully direct him back into the practice. Other times George's space-travels get him too far, so he begins to run around acting like the silly cute kid that he is. You poke in in the ribs lightly with a finger, making him bounce (stick). "Come on George, you should be getting back on track now", you say **with a smile**. Then you cheerfully direct him back into the practice. When George later makes an effort to keep in control, you may hug him or positively tap him on the shoulder (carrot). Then at the end of a class when he really tried hard, you will say in front of all the other children, that George has made the most progress, and explain to them why his achievement was relatively great due to him having difficulties in keeping in focus and overcoming them (carrot).

- Roger is a 34 year old who has been studying with you 7 years. You tend to trust him. Lately he has been slacking off, for various reasons. He has been having a hard time but could have made the effort to attend more classes. Last week he even missed a seminar with your own teacher, which you felt was insulting and unfitting of his position as one of the school's more veteran students. You give Roger a call and ask how he is doing in life, trying to be empathetic, offer help and provide advice (carrot). Then you gradually change the topic to his need to get a grip and set himself straight, emphasizing your discontent from his recent behaviour (stick). You explain to Roger that since he is a more veteran student at the school others look up to him, and missing classes and seminars delivers the wrong type of massage to them. People may begin to sense that perhaps something is wrong with Roger, or maybe Roger is disrespecting you for some reason. Then you tell Roger how much you appreciate him and why (carrot), and that you hope to see him again soon in the next class. Roger sets his priorities straight and begins to attend classes more regularly. So after two weeks of this, you ask Roger to stay a bit more after class, and spend 20 minutes to teach him something special – perhaps something he has been yearning to learn for a long time (carrot). You tell him: "*I have been watching you for a while and I see you are trying, so I wanted to repay you for this in kind*".

There is also much to be said specifically of using pain. It is crucial that whenever you inflict physical pain upon students for the sake of making a point or offering a 'stick', they know that this was either for a teaching purpose or to get them in line. A student must never think that you have hit him because you were angry with him. Also, force should always be used in moderation, never to injure, and be adapted to the student's capacity and willingness to accept pain.

The general rule of thumb for me is, that I use more force the longer a student has been studying with me, and the more I can trust him. Newer students tend to require minor physical cues (small mildly painful hits and slaps) to get them in order, but only some will receive them by my hand (as many are too sensitive). Such students – those with sensitivities, I never hit hard when demonstrating techniques. Veteran students usually do not require much in the way of physical cues as such, but do get hit more seriously in demonstrating techniques, in order that they could understand how to apply and use them well, and sometimes to toughen their bodies. But even with them, using a lot of power and inflicting much pain should not be utilized too frequently. Even once in 10 demonstrations of a given technique will do. Those who to begin with are not interested in the martial side of things, there is no need to use a lot of power when demonstrating with them.

You must however accept the reality of your need to inflict pain. It is a part of the job. When taught by others, people unfortunately learn best through either pain or play, but only pain can get them to focus and remember well nearly 100% of the time. Your skill as a martial artist is in part measured and tested by your ability to assess what type of pain and how much pain (if at all) is appropriate at any given situation when teaching. The best way to learn this is to practice it, and begin on the safe side. Each student should be gradually tested for their pain tolerance and their psychological willingness to accept pain from their teacher, by spending months moving from very gentle slaps and rubs to possibly pretty hard hits, locks, throws, etc. Some people will never pass a low threshold, and that is quite alright. You would be surprised perhaps to discover that there are also in existence some people who barely feel any form of pain, due to either a very high tolerance (born or trained) or sometimes a nervous system disorder of some sort. Such people in fact require you use a lot of power while working with them (as long as it is not injurious), as otherwise they cannot correctly comprehend the meaning, effects and purpose of various techniques.

Remember that people tend to subconsciously believe that others think and feel the same way that they themselves do. Because of this error, someone with a high pain tolerance can end up accidentally being quite brutal with fellow students in class, taking them to be as resilient as himself; while more gentle characters might refrain from executing techniques to their fullest, because they pity the pain their partner might be 'suffering'. This calls for you to not only regulate your own presence, but also that of students as they work in pairs. By being attuned to anyone going overboard or not trying hard enough, you can prevent a lot of arguments and frustrations on part of the students.

Why Good Answers Make Dumb Students

In modern Western culture, we like to elucidate everything to the utmost. This was not the way in which traditional Oriental martial arts were historically taught. Usually, the teacher would create an element of mystery by abstaining from providing too concrete an answer to everything, and not revealing the full extent of anything until the student is already quite advanced. There are several reasons for this:

1. People want mysteries! Without a mystery there is no challenge in solving it, and without a challenge there is boredom and unwillingness to learn.

2. Revealing too much, too early, will overwhelm and frighten beginners, causing them to flee in confusion from the learning process and from your school.

3. Confucius said: "**I hear and I forget. I see and I remember. I do and I understand**". Most of what you verbally tell your students, they will forget. Only some of the things your students see you teach, observe their friends practice or read about with their eyes – they will remember. But allow the students to physically do what they need to learn – and they will eventually understand. After you truly understand something, it is not easily forgotten. **Therefore, a thorough and satisfactory answer and explanation from the teacher is in fact inferior to helping the student to realize something on his own.** Instead of offering the student everything on a silver plate and spoon-feeding him, give up your urge to control the teaching process and trust in him that your wise and well positioned clues will lead him to the right path.

4. A student who thinks he has all the answers will at one point begin to neglect consulting his teacher, and will not be a cooperative member of the student community. Part of the formula for creating a cohesive and supportive community as such is to make the students work with one another to solve problems. The joint effort put by students, into making sense and solving the mysteries of the art together, is a strong-bonding and resilient social glue. Therefore, do not piece everything together for the students - allow them to make this a communal 'construction project'. Encourage them to work together and offer proper supervision to guarantee they do not mess up.
For example - often I will notice students practicing together before or after the class. Commonly I will not interrupt them, only watch from afar. I need to provide them with a space and time for mutual experimentation without guidance.

The Art They Never Knew

Master **Henry Poo Yee (1939-2018CE)** was my Shigong (grand-teacher) in Jook Lum Southern Mantis. His mannerisms were always a contradiction between simplicity and mystery. His lifestyle, on the surface, was quite frugal. The majority of his time was spent training, teaching and healing patients. He lived in a plain house and wore modest clothes. His spoken English was broken and unsophisticated, and he hardly wrote anything down. A man passing him by on the street could have easily mistaken him for a newly-arrived Chinese immigrant to the United States, or a harmless ignorant grandpa. But his inner life was richer and far more intricate than people had imagined. He had been a true master of a very complex martial art, holding unto secrets few people know even existed. He was a skilled doctor of Traditional Chinese Medicine who got people out of wheelchairs with herbs, needles and Qi Gong. Despite his strange manner of speaking, his intellect was quite sharp, and he was highly educated and well-traveled in all respects. He could be kind one moment and vicious the next, and his unique personality kept people on edge. His uncanny patterns were to him not a liability, but an asset.

The many contradictions to master Henry's personality kept people guessing. Even students who had been with him for a long time, were often unsure of how well they knew the man. Being apparently very aware of the situation, master Henry used it brilliantly to his advantage, and encouraged his students to maintain that image. He would for instance tell a student one story, and to another student the same story with slightly modified facts, or from a different point of view. He sometimes did the same with the curriculum of his martial art. For a number of years he might practice a form one way, and then later change a few movements here and there. Some of his students would be taught the original variation, and others the newer one. It would seem to me that he expected the students to struggle to piece together his stories and teachings. But though it was within their reach, many of them felt that only he knows better.

At times this was the objective truth, and other times, the truth he wanted them to believe.

One thing master Henry was particularly fond of, is telling his students: "***You have never seen my real Kung Fu!***". How odd a thing to say. The outside observer would think this does not make any sense. What kind of martial art were the students seeing, then? A fake version he was teaching them? A mockery of real teachings which he was withholding from them?... Quite a baffling statement it was.

But the longer students remained by Henry's side, the more they came to realize what he had meant. This was his incoherent manner of conveying the idea, that there was more to the curriculum of his martial art than was publicly shown. With his skill far surpassing that of even his most veteran students, such a statement was considered legitimate and reasonable by most of them.

Yet Henry was relentless. He kept repeating that sentence over and over for decades. In the beginning, people were inclined to think that they would one day become 'enter-the-gate' students, gain access to secrets, and would then finally witness "the real Kung Fu". But master Henry kept taunting them with that sentence even past their 'enter-the-gate' ceremony. Eventually he even accepted a number of students as 'disciples', a level he considered above 'enter-the-gate', and still he would continue to utter that inexplicable sentence over and over again. "***You have never seen my real Kung Fu!***".

Logically, that sentence did not make much sense. Neither was it particularly convincing. But every time it was repeated, a figurative bucket of water was spilled upon the students' heads. Over years and decades, all of these small batches of cooling liquid had formed among the students an entire lake of uncertainty. Could it be, truly, that even those who had spent 10, 20 or 30 years with the master, have never seen his true art? The real roots and methods of his immense skill?

I was never a believer in that. I do not think he really held back from those students whom he trusted, and who had been with him for many years. But then again, I was not there when that lake of uncertainty was formed. In my opinion, there had been a few students of late master Henry who managed to learn at least 85-90% of the all the material he himself knew, which is a respectable amount of material to be passed on by any teacher. But by the time master Henry joined his ancestors, nearly all of his students were absolutely convinced, that they had never seen his real Kung Fu, and one could not sway them from this firmly held belief of theirs.

Through this story and his actions, master Henry could teach us two important methods for working with students long-term.

Soft power accumulates slowly: Even with a weak, ill-pronounced and unreliable message, master Henry was able to subdue the minds of his students completely. They came to believe his truth without question, and this solidified his power immensely.

We could use the same strategy, but with different, more positive ideas. In my academy for example, I strongly promote the idea that we rise and fall as a community, and have strength in unity. This sort of belief I express to my students in class and outside of it, commonly more than once a week. When I first began teaching, convincing people of this was challenging, especially as everyone came from different backgrounds and education. But within several years, the message seeped deeply into their being. Students were beginning to put this moral philosophy into practice without the need for me to enforce it or even encourage them. The longer I taught and kept repeating the message, the stronger it became.

Students should be kept guessing: I always tell my students that I will not keep secrets from them. That much is true. But this does not mean that everyone receives access for viewing all which the curriculum has to offer. Having been blessed with great teachers, and having studied and practiced for many years, I have a lot to teach. This means that much of what I know, the newer students had never seen. It can take a student who trains and sees me every day, for several hours a day, as much as 7-10 years to study all that I can teach. Those who come by twice a week, may require a far lengthier period of tutelage. This brings about the situation in which, the more advanced parts of the curriculum are not commonly taught.

This, I use to my advantage. I frequently pick and choose small bits of fascinating advanced materials, and teach just a tiny fraction of them to a class, only to withdraw them later for months or years. Or if these are too advanced for the students in a given class, I might just show them once or twice, and be restrained with sharing details and explanations about what I had demonstrated. I may be willing to elaborate a bit more if questioned in private, but will mostly keep to myself, if the student is not ready to learn what I have shown.

The students are then kept guessing. An aura of mystery is created. Stories and rumours are told. Ironically, when this is <u>moderately and carefully</u> executed, the community is strengthened. Now, they have more to aspire to, and reasons to work together to achieve their goals.

What is important to remember and consider, is that such social manipulations will mightily affect your public image, and the direction that the school would be taking in the years to come. Therefore:

- ☯ When you plant an idea in the students' minds, make sure it is a positive and constructive one!

- ☯ Keeping the students guessing, have them also believe that there is light at the end of the tunnel – that they **<u>CAN</u>**, with time and effort, learn more. That learning more is not dependent on personal favours.

- ☯ Though you might wish to become a riddle your students yearn to solve, be not a thing they feel they cannot grasp. While oozing mystery, you should also convey stability. The students need to feel and believe that despite being somewhat enigmatic to them, you are still with them and supportive of them.

- ☯ Encourage the students to work as a team in order to 'resolve mysteries' and fulfill the school's agendas. Otherwise, dirty politics will one day overcome the school, as each student will operate independently for his own benefit.

Painter and Gardener

Aside from teaching the martial arts, I have several hobbies, one of which is gardening. My dearly beloved wife, on the other hand, is a painter. Consider for a moment, the innate differences between the methodology of a classical painter and that of a gardener.

The painter is an artist whose task begins with an empty canvas. He is drawn to fill in that blank with his vision. Little by little, more colour is added, one stroke aside or atop another, until a piece is formed. Frequently, judgement will dictate that constant remodeling of a corner or a scene be done, until perfection is attained. Many of the best painters past and present take months and sometimes years to complete a single image, because of this process of self-correction. The ability to revise repeatedly as means of achieving the ideal is considered a mark of technical excellence.

The gardener however is faced with a different reality. His work begins not with emptiness but rather with an already-extant substance with its own vision – a seed. Then, despite the fact that many plants require maintenance and management in their growth process, this is not considered effective. Under perfect conditions, with the right soil, proper sun exposure, adequate rainfall, timely sowing, harmonies companions and the likes of these, the organism will reach its optimal growth and yield on its own. The best of gardeners, past and present, work relatively few hours at their masterpieces. When meeting the conditions for which they were born, nature's green children can find their way independently, and further human judgment and intervention is not necessary.

How ironic then, that in teaching the martial arts, I was always more of a painter than a gardener. I like my students to know what is expected of them, to correct their faults frequently, and to continuously revise their movements and thoughts until they can reach a satisfactory manner of performance, relative to their physical condition, age and experience: like a painter shaping his canvas with colour.

Yet, over the years I have learned to also operate more like a gardener when teaching. That is, to refrain from correcting people when they are succeeding, even if there are some mistakes. To not always reveal the answers for every twist and turn. To allow the person to express himself and his Self in movement and be patient with such exploration, for each student is a seed with its own vision and potential.

The best martial arts teachers can conduct themselves as neither the classical gardener or painter, but as the master of the art of Penjing ('Bonsai'). Such people combine the foremost positive qualities of both former arts into one. They take upon themselves the care and maintenance of a miniature tree. In the process, is created a balance between the vision of the artist and that of the tree itself. Because the tree is kept at a modest size, each small modification to its structure may yield substantial repercussions. For this reason, the Penjing master must carefully choose and gently apply only those changes to the structure of the tree, which the organism itself is in agreement with. Eventually, the tree grows into a magnificent form which pleases the master and everyone who looks upon his creation. But this can only be an articulation which the plant itself saw fit to be molded into, for otherwise it would not have grown well.

Some penjing trees live for centuries, and are catered for by several generations of individuals. The penjing tree is akin in that respect to a martial art, and each generation of practitioners manifests a unique and ever-changing relationship with it. The art likewise, has its own vision and a distinct manner of growth and expression. By adhering to these principles, which stemmed from the original seed, the art continues to thrive. This is the root of all traditional martial arts.

The Power of Suggestion

Though in this book I do support the notion of having a form of 'dictatorship' enacted in one's school, this does not mean coercion requires brutality. People do not like to be told what to do. Many things then, can be suggested to them, without having to give a direct order. Here is a very good example:

In the social circles of traditional Chinese martial arts, it is an acceptable norm that the teacher is paid for by his students when they frequent restaurants together. Yet how can one convey such an idea to Western students? It would be highly frowned upon in most Western societies to have someone request for his underlings to pay for his meals. Such an action, if it were to result from a direct order, would be interpreted as an abuse of power, rather than a sign of respect. But the problem remains. It is said that true respect cannot be taken – it can only be earned. Yet though one may earn the students' respect, it does not telepathically convey to them the traditional concept of feeding one's teacher. They must somehow be introduced to the idea, while still considering the delicate nature of such a scenario.

The only person then whom I have ever told about the need to pay for the teacher's meals, directly referring to myself, was my first disciple. I have twice or thrice mentioned this to him, knowing that our relationship is as that of family. I knew then that he would convey the message onward.
This was not enough however, to ensure the sustainability of such a habit among the students. I therefore used additional means of indirect suggestion. I would frequently speak of how I myself cater for my own teachers and the things I happily do for them, including paying their bills at restaurants. Then whenever my teachers were around, I would prove that I was up to my word. In the presence of my teachers, I would not wait for students to pay for me – rather, I would be the one to take care of the check, organize the collection of money, and pay for both myself and my share in covering my

teacher's expenses.
Another very important thing I have done, is to write down my expectations of students, in articles and books of mine, and encourage them to read such works. That way they could know exactly my expectations, but would not be offended or irritated with some of them, as in when they may have heard me speak the same words to their face. Paper usually arouses less hostility and more tolerance as compared with the real-life presentation of facts and demands.

In going about such tactics, one has to be a sly politician. Often to make a point, an idea needs to be said to one student, calculating the descent of it down to whomever ought to be the real recipient. I cannot say that I excel at such maneuvers, but when I did manage to pull them off, they worked brilliantly.

Western culture typically glorifies the 'Truth', and the need for it to be said directly. Chinese and especially Japanese cultures, understand the beauty that exists in saying one thing, and meaning another. An ignorant Westerner would be quick to interpret this notion as being innately deceitful. Sometimes it is. But for the most part, the Oriental tendency to be more indirect is not meant to be misleading, but rather come across as more polite, acceptable and harmonious. There is much elegance and grace to when people interact in perfect harmony without having to clearly state their intentions. It is the hallmark of couples, partners and groups who have been coexisting with superior mutual understanding, that they can function like that – as if reading each-others' minds. That is the aspiration of traditional Oriental cultures like those of the Chinese and Japanese – to create social units in which such kinship is possible.
Such Oriental societies have hierarchies same as in Occidental cultures, sometimes even stronger or more oppressive. Therefore, to speak and convey orders and intentions indirectly, does not mean to lose touch with one's status as a teacher or a leader. Rather, it means to meet with the other person without causing rise in resistance. Which, if you think about it, is essentially a theme in all of traditional martial arts.

Considering this reality, how can you make a student understand your wishes, while avoiding hostilities arising from within him? Earlier I have touched upon the political answers to this question, but there is also the physical side to it.
What I have found over the years was, that people can be manipulated in their learning process by the use of movement cues. Think of yourself as an orchestra conductor, who also happens to be a dog trainer at the same time. What these two professions have in common, is that they use body language, facial expressions and sounds (in the trainer's case) to control and guide their subjects into the right kind of behaviour and attitude. This sort of approach works best with children, but is also very effective with adults.

The idea is to become more theatrical. This can be challenging for some, so start with small experiments. Use rising sounds, like turning on the volume intensity on a music device, to denote to a student the correct rhythm and intensity when expanding his body. Use diminishing sounds, as in something collapsing unto itself, in hinting to the same student the correct rhythm and intensity when shrinking his body. As in traditional martial arts we go from opening to closing and back again all the time, it would not be difficult to find several movements with opening followed by closing or vice-versa, and test such an idea with them, on the same student. Likewise can be used facial expressions of opening and closing on your part, and making similar suggestions with the entire body. This sounds silly, but can work miracles with many of the more problematic students, who otherwise do not deduce well one's verbal intent.

These suggestions I speak of then, are no a matter of hijacking one's consciousness, as with hypnosis. Rather, it is the process with which a teacher uses strategy, empathy and sometimes politics as well, to obtain greater harmony, without arousing resentment or distress.

The Truth Which Works

My mentor, friend and colleague, Shifu Stephen Jackowicz, is very well-traveled. For many years, Stephen lived in Korea and China, and was exposed to countless cultural phenomenon that Westerners often miss, when they hover innocently between tourist traps. A lot of the nuance Stephen saw in Korean and Chinese cultures, is only revealed to a person who was born there, or had been living among the natives for years. Luckily for Stephen, due to his willingness to learn the local languages and customs, many doors were opened before him.

When Stephen was studying traditional medicine in Korea, he had a famous professor as one of his teachers. Stephen and many other students would routinely escort the Professor on his treatment shifts and act as his aids. Such is the common model for the Asian traditional medical traditions.
One day, a patient came in the clinic who evoked a very unusual response on behalf of the Professor. The patient was examined as any other, but was diagnosed with a rather exceptional condition. Whilst looking solemnly at the patient, the Professor exclaimed: **"Oh!... Uh!..."**. The patient, anxious to know what was the matter, inquired. The Professor answered with the severest of tones: **"I am alarmed to see that you have what we call a 'Death Pulse'!"**. The patient was awe-struck, and the Professor continued: **"According to this type of pulse that your body presents, and the rest of the diagnosis, you may die within a year! HOWEVER, do not fear! The condition is treatable. I would need you to come to us in the near future and receive treatment at least six times. You are lucky to have arrived here early. With six or more accurate treatments, your condition can surely be completely reversed"**. Shaken, but seemingly determined to make things happen, the patient scheduled the following six treatments and left.

Stephen and the rest of the student interns were perplexed as to what had transpired. They have never heard of the terrible 'Death

Pulse'. Everyone were reluctant to ask the Professor about it, fearing they would seem as fools for doing so. The other students urged Stephen to approach the Professor: "**Hey, you should be asking! You are a foreigner, and would be excused even if the question is silly**". Finally, Stephen agreed, and approached the Professor, who had an interesting answer:

"Death Pulse? Of course there is no such thing in this case! The man simply had kidney weakness resulting in lower-back pain. But you must be interested in knowing why I gave him that explanation... Well, take a look at his medical file. See something there? This man had already visited quite a few other clinics, but no one was capable of helping him. Can you see why?... It was because he never came by for more than two consecutive treatments.
Knowing this, how could I have motivated this man to heal himself? I knew that with about six treatments, we could surely significantly improve his condition. So now that he had heard that his 'Death Pulse' demands at least 6 consecutive treatments, he would be far more likely to attend all of them".

Stephen added a moral to the story:

"When you meet a person on the path, and he has not yet attained a greater understanding, you cannot reveal the whole truth to them. Sometimes, revealing the whole truth to a person who is not ready to accept it, is to tell them a lie".

In the story I told you just now - when the many doctors were too honest and straightforward with the immature patient, their approach ended up being not only useless, but deceitful. It made the patient stray off the path, due to his inability to comprehend things at their level of expectation. The patient needed a version of the truth which appealed to something like Fear, which he could more easily relate to and function by, rather than operate based on a higher concept, like personal responsibility.

Stephen's wise words with respect to the 'right type of truth', apply to all forms of education. Consider how parents avoid exposing and explaining the full extent of human sexuality to children, until they have matured enough to be able to psychologically embrace that reality. It is universally understood that if that truth is to be fully revealed to someone at too young an age, that child can manifest some serious problems. The same logic is also relevant to out students in the martial arts.

As teachers, we are eager to teach at the level at which we ourselves practice. Especially for a young teacher, or someone who has opened a new school, one of the most depressing aspects of the job is knowing it would take several years until students attain a technical level of skill which would be interesting for you to work with. Then we face the temptation, all too often, of presenting the innocent martial arts toddlers with some facets to our practice, which are way over their heads. Sometimes we are lucky, and such actions are harmless – they simply fail to grasp most of the explanation, and no harm is done. But other times, this can be dangerous. A lot of things can go wrong:

A student can use a technique beyond his skill level and hurt himself or someone else. A student may adopt, as a result of a higher principle or method revealed to him, a false conception of the art, and continue to attach himself to wrong ideas for decades to come. There are those who may develop a sense of entitlement by having been told 'precious secrets', while others would be completely discouraged as they would feel unjustifiably overly challenged.

Whatever the outcome, much of the time, a completely honest truth, handed over to a person who cannot handle it, results in a negative reaction, as if the truth was a lie. The truth is not a lie, but its interpretation at the hands of the inept, makes it so. Therefore, quite paradoxically, a well-articulated half-truth – a white lie, can be more benevolent and considerate than a complete truth too earnestly shared.

Ways to Approach a Curriculum

In my career as a martial arts teacher, one of the surprising aspects for personal growth for me has been the development of the curriculum of the arts I teach. This process was never smooth, and always caught me off-guard, demanding that I change my biases and ways of thinking. A good curriculum and training regime are essential for the long-term success of any martial arts school. Here are then the more vital aspects to which you have to pay attention when you tackle this subject.

Make the curriculum visible

You may know these couples, featuring two people who have been together for years, but carry a strong sense of unrealized potential and hidden expectations. They say they wish their spouse or partner would have been this or that. Often, they are at fault too, though – they simply forget to tell and emphasize to their loved one how they wish he or she would act, in daily endeavors, financially or perhaps in bed. The lesson to be learned is that in relationships, especially long-term relationships, you need to let people know what is expected of them, and better sooner than later. Teaching the martial arts is the same. Sharing the general outline of your art's curriculum from day one is making sure the students know what is expected of them.

It is wise to put the written curriculum of your entire art on the wall of your school [21], as well as the requirements for testing (if tests exist). For some strange reason, many teachers refrain from doing this. It only leads to problems. The students are not as immersed in the art as you, the teacher. They usually do not remember everything by heart, not even the more experienced among them. Make sure therefore that the curriculum is before their very eyes. But do not stop there. Make it a habit by the end of each class, to take them to where the curriculum is hung and point to the components in the curriculum you worked on today. You will be surprised as to what these extra 60 seconds following each class can do for you and for them in the long term.
On the curriculum list, there is no need to write everything down to the tiniest details. Simply specify in very general terms the subjects, techniques, methods, forms and exercises being taught at each stage of learning.

This is also a good organizer for you, the teacher. Simply being able to view the entire curriculum whenever I am at my academy helps me maintain a sense of long-term strategy with my teachings, and eases the choosing of topics for classes.
Making the curriculum visible is important for another related reason. As student numbers grow, it is difficult to follow their progress. Even when various students share the same 'stage' or 'level' of training, within that framework one student may know a certain amount of material, while the other has so far studied less. It gradually becomes impossible to keep track of student progress to the smallest details, but failing to do so results in problems with teaching and student progression. A curriculum which is hung on

---

[21] The curriculum I teach, I have also made available online for anyone to view on our website, and so it would be even more accessible to students. You need not fear such exposure – if what you teach has depth, then how could an outsider possibly 'steal' anything meaningful from your curriculum? Even if you listed every single movement and method your students practice, they cannot be 'stolen'. Place your teachings out there for anyone to see and take pride in them! Those who have some experience in the martial arts would be able to tell that your school has something substantial to offer.

the wall and is accessible at all times, allows both teacher and student to keep track of where the student is at and what he or she should study right now, based on their past learning.

That being said, be careful to not reveal the full scope of the time and effort the higher levels of practice can demand. A lot of teachers are too keen on letting people know from the first day that they are about to undertake something which will be life-long and tremendously challenging. I suggest you do the opposite - intentionally omit or de-emphasize such information when speaking with beginners, so that you do not frighten them. Rarely does someone walk into a martial arts school believing that training 3 hours a day, 7 days a week, is their dream. Do not go there. They will understand when they are ready, without you needing to say anything explicitly by that time. Failing to abide by this will result in unreasonable assessment of the situation on part of the student. The reality of it is that most people will only reach a low or mediocre level of practice and stick with it for life, never making the most they can from what you teach. That is OK. Others will continue to push themselves to the utmost and attempt to take whatever you and the art can give them. That is OK also. But the process needs to be natural, and neither type of result should be encouraged. Be clear about what the art has to offer and what is expected at each stage of practice in general terms, but avoid getting into the nitty-gritty details of it with those not yet prepared.

It is fine to change the curriculum a bit from time to time, as long as you are qualified to do so. Just be sure to let the relevant students know, show them the changes physically if required and point to the differences on the printed sheets of paper hung on the wall. People can react negatively to such changes, but are far more inclined to cooperate and take it easy if they have a coherent and convincing explaination. This is also a test for you – be sure you can convince yourself the changes make a lot of sense, before you try to convince them. In my opinion, your most veteran and trusted students should be questioned about such changes to the curriculum before you make them. Ask these students of their opinion, and also of how they think the other students will react, in order to anticipate things you did not consider, and be able to tackle the mission in the best way possible.

In implementing your curriculum at the school there are, generally speaking, three approaches for teaching it: **Brick Laying, Segmenting and Cycling**, and a **combination** of the two.

Brick Laying a Curriculum

The idea with 'brick laying' is that you build that 'house' which is your school brick by brick. Each brick is a piece of knowledge – a chunk from the curriculum. You teach one thing, and then the subsequent thing is taught only after the previous brick has been firmly established in place. Then after a long period of time, perhaps a year, the brick-laying begins anew, with the construction of another 'wall' aside the previous one. This is a very straightforward and simple approach to teaching. It assumes the students will not miss out on too many bricks (classes), and so when their 'house' is built, everything is supposedly well in order and strongly bonded.

Let me tell you a bit, about what professionals originally told to me of this method, and what life and experience had taught me soon thereafter.

At one point in time, Israeli government officials decided, based on confused sports committees, to enforce a nationwide standard for martial arts teachings. All martial arts teachers in the country were subsequently required to undergo an officially sanctioned basic teaching course, roughly 200 hours long, and pay for it, to receive a diploma. Without such a diploma, it is impossible for one to have insurance for his martial arts school in Israel.

I was lucky to get my course done in a traditional Goju-ryu Karate school, headed by **Rony Kluger** Sensei, who is a respectable teacher in the local martial arts community. In that course I was introduced to many ideas. Among these ideas was the notion of always having a 'lesson plan'.
Israelis are big believers in the lesson plan paradigm. This idea originated from the methods used by the Israeli Defense Forces, and subsequently became common in the ranks of the national education system and Scouts movement. The idea is quite simple – you work hard in advance prior to the classes to create a very structured curriculum teaching program, focusing on long-term planning. You ought to know what you would like to teach in each and every class, what are minor goals to be achieved in teaching students in the coming few weeks, where the learning is going to reach within a few months, and what you expect will happen with the students' knowledge and ability within the span of several years. Apparently, many Israeli teachers work in this manner.

Well, I was thrilled! I did not experience such a structured environment in my traditional learning up to that point, when I attended the teachers' course. I figured that this type of strategic thinking fits me like a glove. I could not wait to implement these important lessons and make my future school operate smoothly and logically.
Sometime later, within one month of teaching, reality slapped me so hard in the face you could hear that echo on the other side of the city. Why? Well, here is the thing.

Lessons plans are meant to work with perfect students, and nobody is perfect. The perfect student arrives at every single class, on time. The perfect student listens to everything you say with the utmost attention, trains home every single day, does his own research, etc. The perfect student is always cooperative, attentive and thoughtful and will only ask good questions, often. Alas! <u>Very few such students exist, and no student is like this during their first few months of learning.</u>
You come to class with a plan, and then you realize the scope of your

fantasy: There is frequently a student who, for whatever reason, is a bit late, and is going to miss on some of the training. The class is seldom 100% full, and now some will miss on what you teach. One student forgot half of what you taught him last time. Another student was not even present in the preceding two classes. A couple of them are tired from work, or possibly have a headache or a runny nose and are not at their best. You wanted to do some special training but not everyone brought the equipment they needed, so you think of perhaps taking them to train outside instead, and then a sunny day becomes rainy within minutes. Shockingly enough, life tends to mock the supreme planning skills of martial arts teachers. **Every single time**.

Considering that by this approach of **brick-laying** curriculum the teacher will not often repeat the same material (assuming it was already understood), perhaps once in a few months or once a year, any knowledge conveyed when a certain student was absent will take a serious toll on his learning. Chance has it that a student can and will often miss a specific class (one focused on specific topic) not once, but twice or even thrice over the course of months and years. Such a student is now forever lagging behind. This student will be confused. He will more likely make mistakes. His unfamiliarity with lost material will drag his entire group back. He would be more inclined to leave the school. This is made worse, then, by the fact that every student would have different holes in his version of the curriculum.

You can of course still follow-through with your plans, and continue to lay your bricks. You can decide that you **<u>will</u>**, no matter what, teach each class as designated according to the plan, and follow a yearly program. But in the long term, you will pay a heavy price for such a decision. For you will produce inferior students, compared with how they could have been under your tutelage. You will have a school 'neighbourhood' full of 'houses' with missing doors and windows, with big holes in the walls and a leaking roof. You would notice, your students would notice, and yes – everyone else with experience in the martial arts will notice.

When I see a large group of students from any given school practicing the same thing together, especially a movement form, I can immediately tell if, where and how the brick-laying failed. It is obvious and stands out, for you tend to see one house features a strong corner but lacks a gate, while another has a huge hole in the corner while featuring the fanciest gate I have ever seen. You watch this group of students and their issues stand out like fireflies in a dark night, illuminated by the black gaps in the movement, body method and technique of their peers. A uniform standard of excellence cannot be attained or maintained, for each of them missed out on several key points in the 'construction process'.

Perhaps an MMA instructor would not mind, for in sports-fighting you wish to flesh-out and develop mostly the fighter's strongest attributes, and while working on weaknesses, they are not emphasized in a major way. But those among you who teach the traditional martial arts, know and seek the construction of a whole person, and look to tend to all of his or her many parts and facets. Because of this, especially in the Internal Martial Arts of China which I teach, more emphasis would actually be given to a person's weak points than to his natural strengths. This demands all structures to be built uniformly and very accurately, without deviation, before the student is ready to personalize his art.

For these reasons and several others that you may discover on your own, a brick-laying and an overly planned curriculum are actually detrimental more than they are beneficial.

There are two big exceptions. One is when teaching children. The difference here being that:

- Children study a simplified and shorter version of the curriculum to begin with.

- Children are OK with repetition. In fact, they absolutely love it. You wanted to teach something important on a given class but only 3 out of 10 children arrived? No problem. Teach the exact same thing next time when they are all present, and those who were already working on it last time are unlikely to complain. Chances are they will even rejoice, if the teachings are fun and include small modifications.

Children up to the ages of 12-13 (early puberty if you will) can therefore be dealt with successfully using a long-term lesson plan program. They have a low tolerance for more chaotic forms of teaching a curriculum. A child up to that age is like a sponge. He or she will absorb knowledge and skill quickly, but will lose them just as quickly. Teach them something very well for two weeks, and watch them forget much of it if you have not mentioned it for two weeks later. Make them capable of executing something brilliantly after a month of dedicated training, let it go for another month, and be shocked to discover how they can barely repeat it on their own. Even children who have practiced martial arts for years – if you allow them for a few additional years devoid to martial arts training following that, they will forget almost everything they were taught. This is a child's evolutionary coping mechanism. Children are made to adapt to new environments. Then by the time we become adults, evolution expects us to have already settled into a more regular life pattern as well as a specific geographic location. Because of this, compared with children, adults are better at remembering and preserving skills, but are much slower at learning new things – because they are less 'spongy' – not as adaptable.

The other big exception is when you teach a small group of dedicated adult students. When teaching 5 people or less at a time for years on end, if these people train daily and arrive to most classes, it is possible to follow through with a well-organized plan and yield wonderful results. It is most unfortunate that few are the teachers who have been blessed with such students. Usually this is made possible among those who either do not teach martial arts for a living (can pick and choose students), or among those opt to have more serious study groups along with those intended for the general population.

Segmenting and Cycling a Curriculum

In 'Brick Laying' we work in long cycles, but they are rather long, and follow each other in a logical order. One cycle has to be the foundation for the next. Segmenting and Cycling takes a less formal and more modular approach to 'building a house'. One to three classes will deal with the windows. Another few classes will address the basement. Then the teacher may move to the painting of the walls. With accordance to the vibe of each week and class, the teacher will choose a more fitting subject for everyone to work on. Then eventually and gradually, he will help them see the whole picture and put the entire house together.

I have used this method more commonly because of the chaotic nature of group classes in our society, in which circumstances change and vary considerably from class to class, as I have explained earlier. It keeps classes more interesting for both teacher and students, and allows for considerable maneuverability in one's teachings.

This method works well with that sort of chaotic environment, but the chaos is also its downfall. For not a lot of people are adept and skillful at examining a myriad of ideas and being able to put them into a single, coherent picture – you have to do this for them. Thus, the biggest issue this method is student confusion in the long term, unless the teaching is extraordinarily lucid and exceptionally well-articulated. Also, here too the teacher can accidentally create a situation in which many students have 'holes' in their knowledge, and it is easy for him to forget to teach something important for long periods of time. This approach therefore has many flaws, just as the previous one, although for me personally it worked better.

One of the big advantages of the **Cycling and Segmenting** system however is its adaptability, and this works especially well with those students who are for some reason struggling. Often in a given class one student will come with some problem – may it be illness, fatigue, injury, mood swings, or something else. Sometimes more than one student has issues. The **Cycling and Segmenting** approach allows the teacher to then casually change the topic and structure of the class to suit such conditions, in a way which will be beneficial and fitting for everyone. Some examples:

- You notice that there is an atmosphere of aggression or angst in the audience tonight. Perhaps something of a political nature occurred outside the school and upset some people. Maybe the economy suddenly took a bad turn. Could be anything. You then change the class into a partner-practice only lesson, in which the focus is placed on softness, yielding and relaxation. You choose drills which force the students to let go and relieve their being. By doing this you have sent them home rejuvenated and ready to face today's and tomorrow's challenges.

- You wanted to have a high-energy class tonight, but then just before starting you realize that it is the Winter Solstice. Medically and spiritually, this is a time to focus inward and conserve energy, rather than burst outward and expend it. You tell the students: "*Today I have a surprise – we are going to make this a special meditation class, and we are also going to talk about how the martial arts can help us with life in practical ways, and make an open discussion about it*". The opposite may have been true for the Summer Solstice.

- There was some movement-form you were in the process of teaching a few of the students and hoped to complete during this evening's class. On the news that week were reported several instances of stabbings by gang members. You can tell the students are worried and talk about it among themselves. You turn that class into a knife-defense class, and then also make a follow-up seminar on that subject on that weekend, and use the seminar setting for a social gathering as well.

Finally, it should be noted that **Cycling and Segmenting** is especially challenging to do with children, for two main reasons.

First, as stated earlier, they prefer linearity, as they cannot make connections and themes and lack a holistic viewpoint of anything whatsoever. Secondly, working in this manner provides children with a broad focus, which makes it difficult to direct special 'end of the year shows' – a popular attraction for parents, who are all too eager to see 'proof' their money yielded some results [22].

Creating a superior combination

Planning is in fact good. Overdoing it is what causes harm. The curriculum in general needs to be structured. That is, in the sense that students have 'levels' or 'grades' to pass through. It matters less whether passing through such levels requires a test (though it is beneficial), or if the student is rewarded with a diploma, a belt, a sash or similar. What the students need is a sense of **where they came from, and where they are headed**. This is absolutely essential. Make sure the students always have a Past, Present and Future. The **Past** are the oral and written traditions, as well as what the student has already achieved. The **Present** is today's class. The **Future** is what you expect of them, what they should expect from themselves, and what can be achieved. Therefore, in every single class you teach, make sure the students have these elements included verbally: Past, Present and Future.

---

[22] I personally strongly dislike these special end-of-year parent shows. These are products of modern 'community center culture' – not related to traditional martial arts. They tend to detract from more important aspects of the teachings. The children are herded like circus animals for weeks in order to prepare, and all of this is being done to justify and prove a point for the parents. I do not teach for the parents. In fact, I do not care much for most parents. They do not matter – my students matter. I have nothing to prove to anyone, especially not to people who usually do not really understand what I practice and teach. Good teachers can deliver the 'proof' via marked and notable improvement in the child's behaviour and thinking in all walks of life. I am paid to help people become better versions of themselves, and not to groom stage actors. All that being said, one has to admit that such shows are a good financial investment and leave a strong impression on most parents.

I have never in my life taught the exact same class twice. Neither should you. Teaching the same thing over and over again for years is a surefire way to drive any teacher mad and depressed, sucking all joy out of your profession. In this respect, you can see that I tend to follow more the approach of Segmenting and Cycling.
But this does not mean that I do not lay my bricks. What I actually do is following the **Brick-Laying** approach in the long term, while preferring **Cycling and Segmenting** for the short term. When I come to teach a class every day, it is seldom pre-planned. But in my mind and sometimes in writing, and definitely in terms of the written curriculum of the entire art, the long-term plan is well-organized and quite rigid. Whichever order, shape or form the yearly classes may follow, they would still lead a student down a pre-destined traditional path. That is partly the definition of a traditional martial art, is it not? To have a tradition means people follow a way with clear borders and guidelines. Otherwise, it is simply all chaos.

A Curriculum – when is it too much?

Many practitioners 'hit a wall' when the curriculum they practice exceeds the capacity of their memories or the time they can allot to practice all of that material. When a martial art is rich in knowledge, then it is only a matter of time before a practitioner feels overwhelmed.
The cure for this is to let all that information and skill sink in – to not practice anything new until the mind and body feel that they are 'fluent' with what they already have.
The prevention for said illness is therefore to avoid learning too much, too early. As teachers, this is something we must be cautious with. It is easy for us or for our student to get excited, and in the zeal of teaching and learning to drown a person in methods and techniques. Usually, the student will not realize he is 'drowning'

until the 'water' has reached his nose! Then once that happens, he or she will panic. They will feel confused, overwhelmed and insecure about their past and present achievements, because of their inability to deal with the scope of the curriculum they now possess. At this point their reaction can be negative. They may under such pressure devote less time to training, which in turn will only further their sense of helplessness. Some people can quit the martial arts altogether because of this, because they will develop a false belief that 'the art is too big and complex for them to handle'. Be mindful then of how much you should really give a student at this point in his development, and give just enough for him to progress, but not too much as to fluster him.

There is also the issue with your own progress as a teacher. You too will be tempted to learn more and more from your teachers, colleagues, and perhaps make up things which are innovative and uniquely yours. But this can be detrimental.
My own late Shigong (teacher's teacher), master Zhou Jingxuan, in the course of his short lifespan of 50 years, studied more than 13 martial arts, and was capable of teaching about 6 of them. Yet at any given point in time during his life, he was only proficient at two of these at a high level. It is my belief in light of his life, that of other teachers and my own experiences, that few people can maintain a 'master status' in more than 1-2 martial arts, with the greatest of teachers attainting supreme skill in three styles. While many people practice a multitude of arts, the constraints of time can only allow proper practice in but a few, often just one.
I started my journey in the traditional Chinese martial arts with Xing Yi Quan. Then after a number of years, I began to very gradually undertake the study of Pigua Zhang as well, which was made easier by the fact that the two arts were taught to me by the same teachers (master Zhou and his disciple, Shifu Nitzan Oren). But once I had begun the study of Jook Lum Southern Mantis, I had to gradually let go of my Pigua Zhang practice, eventually maintaining only that art's weapon methods and forms, which are dear to my

heart. Though I continued to teach the empty-handed curriculum of Pigua Zhang at my academy on a daily basis, this was no longer a style I active pursued as vigorously as necessary to be considered a devout practitioner. My Pigua Zhang ironically continued to improve due to my teaching of it, the many hours allocated daily for my other arts, as well as the weapons practice mentioned earlier; but it was no longer purely 'Pigua Zhang' as traditionally intended, but a different type of gongfu – practical, effective and interesting – but different. However, I continued to teach that art traditionally to my students, as was necessary for their development, for several years. Later, my Jook Lum Southern Mantis practice gradually faded, to make room for Bagua Zhang.

Personally, for me, the marker and guide for having 'too much' has always been whether I can practice everything I know in the scope of 14 days' time. Whenever the total knowledge of the arts I knew and taught could not be practiced properly within 14 days' time (training 3-4 hours a day by myself), I chose to either omit some of my knowledge or merge it with other parts of my training. It should be noted that alongside this, I was also 'training' during the many teachings hours, which I never count as being part of my personal training time.

This approach has over the years forced me to make some very tough and heartbreaking decisions, but I never regretted it. Part of the process of growth is knowing to let go of your older self and accepting a new reality.

Now some people are more talented or dedicated than I am, or perhaps have better 'muscle memory'. My Shifu Nitzan Oren has been capable of preserving a lot more knowledge in a given time frame than I ever could. Master Zhou literally remembered hundreds of forms, empty-handed and with various weapons, and although he could not demonstrate many of them well, somehow they were engraved into his mind like prehistoric footprints set in stone.

You alone can tell what your limits are. You should know by the feedback your memory and body provide you. Think of some techniques, methods or forms you have failed to practice for a long time. When do you begin to feel, on average, that the memory of the exact requirements begins to evaporate from your perception? That you could no longer execute the movements as well as you would have liked to? You may find that it takes several months, or just several days. As you grow older and more experienced, many of the things you know could probably go untrained for whatever reason and still be relatively 'fresh' in your mind and body a long while after. But there would still be this critical time frame, to determine the longest time following which you can definitely sense a specific skill deteriorating, even a little bit. For me, that is two weeks' time, and with some of my more refined skills or those I like better – could be a month. But these are my limits. Find yours and do not go past them. Create a training regime for yourself which encompasses the entire curriculum within the confines of what your mind is capable of. Fail at this, and you will never achieve true mastery or be able to guide your students well on the path.

Better Than You

I have known many teachers who hold back on their curriculum. Professionals who refrain from sharing a lot of their knowledge, and sometimes make students wait years and even decades until they are granted permission to study something which they are eager to learn.

Granted, sometimes there are good motivations for this behaviour. Most often, students are simply not ready for a certain level of training or comprehension. Other times, secrets require keeping for some reason. But, more commonly, the teacher simply has a subconscious desire to keep to himself, even when the student is objectively technically prepared to progress through the curriculum.

Let us be honest here. We are human just like anyone else. We too have the inclination to fear a situation in which people leave us because they feel we are no longer of use to them. Or, as also happens, become anxious that our students will transcend our skill and understanding, which might somehow lead to conflict. But we must realize, that distressing over such thoughts makes for a negative eduaction.

The bad news is, that the majority of students will one day leave us. The good news is, that many of them will do so as better people than they were when they came in our door. The role of the good parent is to grow his or her offspring so that one day, they could spread their wings and fly away on their own. Our role as teachers is the same.

This truth stands in direct opposition with financial interests. The best possible economic situation for a teacher would have been, to gather a group of a few dozen to a few hundred students, and have them all stick around for 50 years. But this is not in the student's best interest, because most 'children' should not be living with their 'parents' for 50 years.

Now going beyond the philosophical principles here... let us troubleshoot the problems I have detailed earlier. Why do we hold back, and what can be done about it?

Students "learning too quickly": This is usually the result of a short curriculum, which many can get through in 4-5 years. The solution can be arrived at in two ways, or combination thereof.

1. The teacher may expand the curriculum. That is not always feasible in a traditional martial art, especially when one belongs in an organization. But even in that sort of situation, it is possible to add 'complementary material' from outside the official curriculum.

2. The teacher may add an additional martial art to his arsenal. Then when students are done studying the technical curriculum of their first art, they can be encouraged to continue to practice and excel in it, while picking up the study of the teacher's second art.

Either way, the solution here involves the teacher seeking further instruction.

Students "becoming better than us": For good teachers with many students, this is often unavoidable. There is always a bigger fish in the pond. The teacher becomes older, while students keep coming in young. The hardworking adolescent student you received in your 70s , you will likely not be able to fight in your 80s. That can even happen decades earlier.
Beyond motivation to train more, the solution is not at all technical and has nothing to do with skill. To resolve the problem, the mindset of the students and the school has to change. The teacher is not someone competing with his students. He is a leader and a mentor, from whom the students can learn

not solely the art, but life's many lessons as well. Then, becoming more skilled or combatively capable than the teacher, is but a minor goal, in the scheme of a far broader and more comprehensive quest for excellence.

Consider the following real-life example:
Cus D'amato was one of the most successful Boxing coaches of all time. He is well known primarily for being the coach of Floyd Patterson and Mike Tyson. D'Amato was also a good parent to his boxers. When he took Tyson under his wing, the latter was a troubled teen with a rich history of violence and crime. He brought Tyson to his estate and treated him like his own son. Without this emotional, financial and educational support, Tyson would have never transformed into an international superstar. D'Amato likely had in mind the aspiration of all worthy parents – he wanted Tyson to become greater than he was.

But there is a difference between the type of relationship that D'Amato and Tyson shared, and that a traditional martial arts teacher has with his students. D'Amato, like many other parents, sought the success and growth of his child in a career a bit different to his own. D'Amato was a boxing coach, and Tyson was a boxer. Therefore, Tyson's success did not overshadow that of D'Amato – they only complimented each other. This is in fact not the case with traditional martial arts teachers, for when we are to wish students to become better than us, it means exactly that – in our particular martial art or set of skills, they should become greater than we are. Through this important difference is indicated a sacrifice which needs to be made. We need to put aside our Ego in order to allow the student to surpass us. This can be difficult.

I remember that during the first few years of teaching, though I was aware of this issue it did not bother me at the least. The students were too deep in novice territory to offer me a serious challenge. But as students were slowly passing the three-year mark, things began to change. Their abilities were increasing to the point in which even during cooperative demonstrations, through their unconscious will to protect themselves they could pose quite a challenge sometimes. They were becoming increasingly difficult to execute techniques on, as I have taught them how to avoid and counter many scenarios. Ironically, they were not yet at the level at which they could observe that they were occasionally interfering with demonstrations due to their increased skill and subconscious resistance.

Student progress is a natural process, so all teachers eventually find themselves at that position. There is a moment of teaching enlightenment when the teacher suddenly realizes: “Oh my, these guys are beginning to catch up to me!”. It is at that point, that teachers make a decision in their mind, which is not always conscious. They will have to deal with the situation, with either a positive or a negative approach.

The bad teachers are those who choose the negative approach. What they would do is to make sure their students will not get the full picture. They will withhold knowledge, sometimes even imparting incorrect knowledge, so that their students will forever remain beneath them.

The good teachers are those who choose the positive approach. Their path then becomes a lot more challenging. They will on one hand vow to make the most so that they can increase the skill and understanding of their students. On the other hand, they will pledge to train as hard as possible so that their skill will increase and it will not be easy for the students to surpass them.

It is but inevitable that, if the teaching is very good, some of the students will eventually surpass the teacher or at least reach his level. This is because the speed of skill progression eventually diminishes with age, and also with experience. But the teacher should nonetheless aspire to reach as high as possible before the students can catch up with him. The higher the teacher climbs, the better he can help his students climb further.

“Poor is the pupil, who does not surpass his master”.

– Leonardo Da Vinci

Some teachers fear that once the student reaches their level or nears it, he may leave them. This indeed frequently happens. But if the teacher is highly knowledgeable, the art is rich in content and the relationship is strong, then there is no reason for this to happen. For even if the student were to surpass the teacher, they still can view the art from very different perspectives and learn from each other. So a student well-educated in the arts knows that a true teacher is for a lifetime. I am happy to tell you that I have maintained long-term contact and continued to learn from all of my traditional martial arts teachers, and I am afraid a lifetime would not suffice to learn everything from each of them. Do your best to instill the same feeling in the hearts of your students, and you will not be left alone. Begin though by showing them, truthfully and honestly, that it is in your interest to help them become better than you. Then they will come to know and appreciate the sincerity of your intentions.

“I don't succeed when I make a guy or help a guy become champion of the world. I succeed when I make the fellow champion of the world and independent of me!

'Cause when he is independent of me, I have succeeded. He succeeded when he becomes a champion. I have succeeded when he doesn't need me anymore”.

– Cus D’Amato

The Real Lesson Plan

In the previous chapter pertaining to the building of a curriculum, you may recall I told you about the challenges of operating by a fixed 'lesson plan'. More often than not, you cannot force your plans upon the students who attend a given class. Their personal circumstances at the time of that class, and the atmosphere these create in the group, should set the agenda for that day. But how can a teacher know what kind of approach to take in teaching every class and student? What method should really determine the 'lesson plan'? Luckily, there is a rough system for sorting this out. Here it is before you:

Self-actualization

Esteem

Love/belonging

Safety

Physiological

You ought to know about this famous illustration, called **Maslow's Hierarchy of Needs.** It is a renowned paradigm in modern psychology. Its basic ideas are expressed in this pyramid here before you. The premise is very simple:

Every human being has to get some 'needs' sorted out (bottom parts of pyramid) before he can make time and allot resources for other 'needs' (top parts of pyramid). There is a 'hierarchy of needs'. The most fundamental human needs, seen at the base of the pyramid, relate to survival: Breathing, Drinking, Eating, Sleeping, etc – our physiological needs. Once we can survive, we can take care of our personal safety (second tier). Being safe can relate to our capacity to fend off a wild animal, be associated with financial security, remain free of illness, or otherwise be capable of dealing with 'threats'. As we feel safer, there is room for experiencing love and belonging, in the family and the community, as well as within a martial arts school (third tier). Once love and belonging are established, then we may work on our self-esteem, self-confidence, self-respect, social status, etc (fourth tier). Then when all other things are in order, and only then, we can evolve to the utmost human potential and strive for what is called 'Self-Actualization' (fifth tier). The latter, the end-result, being the fulfillment of our truest and most appropriate personal potential in all of our endeavors.

Now, I shall demostrate what can happen at a typical martial arts class, and how this theory makes a mockery of your plans for that class, but also offers solutions.

Here comes Russell, one of your favourite students, kind of dragging himself through the door. What happened Russell? Well, he had a difficult day at work. But worse yet, an hour ago he was on the receiving end of a lawsuit from a former client. Russell is a talented surgeon who cares deeply for his patients and is overall very professional. But one ungrateful soul heard your student Russell is a millionaire, so he brought in his cousin, who happens to be a hot-shot lawyer, and together they are suing Russell for negligence and malpractice, for the sum of 5 million dollars. Now, Russell enters the martial arts school with the knowledge that there are people who want to take everything away from him, for no reason but greed. Russell will survive the moment, no doubt, but how about his long-term safety? Does he feel safe right now? Take a look at the pyramid. See where **Safety** is located. In accordance with this well-established theory – do you believe that Russell is now inclined and prepared to feel self-confident, for instance? Is he prepared to fill his heart with a deep sense of love and belonging? Surely, it would be difficult for him. Russell does not need that sort of talk. Russell needs you to make him feel safe and to provide him with the tools to make himself feel safe later at home and on the job. Russell would not be capable of handling, for instance, the notion of meditation at this particular point in time, unless quite experienced with it already. He instead needs to feel being in control of his physical body and the bodies of others. Help him regain a sense of control and safety to his being and future, and you would have done a great service unto him that day. Moreover, by helping a certain 'Russell' in that manner, then he would then or in time feel grateful, loving and a part of the school's community. Trust that people tend to remember, who made them feel safe in times of need.

In steps another student, Vicki, charming and energetic as always. But you can see that today, her smile casts a big shadow. Oh, what plagues poor Vicki's mind? You see, two weeks ago she broke up with her boyfriend of several years. They were close, and now that he is gone she is lonely, as the rest of her family and friends live in country far away. Vicki does push through the drills and forms, and surely she feels safe with a stable job and martial arts skills honed for 10 long years. But her heart is shattered, and her self-esteem is at an all-time low. That may not be the best time to have her contend in sparring, especially not with people who may pose a great deal of challenge to her. Sparring is too reminiscent of the hostilities of life, and begets antagonism, not benevolence. She has enough of an emotional challenge as it is. But allow her to work on partner exercises with which there is much positive feedback and comfortable mutual touch and 'massage', and perhaps you could make a big difference for her during this strenuous period in time.

Likewise, there is no point in allowing a student into a class to begin with, wherein he or she arrive seriously dehydrated, malnourished or under-slept - physically or spiritually. Such people require rest and sustenance, as they waddle and wade at the base of the pyramid. Let them sit aside for at least a few minutes, have them eat and drink. Tell them some jokes. With subtle permission, make them into a comedic co-commentator on class events and enliven their mood. Allow them to encourage their friends from afar to make them feel that they still belong and take part. Make sure they breathe deeply and encourage them to gently self-massage and stretch about. They can be a part of the class, even in modest ways, but you have to be smart about the manner in which this is handled.

The wisest and most skillful of teachers know better than structuring an entire class around just one level of Maslow's pyramid. Instead, they teach everyone the same topic and subject, but make each student feel that for them personally, that class supported exactly the level of the pyramid they were more inclined towards that day.

What Do They Really Want?

Once, mankind had a traditional approach for passing information from one generation to the next. This method was that of the Master and the Apprentice – a Discipleship. It allowed for a profound transmission, which transcended knowledge and embodied the very spirit of one's ancestors in his art or trade. Today, most professions and fields of interest have lost this important method. People tend to either get formalized education in a sterile, homogenous environment, or they simply make up whatever they like as they go. Martial Arts are one of few respectable occupations in which teachers still commonly follow the old-school of learning. Be appreciative of this, for you, whoever you may be, are the keeper of a flame, and the living representative of something greater than your Self.

What will you do with this great responsibility? Try this: every time you open the doors of your school, recall that question: "What am I doing with my great responsibility?". Then you could remind yourself, why you are standing there in the first place, and what needs to be done. This is easier to forget than you might think.

Over the years, the school becomes many things. It is a place of study; a community; a medical clinic; a temple of sorts; an island for people to escape to from their daily realities; a gym; a psychological support group; a window to other cultures; and much more. Then there are also countless issues that arise, which do not necessarily relate directly to the martial arts, such as: celebrations, disasters, marriage, divorce, tests, promotions, ceremonies, the comings and goings of individuals, the growth of everyone together and other hallmarks in the life of a school and its people. With all of that fuss and the extra challenges of running a school, you may forget your true calling. This is why you need a frequent reminder.

Then what is your true calling, really? People often speak of why they practice or teach the martial arts. They name things like: a spiritual connection, self-defense, fitness, flexibility, tradition, a sense of belonging, having fun, health, etc. But these are not the real reasons people practice or teach the martial arts. By the end of the day people do things, martial arts included, because they believe that what they do will make them happy. This is the whole thing, in a nutshell. They may talk of deadly techniques. They may show interest in getting their breathing in order. They may want to be someone. They may seek a prize or a medal. They may wish to walk down the street without fear. But they all want the same thing: **to be HAPPY**.

Then who are you really for them, as a martial arts teacher? You are the person who is expected by others to make them happy! This is your real job. This does not mean, of course, that you need to prostitute the art in order to achieve that goal. Quite the contrary. Often, people are very mistaken in their belief of what will make them happy – their outlook and belief system can be perverted in that respect. It is up to you, the martial arts teacher, to find a path – a noble way – to help people reach happiness in their lives and the lives of those who matter to them, through your teachings.

There are only two things in the world money cannot buy: **Happiness** and **Time** [23]. Even love, though it cannot be bought per-se, is sometimes easier to attain when you have more money. Then consider, that you as a martial arts teacher can give these two things to people – **Happiness** and **Time** – the things which money cannot

[23] Research has shown that happiness is innate and deeply ingrained in one's personal psychology. It is not easily modified for the better. Even people who have won the lottery usually only demonstrate a rise in happiness for a brief period of a few weeks, and then their 'happiness levels' tend to drop to how they were before they became rich. Profoundly affecting happiness in the long term requires a deep and complicated internal process of change in one's perception of himself and the world.

buy. You can provide them with Happiness, through the classes you teach but more importantly – through the tools you give them. You can provide them with Time, by both teaching how manage themselves better, and making sure they live longer and not waste time on pity actions, silly thoughts and illness.

Now here is the irony – the students are usually completely oblivious to this, even when they reap the benefits! As a general rule in martial arts teaching and life, do not expect people to guess what you have done for them. Gently, politely and modestly, make sure they know. Communicate with your students about their lives, but most of all in this context, convey to them what they are achieving and receiving from the classes, and speak up when you notice they have attained greater happiness or health. Also, let them know that their happiness, health and time are precious to you. Not once or twice – repeat the message weekly. Then believe in it. Then make it happen.

Watch each student as he or she enter the school. Be mindful. Examine their facial expressions as they say hello. Take note of the tone of their voice. Observe their gait. Appreciate their rhythm. **Are they happy?** If not, act to help remedy the situation. An unhappy student does not learn or cooperate well in class. He may even end up hurting himself or others. An unhappy student is likely to eventually associate his condition with his current life choices, and attending your school is one of them. Be for him a solution, not a part of the problem. Be the man he expects you to be, perhaps even subconsciously – the one to make him happy.

Then you will see that gradually, by this following this mission of happiness, all other things will tend to naturally come into order.

How to Be Happy

This chapter relates directly to the previous one, **'What Do They Really Want?'**, and continues where the former left off. Much of the content contained in this chapter is based on the wisdom of **Paul Chek** [24] – a man whom I deeply respect and admire.

In the process of attempting to manufacture and maintain smiles upon the faces of my students, I was led to write this important chapter. You can use it in your own personal life as well. But more importantly – share this information with your students, and augment these ideas to suit the type of classes and martial arts that you teach. You will not regret it. Happy students are key to a thriving community and a flourishing martial arts schools.

When we try to think of what human beings cherish more than anything else in the world, we should consider what every parent would wish his or her children. Would that thing be money? Fame? Success? Greatness? Love? An amazing career? Talent? Perhaps parents would wish their children some of these things, or all of them. But all parents, without exception, will primarily wish one thing for their children: for them to **be happy**. The great Greek philosopher Aristotle acknowledged this too, thousands of years

---

[24] Paul Chek is a great scholar of our time, and the author of several excellent books. Originally a fitness and nutrition specialist, he has worked tirelessly for decades to expand his vision of a healthy living for the body and mind into a complete system of teaching and learning. He has founded a private college of sorts, called the 'Chek Institute', in which people study professional programs to certify as 'Chek Practitioners'. The level of studies offered at that institution is second to none in the fields of nutrition, fitness training, philosophy and spiritual practice. Chek practitioners operate worldwide, in many countries, and work with everyday people as well as elite world-class athletes of every imaginable sport. Paul makes all of his students at the Chek Institute follow a healthy lifestyle, and one cannot complete even his first year studies without doing so. Therefore, Paul's students tend to be very healthy and vibrant individuals. Another important aspect in Paul's teachings is personal development in all walks of life. Achieving a state of happiness is key to this vision. You can read more about Paul Chek and his fantastic work on his website: www.chekinstitute.com

ago. He also said that the final aspiration of all humans is for happiness, though they tend to disagree among themselves what it takes in order to achieve that state.

A related amusing tale: Famous artist John Lennon remembered that since he was 5 years old, his mother used to tell him that "happiness is the key to life". One day at school, the children were asked to write down what they wanted to be when they grow older. Lennon wrote: "To be happy". The teachers told him he did not understand the task. He told them that they did not understand Life.

Then why is it, that if happiness is likely the most important thing for humans, that it is so difficult to attain?

Confucius suggested that the problem with happiness is as follows: "Men look for Happiness in that which is above or below them. But Happiness is at the same height as man". **Meaning:** The source for happiness is in man's knowledge of what is fitting of his measurements, situation and character – that which 'matches its stature'.

Despite this, most people look for happiness in what does not suit their being – that which is above or below them. A tall man finds pleasure in the thought of those shorter than him, and a short man the same by thinking of how tall people experience problems because of their height. A rich man borrows some emotional support in wondering of the fate of the poor, and the poor man comforts himself pondering the troubles the rich might have with all of their assets. A man of mathematical talent tries his luck in theater, of all things, to escape a challenging career, and a man with a heart in the woods finds himself sitting in an office all his life because his parents told him that this is his destiny. A man who requires a gentle and understanding partner, marries a strong and dominating woman because she has attributes he himself lacks, and another woman finds herself without partners, because she is always chasing men who are not at her level, fearing a partner who could equal her. As a general rule then, he who does not know how to fulfill himself and his ambitions in a balanced way, will witness happiness evade him.

The problem with Confucius, as is with many other Chinese thinkers, is that he does not provide us with directions. He does not tell his students or readers how to achieve happiness. Rather, he simply offers a very broad outline to follow on the path to happiness, and speaks of what will keep us away from it.

How then ought we attain this most evasive treasure, in our own lives and those of our students?

We can use the Japanese map to happiness. It is called **'Ikigai'**. The Japanese believe that if you have Ikigai, then you have necessarily attained happiness. The word Ikigai is possibly the most ingenious concept ever invented by a human society. It means: "A reason for living", or a "life calling". But more accurately, Ikigai refers to something in your life, something which you do, which encapsulates all the following:

The path to happiness then, is plain and simple. We require only to establish two things in our lives: Balance and Ikigai. To attain balance, we can follow the advice of Confucius concerning it, which I have written of earlier in this chapter. Balance then will lead us to Ikigai, and will help us sustain it. To achieve balance in life is relatively easy, since it mostly entails avoiding bad thoughts and habits. But Ikigai is trickier. Let me then break down the process of finding one's Ikigai, which in turn will undoubtedly yield much happiness in your life.

Ikigai, as you can see in the chart on the previous page, is made up of your component: "What you love to do" , "What the world needs" , "What you can be paid for" and "What you are good at". I have written these four components in this order for a good reason.

What you love to do – finding your Dream: This is the first order of business. You cannot be happy in life if you are not doing something you love. But this 'thing' has to be special. It needs to challenge you and satisfy you at the same time. It must resonate with your inner being.

What we truly love doing, is dictated by our 'Original Self'. All humans have this 'Original Self' inside of them. The Chinese call it the Hún 魂 – an 'ancestral spirit' [25]. We are not born a clean slate. Every person born has within him or her already a 'character'. This is our Original Self. It is who we were before we had bias – prior to the creation of our clearly defined Ego and personality. The latter are merely the masks we wear. The Original Self is who we really are at the core. Though you may forget how that Original Self looks and what it wants, you can be sure that your Hun does not forget you! Yes, the Original Self continues to lurk in the shadows of your consciousness, and is involved in your everyday decision-making [26].

---

[25] The **Hún 魂** is an ancient concept in Chinese philosophy, medicine and thinking. In Chinese culture, the Hun is one of the five components of the human psyche. The other four are: **Po** – the Soul, **Zhi** – the Willpower to be myself and manifest my destiny, **Shen** – the Mind Spirit – the Ego, and **Yi** – my intelligence and the ability to guide it intentfully.

[26] Famous psychologist Carl Jung had his own way of explaining this struggle. Jung noted that the majority of people suffer from a war waged inside of them, between their **Shadow** (Original Self; Hun) and their **Persona** (Cultivated Ego). The **Shadow** is who you really want to be, but are not becoming in reality due to reasons and circumstances. The **Persona** is the mask you wear in public; who you present yourselves to be, which actually reflects little the depth which lies hidden beneath the surface. The great struggle between Shadow and Persona – between who you want to be and who you present yourselves to be, creates major tensions within your psyche. For a person who completely fulfilled his dreams, shadow and persona become one – who he wants to be is who he has become. This is another important reason for pursuing one's dreams and finding one's Ikigai.

Children know their Original Self best, because they have yet to learn enough bias from the world around them, to be otherwise. When we are very young, typically before the age of 12, we know what we truly love and wish to do in life. But at that age we have a problem. We are too stupid and inexperienced to make sense of our thoughts. Thus, children go about 'changing their minds' every few hours, scattering in all directions. But inherently, they have a few decisive and clearly evident inclinations which point to what they love doing above everything else. Connecting with the inner yearnings and aspirations we had as children will lead us to an understanding of what our Original Self wants and loves to do - what we authentically desire.

Connecting with the Original Self is one of the main goals of all true spiritual practices, the traditional martial arts of the Orient being among them. Intentful practice of Yoga, Meditation, prolonged exposure to natural scenery, and any skillful practice which is highly systematic and complex enough, can lead one to a better understanding of the Original Self. That is because the Original Self is the source of all true creativity, and whichever aims to draw from that well, whilst silencing the Ego, helps us meet that part in ourselves in harmony.

Apart from deep contemplative practice though, there are also simpler methods for finding our true call. For instance, we can ask ourselves:

What do I love enough to change?

Perhaps I want to learn how to play the guitar. But in reality, I am unlikely to make time for it, because I have obligations which I deem more important or interesting. Therefore I can tell, that learning to play the guitar, while it fascinates me, is not really my Dream, because I will position it as a low-ranking priority in my schedule.

At the same time, I may fancy being a veterinarian [27]. My current line of work may be completely different. But were the circumstances right and fitting - say I had good grades and enough money to study it, I would have definitely made a considerable effort to push aside almost anything else so I could become a veterinarian. Despite the fact that studying veterinary medicine is considerably more demanding that learning how to play the guitar (as an amateur), for a career as a veterinarian I would have moved mountains and transform my life completely - which I would not have done for simpler aspirations. Therefore, becoming a veterinarian would be my true Dream.

In this manner, by asking oneself (or one's students) questions and answering them, we could to those things which we truly prioritize, and locate our deepest and most honest dreams. Remember once more the first and most important question to be asked here: **What do you love enough so you would change your life for it to happen?**

---

[27] I do not of course wish to learn to play the guitar or be a veterinarian. These are examples for the sake of explaining things.

Unfortunately, even with this question in our arsenal, some people will still have difficulty locating their dream. This is common. Many of us have gone so far from our original Self and natural state, that we now lack proper introspection, needed for us to find the dream within. Wherein you find that you or one of your students still cannot locate the dream, then ask a different question:

What will motivate me more than my biggest nightmare?

Some people are terribly afraid their spouse will leave them. Of losing their jobs. Being mocked at for a specific reason. From eternal loneliness. Or being abusive of others.
There are many fears in the world, and people are usually aware of what really frightens them. So instead of going after their dream, which they cannot find, ask them instead: "what do you fear the most in your life?". They will know.
Now continue that thought process in another direction: "Let us assume for a moment that the worst has happened – what you fear has come true. What can you now do or become, which will change you so much that you could completely forget about and transcend the previous terrible experience? What is that thing that you can do, which will make you greater than that trauma? That thing which is the answer, is the person's dream.

Then if by some strange means the person still has difficulty locating his dream, it would be wise for him (or you) to consult people who have known them for many years, are very close to them and want the best for them. Good old friends or loving family. By spilling one's heart to such a person and talking to them of one's fears and aspirations, it is sometimes possible for them to help one locate that memory of a dream within, and serve as a mirror for the original inner being.

Other guidelines include discussing what in a person's life feels like a trap. What chains one to routine and does not allow the person to be who they really want to be? Is it family? Work? A romantic partner? Fear of change? Lack of self-expression or artistic expression? Fear put into one's heart by others? These are the things which the dream needs to help one resolve. One purpose of the dream is getting the person out of such traps.

When considering your dreams and those of your students, please solemnly ponder the following truths:

The true measure for a person's wealth is how much he would be worth to those dear to him, if he had lost all of his money.

Following this logic, wherein a dream involves causing others troubles and pain, it will produce more suffering than happiness.

Then the second truth you need to pay attention to is:

The value of time is greater than the value of money. You can always get more money, but above a certain threshold, no man can get more time.

Thus, if the essence of your dream leads you to invest all of your time in making a fortune, the dream is inherently problematic; for the time available for you to live outside of work is more essential than the money you can earn. Therefore one must establish a reasonable balance between enrichment and investment of time, wherein the dream involves acquisition of financial means.

<u>What the world needs and what you can be paid for:</u> Having a Dream and doing what you love is great, but having **Ikigai** calls for a sense of practicality as well. Most people will enjoy eating a good chocolate cake. But eating a chocolate cake is not what the world needs, and neither what most people can be paid for, nor something you can get good at without hurting yourself [28].

The circumstances also differ from place to place. Say you aspire to open a martial arts school. Surely, if you are qualified, skilled and capable of bettering people's lives, that is what the world needs. But if in your neighbourhood there are already two schools from the same lineage you teach, then perhaps this is not what the world needs ***at that particular spot***. I once joked about this with a colleague of mine. He sought to retire to Okinawa, the birthplace of Karate. But being a Karate teacher, he was in no position to make a living there. In Okinawa, there must have been several Karate dojos in every single neighbourhood. Therefore, despite Okinawa being very alluring to him, his Ikigai – teaching traditional Okinawan Karate – was ironically not to be manifested at that location. The Okinawans really <u>did not need</u> any more Karate where they lived.

Then there is the question of: can I be paid for what I love to do? This often depends on your business model. In a small, rich community of 1000 people, one cannot possibly build up a school of 200 students. The notion of being a part of a large school is commonly less appealing to the rich who live among themselves, and the notion of having one out of five people in a given community

---

[28] A wisecracker might attempt a silly argument here. Someone might say: "I love eating chocolate cake; I can get a job as a taster at a cake factory and be paid for it; the world needs people who make decisions about the qualities of cakes; and I am quite good at it! Is this not Ikigai?". The answer is no – because there is no true skill in it, and the world can arguably do without it. But even if it had been Ikigai – still, it will not lead to happiness, because it lacks Balance.

as your student, is highly improbable. But that same community, would likely react better to an exclusive 'club', in which people are taught either privately or in very small groups - preferably even at their own estates.
The opposite is true for a large, poor community. Teaching at a rough neighbourhood will become a financial disaster wherein the teacher opts to charge an above-average sum for classes and aim for a small, 'exclusive' school. In such a place, low fees and a larger number of participants would be the way to go, most of the time. Charing too much may even attract negative attention, as in difficult neighbourhoods, those with a strong financial backbone are often people associated with crime.

Through this we see, that whether something can become your Ikigai depends not solely on how much you love to do it and whether it has objective value for the community, but also how well you market it or how much the community desires it.
A good example would be my native country of Israel and its initial exposure to the traditional martial arts. During the 1960s - 1990s, very few traditional martial arts schools existed in Israel. The people were eager and thirsty for that type of knowledge, being that various martial arts films and Hollywood action-flicks were very popular. During these decades, anyone who opened a school and made even little marketing efforts, tended to attract masses of students. My Southern Mantis Shifu, Sapir Tal, opened his school in 1997CE. Within a few short years, he had over 300 students. He was working so much, that he could eventually afford to take a sabbatical year off, to spend more time with his family, before returning to teach. Many other Israeli teachers, who opened schools in earlier decades, became rich from teaching the martial arts - something which is highly challenging to do these days, if you are not a charlatan (exceptions do of course exist and abound worldwide).

<u>What you can become good at:</u> A person may love to do something, be engaged in a profession which the world needs, and also be paid for it. But this is not enough. One must also be proficient at his vocation – otherwise, it is not truly **Ikigai**.

We sadly encounter this a lot in the martial arts. There are swaths of ignorant charlatans who teach the arts, and are certain that they are doing a great service to the world. They often truly and honestly do no understand, that by providing instruction on something which is entirely self-taught or self-made, or that they have not learned well enough, they are causing more harm than good.

But sooner or later, this lie will catch up to them. No charlatan can maintain his ignorance for a lifetime. People eventually realize their folly. Then, even if they continue teaching knowing that they are unqualified, they will never be happy or content. They will always know, within themselves, that they are cultivating and selling an illusion. This is the reason for which Ikigai requires skill in one's vocation. Without skills, there cannot be a sense of attainment of fulfillment, and without these, happiness will not manifest and sustain itself.

Dreams and skills seldom come easy. Making a dream come true usually involves **personal** sacrifice. So when considering what I may become good at, this is not solely about the technical or physical challenges. It is also about your willingness to make the sacrifice to gain that skill. Which in turn, requires you to literally demolish your routine, step out of your comfort zone, and work hard at something. When you do not have enough motivation to make such a sacrifice, then perhaps that thing you are considering is not your **Ikigai**.

IS THIS SOMETHING
I ENJOY DOING?

IS IT SOMETHING WHICH
IS TRULY MEANINGFUL?

HAVE YOU YEARNED TO DO THIS FOR A LONG PERIOD OF TIME?

IS THIS A REFLECTION OF YOUR TRUE SELF - YOUR ORIGINAL SELF?

IS THIS DREAM POWERFUL ENOUGH TO MAKE ME CHANGE,
AND SOMETHING STRONGER THAN MY NIGHTMARES?

CAN
YOU BECOME
SKILLED AT IT?

DOES
IT NOT
HURT OTHERS?

ARE YOU WILLING TO MAKE
SACRIFICES TO BECOME SKILLED AT IT?

ONCE SKILLED, CAN YOU BE PAID FOR IT WELL,
VIA MONEY, SERVICES, BARTER OR OTHERWISE?

IS THIS SOMETHING WHICH THE WORLD - OTHER PEOPLE,
ANIMALS, THE PLANET OR OTHERWISE - CAN BENEFIT FROM?

Fully pursuing one's Ikigai: The complete manifestation of one's Ikigai, will undoubtedly involve a tremendous personal transformation, and an even bigger change in one's relationships. You have to take into account and be prepared to deal with the fact, that having your dream manifest will bring out the best and the worst of everyone you interact with. The majority of people whom you are in touch with will react in a significant way to the change you have made, and their reactions may at times be extreme. **Remember then and believe that your right to be happy and fulfill whom your truly are is more powerful and important than other people's fear of change** (that last sentence is good to repeat for your students). Notice how those who react negatively to the change you make in your life, tend to be the people who are having a difficult time making a positive change in their own lives. Such people may abandon you on the path. The opposite is also expected to occur. As your dream manifests into form and others become aware of it, so through the months and years more and more people who are like you – who have worked tirelessly and made sacrifices to fulfill their dreams, will find their way into your life. These people will offer support and be good friends on the journey.

Finding your Ikigai and fulfilling the Dream will almost certainly require the aid of one or more mentors. The mentor is a person who had already done what you seek to achieve (or similar), managed to do it well, and is possession of notable expertise in all of the technicalities of what you are trying to accomplish. This could mean a capacity for financial understanding, psychological insight, paperwork, laws, professional knowledge, familiarity with a 'scene' or a place, or anything which can be of aid to you directly. It is your duty to locate those who shall be your mentors, and demonstrate before them honesty and sincere will to make things happen. It is vital to find people whom you can both trust and personally relate to. Especially, those who possess moral values which you share. A mentor whose choices, values and personally mismatch with yours, will offer your ways which will not lead to happiness. The mentor will be a 'father figure' (or mother) for all matters pertaining to your

dream and the pursuit of it. You need to honour such people, but not worship them, and be cautious of them taking advantage of you financially, emotionally or physically.
As far as students go, you are often one of their mentors. This book as a whole is meant to advise you on how to fulfill such a role in the best and most adequate fashion.

As one's dream comes into fruitation, a person can be reborn. One's energy reservoirs are refilled, he feels younger, and the body is stronger and more vital, even if no major physical or diet-related changes had taken place (though these are of course also very important). Good opportunities and circumstances will seem to arise naturally and spontaneously all the time, and be in one's direction. The person becomes more creative, and makes better decisions about his life and future.

<u>**Confucius said:**</u> "***Humans beings live with honesty. Those who are dishonest, live feeling they are ruled by fate***". There is honesty towards others, and sincerity for ourselves. He who is dishonest, society shall easily find out about his lies and half-truths, and people will take note of his fickle nature. Then he will be haunted and attacked by others without being able to anticipate the blow. A man insincere with himself, would not know what he wants, and will find himself making decisions which are unfitting of his true Self and true wishes (again, a problem of Shadow vs. Persona). Furthermore, lying to one's own psyche, he would be attempting to hide the real reasons for why this or that happened, and blame things on unrelated things and circumstances. Such a person is doomed to live feeling like "he is fated"; things will simply 'happen to him', instead of him making them happen, and he will not understand how they came to be.
Fulfilling the dream is manifesting sincerity, by which we also gradually become honest with our surrounding environment. Only by fulfilling our dreams are we able to detach from the feeling that we are victims – that the world has done so and so unto us, and stop living as if we are fated. In other words – fulfilling our dreams is the

cure for the victim's mentality, and a victim's conception of the world as something that happens to him while he is a puppet in the hands of other people. Such is the development of a man into a mature and responsible individual who takes his life and fate into his own hands.

Now that I have already discussed what Ikigai means and how to find your own, it is also important I discuss how to balance the different types of happiness. Yes, there is more than one type of happiness! There are in fact three of them:

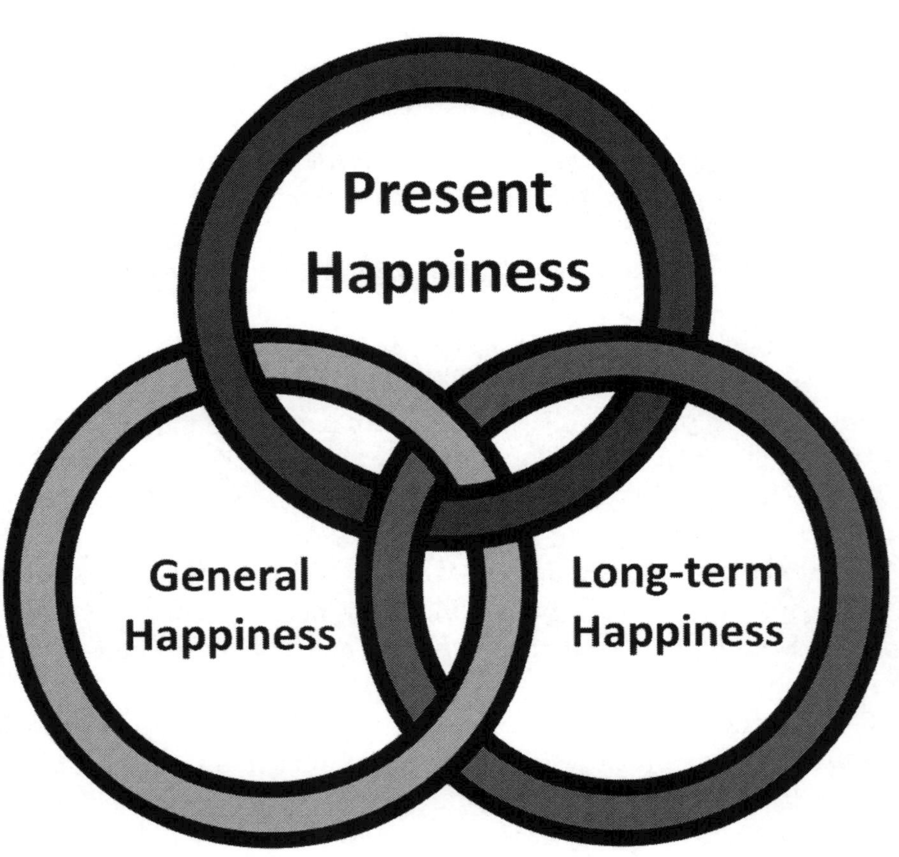

Present Happiness: It is very simple. How happy are you right now, at this very moment? Are you feeling good or bad? Are you, as of now, happy or sad? This is the measure of Present Happiness.

General Happiness: How happy are you, generally speaking, of the state of your life and being? Is your general state of living, thinking, feeling and working a source for happiness? Having **Ikigai** is essential for General Happiness and contentment in life.

Long-Term Happiness: How happy are you with your life over a long cross-section of time? Looking to the past, present and future of your life, together – is this great continuity satisfying to you and brings you happiness?

In order to truly be happy, you must balance between the three types of happiness. A person's happiness is only full and sincere when the three types of happiness are synchronized.

<table>
<tr><td colspan="6">The person is suffering, and likely experiencing depression.</td></tr>
<tr><td>Present Happiness:</td><td>✗</td><td>General Happiness:</td><td>✗</td><td>Long-Term Happiness:</td><td>✗</td></tr>
<tr><td colspan="6"></td></tr>
<tr><td colspan="6">The person has experienced a positive and uplifting experience at a given moment, such as eating a good meal or having sex. Yet within a few minutes or hours, his spirit diminishes and he resettles in sadness or bitterness, as he remembers that his joy cannot go beyond momentary pleasures.</td></tr>
<tr><td>Present Happiness:</td><td>✓</td><td>General Happiness:</td><td>✗</td><td>Long-Term Happiness:</td><td>✗</td></tr>
<tr><td colspan="6"></td></tr>
<tr><td colspan="6">The person is happy some of the time, and does have Ikigai. However, he may consider himself a failure, or believe too strongly that he has much room for improvement. Despite enjoying life and being pleased with it in general, he might be haunted by the sense of not having created meaning, which can then lead for him looking for it later in life, as he grows older. The scenario described is typical for younger people, but could also manifest among those who have no children or who otherwise lack a personal legacy to leave for future generations.</td></tr>
<tr><td>Present Happiness:</td><td>✓</td><td>General Happiness:</td><td>✓</td><td>Long-Term Happiness:</td><td>✗</td></tr>
<tr><td colspan="6"></td></tr>
<tr><td colspan="6">The person might seem to 'have it all', but in truth he lacks Ikigai. He indulges in things which please him at present, and has a sense of meaning over a lifetime. But in general, he feels that his life at this time is at the place in which he does not wish to be, and he would rather change that reality. He does not feel like he has something positive to wake up towards in the morning. This is the classic scenario in unhappy marriage or being at a workplace which is unfitting. Also a typical scenario for 'mid-life crisis'. Wherein the person shall not act to remedy the general situation in his life within months or a few short years, the other types of happiness will naturally also weaken and fade, causing his suffering to worsen.</td></tr>
<tr><td>Present Happiness:</td><td>✓</td><td>General Happiness:</td><td>✗</td><td>Long-Term Happiness:</td><td>✓</td></tr>
<tr><td colspan="6"></td></tr>
<tr><td colspan="6">The person is generally happy about his life and the way in which he has led them so far. At this particular moment he may be suffering from a pain of sorts, either physical or emotional, but within a short while, minutes to days, the situation will change and his happiness will once more rebound.</td></tr>
<tr><td>Present Happiness:</td><td>✗</td><td>General Happiness:</td><td>✓</td><td>Long-Term Happiness:</td><td>✓</td></tr>
<tr><td colspan="6"></td></tr>
<tr><td colspan="6">Such a person's happiness is full, honest and sincere.</td></tr>
<tr><td>Present Happiness:</td><td>✓</td><td>General Happiness:</td><td>✓</td><td>Long-Term Happiness:</td><td>✓</td></tr>
</table>

The Quick Path to Happiness

Thus far was a big discussion of how people can become very happy in the long-term, mostly. But how about the here and now? After all, modern humans are impatient, and demand 'a bang for their buck'... Here this is Happiness, simplified.

All humans on this Earth, primarily yearn for three things:

Happiness
Meaning
Continuity

Meaning and Continuity can be manifested through martial arts practice, but take years and often decades to attain through our teachings. About Meaning and Continuity, I have written elsewhere in this book. Happiness, among the three, is **RELATIVELY** easier to come by.
To have Ikigai is the ultimate path of Happiness, Meaning and Continuity. That should be the long-term goal. But in the short-term, the quickest way to gain Happiness through martial arts is by improving the student's Health.
On the physical side of things, there are only three major components to Health: **Food** (and drink), **Sleep** and **Movement** - in this order of importance.

So, assuming you want your students to be Happy, the quickest way to go about that, long before they can find and cultivate an Ikigai, is to make them healthier. Why am I even writing about this?

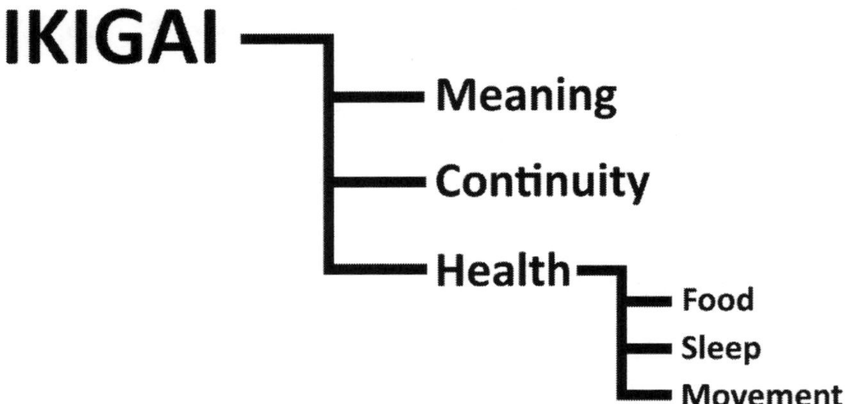

The reason I am writing about this, is that many martial arts teachers do not think it is their job to cater for the students' sleep patterns, or what they put in their mouths. In our overly-specialized Western societies, people dislike stepping out of their own little box – even martial arts teachers. They tell themselves: "Oh, I am not a doctor, a sleep specialist or a dietician; neither am I that student's mother! ***It is not my job to take care of it***!

Well, I am here to tell you that this type of pinhead attitude to teaching in life is not only ill-fitting and offensive to our profession, but also practically harmful to your school. See above – THREE components to Health – Food, Sleep and Movement. An unhealthy person is an unhappy person. So how do you expect to have happy students – lasting and capable students – if you are only going to look after their movement, but say nothing of their sleeping and dietary habits? This is self-delusion.

Granted, at least 50% of the trick is to set good personal example. When you are without excess weight, avoid smoking, do not drink too much if at all, get enough sleep and go to sleep early, avoid any food containing preservatives or refined sugar, and overall lead an openly healthy lifestyle – then your students are likely to follow your example. But for them to acknowledge your virtues and be swayed by them, can take years. This is why actual conversations are important.

What goes on these days with the world of allopathic "Medicine", sickens me. People arrive at a doctor's office who are hardly fit to be called a functioning human. They feature the most horrendous ailments of their own making, and suffer immensely of pains of the body and mind. Yet seldom are these people provided with true healing, which are in fact practical tools for changing who they are from the inside. Instead, they are given instruments for waging "war" against various microscopic creatures and cells. War has never healed anyone in all of human history. War is the excuse for not dealing with the greater issues of self-change, which most medical doctors are ill-equipped to contend with. The best that some earn from their encounter with the doctors of today, are short-term solutions for problems. This often saves lives, but is not real healing; and truth be told - allopathic doctors kill more human beings every year than most types of diseases. This is in the official statistics of all 'developed' nation.

You know what the difference between you and the modern doctor is? He can barely, gently and politely sort of hint to his patients that they ought to lose weight. You, the martial arts teacher, can come close to ***commanding*** them to do so! With proper courtesy, finesse and a positive attitude, of course.
It this not our duty, anyway? Beyond the striving for Happiness, you know just as well as I do, that an obese person, or even a moderately fat man, is usually not going to be a good martial artist (though exceptions abound), and even if he succeeds in his trials, would be far more prone to injury and illness. I say, it would be malpractice and negligence on your part, to not tell this to people - that they need to lose weight not only for their health, but also to be better at martial arts relative to their own potential.

This whole discussion is directly related to sleep. Without enough sleep, one is prone to gain weight, suffers from adrenal imbalances, and is at a greater risk of hurting himself and others during practice due to lack of focus, concentration and energy. All that, and being less happy overall. I would gather these are good enough reasons for any martial arts teacher to care for how well his students sleep, and how much.

I see that today a lot of teachers like to spend time on analysis and discussion of professional fighting matches. Even I might do this twice or thrice a year, for a few minutes. Or maybe, students are brought together to watch martial arts films. This is also very nice. But how about focusing more of the attention concerning theory, on healthy living? Moving from talking much about other people, to discussing how the real lives of the members of the school could be improved?

Every year, I have at least two short seminars, lasting 2-3 hours each, in which I teach sleeping meditation. I routinely asked health professionals whom I trust and respect, to come and lecture to my people. The students get at least one long recorded message from me every 48 hours, and a large percentage of these have me mention subjects related to healthy living. When a student comes to class extremely exhausted, I would sit them down for meditation or teach them rejuvenating breathing methods, before sending them home to rest. Our school is free from all refined sugars, preservatives and other poisons. Proper posture is enforced at all times, including when resting, washing dishes or cleaning the floor. No mouths are allowed to remain open unless absolutely necessary for hard breathing during strenuous exercise, speaking or eating. High-heeled shoes are frowned upon and strongly discouraged outside of class, and in class people only train barefoot. The state of a student's teeth or hair can become an interest of mine if they are inclined to share, and I certainly express interest in more serious concerns as well, and advice to the best of my knowledge. These conversations, the students are furthermore encouraged to have among themselves.

There are people who may find this excessive and intrusive. My students find this caring and thoughtful. In fact, few are the people in any of my students' lives who become as engaged with their physical well-being as I am. Sometimes, I am the only person who talks with them about such important health matters. This too, is a catalyst for Happiness – to have someone in your life who cares, in this alienated modern society in which so many people are depressed, because they feel no one is genuinely looking after them.

To take care of the health of your subordinates, Confucius teaches us, is in fact a part of being a worthy leader and Junzi. In Confucianism there is the concept of **Xiào** 孝 ('Filial Piety) – the proper etiquette and relationship between people of different social standing. When Confucius spoke about Xiao, he gave a lot of examples for the proper relationships between parents and children, emperor and citizen, teacher and student, older brother and his younger sibling, etc. Confucius was very wise in drawing anecdotes and allegories which taught why Xiao was important.

A person once asked Confucius about the principles of Xiao (Filial Piety). Confucius answered [29]:

"Your parents' greatest worry would be your health".

This answer of Confucius puzzled me for a while. Surely, there was logic and reason in suggesting that parents should look after the health of their children. Or in paraphrasing – that perhaps we martial arts teachers – our greatest concern should be the health of our students. But why should this particular aspect of care be more important than all else? This is cleverly revealed in another saying

[29] The Analects, Chapter 2, Verse 6.

of Confucius. When a disciple asked him about Xiao, in replying to that man, Confucius posited a theoretical situation and asked his disciple what he thinks of it [30]:

"Subtle is the countenance. The young bear the burden in work, and the elders enjoy the first choice in food and wine. But can this be considered Xiao?".

The image Confucius draws supposedly oozes dignified etiquette and respect. Via but subtle facial expressions and cues, it is understood between the parties that the young people have to do all the work, while the elders get to eat the finest food and drink the best wine (which in ancient times were scarcer). This looks to be a most excellent situation. But Confucius asks – is that really Xiao? The surprising answer, is that it is not! Here is why:

Earlier, Confucius posited that "your parents' greatest worry should be your health". How can parents be said to care most for their children's health, if the offspring are the only one doing any work, while the parents rest and do nothing? Or otherwise, when the elders get all the best food and drink, and the younger folk only the scraps? For there are many a time, when the young are sick, and do require better food and less work for nourishment. Furthermore, if the young do all the labour, they need more food and of a higher quality, to maintain their health. Confucius therefore provides us here with a brilliant allegory, which hides important moral principles:

1. Mere actions do not make for Justice. Correct Xiao – proper Filial Piety – is dependent on circumstances, not empty actions without

---

[30] The Analects, Chapter 4, Verse 8.

thought given to them.

2. When the greatest concern of the parent is the offspring's health, then it is possible to overcome a situation wherein the parent becomes spoiled, and is worshipped by his offspring at the expense of their well-being.

3. Xiao (Filial Piety) is a two-way relationship. Only by upholding its standards on both sides, can it be just and proper.

What we martial arts teachers can learn from this, is that it is in fact our sacred duty to care for the health of our students. This duty does not arise from professional status, but rather from sound moral and humane principles. It is our caring for the students' health which helps them cultivate their happiness, and also what is required to achieve balance in the relationships we have with them. Moreover, as in the example brought forth by Confucius, we must partake in the labour within the school, and be willing to do more than the students and alleviate their burden if that would support their well-being.

Their Special Moment

It was a lovely Italian night in the year 2017CE, when my friend Keith and I were strolling along the streets of Pisa, sharing stories and tales [31]. Master Keith R. Kernspecht, with no less than 60,000 students in his EWTO organization, sure knows a thing or two about teaching. During the course of our discussion, he and I were keen on getting to the core of what were the most important elements in teaching. As we were conversing, Keith brought up a crucial and perhaps surprising aspect which he deemed imperative to his great and unsurpassed success in the spreading of his teachings.

All of his adult life, Keith had a talent for getting at a certain something. He could tell when people needed his help, and what was required for him to do in order to draw out their full potential. He could look at someone from afar and observe him or her, and if the time was right and the connection was to be made, he would feel compelled to act in order to make their interaction happen. Sometimes he could even do this by simply watching a video of a certain person, or reading a text someone has written. Keith's intuition about his need of a new and fascinating human relationship seldom failed him.

Then upon becoming acquainted with new people, Keith would use a very unimposing and rather friendly demeanor in order to lead them on the right path. After having befriended them, he would be able to make them follow and be guided into a situation which will eventually give rise to "their special moment".

What was that 'special moment'? Keith described it as the moment in which an individual had experienced a difficulty, was able to

---

[31] I became acquainted and later befriended master Kernspecht after he had read my first book, **Research of Martial Arts**, which he really liked. Following a friendly correspondence of about 2 years, he invited me to spend a week with him in Italy while on vacation there. He is one of the kindest and most pleasant human beings I have ever met.

overcome it, and by passing that sort of personal test would have a revelation about his true potential and calling. The type of difficulty the person, typically the student, had to resolve, could have been trivial for some. It may have been a form of public speaking or teaching. Perhaps it was a requirement to use force in order to overcome a strong partner in class. Whatever the thing was, it needed to be something that the student would not normally be willing to do, but that Keith was able to cunningly manipulate him or her into doing nonetheless.

Then upon completing this minor quest and experiencing that special moment, the student would acquire the blessing of three powers: faith, hope and self-confidence. From then on, the student could have a vision of a better version of himself, and believe in it. The special moment would ignite a flame, which could burn for a lifetime.

Therefore, Keith considered it imperative that the martial arts teacher be able to **lead** each student on a path which would eventually place him on that platform of challenge suited especially for them; the place in which he or she could be tested on their own terms and arise triumphant. More often than not, that would be a very personal kind of journey and victory, to be walked and attained outside of the regular school curriculum and classes.

Through this exceptional moment in someone's life then, it becomes possible for the martial arts teacher to inspire his student to believe that he or she can be more than they ever dreamed of, and achieve great things. By leading them to that moment and being there to support and cheer as they cross, you the teacher then becomes an instrument for enabling their success. Most people will cherish this sort of inspiration and support for a lifetime. Then it is possible also, for the teacher-student relationship to transcend the mundane – it becomes a manifestation of destiny. When you can make students feel this way, they will likely never leave your side.

Your Invisible Assistant

So much is being said and written about marketing, in particular for martial arts schools, and most of it is focused on the actions you are supposed to be undertaking. "Hang these signs", "pay for those advertisements", "say such things over the phone", etc. All this considered, there is a whole lot of value, perhaps even more value, in what happens when you are not doing anything! Here then, is a Daoist view on marketing.

"The thirty spokes unite in one nave; but it is on the empty space of the nave, that the use of the wheel depends. Clay is fashioned into vessels; but it is on their empty hollowness, that the use of the vessels depends. The door and the windows are cut out of the holes to form a dwelling; but it is on the empty space of them, that their use depends. Therefore, benefit comes from what is there, and usefulness – from what is not there"

– The Dao De Jing, chapter 11.

In your martial arts career, as in the life and career of any other person, there exists an invisible ghost. The name of that invisible ghost is: **Reputation**. The ghost which is reputation is an entity which you do not commonly see, but its effects are felt and often observable. The ghost of reputation hovers among people and tells them about you. Unlike paid advertisements and marketing schemes, Reputation cannot be told what to do – it manifests as how people take you to be, and not as you wish them to think of you. To be aware of one's reputation, and to consider it as a true entity whose actions bear consequences, is in my opinion one of the hallmarks of true adulthood. Without catering for reputation and its needs, one cannot achieve success in anything.

Confucius, speaking about Trustworthiness, which is but one aspect of reputation, had said [32]: ***"I do not know what a man without trustworthiness may accomplish. Be it large or small, how could a carriage move without its yoke-bar?"***. By this Confucius means to say, that when a person is lacking in a crucial element of good reputation – when people do not think someone is trustworthy, then that man cannot move his 'vehicle' forward and succeed in whatever he aspires to do. Because by being considered 'not-trustworthy', others will not present you with the opportunities you need to advance your life and career.
I can tell you that the opposite is also true. Once a person reaches a certain threshold of positive reputation, he needs no longer advertise himself, sometimes for the rest of his life. Ask around and you shall find, that many successful martial arts teachers, as well as other small business owners, invest little to no time or funding in marketing [33]. Perhaps they give it a minor push for encouragement once or twice a year, but they do not have to work hard at it. The reputation ghost creates word of mouth for these martial arts teachers, and the word of mouth is the most powerful form of advertising. Word of mouth is the most powerful form of advertising, because it tends to not simply bring along 'customers' – but the types of customers who are best-suited for your type of 'business'.

---

[32] The Analects, Chapter 2, Verse 22.

[33] This work well for a smaller business. A martial arts school which is always striving to grow, or a martial arts organization with several schools which keep expanding, will always need some marketing done.

So how does one go about asserting, that the invisible ghost of Reputation becomes his loyal servant, and creates positive word of mouth? Before anything else is said, it must be understood, that this is going to take several years, at the least, for the reputation ghost to get working for you every day, whispering in people's ears; and, for the first few years, there would be little evidence to suggest that your invisible assistant is doing its job. The invisible ghost called Reputation requires a long-term investment based on faith. You have to believe that it can be done, and over time it will happen. Building a good name and reputation is older than the pyramids and a wheel. It was done countless times, and you can do it too.

The first order of business, is to make sure that people know you are in the business. The only thing required here is a habit – that of refusing to shut up about what it is you do. Be aware though, that this can come off as annoying. You cannot simply tell people that you are teaching the martial arts. You must bring about the subject in a flowing conversation, and ascertain that it is relevant for those with whom you speak.

For example, say you are at the supermarket and happen to overhear a chat concerning an injury or illness. Being tactful and polite, you may interject at an appropriate moment and comment about someone you know who had an identical or similar affliction, who was helped and recovered. Upon the parties questioning who and what were the circumstances, you tell them it was a student of yours and how you helped her. Or otherwise, when there is in a place you frequent, a discussion about bullying among children. You can stick in at the right time, and move the talking gently and wisely in the direction of your manipulative marketing ploy. Truth be told, the real cure for bullying is education, but in the short term, martial arts teachers have superior answers, which you need to make people aware of.

It is far superior to do things in this manner – flow into an already extant situation and conversation, as when you do this, people then do not tend to come up with immediate biased rejection of what you may have to say. Also, take note of people's need to hear something

which bears relevance **for them**. When you pitch the wonders of your teachings out of the blue and out of context, that is about what is right **for you**. Things work better when the foundations for the discussion concerned other people's interests. Then, they are more eager to listen.
Another important factor here is to give before you receive. When coming to 'preach' at a business location – first show an initiative and willingness to do actual business in that place, and THEN deliver your message. Otherwise, people can commonly tell you only stopped by due to having foreign agendas. Carry the full grocery bag before you open your mouth. Sit in the barbershop's chair prior to your martial arts storytelling. Talk about the terms of buying the car in advance of pitching your classes.

The point here being, that by frequently talking about what you do with everyone who meet you in your social and professional community, you become 'that guy'. People may ask: "Who should I send my son to teach him martial arts". The answer: "Oh, I know! To ***that guy***". Or: "I do not feel safe walking down the streets at night". The recommendation: "Oh, you should definitely attend classes by ***that guy***". Be that guy they are talking about. When you make it a habit to share positive things from your professional scene with everyone around you – family, friends, acquaintances, businessmen and random people you meet – you can become that guy. This is the beginning of the process. This is what awakens the ghost of reputation, and encourages it to go and whispers in people's ears.

"Your brand is what people say about you when you are not in the room".

- Jeff Bezos

The greatest apostles of your own personal gospel are your own students. But oftentimes, the students are not skilled at this task, or not even aware that this is something they ought to be doing. Few are born salespeople, and among those born with a gift of salesmanship, fewer still are martial artists.

The students need to be helped with understanding, that the growth of the school ought to be a major interest of theirs as well. This is not always obvious. Sometimes students might even perceive a conflict of interest in the works here.

Assume for instance, that you have 30 students split in two major groups, of 15 participants each. You do not show signs of being willing to create an additional group – as far as the students can tell, whatever the number of students, you will still have two group. The students can do the simple math. They know they belong to a group of 15 people. They realize that if ten additional participants were added to any of the groups, its number will grow from 15 to 25, and that makes a whole lot of difference in terms of how much attention they themselves can get from their teacher. Then, either consciously or subconsciously, students will in fact avoid 'spreading the gospel', or might even discourage people from coming to classes. Why? Because they are anxious of losing the little attention they already get. Even 'good people' who are otherwise moral and thoughtful, may end up doing such things.

Therefore, the aid of students in bringing in new people, must be presented as an advantage to them. It is a positive civil duty. It will bring more funding into the school, allowing for superior equipment and possibly a larger training facility. You will take more seriously and allot more time to a student who brought newcomers. More students would lead to the creation of additional groups, allowing for more versatile class hours for everyone.

Such are good incentives for students, but they need to be uttered verbally and frequently to be effective. All the better if these things are written down somewhere. Over time, the veteran students will come to carry forth such messages for you, as the notion of the duty of being the school's willful ambassador would become an integral part of your communal culture.

You also need to provide your students with a clear vocabulary for how to describe what they are learning. Otherwise they cannot carry forth the word of mouth 'marketing' for you. Over the years I have many a time encountered the following script, told by one of the students: **"I met with so and so yesterday, and sought to tell them what it was that we were doing in class. But the person I spoke with did not quite understand what I was trying to convey, and I had difficulty answering their questions. I told them that it is best to come and have my Shifu explain it to them in his own words".**

I heard this sort of thing hundreds of times. The result was usually that the student who was telling of what happened, was not successful in persuading the other party to come to class. There are two ways of tackling this challenge.

When you hear students tell these stories, make sure to spare some time outside of class, to educate them personally on how to better communicate the messages which are relevant to the school. This is one important solution. The other is, to hand over to students a 'bag of tricks'.

I am not a fan of selling 'tricks' to people. But it is useful that your students be familiarized with various easy-to-execute techniques, which tend to leave a good, awe-inspiring impression on people. These techniques should be things which are perhaps unique in the manner that you teach them, or at least unusual enough for laypeople and casual martial artists to be impressed by. Using these, students can become far more effective in persuading others to attend your classes.

We martial arts teachers are often surprised finding out though, that while students arrive rejoicing to class, certain that they have convinced their friends to visit, those people they speak of seldom arrive. What happens is that we live in a time and age wherein communications bombard each and every one of us with 'invitations' on a regular basis. The average person is offered invitations for more events and activities than he could possibly attend, and these all 'compete' with his or her intentions of visiting your class. Due to this reality, to ensure that new people do come over, your students need to be taught to finalize three things: **A Date, A Time, and a Joint-Adventure.** Unless your students manage to physically make their friends schedule a date, a time and mark them in their diaries, their presence could hardly be guaranteed; and aside that, it is preferable if the parties involved come to class together, to have a 'joint-adventure'. Without these elements I just mentioned, the talking would not commonly transform into doing.

Your reputation, whether carried forth by family, friends, students acquaintances or even strangers, is highly dependent on consistency of character. Are the stories about you the same as the person people meet during their first class? Is the teacher running the show similar to the man people were earlier speaking with over the phone? Do your writings and other publications reflect who you are? These things matter. Think about it this way: consistency of character is like highways through which the ghost of reputation travels. Every time people discern an inconsistency about who you are perceived to be, another highway you have paved is destroyed. Then the ghost has to take a longer route, or becomes limited altogether from reaching certain eyes and ears.

Consistency of character is not solely about what you say as compared with how you appear. It is also about things like compatibility between your philosophy and actions. Suppose you present yourself as being noble, but you are witnessed throwing trash on the street or cursing someone terribly (even if they deserved it). A single person watching such inconsistencies can do you major damage.

The same is true for getting caught up in martial arts politics. When we become involved with such politics, others may come to view inconsistencies in us which can damage the workings of our reputation ghost.

Once, many years ago, I was contacted by another martial artist,

who was asking me some questions about many teachers and lineages. Among these people that martial artist was asking about, was a colleague of mine – Shifu **Robert** (pseudonym), whom I have never met up to that point. I told him of Shifu **Robert**'s background, as I saw it – who were the men he studied under, and for how long. My answer was given in few sentences, punctually and without criticism or ill-intent. My words were not meant to offend anyone or cause trouble – only answer the inquiry of someone who appeared curious and eager to learn. I did not think much of it. Some weeks later, my colleague Shifu **Robert**, reached out to me, angry that I had "**spoken with a former student of his about his training experience, and provided him with false information**".
I had not realized that this teacher wanted to hide his inexperience, and that by discussing his background with someone I did not know, I could be corresponding with a former student of his, and causing him trouble!
This went from bad to worse. Two weeks later I took the offended teacher, Shifu **Robert**, to eat lunch at my expense, apologized, settled my matters with him, and thought this was over. But apparently, some time before I have made peace with my colleague **Robert**, he had already told a bunch of other teachers that I was speaking ill of him. In the years to come, I learned this had negatively affected my reputation among some members of the local martial arts community, and the damage took a while to mend.
It was around that time, that I had nearly completely withdrawn from public engagement in martial arts politics; as in, speaking my opinion of specific people who are still alive, as opposed to causes, histories and ideas. I would encourage you to do the same. You would not like to have the ghost of other teachers chasing after yours. It is one thing to contend with a man using your hands, and another to deal with his own invisible assistant.

Park Bait

When you have your own school, whether it be a garage, a community center hall or a fancy independent facility, one thing is certain – it is very easy to get spoiled and comfortable. Before I had my own school, I used to train outside almost every single day, even in the scorching heat of the Israeli summer and the bitter rain storms of our wet winters. Then once I had my own place, I quickly became the air conditioner's best buddy, and found myself less and less outside. I had to force myself to get back in touch with nature, which I did, but it took a while.

There are countless good reasons to train outside, especially barefoot on exposed earth or grass. Simply put, it is good for your health – physical and emotional alike. But moreover, it keeps things real. The flat floors of martial arts school, often covered with soft padding, do not reflect the realities people live in. In there, you and your students are like hamsters in a cage, and that wheel is nothing like the hill you will need to climb when the cat comes around. So, getting out there is good for everybody. But there is another decent reason to conduct your own personal training and some of the classes outside, which is the simple marketing method called 'Park Bait'.

I will tell you outright – Park Bait is not the most efficient of marketing methods, and it will not serve to build a school on its own. But I cannot argue with one thing – this is the manner in which I found and 'recruited' some of my best students. This has to do with the nature of the method, and I shall now explain why and how.

It matters a lot whether someone came to you of their own accord due to their own interest and by their own will, or were convinced by you to become students. Most students arrive at your school via persuasion, either by you, a friend of their, some marketing piece they have seen, a video perhaps, and similar. A smaller portion of

the students become members of your school completely of their own volition. Not only have they found the school on their own when they were in the process of seeking something roughly like it, but also chose to join in without any need for convincing, and based purely on their own sound judgment.
Why does it make a difference whether someone joins the school of their free will, as opposed to joining by persuation? When someone makes a big decision based on external persuasion, whenever they want to change their mind or quit, they easily find a way out by consciously or subconsciously telling themselves: "***Oh, but this was not really my idea anyway... I was pulled into this, so I can just as well give it up***". But when someone made a genuine, deep emotional decision to join which is his, and his only, then they are invested in that decision, and its power on them is much more powerful. At least, such is how things transpire with martial arts students.
Beyond that, the inner motivation for joining the school is also a decent predictor that a student is likely to last more than others. This is because such a decision tends to be more subjectively right for that student at that point in his or her life.

While in the park, you are like a magnet for all sorts of people to approach. Most commonly, they will be clueless idiots who simply are looking to have an amusing conversation or impress their friends. These can be either ignored, or done away with by pretending you are practicing something which does not interest them (getting rid of hostile imbeciles is an art, but unfortunately this would require an entire chapter which is beyond the scope of this book). Case in point – a short funny story:

One day, two idiots approached my martial arts class at the park. Walking on the trail aside us, they decided to convey out-loud their educated scholarly remarks about what we were doing.

Idiot #1 spouted: Look, it's Yoga!

Idiot #2 retorted: No, it's Ninjas!

Facing them with a solemn expression, I replied:

"It's the Yoga of Ninjas!!"

The idiots, ignorant of the joke played upon them, said: "Ooohhhhh...", and left the scene promptly, certain they were both correct. Though the joke is apparently on all of us, as I later found out there was in fact at least one teacher in the country who marketed his classes as "The Yoga of Ninjas".

Jokes aside, when you are in the park, you are also attracting a more important group of people. These are the type of potential students I was writing of earlier, who wish to make a wholehearted decision about joining a martial arts school. How do you tell the difference? Simple. Look for these people who, upon beginning to speak, express a genuine interest in what you do, and are very curious to learn more and be a part of whatever you may represent. These people can become some of your best students, or send your way appropriate individuals who are their family members, friends or acquaintances.

For those who are more serious in their intentions, it takes a while for them to approach you or your class. Seldom would they would draw near on the first instance of seeing you teach. One must be patient with this process.
It is often stated in marketing that it takes a person at least three times of observing an advertisement in public, before its message begins to sip in. With the park bait method, it can take as much as months and sometimes years for some people to make their move. But once they do, they are ready for a real conversation, and will likely express a serious interest.
Not everyone are brave enough to simply step in your direction.

Sometimes they prefer to stand some distance away from you and watch. I like to wait and see if they can stick around for a few minutes, which reveals whether they have a little bit of patience in them. Then if they continue to observe from afar, I will gesture them to come closer and issue a loud, cheerful and friendly invitation. At this point they usually approach. The first thing I do is greet them and ask for their name, which is to be remembered and used frequently throughout the conversation. Depending on the circumstances and the character of the person involved, I may spend anywhere between 5-20 minutes talking to such people (shorter if I am teaching a class, longer if I am by myself). I will not limit the conversation to my martial arts, but rather find out about their personal lives, what they are having challenges with, and look for ways to explain to them how I may be able to help them with their problems through my teachings. By showing real empathy and appreciation of them as fellow human beings, they buy into what I have to say.

Remember that you are not approached randomly. People reach out to 'experts', and those whom they stereotypically perceive as a 'martial arts master', because they see in them a certain **something** which they wish they had in themselves or that they could give to others. You need to find that **something** and make it the point and purpose of the conversation. Then you end the interaction by making sure:

- They know how to contact you and have your contact details written down (a business card will work).

- You have their contact details. Even if you do not plan to chase them later, it is only respectable that you take their details as show of interest in them.

- They will contact you on date X and hour Y.

- They are committed to either come to class themselves at some point or talk to person Z about coming to class.

Once more – be patient. These people may not call immediately. Some may come back to you after weeks and months. Others you will never hear from again. But your name gets out there. Through discussions with such people (which others in the park also notice), and by your very presence in the area, you become a part of the scenery. You are that martial arts guy in that park. People who come by expect to see you around, for you are like a fountain or a tree they like, which is always there – a predictable and notable aspect within that environment. When you are gone for a while, they wonder where you may have disappeared to. When someone brings up the topic of martial arts in conversation, they often talk of that man who does strange movements on their regular jogging path. Your presence lingers in their minds until, one day, they cannot hold that curiosity anymore and just have to ask – either you or someone else in the vicinity. With persistence, charm, personality and kindness, you can become a focal point of the park experience, and in time, this will reward you in unexpected ways.

Finally, when considering the value of the 'park bait' method, do realize that it complements well your reputation. Remember what was discussed in the previous chapter, titled **'Your Invisible Assistant'**. Think about the impact you can have, by having dozens of thousands of people physically seeing you practice and teach over a long period of time. Those who remain confined to their school between four walls, only ever get to present their abilities and skills to the folks who come and visit them. But in a single evening of having martial arts classes taught at a central spot in a popular park, more people would be exposed to your teachings than those who will enter the doors of your school in the span of an entire year! It does not require planning, it is free, it is healthy, and in the long term – it works. Do try.

The Fine Compromise

I remember a father who called me on the phone some years ago. He used to be my principal in high school, and remembered me fondly. He had a son, 13 years of age, who was a brilliant computer nerd. The father wanted me to put some martial spirit into the boy, and help him build his confidence. Then he said: "You know, I figured the best way for this to go about is for you to give him a short course on self-defense".

That last sentence had me triggered instantly. I am very much annoyed be those clueless people who honestly believe martial arts are akin to learning how to drive – a few classes, and we are done... You now have the skill for life! What an ignorant manner of thinking of our teachings and profession. [34]
No doubt, a much younger me, a decade earlier, would not have been mature enough to stop himself from explaining to the father, that this is not how it works. But fortunately, as we grow older, we learn the fine art of compromise. I said nothing of his comment, accepted his suggestions, and began to instruct his kid the next day. Within a few classes his curiosity intensified, and he eventually became a wonderful member of my academy, studying the martial arts diligently and traditionally, as I wanted him to.

We teachers, especially those who are involved with the traditional arts, tend to go about our professions with a religious

---

[34] Note that this is very different to women's self-defense courses. With women, the emphasis is on building confidence and teaching scenario-specific skills, which by nature tend to be well-defined and limited. However, men who are not soldiers, guards or with law enforcement, are required to prepare themselves to face violence which is usually not scenario-specific and which requires a very broad specialization. Therefore, while I support the concept of women's self-defense 'courses', for most people the solution should be more in-depth study of the martial arts, and in general, courses are a very lowly and shallow compared with a serious commitment.

zeal and much idealism. We have an image in our minds of how things ought to be, and we attempt to create that image in real life. After all, this is what most of martial arts are about, is it not? Making the fantasy a reality. But in the course of doing so, we have to deal with individuals like that father I told you about, who have a very different image in their minds of what martial arts are about.

The trouble with this is that a single conversation, particularly over the phone or via text, is not nearly enough to change the other person's image of what we do. Consider how long it takes to initiate a new student into the mindset and culture of your school. You are lucky if they 'get it' within a few short months. Then for a complete stranger, this is an impossibility. We have to be wiser and recognize, that the person with whom we speak for the first time is not going to understand our point of view. Therefore, we have to compromise.

The compromise should strike a balance between the wishes of potential students (or their parents) and your vision of how training should be. You want and need to eventually enforce your vision of things, but they cannot be told that. This does not mean however that you must lie. Rather, you provide people with a chunk of the truth which is small enough for them to chew and swallow. So, taking the example from earlier – instead of telling the father: "martial arts are a long-term commitment and your kid will require several years to become proficient and then will have to keep practicing for a lifetime to maintain the skills"; rather you say: "Great! Let us try that self-defense thing for a while, and see where it takes us. Then if he is still interested we can take him to the next level".

Likewise in class, some students require gentler and more compromising treatment than others, during their first few lessons. In our early 21st century society we currently experience a profound imbalance between Yin and Yang, Male and Female.

We see this manifesting in people going to the extremes of masculinity or femininity, and in those who have blurred the differences between them. I say this without being judgmental – this is the reality we face, and I myself try to be tolerant to a degree. I have stated this because the result of this imbalance is that a lot of people come to classes with related issues. Some examples would be:

Men who possess a weak and frail character with no backbone, a skinny-fat constitution and a feeble personality, prone to anxiety and depression. Women who are out to prove they are 'the biggest gorilla in the forest', concerned with waging wars against other people and various causes, who are bitter and angry, always on the lookout for conflict. Then there are those with an inability to define who and what they are, in all respects, floating like clouds at the outskirts of society, wandering about aimlessly, all too afraid of taking and making a stand.

These are not healthy individuals, but are nonetheless types of people with whom we may have to deal when we operate a commercial school. These people, 'the gentle snowflakes' with sensitive emotional triggers, cannot fit into a vision of a curriculum intended for the strong, healthy and confident – they require a temporary compromise. [35]

So, when teaching those with more challenging aspects to their being, like those I have described or other difficult characters, for the first few classes one needs to find a meeting ground between their vision and yours. Often such people are used to receiving a 'special treatment' from society, augmenting their wishes and needs. Be patient and try to chime with their rhyme for a short time, all the while gradually pulling them more and more in your

---

[35] Why compromise under such circumstances? Good you asked. First of all – they are paying, and you need to eat and support other people. Second of all – the compromise provides you the opportunity to help them become better versions of themselves, which ought to be a part of your calling. Additionally, those who have turned their life around by your influence can often become more dedicated and loyal students than those who did not undergo such a process.

direction and that of the school. There can only be two possible outcomes with such people – either they conform within a month or two, or they will have to leave. Do not allow a situation in which you have a constant game with any student, in which each of you continues to make compromises for the other. Some of these people really like these sorts of games, but they make for a very poor relationship, in life and certainly between a teacher and student.

Then there are these instances where you should not at all compromise, when people truly challenge your personal or professional integrity in some way. Here are some examples I have experienced and choices I have made:

- In Israel, a majority of orthodox religious Jews, maintain a rule which says that they ought to avoid touching members of the opposite sex. This avoidance of physical touch always holds with strangers, and is sometimes maintained even inside the family, with the exception of one's spouse. During my career as a martial arts teacher, I have received numerous calls and visits by religious Jews who wanted to attend classes at my academy. All of these people have told me, over the phone or during their first class, that they need to refrain from touching women, so they cannot participate in a class in which women are present. My answer was always the same: "***There are women at our academy. Furthermore, all academy members must at one point or another practice with all other academy members. We do not allow a person to refrain from practicing with another based on race, gender, religion, ethnicity or any other such reasons. We consider this to be disrespectful. You will either practice under these rules, or you will not be a member of our academy***". Sadly, most of these people opted to not participate. However, over the years, a few of them chose to forgo their religious dogma in this matter, and usually stayed with us after they did so. Once they came to know our lovely ladies in person, they forgot about their biases and treated them equally and respectfully. They have nonetheless maintained their religious beliefs and were not coerced to abandon them – by our ethical and honorable ways, it was them who learned to compromise. Some of those religious folks who called even offered to help me set up a 'male-only' group solely for their crowd. I refused that also. Though I have lost a lot of money by the action of not taking in these religious Jews who insisted on sexual segregation, I am proud of taking a moral and professional stand on the matter. A teacher's personal integrity is the backbone of the entire school.

☯ Over the years I have received countless calls from parents who wanted me to teach very young children, often as young as 3-4 years old. Obviously, such people have watched too many movies, and thought this would be akin to leaving their baby at the footsteps of the martial arts temple. I have always refused to teach very young children, and was patient and thorough in explaining to parents why the children were too young to learn anything remotely similar to martial arts, or to develop any practical skill pertaining to self-defense or fighting. Although it is true that once in a while a young child is seen performing well beyond his years, these children are the product of very intense and rigorous training, always in a private setting and often taught by family members.

With time and experience, I have come to realize that it was a waste to allow these parents to continue to wander about, as it was likely that right after they called me, they would have simply called the next martial arts teacher they found who was willing to give them what they wanted. So, I also collected the contact details of various professionals in the field of teaching movement to young children, people I could trust, and referred the parents to these people at the end of each conversation.

☯ Years ago I received a call from a school principal who wanted me to teach self defense to all of their students in a given age group. But the offer had the following caveats: I had to teach group of over 30 children at a time, and only for 45 minutes at a time, with each group having only one weekly session. Despite my best efforts to bargain for a better arrangement, this was to no avail, as these were the instructions issued by the Ministry of Education. Without these terms, the school would not have received the State funding. I therefore politely refused this very lucrative financial and career offer. I did so because I could not honestly teach anything of substantial depth or meaning to such large groups of students, in such short classes, to be held once a week only. This was in too great an opposition to my method of instruction and the contents of what I personally teach, and for this reason I declined the offer. While other teachers may have readily jumped at the opportunity, I felt that for me this was the right decision in the scope of my professional integrity. This is, in the end, a major component of what matters in teaching and life – whether you can live peacefully with your decisions.

You, the teacher reading this, do not necessarily have to follow my example. Rather, use these anecdotes as the basis for thought experiments with yourself, to examine and see where you want to draw the line. The fine art of compromise is an instrument which augments itself according to your vision of how your teachings ought to be. As long as you follow the Middle Path in drawing these lines, it will lead you to success.

That First Class

I have observed that there is disagreement among teachers as to how a person should be treated during his or her very first class, which is usually a free trial lesson [36].

Many teachers opt to place a first-time visitor solely under the supervision of a veteran and trusted student, who 'babysits' the newcomer for most of that class. All the while, the teacher tends to the rest of the students, and works on more advanced aspects of the curriculum with them.

Alternatively, there are those teachers who attempt to treat the newcomer as they would any other student, and do not make an effort to change the lesson's curriculum for him or her. Whatever the teacher and students were supposed to practice on that day, the newcomer is expected to tag along and try to follow. By doing this, such teachers hope perhaps to give the newcomer an honest sense of what is to be expected of them in the future. Sometimes teachers even go as far as to demand newcomers should have a real sparring match, or several, during their very first class.

In the distant past I too have experienced both approaches as a beginner who was passing from school to school, looking for a new teacher. I never liked either of these approaches, and nor do I believe they are popular among newcomers in general.

---

[36] It is in our time an international standard in the martial arts community, to allow at least a single free trial lesson to all newcomers. Based on your business model and advertising strategies, you may choose to offer more, or less 'incentives' to new students. But that one free trial lesson is definitely the bare minimum. Not only is it justified by means of pure reason, but refraining from offering this will place you in a bad position in light of the fact that nearly all other schools offer such an option. People agree to go on 'blind dates' knowing that they can leave the premises at any time. But almost no one will agree to such an idea if the blind date required you pay for the other party in advance...

The exception here is the private lesson. With these, I do not believe in free lessons, and it would be a mistake on your part to offer such things, especially to strangers. People have a tendency to take this the wrong way, and it is a bad setup for a teacher-student relationship, as the student-to-be may consider himself to begin at a position of power over the teacher.

The first approach, of assigning a 'babysitter' to the newcomer, seems logical and considerate to teachers who use it. But it can be experienced in a very different way by someone who is not a member of the school. Such a person can and will often consider the 'babysitting' thing somewhat insulting and belittling. A novice might feel he came to that school to take part with everybody else, not to be put aside and catered for like a 'special needs child'. No matter how slow or challenged a person is, no individual wants to be the one who is different, especially when he has not even received an opportunity to prove himself. Then in the event that the new student is actually versed in the martial arts, such people too may react negatively, as based on their former training they do not consider themselves to be needing a babysitter, even if objectively they do.

Also, the teacher is usually the 'face' and 'brand' of the school. The teacher is commonly who that person spoke with over the phone, establishing the first interaction and trust in coming in contact with a new environment. Then when the newcomer arrives and is distanced from the teacher and put into the hands of a complete stranger whom he had never seen or heard before, this has implications. I gather, that teachers have long ago forgotten what it is like to look for a martial arts school to study at, and that newcomers tend to construct a certain scenario in their mind before arriving in order to be able to deal well with the situation. You can be rest-assured that the movie script people had in mind before they came to your class, did not include a babysitter being assigned to care for them. Then when this happens, luck plays a part. When your trusted student can execute the job fabulously and connects brilliantly with the newcomer, then you will have a new student, who even felt as if he was given a private class by a great teacher and is happy about it. But anything else will be a disaster. The babysitter and newcomer may not get along, and that means a whole class of not getting along, stuck together. The newcomer may envy the other students or feel left out. The newcomer could be upset with the teacher not providing enough attention. The newcomer may notice the babysitter saying one thing while the teacher says another. A lot can go wrong. This is why I do not abide by this method.

Then we have the other approach, of throwing the baby into the swimming pool to give him a good taste of water; treating a newcomer like you do everyone else, and perhaps even testing his character. Honest, is it not? Yes – honest, and intimidating. People seldom arrive ready for a real challenge. During my days in the boxing gym, when I just started out, I saw dozens of potential students forego their second class because of the ridiculous intensity of the training expected from beginners. 'My way or the highway' works well when you do not care at all for making an income, and only look for very specific types of students. Even that can get excessive though, and some people end up with few or no students at all after decades of 'teaching'.
One should also consider that it is a false assumption to think, that you can get these specific students you want most, by throwing everyone in the water the first time around. The truth is that in the martial arts, many people only begin to show their true potential after several months to several years of training. When I began training as a teenager, for the first several years there was absolutely no indication that I was to become a serious teacher, let alone a notable author on the martial arts. Although I was perhaps a bit more on the dedicated side than others, it took a while for me to make the leap from an amateur's mindset to that of a real professional. Likewise, you too often cannot tell who among your students, especially the younger ones, is going to become your successor, a great master, or simply a very good practitioner or teacher. People change. Tackling them with the full harshness of your art during their first few months of training is therefore an inappropriate strategy.

The worst of it is manifested in schools which make people go through sparring sessions during their very first class. Though it can be balanced by a teacher of good character, this habit tends to attract to such schools a large number of people who are all too eager to fight and hurt others. This can shape the destiny of the school and of the teacher for years to come. A school solely made of fighters is not a friendly community – it is a brotherhood of gladiators, who albeit having common grounds still look out to hurt others at any given opportunity. That is not to say that all students who will survive that first sparring session and return are hostile brutes. Once more, a teacher of good character and a kind heart can balance this well. But it certainly sets a tone for what the school is about, and bears consequences. I have seen with my own eyes how several such schools disintegrated within a few years, because of great inter-personal tensions. One's first class tends to memorably imprint an attitude upon the student. An attitude of conflict and survival is not conductive to a relationship of learning and respect.

My approach to dealing with newcomers is altogether different from those I have described so far. The fundamental rule is that the newcomer should be center of attention for me during his first class, to the extent that he or she feel comfortable [37]. The class will begin with the newcomer doing everything along with everyone else. I may approach the newcomer in a discrete or gentle way and offer him an easier manner for the executions of techniques and methods. I never present this to be a 'lesser' version of the things others practice – rather, I tell him: 'Here is a more comfortable way for you to do this'. In doing so and with other teachings, I refrain from any complicated technical explanations. However, when the newcomer wonders out loud where something can lead him, I call upon a student who can do it well, make a demonstration with him, and promise the newcomer: "This student was able to achieve this much in that amount of time – so could you, if you choose to stick around".

When required to work in pairs, I <u>interchangeably</u> team up the newcomer with my most veteran and trusted students, allowing him to practice with several of them. I care to educate my students in advance that newcomers require 'special attention' to show them the best of what we have, and therefore my students aid and assist

---

[37] I am always mindful of the newcomer's feelings and body language. I provide a lot of attention, but immediately back off when I sense that the newcomer wishes to operate on his own and beings to feel uncomfortable. Then the newcomer can sense that I am being respectful and thoughtful.

with pleasure, understanding the situation. I care to remind students that they too were once newcomers, and that back then I also made an effort to treat them similarly.
Thus, the class goes on as usual, but the newcomer receives more attention than the other students – again, only to the extent at which he feels comfortable. This extra attention should be provided more on a personal basis, and avoided in group explanations. Newcomers do not like excess attention in a group setting, and those who covet such attention will inevitably cause problems if they are provided with it.

Important focal points for providing newcomer attention are <u>before and after the class</u>. During class, there is not much time to explain to the newcomer what the school is about, and the preceding phone call is also not the best opportunity to do so (as it should be focused on generating commitment to come to class). For this reason, remember to ask people to arrive early to their first class, preferably 10-15 minutes in advance, so you can sit down and have a chat with them (preferably in your office, if you have one). Make this conversation about them, and do not be tempted to cut the conversation in favour of chatting with your students.

I remember once, when I was a beginner in the martial arts, I went to a Taiji Quan teacher's class. When I first called that Shifu prior to class, to introduce myself, he requested that I arrive at his TCM clinic a whole hour before the class began. We had a long chat. He asked of me to arrange a set of information cards, on which he had the details written down for various clients of his. Obviously, he was testing me. He wanted to see how patient I was, whether I was organized, if I am cooperative and open-minded enough to indeed arrange the cards as he requested (which I did). The task took a while, perhaps as much as 10 minutes, during which time he was treating a patient with acupuncture. During the last ten minutes before we left for the class came a young, good-looking lady. He did not take her as seriously as he did me, and his manner of speech towards her was quite different. I did not appreciate this. Later the

class was alright, but the teacher left his veteran student to babysit me alongside that other young lady. Her good looks were enough of a distraction already, but making it worse was the fact that she had no experience in the martial arts, while I by that time had trained for a while. This perplexed the babysitter, who was not skilled or experienced at this type of thing. I remember the whole ordeal very well to this day, but I never returned. The babysitting experience in particular, which I have also experienced in other schools, I did not appreciate or feel comfortable with. The fact that I was knowingly tested, too, was not a great choice on part of the teacher, as it created an atmosphere of distrust.
So in light of the story, take this to heart – a good conversation before class is a good thing, but avoid overdoing it, especially if the newcomer is not keen on talking at length. Use that conversation to state what the school is about and what it can do and has done for people. Focus on the school and its community, and do not talk about yourself. Chances are the newcomer already did some homework to check who you are, and this visit is about him, not you.

Then there is the post-class conversation, which is even more important. Here you must be attentive and empathetic. Approach the newcomer carefully and gently after the class is finished. Try to initiate conversation in a discrete manner, as far as possible from other people present in the vicinity. Any student who approaches, signal them to back off. Cater to the feelings of the newcomer. Make it very short. You goal is to check whether there is a chance that he or she would come again, and if so – try to state a date and a time for that. Even if they say: "yeah, I will come", make them repeat it at least twice, but not too much. Once during this conversation, make the all-important reminder about when and where they can come again. Then just before they go out the door later, call their name again and make that reminder once more. **<u>Then forget about them</u>**. Whether they come back or not, it is up to them now. Chasing them with messages and calls is not a good strategy, but you may send a single message a day before the next class they are supposed to attend, with a reminder. Most people who come to trial classes never return. This is the reality for all martial arts teachers. I repeat - do not chase them. There is no point. A person without even the smallest motivation to come again, is not someone worth wasting energy on – your attention is better spent with real students.

Additionally, by overtly chasing someone after 'the first date' you begin a sort of psychological game between you, and playing such games is one of the worst things that can happen in a teacher-student relationship. I know that you want to make a living and that it is important for you to increase the student quota, but as teachers we ought to first act to preserve integrity – ours and that of other people. It is only respectable and reasonable to allow the other party to decide, as a mature adult, whether he or she wish to return. As explained in the chapter titled **'Park Bait'**, people who make this decision wholeheartedly and of their own volition will tend to make longer-lasting students. A single student who shall be with you for 5 years is better than twenty students who only last a month – both financially and community-wise. Therefore, make each student count, and do so in part by thinking about where the relationship with the students begins. Does that occur at the point of one side being chased by the other, or at an instance when two mature people chose, each independently, to trust one-another? You call the shots. You make it happen.

People and Their Reasons

When a new student comes to my academy, I always question him or her about their reasons for wishing to study martial arts. Even when they have not a clue as to their true motivations, their lack of an answer is also something to learn from – now I know that they are somewhat lost, and disconnected from their inner selves. For such students I can offer guidance and ideas as to why they want to join, and then they often pick a reason even when they are unsure. It is better to provide them with a sense of dignity and the ability to supposedly make a choice, then leave them wondering why indeed they are here in the first place.

Then what I do is to use that reason or reasoning to ease the student's assimilation into the school's curriculum and community. It really does not matter what the reason was – it matters that I can genuinely and convincingly show the student that the school can provide him with the answer. I simply stress and emphasize whatever is important to such beginners. Are they here for self-defense? [38] Then for their first few classes, I will make sure to communicate and show them how the art they are studying is practical for that purpose. Are they here to improve their health? Then even if their first classes happen to revolve more around self-defense or some other aspect of training, I will show them how through this they can attain what they are seeking. After 1-3 classes, if they stick around, then there is no point in further 'convincing' – either they chime with our rhyme, or they naturally vacate themselves from the area. Do not force the process, as allowing people to make independent and calculated decisions is more important than pushing your teachings. **<u>Remember</u>:** Good students

---

[38] The majority of students coming to martial arts classes will tell you that they are here for "self-defense". But frankly, they commonly use this term as coverup for more profound yearnings, for things like self-confidence, self-esteem and self-respect. They may also possibly be on the lookout for living out a specific fantasy of theirs, which is something to beware of.

are only those who voluntarily and wholeheartedly joined the cause. They need to believe they want to do this, otherwise only trouble will come of them.

We teachers need to keep in mind, that whatever reason prompted a person to our doorstep, is usually not the reason he is still with us several months later, and seldom the reason he continues to practice for years. People change, and their motivations do with them. It would be unwise to consider the student as having the same motivations and accordingly treat him in the same manner after a long period of study. Whichever reason it was that brought him in, after a certain period of time it ceases to matter entirely. Therefore, there is no longer a need to speak of why people are here. This is an incorrect mindset which can only yield doubts and disappointments. Instead, focus on where they are heading, how they can evolve as human beings to their utmost potential, and how this process is part of the evolution of the entire school. Reasons are for outsiders. Communities live and thrive for their own sake – they are self-perpetuating.

Contracts and Payments

Two great historical scholars and educators, the Chinese Confucius and the Roman Seneca, made the exact same observation: "***The more laws there are, the more corrupt the populace***". This is easy enough to understand. When people are upright, they manifest the best of human qualities, acting with compassion and a moral compass. The less they are so, the more laws are naturally enacted to 'educate them' or 'put them in place'. It is a natural process in the corruption of nations and societies that the worse people become, the more laws they have. This is true for martial arts school as well. But it is not only bad behaviour which encourages the creation of more laws – the opposite is also true. When people attempt to follow countless laws, then gradually the written word replaces reason, common sense and empathy. Thus, in Law School I was taught that there is 'factual truth' and then there is also the 'legal truth' – the two are not the same. This is the face of dishonesty and corruption. As martial arts teachers, is that the reality you want to represent? I hope not.

Contracts have no place in martial arts schools. Take this from a person with a law degree with two lawyer parents and a family full of lawyers. Contracts are a replacement for trust. When you hand over a contract to a person, you are bluntly telling him: "*I do not trust you. Here is a piece of paper that guarantees that a person such as yourself, whom I cannot trust, will not take advantage of me in the future*". These words of course are never said, but this is exactly what is being implied. Because if you could trust them, you would not have been using a contract, would not you?

Consider then the implications of this. A newcomer arrives at your school and is about to join. The first 'official sanction' of his entrance to your community? A document stating that you do not trust him. Is this truly a humane and worthy way to treat a fellow human being? Is this really the society we need to live in, and a method which we must use in order to keep us safe? In fact, what does it say of our self-confidence as teachers of the martial arts, if we feel we must use contracts to 'keep us safe'?

I am not sure what lawyers have told you about this issue, but lawyers are the devil's advocates when it comes to contracts. In the world of Law, everything is done with contracts. Lawyers need contracts to operate much like Mathematicians need equations. Do not expect a lawyer to find a moral dilemma here – the contract is to him in his mind like a wheel to a race-car driver... nothing moves without it.

Let me enlighten you though, on the fact that contracts need not be written to be manifested or enforced. You do not need a written contract to sue somebody. Contracts are, by law, also created through behaviour. It is enough that a student came to class to study. That is a contract between you and the student, just by him attending the classes, which implies that he receives instruction and should pay you for it.

To enforce payments, you do not need contracts, either. What you need is proper and smart planning. I will give you an example. I used to collect money from everybody at the beginning of each month. Big mistake. I had to chase people around too much and it was a major headache for everyone involved. The best solution is to encourage, but not force people, to pay in advance. At one point in time I used to charge adults 300 Israeli Shekels a month (equivalent of 85 US Dollars at the time). Students could come train every day of the week, as part of their class or beside another class. I then changed the payment model to be as follows, in the beginning of a school year:

Pays in the beginning of each month	**375**
Pays for 3 months in advance, either cash or checks	**350**
Pays for 12 months in advance, checks	**325**
Pays for 12 months in advance, cash	**300**

Before this arrangement, 300ILS was the sum everybody paid, and there were no incentives. Now, as I explained to students, those who were more dedicated and willing to commit would pay less, and those who were not as dedicated and willing to commit would pay more. Not a single student quit because of this decision, and I believe this was due to the fact that I presented it well to everybody, was polite and reasonable about it, and provided students with a sense of justice to that sort of payment model. As soon as I changed to this model, nearly all students deposited checks for either 3 or 12 months in advance, with only two opting to pay in the beginning of each month. Not only have I solved my payment headaches – I have also increased my revenue, and did so in a way which respected my students and their freedom to choose. For this process, absolutely no contracts were required. All that was needed was careful planning and good relationship skills for making the idea acceptable and successful.

At my school, the students do sign a 'contract' of sorts, but it is very different to a traditional document of this type. The 'contract' is a single piece of paper upon which they fill their personal contact details and place their signature. This paper details the etiquette norms of the school, and signing it helps the students understand that they are entering a place at which they are expected to behave properly. But as far as contracts go, this means nothing, as school etiquette is not legally enforceable. The only crucial element on this piece of paper which is truly of a legal nature is a paragraph which lawyers would call a 'non-competition clause'. This paragraph states that the students agree to:

1. Never teach the martial arts they (the students) were taught by me without my permission **in writing and in video**.

2. Never to teach these martial arts in the same city in which I teach without such permission.

3. Never teach students who are my own unless permitted to.

As much as I dislike using contracts in the martial arts, I have to advise that these three things, you do make students sign up on. It sadly happens often to martial arts teachers that after many years of study, a student 'betrays' them in some way. He may go about teaching without their permission, become their 'competition' in the same city, or sometimes 'steal' some of their students. These types of things are unfortunately quite common in our community. I was witness or have heard of dozens of cases as such. When this happens to you, and betrayal burns a deep hole in your heart, unless you have such a document at your disposal, you are completely helpless. The only solutions remaining to resolve the problem are then illegal. Having students sign up on such articles is for you an all-important insurance policy. From the newcomer's point of view however, they have no understanding of this and they do not care. Such wording describes a reality which is usually beyond their wildest dreams, and unlike martial arts teachers they cannot imagine this type of scenario happening 5-20 years from now. They understand you are concerned about something and they sign up. Then you take this document and carefully preserve it in a safe place, with copies too, and forget about it until the day it may prove essential.

But do not let that day arrive! Remember the beginning of this chapter: "***The more laws there are, the more corrupt the populace***". In the event that you were ultimately required to use the power of such a document and that of the law against a former student, then you have failed, also. You must understand that it does not simply come about, that after many years a student 'suddenly' becomes a villain. You were watching him being a villain the first month at your school, or could have observed him transitioning into one through countless hours spent together. When such a student betrays, shame on you if this was a surprise! You ought to have kicked him out years ago, or better yet – work as his teacher to save him from the ocean of darkness into which he unwittingly plunged. As the saying goes: "A smart man can solve the difficult situation which the wise man never gets into".

One more thing to consider is the need to disengage within the student's mind the connection between Money and Time. A typical modern student considers martial arts teaching a sort of "service", which is purchased via financial means. Therefore, it is like renting a vehicle – you pay for a certain number of hours and days, and then you are provided that service for that time period. When students think like this, your relationship with them deteriorates to a form of business transaction – which in turn means they owe you nothing, as they can simply move on to the next vendor.

Another issue in this respect would be with students then sometimes demanding 'refunds' in the event that they missed some classes – something which you ought to never agree to, unless there had been unusual circumstances. At my academy the rule is as follows: A student who was ill for over two weeks can receive a 50% 'discount' on next month's payment. A student who went on vacation for over 30 weeks will receive the same 'discount'. I do not however 'refund' money.

In order to strengthen the validity of this approach, you have to exemplify in your actions the belief that your school is about more than financial transactions between willing parties, and that time does not in fact equal money in the same manner that it does in everyday business. The notion that the school is more than a paid service is established by grooming a community, which is the subject of many other chapters in this book. The idea that time can be detached from money ought to be encouraged by the teacher making 'time-consuming sacrifices' for his students. This includes allowing classes to last for longer than originally intended, providing free extra teaching time outside of class once in a while, and spending time engaged in helping students with personal issues. I go further than most by writing a lot of content for my students and providing them with countless learning materials. Then, these actions by the teacher should be clearly articulated and emphasized in class, making sure the students understand that in a communal relationship this is what is expected of them – to contribute by going outside of their comfort zone and not bicker over the value of their payments. Remember this well: **All speak highly of the virtues of Modesty, but nobody wants to buy her products.** You cannot do much for the students and then expect them to appreciate your efforts, if you do not make them take note and consider such things solemnly. Timid altruism is a recipe for disappointment.

Leading by Virtue

Speaking of rules and regulations (see previous chapter), we can draw inspiration from another fine quote of Confucius[39] :

"Lead by setting policies, discipline through punishments – and the people may be restrained, but without a sense of shame. Lead by virtue, discipline by ceremonies – and the people will have a sense of shame, and their conscience will improve".

[39] The Analects, Chapter 2, Verse 3.

In light of the quote on the previous page, consider the role of a parent. There are a lot of things which parents wish to convey to their children, to guarantee their arrival to adulthood with an upright bearing. But commonly, whichever principle or belief that the parent cannot back up by demonstrating through personal example, the child will decline to follow.
This is frequently seen among parents who smoke cigarettes. No matter how many times they may lecture to their children of the dangers of smoking, as long as they themselves have smoked for many years, the children will possess a very high change of catching on to the habit themselves.
Such negative examples could even arise in a more covert fashion. At one point, I taught a child of 11 years, who was fat. Upon a deep inquiry as to his reasons for over-eating, it came up that his father, who was by then a muscular and impressive man, told him keenly that when he was a child, he was quite fat as well. Then the child with his meager mind, came to the silly conclusion that being fat for a number of years was the right course of action in his quest to be like his father. He would repeat that line of reasoning many a time – that he father used to be fat, and thus so should he, and was honestly self-convinced that his path was righteous and proper.

Your students are the same. Rules and regulations will only carry them so far. Such laws are superficial, and merely aid in sustaining peace in class. These are trifles and bear no lasting effect, when compared to leading by virtue and setting a good personal example. As for the 'how' of setting a personal example, the rest of the book deals with that.

The order part to that quote, discussing the proper way for leadership, concerns "discipline through ceremonies". In the context of a martial arts school, ceremonies are many things. The opening and closing of a class is a ceremony. The testing of students and bestowing rank, are ceremonies. Dining with students ought to also be a ceremony. Martial arts seminars are very intricate and complex ceremonies. Even the interaction between two students as they choose each other as training partners, before they touch hands, is a type of ceremony in the traditional martial arts. There

are many such examples.
The discipline arises through ceremonies, not by coercion, but instead through mutual willful participation and imitation of another person's appropriate behaviour. By this Confucius rightfully discerns, that education is far better delivered not by ordering people what to do, but rather encouraging them to follow those who are worthy. For even when forced to go about something, when the educating figure is not worthy, the students will know, and therefore be inclined to not embody the lesson at hand.

More so, in leading by virtue and through ceremonies, it is possible to make people develop a sense of Shame. The reason for this is, that people are naturally inclined to view themselves as "the heroes of their own story". A person who believes himself to be a villain quickly becomes depressed, and may even opt to end his life. True villains seldom exist. Even the most vile and hurtful people, usually hold an inner conviction, albeit twisted, that their actions are good, just or necessary. Therefore, people cannot stand when their improper ways are transparent to all. Then, they feel ashamed.

My student Jechiel once told me this story: Many years ago, his business required him to deal with a infamous local mobster. The mobster was not happy that Jechiel's company operated in his territory without asking for his permission. He got into a room with Jechiel, just the two of them, and locked the door. The Mobster then stood right in front of him and began shouting and cursing like a menacing maniac, making the nastiest of threats. His tongue had Yehiel's house burnt, his wife raped, his arms and legs chopped off, his dog drowned... you name it. He was notorious enough to be believed, too. Jechiel just stood there and listened without interruption. After one or two minutes, the mobster paused, feeling that he had spewed enough intimidation to make his case and cause Jechiel to pay. Instead, Jechiel looked him right in the eye, and with sincere empathetic friendly demeanor told him: "Hey, why ought you say things like that? This is unlike you. We have spoken before. You are a better man than this. You are a good person, so why use such language? This is not who you want to be...". The mobster was utterly shocked. After a few moments of silence, almost shedding a tear, he told Jechiel: “You are right”. He then went on to tell Jechiel about his childhood and business, the wrongdoings done to him and his family, and all the people that upset him recently. He spoke continuously for many minutes, then paused, and said: “Uh, I like you. Let’s forget about that. Whenever you have trouble with anyone around this city, just give me a call”. He then left, and Jechiel never saw him again. [40]

What Jechiel was capable of doing was to lead by virtue and teach by ceremony. He recognized that in the person standing in front of him was a hidden sense of shame, and was wise and experienced enough to know how to draw out that sort of emotion. By showing an unruly person empathy rather than attacking him, and by being courteous and polite in his manner of listening to a hoodlum, he demonstrated a most honorable pattern of behaviour. The latter, we can conceive of in the context of the ‘social ceremony’ between two people. Upon witnessing Jechiel’s actions, the mobster’s subconscious could only react with shame, for he knew that he had chosen to act in a lowly way towards a man who was better than him. This sense of shame, by itself, had resolved a complicated and dangerous situation, without having required the aid of laws or regulations.

Such are also the ceremonies conducted within the martial arts school. When the teacher and veteran students have a dignified bearing in the manner of going through such ceremonies, then all other students will improve their conscience, and develop a sense of shame, that would prevent them from offending or transgressing the expected norms.

---

[40] This story, by sheer coincidence, bears some similarities to a story called ‘The Man Who Spat in Buddha’s Face’, which I have included later in this book, in the chapter titled ‘**A Spit in Your Face**’.

To Err is Humane

Confucius said[41]:

"When the Junzi makes a mistake, it is like the eclipse of the Sun or Moon. He makes a mistake, and everyone sees it. He corrects, and all men look up to him".

Do you ever make mistakes? Have a look at these pages – this book is full of mine! But put to good use, they have value.

Confucius tells us, that when the leader errs, his mistakes are worst than those of the everyday person. That is especially, when the leader is a Junzi – a man of high moral standards.
However, the Junzi has the advantage of being a beacon of integrity and righteousness to his followers. Though his mistakes could have grave consequences, their correction, done in a manner which is public, is an act of tremendous power.

Consider for example, the quite common scenario, of a relationship with a student which turned sour. Has it not happened to all of us teachers at one point or another? Likely, many times over in your career, as it did to me. But in such dire and uncomfortable moments, is hidden a gem of an opportunity.
When and if the greater community of students observes, that you had managed to rebuild and even enhance a formerly troubled affair with a specific student, this tonifies and empowers the entire school. The students come to understand that their teacher can be above petty grudges, and is not vengeful. They come to believe that even difficult points of contention with the teacher, could be resolved. Thereby, even at the backdrop of a misfortune, can be obtained a superior position.

---

41 The Analects, Chapter 19, Verse 21.

Five Lessons From A Businessman

Jeff Bezos is one of the richest people to have ever lived. He founded and heads one of the most powerful business conglomerates the world has ever seen: the **Amazon** company. During the onset of the 21st century, there was hardly a country in the world which was not strongly financially affected by the enterprises of Mr. Bezos, in some way or another. Not everyone appreciates Bezos' style or character. But we all can sure learn a thing or two from his business tactics and strategies.
I read once, that Bezos is famous for following five major principles in doing business. These are: 1. A focus on customers and not competitors, 2. Taking risks for market leadership, 3. Facilitating staff morality, 4. Creating a 'company culture', and 5. Empowering people. Now, whether or not these are essentially followed by his own conglomerate much of the time, is a matter of interpretation left for you to decide. However, not matter the opinion, it ought not deride from the validity and wisdom contained in these ideas.

Focus on customers, not competitors: In the years prior to writing this book, I have read a lot of literature, in the form of books and articles, about the subject of teaching the martial arts. Many of the authors of said materials were very keen on conveying the '*secret formula for success*'. Every action the teacher undertook, they considered to be some form of '*marketing science*'. Their essays were drawing upon the '*winning strategies*' of the '*top schools*', and '*how to imitate* them'. It is a pervading mindset in business nowadays. People seek "to beat the competition by copying the competition and doing it better than the original". All that is exactly the opposite of what what Bezos recommends. It emphasizes focusing on the competition, rather than the customers.
Yes, the school next door may have 300 students, all extremely enthusiastic, the head-teacher drives a Ferrari and they have been

at it for 30 years. So what? They are not You. Why would you want to be them? You are you. You are about what you teach. To be them, let go of everything you do today, practice their martial art and their lineage, act and think like them in every way. Uh, not that enticing now, is it? There is a reason that You like and want to be You – otherwise, you would have been someone else. But you cannot simply be 10% of someone else. This is bound for failure, especially as a 'small business'. Not only will you not be effective in imitating the mannerisms and ways of another person, but other people would also see the sham in your efforts. Even a professional actor, can hardly pull-off a semi-convincing show for a few short hours, and only after much rehearsal, within a very confined and pre-determined script. Therefore, do not try to be the 'competition'. Be yourself. Trying to be other people is a highway to misery, and a magnet for mockery.

Our so-called 'customers' are of course the students [42]. We should focus on them, not on the competition. Do not try to mimic what someone else is doing. Rather, ask yourself – what do my students want, what do they need, what I wish to teach them, and how will convey this during class in the best way possible. Solve that problem, and there would be no need to be like anyone else. As for how to solve it – that is discussed in most of the other chapters in this book.
Note that a student-focus means not that you need to re-structure your martial art or its philosophy because that is what they would prefer. In martial art, the 'customer' is not necessarily right. In fact, he is wrong most of the time. But his innate and often covert wishes do require your consideration. Of this, read more in the chapters titled '***What Do They Really Want***' and '***The Fine Compromise***'.

---

[42] This far into the book it ought to be obvious that the word 'customer' is not one which I like to use when considering the martial arts. The moment you believe your students to be 'customers', in my opinion you have turned from a martial arts teacher, into a businessman.

<u>Take risk to achieve market leadership:</u> This principle is directly related to the previous one. There are hardly any 'market leaders' who are not innovative, or at least were as such before everyone else imitated them.

I sometimes ask my students: "Can you be both ***average*** and ***highly successful***?". The answer is: "No, you cannot". The 'average person' is right there in the middle – an average! He is never at the top. You cannot think average thoughts, say average things, perform average deeds, and then expect to be at the edge of the curve. This has never, ever happened. It is a mathematical impossibility. The only people who are average and gain major momentum and success in life, are those who are pawns at the hands of others, who are themselves not average. Such pawns are many average artists and politicians, who are manipulated by financial interests of above-average masterminds. But as martial arts teachers, we are neither pawns, nor has anyone the interest to promote our careers when our effort or creativity are lacking. We therefore have to take responsibility and rise above what is mediocre[43].

What can be done is completely up to you. But there needs to be a willingness to do what others have not dared or even thought of. Have you ever taught a class in the middle of a train station? Performed a kata on a bus? Put a sign on an entire building in the middle of a city? Gone on talk-show to expose your unique martial art to the world? Sent your students a recorded lecture every day? Brought a giant aquarium into the training hall? Convinced 40 students to spend a week-long retreat in a forest in a foreign land

---

[43] The infamous McDojo model can be successful, economically speaking, but would you consider it a real measure of success in the martial arts themselves? You can have average martial arts and teaching with economic prosperity, but you cannot have average martial arts with martial arts excellence. The question is then, whether you are a martial arts teacher for the sake of making money – in which case your salary is the measure for success, or perhaps for other reasons... I am hopeful that if you are reading this book, financial gain, while ***important***, is not your top priority for teaching the martial arts.

without technological exposure? Had your entire school go and paint the homes of Holocaust survivors over a weekend? Recorded your entire martial arts curriculum on video and shared it for free on the internet, knowing that this does not threaten but rather strengthen you? I know of martial arts teachers who have done all of these things, and much more. We may not choose their path, for ours is different, but we have to follow their example and aspire to their charisma. What is uniquely your own, and is a risk taken based on genuine inner calculated passion, can be unstoppable. When people witness a thing as such, they want to be a part of it. Make it happen, and let them know.

Facilitate staff morality: The greatest threats to any enterprise can often arise from within. Corruption in an organization can go undetected for years and even decades, and as martial arts teachers we have no 'internal auditors' to mitigate this danger. This is why the notion of 'staff morality' is so important. In martial arts schools, a good example for this problem unfolding, would be that of a frustrated younger instructor, who fell out of favour with the headmaster. Such an instructor may form a group of dissident students, and lead them in an open 'rebellion', leaving their original school or organization and setting up a new one. I have heard of this and seen it happen many a time. The major cause might be personal issues between teachers, but more commonly the problem is rooted and stems from a lack of morality on part of the chief troublemakers.

For me personally, teaching the martial arts is a one-man show. I would not like anyone to do it for me, thank you very much, beyond the occasional minor aid or replacement. But many teachers do choose to eventually recruit and hire 'staff'. In a big company like Bezos' Amazon, it can be a tremendous challenge to facilitate staff morality. That is because, people's moral viewpoints as adults are not easily changed in a corporate environment. However, at a martial arts school, the 'hired staff' ought to originate from the core group of students one has been teaching for years [44]. That means that "staff morality" begins not when a student of yours assumes a teaching position for the first time, but during his very first class at a the school. This is due to the fact that morality in martial arts schools, as in other human relationships, tends to set its boundaries at an early stage. Whatever moral flaws you could not correct in a student during the first 4-7 years of his training, it is highly unlikely you would be capable of polishing out later. For this reason, it is of utmost importance that higher ranks are not issued to students without your sincere trust in their good character. This prerequisite should also be evident to all who attend your classes: past a certain rank, there shall be no 'promotion' or further studies, until a man has transformed his character for the better.

Creating a 'Company Culture': This is the subject of the chapter in this book titled ***'Not a Business, But a Community'*** (p.44), and discussed in other chapters as well. It is in essence related to the previous recommendation made by Bezos, concerning 'staff morality'. Trust and morality are more easily fostered and established based on a shared sense of community, rather than mutual business interests. Creating common grounds based on shared culture, guarantees:

---

[44] I personally abhor the notion of hiring people to teach under you who were not your own students, or at least members of your extended martial arts family. Such people can never be fully trusted with the art, unless one previously had a preexisting close personal relationship with them. Even then, it is highly challenging and troublesome to produce a harmony in the curriculum and vision taught at the school, as long as you also continue to teach alongside them. I have little faith in hiring people from outside one's own martial arts family, and I take it to be a sign of commercialization of a traditional martial arts school in the event that this occurs. That being said, from the pure business perspective, for those who regard their school like a company, this idea makes a lot of sense. Here again, the opinions expressed refer strictly to traditional martial arts schools, and not to sports-fighting, MMA and the likes of these.

- Students would feel 'at home'. A place in which the rules and norms are familiar and welcoming, providing security and refuge from the harshness of the outside world.

- Students would be less likely to feel lost or confused, having a broader understanding of what the school is about. This is important for student retention in the long term.

- Students would have something greater than themselves to look up to, shifting the focus from narrow goals to big aspirations and the greater good.

- Students would be invested in an expansive 'cultural universe', and less prone to give up and quit on a whim, since that 'world' does not exist elsewhere. The school culture itself is akin to a relationship the student has with a person.

- Students would have no confusion about the history of the establishment they belong in, and will know their role in and place in the context of the school and its heritage.

- The shared culture would create a bonding glue between the students, providing them with means to bridge gaps of experience and personality.

- It will enable the teacher to have a point of reference for every class. Things you teach would appear more connected and relatable, rather than simply a random collection of techniques, tactics, strategies and ideas, detached from an over-arching framework.

Empowering People: In bestowing more power upon your students, that comes in two forms. The first is to allow for them to have more autonomy and participation within the school environment. That is the subject of the chapters '***The Fine Compromise***', '***You Need Help – Ask For It***', '**The Gift of Trust**', and others in this book. The second form of empowerment you should be exercising is making for your students the connection between their martial arts practice and the improvements in their daily lives. Let me share with you a story about that.

My first-ever student, Jechiel, I had met randomly at the park many years ago, when he was 66 years old. A first student who sticks around with you and is loyal, is in some ways like a childhood friend. He knows a version of you from before you became what you are today. There is a level of authenticity to a relationship which is difficult to attain or come by with other people. Being that he is the CEO of a large company and a man with tremendous life experience, I felt often that Jechiel had taught me about life no less than I taught him. This is also a wonderful type of relationship to have – a sort of 'dual-mentorship'. One day Jehiel told me the following:
"*When I listen to you, I can hear that you have the capacity for making countless associations. You can, in your mind and speech, draw the lines between what we do in martial arts class, and endless topics of interest. You are capable of explaining how our martial arts relate to gardening, sleeping, eating, thinking, woodworking, writing and many fields of knowledge or interest. But your students, most of them do not have this ability. They have other skills, each of them. I believe it is therefore your duty, to cater for the minds of your students. You must guide them in a way that would help them see and comprehend the connections that you so vividly and intuitively understand*".

I listened and considered earnestly Jechiel's words. His observation was astute. Even writing articles and books for my students, was not enough. I needed to physically hold my students' hands and lead them towards the light, in this respect. They had to know how to use their breathing when arguing with their spouse. They had to learn how to manifest mindfulness when eating. They had to understand how to bring about postural awareness even when walking casually on the street. By teaching them such things specifically, not merely describing examples verbally or on a piece of paper, I would be empowering them as individuals. Empowered students are healthier, happier and have more fortitude. Empowered students are those more likely to sustain their practice of the martial arts, and remain by your side even when times are difficult. Empowered students are those, who know the value of your teachings goes above and beyond the participation fee which they pay.

Converging all five principles into a single plan: One of the things Bezos had done over the years, was to allow employees at certain Amazon facilities to bring their dogs to the workplace with them. He realized that for a lot of people, their dog is like a family member, perhaps even a son or a daughter. Employees felt bad leaving their furry friends at home. This caused problems. The employees were perhaps not as focused. They may find excuses to arrive late to work or leave early, to walk their dogs or be with them. They need to make arrangements to have their dogs walked and being taken care of. Dogs who were left alone for too many hours became depressed, and this in turn darkened the mood for the employees who owned them. This all had a negative impact on both the employees and the company.

By allowing people to bring their dogs to work, Bezos manifested all five of his important business principles. He focused on the needs of the customers (his own personal customers – his employees, which he needs to satisfy) rather than the competition. He took a risky decision to manifest market leadership, being among few companies at the time to allow for such a novel arrangement on a massive scale. He helped facilitate staff morality by emphasizing the need to care better for a loved one. He created a strong tenet of company culture. But most of all – he empowered his people, with the ability to make important decisions that matter for them.

The 24/7 School

There are some statistics about martial arts schools which I cannot back up with any research, but I can certainly confirm based on my experience and that of other teachers:

- The longer a student has been absent from class, the more likely it is this student will leave your school.

- Following just two weeks of absence from classes, which were not justified by serious reasons like illness or job requirements, there is at least a 70-80% chance the missing student will not return for the time being.

This means two things for you as a teacher:

1. You better keep track of students who went missing and check up on them. Based on your judgment of the situation you may call them yourself or have a trusted student (who is also their friend) make the call. When calling yourself though, never call more than twice unless the personal circumstances of the student are dire – you do not need to appear desperate to have the student back, and chasing a student with calls create imbalances in your relationship. [45]

2. You should make sure that if the student missed a class or two, he has an opportunity to make up for it.

Here is a common scenario in a martial arts school: a student missed three classes in a row for whatever reason. He is about to miss his

---

[45] A student who has been ill for over two weeks, I gather is worth a personal friendly visit to his home. A student who spends over 3 days in a hospital should also be visited. You should be the first visitor, and then encourage the other students to visit as well.

fourth class because he cannot make it on that day. The causes for his absence do not matter for this discussion. What matters is that if this student usually attends class twice a week, then missing that fourth class would make it two weeks in a row of having not attended classes. Remember what I wrote earlier of missing two weeks straight? Trust me, this is a bad omen.
The problem here was that the school was not able to accommodate for the student's schedule. True that it was his responsibility to get to class on time and when due, but right now you have to deal with the fact that his schedule changed and if you cannot help him reach a class soon, two weeks will pass without his attendance. The solution is found in a commitment called the '24/7 School'.

You need to take it upon yourself to convey a message to the students that the school is supposedly open 24 hours a day, 7 days a week. I do not mean this literally of course, but you should strive in that direction.

- Students should be told that you are available to answer their calls 24 hours a day (though irregular hours are of course for urgent matters and emergencies only). You need not worry, as a student will seldom take up the opportunity to do so. But if and when a student does take advantage and for a good reason, then you should be courteous and helpful to him. Just do it. You cannot begin to imagine what sort of aid your students may require. One teacher for instance told me of a student who called him once in the middle of the night because his wife kicked him out the house and he needed a place to sleep. Make sure to be there wholeheartedly when such calls happen, a few times during your career.

- Optimally the school should be physically open for as many hours and days as possible. Even try and move 'office hours' into the academy just to be there and keep it open. Whether the students should pay more in order to attend sessions beyond their regular classes or simply train at your place – that is up to you. But keep the doors open. Also, allow students who missed a class to attend another group's class without prior notice. Or perhaps have them train at the side and get some instruction from you separately, but do not allow them to make this a habit. These things enable a lot of students with more problematic schedules to not miss too many classes in a row. At my Israeli academy, I had issues with students who were serving in the military, and they were very thankful to me for allowing them to come train outside of their regular classes. I even invite students to train alongside me during my personal training time, and do so 7 days a week (this is considered unusual among martial arts teachers and is my personal preference).

- Vacations: try not taking them until your school is well-established (that is, at least 25-30 students). I have not taken a vacation during the first 3.5 years of running my academy in Israel, and the first 'vacation' I took then was a training trip to China. Remember the two-week rule – when you and a student become absent from each-other's lives for too long, and you risk losing him. This is why long vacations are also a problem. What to do then? Prolong time between vacations for as much as possible, and take more vacations only once a student or two can teach in your stead. It is good to have a big event like testing several students or having a long workshop on a specialized topic just before you leave for vacation, in order to cement your presence right before your temporary absence. Even if you do not have someone to teach when you are away, try to have someone keep the school doors open and encourage students to come and train on their own and help each-other. You may even leave them 'homework' to practice together.

As explained in the chapters '**Not a Business, But a Community**' (p.44) and '**Barter Glues Better Than Money**' (p.238), you should not be thinking about students as business transactions. By allowing students to train more for less pay, or possibly for free, you are not 'losing' anything. Rather, you are gaining more loyal students, who are also becoming more skilled if provided with decent instruction.

Greater loyalty and growth of skill are both decent guarantees and indicators that a student shall remain by your side for a long period of time.

When the students know that the school is open for them and that you are available to them 24/7, then they have more respect for you and feel at ease with their schedule problems. This helps remedy the issues I have presented before, and also relaxes tensions which rise from the student's shame of missing classes, as he or she know that they can make up for it if they want to.
The only warning and challenge is for you to make sure people do not abuse these gifts. Whenever you see a student coming to practice twice or more in a row outside of their regular class, but failing to arrive to the latter, you should warn him that you will not enable him to take advantage further if he does not make an effort to get to the regular class as well. Do not allow for anyone to seek 'special treatment' via these options – they are meant for those with real scheduling issues or who are more dedicated than others and wish to train extra.

Having a so-called '27/4 school' is also a good marketing ploy. Whenever people complain or sigh at the prices you ask for when calling over the phone or otherwise, always patiently explain how the school offers this special benefit of being able to attend many classes and come practice outside of class time. A lot of people are more easily convinced they get their money's worth when they hear about this type of 'feature'.

Tests and Ranks

Who needs tests anyway?... We martial arts teachers love to say that "rank is not really that important", and that "it is all about the individual effort" and "the journey is more important than the end goal". This once more is making the mistake of considering the student as we think of ourselves. Tests and ranks can be done without, when you teach family members or friends. But when dealing with a student community and a commercial school, people have a strong need to gauge, assess and compare themselves with others. Without this they feel lost, as they cannot assert their 'position' within the community.
One should understand that most people are not keenly introspective and are incompetent at knowing fully who they are, what they are about and what they are capable of. They need help with these sorts of things. Tests and ranks are superficial means of doing so, but at least they provide them with direction. There are more merits to testing of course, which I shall get to momentarily.

Tests are commonly used to measure progression and promote one's 'rank', which usually determines if a student is ready to learn more or to accept teaching permissions. Rank has the benefit, and deficit, of providing someone with a social position. It always helps the individual to know their social position within the school, but it can also lead students astray, and make them believe they are entitled or privileged. You must help the students understand that rank is something to live up to – a higher bar set for themselves, and not a crown which bestows upon them power over others.
I know that a lot of schools are 'stuck' with a rank structure dictated by an organization or teacher which is difficult to change. I was fortunate enough to be able to make up my own 'ranking system' for my school. What I chose to do was as follows:

1. I split the curriculum into 18 different rank stages. A beginner is positioned at stage 0, and a teacher who knows the entire curriculum well is at stage 15. The last three stages, 16-18, are based on non-technical achievements. Why 18 stages? Because it is a fitting compromise in my opinion.
Schools with perhaps 5-6 rank stages find themselves testing students once in a very long while. In such a scenario, of a school having just a few stages, a student may test for stage 4, and it would then take him years to reach stage 6. This tends to make students indifferent to the tests because they are very far apart from one-another, defeating part of their purpose (to encourage students to train harder in order to get to the next stage).
Then there are many schools, say of Karate, with as many as 22 stages (12 Kyu ranks and then 10 Dan ranks). This can also be detrimental as the road may appear too long and arduous. Have you recently signed up for any professional training program where it was stated from day one that it will take you 30 years to 'complete' it? People are not thrilled about signing for a decades-long commitment, and that applies to the martial arts as well. Many still do sign up of course, but the overly-long program presentation is, in my opinion, not helpful for student recruitment and retainment.

In my curriculum structure, people who train several times a week can teach (rank 9) within 4-7 years, and know the entire curriculum well (rank 15) within 8-12 years. Even the highest degrees (ranks 16-18) can be obtained then within 15-20 years, whilst in some other traditional schools such a thing may require one to wait 30-50 years.

2. The other thing I did with ranking was that although I test for it, the ranks themselves are not outwardly visible. Everyone sort of knows the rank of the other person (as the tests are public), but there are no belts, sashes or tags to indicate that. Instead, everyone wear the same white shirt, and a teacher wears a black one. This achieves a positive situation in which people know their place, but do not overly busy themselves in comparing their achievements with others. As in class there are also no special sitting arrangements based on rank, and everyone are practicing together, then rank remains more of an individual marker and contribution

and does not easily evolve into a political game between students [46]. The only additional marker for rank are advanced student classes, in which only people above a certain rank are present. But these people are also expected to attend the 'lower rank' classes from time to time.

Testing events are in my opinion like cooking – all about timing, the right amounts and the proper ingredients.

How many tests are appropriate in a given year? Some teachers will test every month or two. This is too frequent and stressful for both teacher and students. This also leads to either a high-failure rate or high promotion rate, both are bad for the school. Then there are also teachers who insist upon only testing once a year. The problem here is that this makes student promotion too slow. Additionally, students often miss tests for whatever reason, and then waiting another 6-12 months for the next test really frustrates them. Trust me when I tell you, that those who only test once a year lose a whole lot of students simply because of unspoken angst developed against this policy. I know this to be true based on first-hand experience of several colleagues of mine.
You have to be mature here and admit that the testing cannot be conducted based on your own whims and schedule. Rather, you should determine the right time for testing and the number of tests necessary in a given year based solely on student progression. You should wait until enough students are ready for testing, and then make a date and let them know at least a month in advance.

There are teachers who like to 'surprise-test' their students, telling them about a test as little as a week or even an hour before the test is due. This also defeats the purpose, which is to have at least a 95% probability of the student passing the test. Yes, optimally you want all students to pass. You do not want it to be easy for them, as without a challenge people lose interest and do not learn, but you want them to work hard and then make it. Failing tests is not good

---

[46] Note how this complements the principle of Egalitarianism, discussed in the second chapter of this book.

for the students or for the school. Let them fail frequently in class, but have them ready to succeed in the test, which is the 'bigger war' they have been preparing for. By surprising them with a test you obviously are 'keeping it real', but this is not the time or place to add obstacles. With each failed test the probability of a student leaving the school rises significantly. Why do this, then? Just to make a point? Do not be childish. People's lives are on the line – yours, and those of the students. Would you rather show a student "he was not ready" so you could prove something to him, or be able to keep him around for the next 10 years? Think about that.

Now this is not to say you should not fail students in tests. I have done so many a time. But failing a student should be on a fair basis, and hopefully with the student understanding that this was their fault and they can make up for it next time. It is however your responsibility more than his, to allow him to test only once he is ready, and not prior to that. Students can get emotionally manipulative or simply nagging about their wishes to get ahead in the curriculum. Here there should be no room for compromise. You need to make it clear to them that you will only let them test when they are likely to pass, and also provide them the means and instructions for reaching that goal.

The testing events are very important instruments in the hands of a teacher for building a student's character, and also a sense of community. Optimally you should have as many people present in each testing session, beyond those who actively participate. Get large portions of the student community together. When the student needs to demonstrate various techniques or partners, pick and alternate as many people 'from the crowd' as possible. Use the opportunity to praise not only the student being tested, but also his helpers. Speak loudly of the importance of them aiding their friend deal with the challenge. Have them bring food and drinks, and by the end of it have a small party. The students who pass, and also those who did not, are the 'guests of honor' and should be applauded for their efforts. For major testing events, take pictures and videos. Encourage those suitable to have short speeches about the tests, comradery and brotherhood. All of this is very beneficial.

Be careful about the length of tests. No street fight lasts 3 hours, and likewise I see no reason why a test should last as long, and I have seen schools which went even beyond that. Remember that you want to make a positive social gathering of the occasion, and people are going to be bothered by sitting aside for 3 hours watching – especially if that happens several times a year. Be reasonable. Perhaps you do not need the person to demonstrate each and every movement in the entire curriculum. Maybe one does not have to really fight 20 people in a row to prove he can handle himself well. This is a martial arts school, not infantry boot camp. Extreme stamina and endurance are better left for those who need them – they are not related to civilian martial arts. The most commercially successful martial arts schools seldom test people for hours on end, unless for one very special rank and such, and often not even for that. A good martial arts teacher can tell how skilled a man is, when observing a person of his art, by simply looking at him perform for 5 minutes. That is true for your students as well. Anything over 5 minutes is simply technical or psychological. Whatever goes beyond 5 minutes, is simply for you to check he remembers and does everything decently, or his need of undergoing a tremendous challenge in order to build character. But you likely know if he passed 5 minutes in, and often before he even tested.

For that matter, my own tests tend to last anywhere between 15 minutes and 2 hours, depending on the rank one is being tested for. The longer tests linger only for the purpose of demonstrating most or all of the curriculum, in single practice, partner exercises and combative applications. I do allow a few resting periods between demonstrations. This is not a marathon, but an inquiry into one's knowledge and skill.

Private in Public

One of the greatest unseen and unspoken challenges of teaching the martial arts is the need to allocate your attention correctly between students. The martial arts class is a chaotic environment, because at any given moment, one of several people is making several mistakes which beg your attention, or literally calls your attention to him or her. Also, the students unconsciously feel that they have to 'compete' for your attention in a group setting. It is perpetually 'losing' situation, as at any point when you provide a certain student with attention personally, you are depriving the rest of them from that attention, and many will notice. There are however several key points for preventing this scenario from causing tensions in class:

1. When you provide a given student with attention, he should be at the 'center stage'. You will do the utmost to ensure that only he receives attention at that point in time – there could be no distractions. The same notion should be followed when speaking with a student (or with anyone in life for that matter) outside of class or even on the phone – do not cut the conversation in the middle in order to give someone else a part of your attention. Politely tell that other person you will be with him in a moment, and then continue what you were up to with the first student.

2. In class, rotate between the students and attempt to provide each with roughly the same amount of time and attention, doing your best to not focus on one person for too much time (unless that is their first class). Worst case scenario, if he still does not understand your explanations, you can come to him later, and in the meanwhile he can work it out on his own or use the aid of a veteran student.

3. Do not be afraid to pause your student rotation, step aside, and witness the class from afar as they practice. You will often observe that most, and sometimes all students are so busy with their training they do not even notice you are not currently teaching anyone. By doing this for a minute or two you can get some rest, and also more easily see which among the students is more desperate and needs your support.

4. When speaking and demonstrating in front of students, constantly shift your gaze. Focus on specific 1-3 people for a few seconds as if you were speaking to them only, and then move your gaze elsewhere. This allows you to keep students in check, making sure they are listening, and them to feel that the lecture is more personal.

In abiding by these instructions, you would be able to make each student feel that every public class was to him like a private class. Through this your students will develop a greater appreciation for you and your teachings.

Latecomers

In countries where being on time is not a fundamental social value, every martial arts school is at one point or another inflicted with the 'latecomer plague'. It begins with one infected individual who, for whatever reason, is always late (sometimes the reason is justifiable). Then suddenly, you find yourself having to deal with some classes where up to 50% of people are late every time. This disease must be treated and cured hastily, or it can shake the very foundations of your school.

Here are several strategies for failure, followed by the one that actually worked for me personally:

- **Talking common sense:** I often tell the students they would not dare be late for meeting with other professionals, such as lawyers, accountants, psychologists, dentists, etc. So why do this to their martial arts teacher, who cares for them more than some other people as such? Well, yes – they get you and this may help at times with aiding them in understanding your point here. But I guarantee you that talk alone will not suffice.

- **Yelling:** The student feels bad enough for having been late, and in my experience often it is not completely their fault either – there are only partly to blame, even if in hindsight they could have prevented this. So adding more blame in the form of public humiliation is not helpful.

- **Go home:** Over 15 minutes late with no justifiable reason? Go home. This tends to hurt people's feelings (perceived as 'banishment' for good will), and defeats the purpose of the student learning anything, and the goal of having more people in class.

- **<u>Shame corner:</u>** I never liked this one, but it is popular in many martial arts schools. The late student cannot speak until spoken to. He sits in the corner outside of the main training area and waits until the teacher feels like calling him over to join the class. This approach can be humiliating for some, but its main problem is that it simply wastes more of the student's time. The student already knows he missed a part of the class, and now he has to miss additional few extra minutes doing nothing. There is no incentive here for changing one's behaviour, and if anything, this encourages the student not to come when he knows he would be late.

- **<u>The boot-camp treatment:</u>** The student is punished by having to execute some conditioning exercises, like running, pushups, jumping, etc. This is more useful and educational than the previous solutions. The problem here is that this type of punishment does not really fit well a wide range of student types and situations. Send an ill student running? An old out-of-shape student to do push ups? A student who did not sleep a whole night for a round of jumping squats? Hmmm... You can see where this is going. This is a solution, but not a well-rounded one.

It is my belief that you can learn from anyone – even a child, a fool or a dog. You simply need to keep an open mind. One day, a kid from a class of mine provided me with the ultimate solution.
When the number of students in class was uneven and one group of student ended up being a trio rather than a pair, one among the trio used to wait by the side until it was his turn. One day that 10 year old kid says out loud: **"WHY CAN'T THE PERSON WAITING DO SOMETHING?! LET THEM DO THE HORSE!!"**. By that he meant, that the person without anything to do in class should simply spend that time sitting in Ma Bu (meaning 'horse step' in Chinese; usually mistranslated as 'horse stance'; called Kiba Dachi in Japanese). That was the moment folks. So simple, and so ingenious. I took the kid's advice and implemented it as he had suggested. But I went further then, and used it to solve the latecomer problem too.

Enter: **'The Stable'**. From then on, all latecomers were jokingly branded 'the horses'; and horses need to be put in the stable. The latter was a corner in the school were people usually did not practice, which was still in the training area, overlooking the class. A horse latecomer who was over 5 minutes late without a justifiable reason would have to go and sit in Ma Bu at the stable. For how long you ask? For the length of his delay! 10 minutes late to class got you exactly 10 minutes of quality time at the stable, and you had to put the time on your watch and get on with it. This was a great solution for several reasons:

1. The activity itself builds skills relevant to the practice in class.

2. The horse may sweat, but he does so while observing the rest of the class, and since he is stuck in place, watching the class and paying attention is the only entertainment and his only mental escape from the difficult practice.

3. There is a limit to how long most people can sit in Ma Bu. Most people cannot bear the challenge and pain for over 15 minutes, so naturally if you were going to be very late, you would rather not come because you would not like to go through such torture. This immediately brings an end to excessive late arrivals.

4. Anyone can do it. Beginners, sick students or tired ones – the practice can be augmented to fit the level of skill of each student and his physical condition during that particular day. A weak student can even hold onto something to make the practice more bearable.

5. The student gets a chance to 'participate' and practice from the moment he arrives, even though he was late. You may even use this opportunity to throw some 'horse jokes' his way in the midst of class

if he is so inclined, making the experience more memorable.

6. And memorable it is! For holding Ma Bu for a long period of time is certainly a thing people remember. The pain plays a positive role here, cementing the memory of "being late is bad". It is a special kind of pain, which you likely know too as teachers, and unlike with fitness exercises where the pain comes and goes, here it sticks long enough to take root in the student's mind.

Within two weeks of establishing The Stable, the latecomer plague subsided, and never returned. It was a tremendous success, and implementing this kind of practice or similar I would highly recommend to any martial arts teacher.

With latecoming children, though you should of course talk with them and educate, the solution is usually to settle the score with the parents. Also, be emotionally prepared to 'pardon' a child and make excuses for him in front of the other children, if the late arrival is serially the parent's fault and there is nothing to be done about it.

Barter Glues Better Than Money

I remember once speaking to a high-ranking Karate teacher who is quite famous in my country. He has been running his martial arts school for over 40 years, with great success. I was surprised when he told me that at any given time, about 17% of the people at his dojo were not paying! In fact, he was the one to encourage them to not pay if they could not. These were all people with financial difficulties who were not capable, so he allowed them to skip payments.

Is this really something we martial arts teachers ought to do? Well morally, of course this is the right thing to do, if indeed people cannot pay. But everything depends on your personal circumstances. The teacher I mentioned had a school with over 150 people in it. He could afford to allow 17% of students there, about 25 of them, to not pay, at any given time. But this can be much tougher financially for a teacher who only has 10-30 students. That teacher with the large school was a tad too generous in my opinion, but he could afford it.

We have several things to consider here. First of all, a student who is not paying is neither a liability nor a loss. Considering no one else knows that he does not pay, no feelings of discrimination arise from the other students. In fact, this is a positive thing, to have such a student around. He is one extra member of the academy, making classes larger and your student count bigger. He now owes you something for your kindness. He would not have been able to pay anyhow, so letting him go would not do you any good, and it is not as if you could have earned that money which he does not have.
Secondly, there are ways to settle the score with such a student. You

can have him do jobs or chores for you which you feel are worth the fee that he is not paying (something you ought to avoid with people who experience great personal challenges). You can for instance send such a student to hand out flyers, have him work on your website, come clean the school, and similar things as such. Or perhaps if his financial situation is obviously temporary (say he will be missing a salary for just 2 months), you can let it pass given he guarantees to give back the money later (do not place a deadline though – this is friendly aid, not a bank loan).

What I like to do is to also require that those who do not pay arrive to class more. You need to skip payment for 3 months? Fine – but you will need to get to class at least twice a week. Miss a class without a very good reason – you are paying for that month, no excuses. The students need to understand that the charity policy comes with commitments and obligations, otherwise they often disrespect your kindness and abuse it.

In my school the charity policy is open for all. You will not pay if you cannot. But there are the rules and caveats, as I have described before. I have never experienced as many as 17% of students in need of using the charity policy. Usually we have anywhere between zero to three such students at any given time. But if you find yourself forced to become too charitable, simply make the demands and requirements tougher for those people who ask for your kindness (those among them who can actually sustain an extra burden). Also, try to avoid having students who cannot pay from day one. Usually I only allow to take advantage of the charity policy to those who have been with us for at least a few months. They better have to prove themselves first before you extend your helping hand, otherwise this is just a waste of time.

Realize however that you cannot stop there, at that agreement with such a student. Because if a student reached a situation in which he cannot pay for martial art classes – classes which tend to not be very expensive, then that student has issues that need taking care of. He got himself into this mess, so likely he needs help. Make sure you help him, and if possible have other members of the student community help him. His problems are your problems, and this was true even before he had to ask not to pay.

Working wisely through such situations with students can be of great benefit to your school and your reputation in the long term. People tend to remember those who have been as kind and charitable with them, even if they do not take the initiative to show it. Whenever such students become well-established in their personal lives and careers, never shy from asking a favour of them if and when you really need it. Likely you will find that you have created some powerful allies in the form of people who love and appreciate you. This type of relationship and appreciation you may have never earned from such people by having them simply pay for all of their classes; for the action of bartering manifests a stronger bond than the exchange of financial means.

This truth I have learned and experienced twice myself. With my first teacher, Shifu Nitzan Oren, he asked me to stop paying him after I had been studying with him for about 5 years. By that point in time I was already his disciple and his only student as he had stopped teaching groups a while back. He felt that we were already close enough to go beyond the financial relationship, and though I tried pushing cash into his hands several times he refused, so eventually I gave up. Since then we have become very close friends, and I have helped him with countless person affairs, from rent contracts to job searching and translation work. He in return continued to teach me from time to time.

My second teacher, Sifu Sapir Tal, I had been studying privately with since my first class. By my first class Sifu had reasoned, with his keen empathic senses, that it would be very difficult for me to pay for his private sessions, as he was charging a large sum, worthy of his status and experience. So instead, he offered a barter deal, though he did not really know what exactly I might be able to do for him. I ended up becoming his personal assistant, and have done countless jobs that he required. From writing and answering letters, to co-authoring a book, documenting our martial art in great detail, assisting with his wife's summer camps, working at his garden or teaching in his stead when he went on vacation – I did all of these and much more. Sifu was very kind in originally offering a '1 for 1' deal, according to which I was supposed to work for a single hour for every hour of private session he gave me. I laughed at his suggestion and told him that I was expecting to work much more than that, and indeed I did. Usually, the ratio would be more in line of 5-10 work hours on my part for every hour of private instruction. But I never complained, and did everything wholeheartedly.

In fact, I gained a whole lot from this latter barter deal. I became closer and more intimate with my Sifu and his family than most of his other students over his decades-long career [47]. I had a chance to be with him in his house a lot, and for every hour of class there were often 1-2 additional hours of chatting about anything whatsoever

---

[47] Despite this situation and the benefits I garnered from it, I would not dare claim that I was ever my Southern Mantis Sifu's best student. Additionally, beside myself there had been over the years a few other students who maintained a close relationship with my Sifu, sometimes closer and more intimate than my own.

(though usually martial arts) and getting to know this man better. I could ask and had time to ask any question about the teachings, and I certainly used the opportunity and kept the questions flowing endlessly every single time we met, taking care to document everything. Being so appreciative of this, I worked as hard as I could at whatever task my teacher issued me, no matter how long it took. My teacher on his part earned a lifetime service for which he would have needed to hire at least 10 different professionals. We were both always pleased with the arrangement, and certainly made the most from it.

You too can be wise about such things. Do not wait for a student to come and ask for the charity policy. Be proactive in offering a barter for certain individuals whom you have known for a while, who show great promise and whom you can trust. In doing this you can within a short while manifest a teacher-student relationship many wish they had, but could never quite establish. By the end of the day, money tends to get in the way. You need it to make a decent living, but do remember – the strongest bonds are not between business partners, but among those with a mighty mutual interest which stems from the corresponding echoes of their hearts and minds. To know a man, is to seek what he has sought, and be able to follow his footsteps on his way there. The majority of students are only handed a map to the top of the mountain. Some fortunate students get to walk the path alongside their teacher.

Those With Prior Experience

A famous proverb states: "***The are no difficult students - only students with prior education***". This is an encompassing statement, referring to any prior education. As martial arts teachers we have to deal with this constantly, and sometimes we do not even notice.

Take this fictional example: someone heard from his friend when they were 10 years old, that "a very strong slap to the back can cause a temporary arm paralysis, and may be used for self-defense". Silly as it may sound, that person is now 30 years old, has never discussed this again with anyone, and that belief stuck with him for 20 years. He has only been attending your classes for 3 months. Now, you find that he tried this in class! He still thinks a slapping someone on the back arbitrarily can cause temporary arm paralysis, because his friend told him that 20 years ago when they were kids. But you of course still have no idea why he did it. Upon questioning him, you learn that he thinks this to be effective. Now, convincing him that this belief in unreasonable would take some effort, simply because it has been long-standing and deeply ingrained.

Commonly we encounter such challenges with students who heard various things about anatomy, medicine, history and whatnot. They can claim the most outrageous things in class, often out-loud. They may appear to challenge our authority sometimes, but more so they generally just wish to protect and affirm a long-held belief of theirs.

The type of former education which casts the greatest and most intimidating shadow over a teacher-student relationship can be a person's past study at another martial arts school. The relationship of a student with a former teacher can often be likened, in the context of your relationship, to his feelings towards an ex-girlfriend or ex-wife. Sometimes, people want to leave those experiences behind and seldom even think about them again. But frequently, people arrive at a new relationship with 'emotional baggage'. In this case, they would be inclined to draw comparisons between you and their former teacher. These comparisons may be spoken to you directly, or even whispered in your absence to the other students. This spells trouble.

Any gossip about another martial arts school, as opposed to a positive and open discussion, is bad for your school. However, wherein you have been wise enough to educate your students to avoid negative gossip, then they will quickly shut down a student attempting to draw comparisons and tell them about it. There are no good outcomes from such gossip. When a student believes that his former teacher is superior to you in some way, then it undermines your authority. When the students believes you are superior and yearns to share it, then your school may eventually come to be known as one in which other teachers are not respected. Therefore the less gossip, the better.

Then it also happens that the student will unintentionally undermine your authority by drawing comparisons in class, in front of other people. "Oh, but when I studied this style, we used to do it that way". That sort of statement carries a very annoying passive-aggressive undertone. It is a challenge to your authority, but in fact encapsulates the student's wish for someone to give him answers. The student wants to understand how can two differing approaches coexist and still be valid. This should be met with patience and tolerance, to the best of your ability.
However, do not be dragged to his level. What the student wants to conceive in his imagination, is you and his former teacher getting into a ring and fighting it out, to see who is best [48]. Because this is unlikely to happen, then he opts to have you engage in a verbal fight ('an argument') in order to make your case. Do not argue – explain.

---

[48] Over the years, I have had several novice students so audacious, as to literally tell me they would have liked to see me fight their former teacher. Their foolish statement was completely innocent of course, but points out to a childish fantasy a lot of students have, which most dare not utter. It is a 'my dad is better than your dad' kind of fantasy, which they still hold on to since childhood.

Do not make this into an 'us versus them' situation. Instead, resolve the conflict with statements that allow room for everybody to thrive in. Rather than attacking the former teacher or his methods, speak of why what you teach may be better for that particular student in that specific scenario. Also, do not run away from this 'fight'. It is all too easy to tell a student: "we do it this way and that is it", or "our way is simply superior". Such answers, when repeated, can be interpreted by some students as intellectual cowardice, and will not yield good results.

Most people get the hint quickly, and stop challenging your authority in this manner eventually. But just as some individuals cannot get over their ex-girlfriend or ex-husband, so are some martial arts students stuck in a former teacher-student relationship which they continue to bring up in class. Wherein despite of your best efforts the student does not change his attitude, then you should carefully and politely direct him or her to seek instruction elsewhere. There are fewer things more damaging, than veteran students who still frequently speak of former schools and glorify them in the presence of other students, at your expense. You cannot allow this to happen. A student who features this type of behaviour does not fully trust you, and you cannot trust him.

The Challenge of Trust

In the past, it was quite common in the United States, China and other countries, in traditional martial arts circles, for a practitioner to publicly challenge another, often a teacher. Usually the word 'challenge' in this context meant that for whatever reason, the challenger demanded to fight the other party. Often, if he lost, a challenger would be begging to become a student of the teacher who beat him. This occurred when the purpose of the challenge was for the challenger to locate someone who he considered 'worthy and formidable' enough to teach him.

I was always of the opinion that such events were ill-mannered and inappropriate. Some teachers are notorious for having attracted that sort of attention, drawing to them the types of characters who sought trouble like a bee yearns for nectar. Such teachers would for instance hang signs outside their schools proclaiming: "We Accept All Challengers". By so doing, these teachers created fertile grounds for hostile and problematic people to arrive at their doorstep.

Assuming a losing challenger was to become the teacher's student – how could the teacher ever fully trust and rely upon him completely? To begin with, the student to be came with bad intentions, and the origin for that relationship was crooked and antagonistic in nature. Furthermore, by requesting to be a student, the challenger is in fact revealing that he is interested in receiving the teacher's knowledge and skill, and become better than him. Although this goal is in-itself respectable and reasonable in a teacher-student relationship, its roots should not be grounded in a competitive urge, but growing out of mutual respect and an appreciation for the art and the tradition being taught.

When such an event is used to establish a relationship, the teacher will forever fear that his student, originally a challenger, will one day fulfill an opportunity to once more 'prove himself' by demonstrating in public that he has transcended him. Alternatively, such a student may be tempted to use the knowledge bestowed upon him by his teacher to challenge other teachers. Even when such a person has perhaps later been accepted as an indoor-student or promoted to a high rank of sorts, the teacher's suspicion of him and his caution will not necessarily vanish. With accordance to this reality, the teacher will be less inclined to wish to share his art in earnest and full with that student, due to the possible destructive consequences of the teachings. Indeed, from the moment such a person had studied the full technical curriculum of the art, what is to stop him from once more challenging his teacher, if not sooner than that?... We should also consider that by the time which had passed since the original challenge, the teacher has gotten older, and he knows that when the second challenge comes, he may already be in suboptimal physical condition.

Among those who have challenged their teachers before studying with them, there are many who under the teacher's influence have turned subtler, more civilized and enlightened. Through such positivity, they change their attitude and outlook on life, and no longer seek conflict or feel they have something to prove to the world. This change can at times be quite substantial, to the point where past issues between teacher and student are forgotten. But a person's character is a fickle substance; a stubborn form of matter which does not easily or quickly molds into a new frame.

It is therefore a bad idea to begin a relationship of trust with an action which embodies mistrust. This is not the best way to establish a heart-to-heart transmission.

I remember that once I was contacted by a man close to me in age. He arrived in one of my classes, participated and was positively impressed with what he saw and practiced. After having expressed his wish to study at our academy, he suggested we conduct a friendly sparring match in order to "check things out". In return I asked him: ***"What good do you think will come of this? You have already stated that you believe what I teach can make you a better martial artist. Now, as for the question of who among us two can fight better – will***

***the answer to this question improve our relationship as a teacher and someone who is to be his student?*"**. The man paused for a moment, carefully considering what I have just suggested. Then he said I was right. Later he studied with me for a few months, and eventually became a student of one of my own teachers. Nowadays he is my gongfu brother and a good friend. I know that I can trust him.

Not all challenges are martial by nature. Every week I experience a few dozen minor and hidden 'challenges' from my own students. One for example has a background in Okinawan Karate, and is used to holding a certain stance with his legs wider than what is the norm at our school. In the past, every time I corrected his foot positioning, he would complain that my instructions “do not feel right” and said he could not see a problem with the way in which he was doing it. Another may not be accurate with the angles of his upper limbs, resulting in failure in the execution of certain techniques, and then protesting that this or that movement was “ineffective”. Yet another could be having a hard time remembering Chinese terms for various concepts in his martial art, and so he utters that “this teaching method (using the Chinese language) is not friendly and is unreasonable”.

All of these and similar occurrences are akin to challenging the trust within the teacher-student relationship. However as a teacher I do my best to not be overly judgmental of students for such things they say or these patterns of behaviour. I understand that their purpose and essence are to express the student’s distress at that particular point in time. Just as a baby cries and shouts out of frustration when he or she encounter difficulties in learning the ways of the world, so does the martial arts student experiences the urge to outwardly express the inner tensions which arise within him, as he feels helpless in handling a new challenge.
Likewise, we can say of one who is seeking to challenge a teacher through combat, that he usually does not act out of anger or evil, but out of a need to tell the world something about his feelings and emotions. He has not the tools to express these in a more constructive manner, and therefore he chooses the physical confrontation – the most primitive resort for self-expression and making a bold personal statement. Being capable of understanding this reality would allow us to find means of creating a true conversation with such an individual, without resorting to the use of violence.

The Gift of Trust

My first-ever student was a CEO of a very large and successful company. His name is Jechiel. We seemingly met by complete coincidence. One day I was training at the park late at night, when this older gentleman, in his 60s, came waddling along the trail next to me. He paused and looked at what I was doing. As he observed, I was in deep moving trance, away from everything. A while passed, and my rational mind made a note that this man had been standing there for a very long time – an unusual occurrence in the park. I decided to strike a conversation, and got to know this pleasant man.

I remember Jechiel telling me right then and there, that he sought to find his Self. He believed, by observing me, that through whatever I was practicing, were means of attaining what he was looking for. He was right. However, at the time I did not consider myself 'a teacher'. Although I had helped my own teachers instruct some people, and had a lot of teaching experience outside of the martial arts, I did not think my skills were up to par for the task.

As we ended our conversation, I opted to begin providing Jechiel with a list of teachers of the Chinese martial arts, who taught similar things to what I was practicing. But, within a minute or two I came to the realization, that in fact none of these people focused on or had the means of conveying, what this man was after. I hesitated for a moment. Jechiel sensed this. He asked me: "Why will **you** not teach me?". I considered the idea for a moment, and replied: "Uh... Why not, really? I am here every night, anyway. Come and train with me". We have been together since.

Over the years Jechiel and I grew close. I have come to learn that he was a very wise man, with mannerism and a style which often go unappreciated. I have learned a lot of lessons from him, as he did from me. More so than with any other person I taught, we were at times uncertain who was the student, and who the teacher.

One of the things by which we always saw eye-to-eye, was the notion of setting a personal example for one's subordinates. Jechiel, having led his company to tremendous financial success for decades without fail, did so much through caring and catering to his employees like they were all family.

It is said that one of the best ways to earn people's trust, is to put trust in them. In a way, this is how I came to teach this man. Jechiel wholeheartedly believed this, and put it to practice constantly.

At one time, Jechiel had an employee put in charge of a complex technical job. His employee had to resolve a difficult construction problem for a company they were doing business with. Jechiel's employee crumbled under the pressure, and failed to deliver a solution in due time. The other company's men became anxious. They took that employee's failure to be a sign of negligence and indifference. Wishing to work with someone who was more to their liking, they pressured Jechiel to let that employee go and replace him with another man whom they themselves thought was more fit for the job. They were not at all subtle about this either, and made sure the employee heard what they had to say of him. The employee, upon hearing this, became quite anxious and unsettled. He felt alone, facing a huge conglomerate who wanted him to get out of the way.

Jechiel had other plans. He told his employee: "*These people, I have been working with for but a short time. The fact that their business with us is worth millions, does not mean that I should value them over you. I have known you for many years. I know that you are a dedicated professional, and that you care about our company. I ask you now – can I trust you to get this job done? I know you can do this if you keep trying. But if you tell me that you cannot handle it, then I will respect and understand that as well*". The employee immediately looked reinvigorated and rejuvenated. His eyes were sparkling. "*Yes!*", he said; "*I will do my best, you can trust me. Give me a week, and I can have this done and executed to the best of my ability. You can trust me*". As he promised, so did he deliver, to everyone's satisfaction.

When Jechiel told me this story, at first I found it inspiring, but did not give it enough consideration. Some years later, as my experience as a teacher continued to develop, I recalled that story and could see more value in it, and in Jechiel's behaviour.

Through this story we can learn the importance of siding with the people who are close to us, and whom we know should be trusted more than those who are newcomers to our lives. By trusting our students, their loyalty, self-esteem and performance all improve. Therefore, next time you step into a class, make sure to take the time to tell each of the students, personally, that you trust they can do and achieve certain things. Then watch them grow and succeed.

The Personal Touch

The martial arts are too serious to be taken seriously. Tell some jokes, keep that smile on. Your students already have enough solemn drama with all this talk of "life and death situations" and "be careful because that technique can accidentally kill your partner". Martial arts classes can get quite intense like that. We teachers tend not to notice. For us, this is simply what we like to do, so there is no stress to it. The students however feel as if they are being tested all the time, because the challenges just keep coming. A stressful student is less cooperative, a worse learner, and is inclined to be stiffer and badly coordinated. This is not what you want. To counter this, a personal touch is required.

Oh, I mean that literally! You should keenly observe for any student who becomes overly stressed during class. Then you should approach and physically touch them. The touch needs to be friendly and encouraging, but not too intimate. You can place your palm on their arm, shoulder or back, perhaps adding a little rub or a few gentle taps. Use two palms to give more energy and support. A depressed student can get a half-hug, or a full hug if you are alone [49]. A pre-puberty kid can get a full hug or a rub on the head. Then with this personal touch, add an encouraging sentence, like: "Hey, everything will be OK"; "Keep it going, you are doing great"; "Do not give up, I am proud of you"; "Take a deep breath, you can do it!". I do such things during every single class.

You cannot begin to imagine how desperately some students need this type of encouraging personal touch. For a lot of people that could prove the most significant act of empathy they have received

[49] Research has shown that after roughly 20 seconds of hugging, the body begins to release oxytocin – a hormone which supports social bonding, reduces pain, fear, anxiety and depression, and makes us feel better overall. When a student is experiencing a very difficult time in their personal life and really needs that hug, and the circumstances call for it, then by all means provide a genuine and long-lasting hug for best results.

in a very long time. Others may get enough empathy elsewhere, but they really need it then and there to push through the challenges.

The personal touch can extend its application as a teaching methodology. In the traditional Chinese martial arts, it was the norm to teach in this manner, and is still commonplace among many traditional teachers such as myself. The idea here is that the student will find it difficult to attain the right type of feeling for body movements, especially the more internal ones, without being able to experience how his teacher feels it. So, the teacher has to allow a student to touch his body when executing certain movements or training various methods, in order for the student to have a kinesthetic experience of what it feels like to be the teacher at that moment. This teaching method is in my opinion essential and crucial, at least in my teachings. I find it unfortunate that most martial arts teachers never allow the students to touch their bodies, due to cultural habits and psychological restraints.

The student should be allowed to touch any place on the teacher's body, apart from sexual organs, but usually ought to be guided by the teacher to the more appropriate locations and how to touch them. This is a problem in modern society, as people have become alienated and estranged for each-other, and now a lot of us sadly consider most forms of touch to be 'inappropriate' or 'sexual' when not with family members or life-partners. Because of this, you should only allow veteran students to touch your body on area considered more 'intimate', and use sound judgment to determine which people are accepting of this teaching methodology, and which are those who make take it the wrong way.

The rule of thumb for me is: if you treat this personal-touch-driven instruction as a teaching norm, it is less-likely to be considered awkward. Still, this method is very limited with the opposite sex. I never use this method with women, because in the society I live in, women are quick to make threats, file a police complaint or issue a law suit for less than that. I also avoid it with students during their first few classes. A lot of teachers solve the problem, or a possible misunderstanding and backlash from some students, by only allowing their disciples or high-ranking black belts to touch their bodies freely. Whoever you choose to allow to touch you, once this method is established and accepted by the students, then they should have 'free access' to your body and be able to politely ask, without fear or hesitation, to place their hands somewhere in order to learn and understand better.

So far was discussed the passive element of this teaching method, with the teacher doing something and the student touching. There is also an active component to it, which I use a lot. To help students understand and move better, I would touch somewhere on their bodies while they are practicing. Then by using empathy I will try to sense where their problem is, and convey unto them through my body and mind the correct sensation. This is done through minute and delicate changes in muscular tension, body language, facial expressions, the use of sounds to emphasize one's intentions, and dare I say – sending into the student's body the right type of energy. This type of teaching skill cannot be taught – you have to experiment with it, and empathy will be your guide. You do, however, absorb much of this skill from your own teacher wherein he himself taught like this. My ability to teach like that, I have inherited from one of my teachers, Shifu Nitzan Oren.

It is by far the most effective method of teaching I know of. This is why I touch my students a lot. I will come to a student while he works on something and place one or two palms on his body to convey the right message, often without having to speak. He will get it, at least in part, and even if he is not capable of changing much at that moment, he understands the message, which is important in the long term. Sometimes I will have the student place a palm on my body and we will perform the same movement together, becoming one entity. Then through this connection the student's body will aspire to harmonize with mine, and by this I can pull him in the right direction.

You may have noticed that in order to allow someone to touch me, or for me to touch them, I need to be with only one or two students at any given time. This indeed is the opposite of the teaching method with which the teacher performs techniques in front of the class and 'leads by example'. I prefer to allow veteran students to stand in front of the class, while I go from student to student to give each one the personal touch he or she need at that moment to correct their issues.

While doing this I do not always create a deep connection with the student. Sometimes I simply 'rub out the flaws' for 2-3 seconds and move on. For example, I may see a student's shoulders protruding. I would rub, tap or slap them into place, hold them in place for a short while, verbally note what I have done, and move on to the next student. When a student fails to hold correct alignment after having been correct twice or thrice, I may come and physically hold his body in the correct position for the upwards of 30-60 seconds to create the right sensation. The students remember these sorts of corrections much better than verbal commands or a mental image of a teacher performing in front of them.

The personal touch is also essential in creating a strong social bond and establishing trust between teacher and student. Humans are primates, and as such we naturally maintain close relations by 'social grooming' [50]. Traditionally in a small community people would have groomed each-other, but in modern society the grooming often became something only to be found within the core family, and even that is on the decline. Teaching through personal touch is a form of social grooming, and is essential in the process of gradually welcoming students into your martial arts family. Therefore, there is nothing unorthodox about this teaching method. It is in fact one of the original forms of human communication, which has merely been obscured by modern culture. Try it for yourselves, and the results will surprise you. But do use moderation, caution and sound judgment, as a lot of people can take this the wrong way.

---

[50] Here is another take on social grooming:

There is a saint among us, whose name is Gabor Mate, and he is a world-renown expert on the subject of Addiction. Dr. Mate often repeats his very important observation, that Addiction is the opposite of Connection. In other words – people who are serially addicted to anything, their basic yearning is to feel connected – to themselves, to other people, and to the universe. The chemical influence of their drug of choice, is of a secondary importance to that innate psychological aspiration. Why are so many people addicted to things, then? Because in our 'modern and enlightened society', we suffer from too great a deal of alienation. There is not enough true and authentic social contact and connection between human beings.

Social grooming is unquestionably a part of the solution for this problem. The more social grooming you have in your school, which is non-romantic, the better, and the less addicted or inclined towards addiction your students will be. In my school for example, myself and the students greet one-another with handshakes **and** hugs.

Mind Their Feet

In this book, it was never my intention to attempt instructing you on how to teach the specifics of your art. This sort of skill ought to be learned primarily from one's teachers. But there are a few subjects of study with which I feel I can contribute to many from my technical hands-on experience, and one of these is the teaching of footwork.

In my experience, the majority of serious martial arts practitioners and teachers agree that the key for developing real fighting ability is in the footwork – regardless of style. I believe so too. I am also of the opinion that lack of proper footwork training is the main reason many martial artists find themselves clumsy in real fighting situations, whether in class sparring, a competition or on the street. Part of the reason that practitioners of Western Boxing tend to not fail in this respect is that they have a relatively limited array of stepping methods at their disposal, utilizing 2-3 types of steps and stances most of the time, and not strongly emphasizing correct angles and positioning (by the standards of traditional arts). With less 'options' to choose from, this makes footwork easier under stress and in real time.

Yet with traditional martial arts, practitioners face the problem of having to be able to change between as many as 10-20 types of steps and stances. That is to say, the traditional martial artists have a lot of 'footwork choice' at their disposal. It is now a known fact based on studies of human psychology, that past a certain degree of choice we become 'stuck' in our thought process, and our decision making is hindered. This is very evident in a supermarket, where the enormous selection causes people to pause in front of product lanes and take a very long time to decide what they really want. Now imagine a fight as supermarket lane, and the steps as 20 different products, with the 'customer' having to decide between them and pick just one within a split second. This is a challenging task for the human psyche.

Furthermore, the choice is actually greater and more complex than simply using a specific stepping pattern, because the steps have to be accompanied with hand movements and other, countless movement parameters. All the while, freestyle transitioning between steps and stances is essential – without this there can be not real combat usage of a traditional martial art.

The natural solution for this problem is to ingrain within the student a sense that he and the art are one, so as when driving a car, he will simply know what to do without having to think about it. To do this with one's footwork, I use a very effective method which has proven itself time and time again. I call it the Natural Stepping Method (Ziran Bufa), and its premise is very simple.

The students are to allow their hands to hang beside their bodies and not use them at all, making them to be like flags in the air. This is very important. Then, the students are presented only two types of steps or stances. They are to transition between these two steps at will, and they should attempt to do so at various speeds, alternating between left and right, front and back, and also moving diagonally (which in itself can be done in several directions). Before they begin the practice, explain to them the many options they already have with just these two steps. The students should be left to explore these options for about 5 minutes, while you correct their angles and body alignments.

Then you would add another step or stance. With only three steps or stances, the students already have dozens of options at their disposal – count and you will see. Now every 3 minutes, add another step or stance to the practice. By the time the students are going through 10 steps, they should have already been practicing this for 29 minutes (5 first minutes for the first two steps + 3 minutes times 8 = 5+24 = 29). The practice is however challenging enough and changes frequently enough to not become boring. Beginner students can be limited to a smaller number of options, while veteran students may be asked to deal with as many as 20 or more options at a time.

After the first 4 steps are introduced, you can add another fun facet to the practice – tell them to now walk until they block each-other's path, but that they are not allowed to touch one-another. They will naturally get 'stuck' when blocked by a fellow student, and will have to pause and consider which step or stance are most appropriate, and in what direction, so they can maneuver themselves out of that situation.

This type of practice has been yielding very good results in my schools. It allows students to learn how to naturally transition between steps and stances without having to spend a lot of time 'thinking'. It teaches the students the appropriate reactions to many types of situations, and develops in them the confidence to use a broader arsenal from what their martial art has to offer. I tend to include this exercise at least once every two months for each group of students. When I accompany my students as they practice this, my emphasis is on encouraging them to develop greater mobility and maneuverability. This is not the time to pose riddles or make things more difficult. As soon as I observe that a student has become flustered, I will quickly approach, offer an efficient solution, and make him adopt and adapt at once. The key for them is to keep moving, and not waste time in pausing, even if the movement is very slow. There is nothing wrong with slow, by the way. Though they should test themselves at all speeds, for this particular exercise, slower is better.

Rules Are for Children

My teacher Shifu Nitzan Oren always told me, that there would come a day when I will need to find additional teachers to learn from. This was not said because Shifu Nitzan had little to teach – far from it. When I met him, he had been practicing the traditional martial arts for over two decades, and the Chinese martial arts for at least 14 of these years. Despite this, it was important to him that I receive exposure to the arts from other people and differing points of view and methods of instruction. This has been the philosophy and mindset he inherited from his own teacher, master Zhou Jingxuan. Back when Nitzan was studying with Zhou Shifu, he was told by his teacher after 5 years that he should look for another Xing Yi Quan Shifu, to expand his horizons. Shifu Nitzan then continued to study under master Zhou, but at the same time was also learning from master Wu Bingwen of Song style Xing Yi Quan, as well as other teachers, of Shuai Jiao and Kendo, from time to time.

A good parent should aspire that his children be one day set free, and then eventually surpass him. It is vital that a martial arts teacher understands this as well in his relationship with students. At one point in time a student should be told that from now on, he is his own master. That does not mean he has to abandon you or consider himself to have mastered the art itself, but should release him from the bonds and shackles of the original form of his practice, into the realm of personal expression and creativity.

When we are children, we primarily follow the rules laid out for us by adults, and periodically we break them in order to test our own limits and those of other people. Without assuming this attitude, we cannot mature properly. As adults, we should mostly live by our own rules, but at times we ought to accept the dictations and borders set upon us by society, and especially people we garner respect for. Acting differently makes us into either blind sheep who are prey to norms and dictators, or into wild men who clash too much with their surroundings.

A student needs to be set straight when he is still 'a child in the art', but also be made aware when he has grown up and matured enough to set his own course. Martial arts teachers usually suffer from students who either perceive themselves to be 'adults' before they have even rudimentary understanding, or those who continue to practice for many years but never quite get out of the shadow of their 'parent'.

The ones who mature too early tend to 'reinvent the wheel', making up a 'new way' of their own which lacks real foundations and is detached from the traditional teachings. They routinely and casually change techniques and methods without a true understanding of the ramifications, and often cause more harm than good in what they then pass on to others.

Those who fail to mature cling to a child-like mentality, in that they always depend on the views of their teacher, and never evolve past his instructions and thinking. Their practice becomes frozen in time, and eventually they degrade rather than progress. Attempting to copy and preserve things without much change, if at all, they end up practicing a style fit for the psyche and body of someone who is not them, never making the necessary modifications and innovations.

Both problems, though different, stem from the same place – an inadequate education as was appropriate for that individual. Those among you who wish to avoid such sad occurrences should cultivate honesty, with themselves and their students, and make sure those for whom they hold responsibility know the time and place for every stage of growth.

A Spit In Your Face

There comes a time, perhaps once a month or two, when you feel either a student or a parent, metaphorically spit in your face. I could hardly begin to consider the numerous occasions in which people were rude or offensive towards me, in some way, as a martial arts teacher. The very fact that we are considered by most to "sell a product" and "offer instruction services", tends to invite tensions and strife. Whatever people paid money for, they are sadly inclined to believe they can own, and because of this, we martial arts teachers end up frequently being mistreated and dishonored.

It is no doubt our responsibility to draw the line, and I usually do not shy away from being upfront and decisive in letting people know their boundaries when dealing with me – in martial arts or otherwise. When parents take you to be a babysitter for their children, it is definitely up to you to make them understand the function and role of a martial arts teacher in their child's life. Likely, they would not educate themselves on what you do or your traditions. Or otherwise when a student steps out of line, commonly it should be made clear – it is either your way, or the highway.

But as stern and strict as I like to be with troublesome or disrespectful people, sometimes there is room for compromise. When a person figuratively 'spat in your face', or simply annoyed you, it is not always a black and white situation.

To illustrate my point, I would like to share with you a Buddhist allegory which I am very fond of. I happened upon this fantastic tale a number of years ago, but alas, I could not locate its original author. It may be a variation on an old folk tale, or possibly a newer literary creation. Either way, I gather everybody can learn something from it. Following this exceptional text, I will relate it back to the original discussion, of how to deal with challenging insults.

"The Buddha was sitting under a tree talking to his disciples, when a man came and spat in his face. He wiped it off, and he asked the man:

"What next? What do you want to say next?"

The man was a little puzzled, because he himself never expected that when you spit on somebody's face, he will ask, "What next?". He had no such experience in his past. He had insulted people and they had become angry and they had reacted. Or, if they were cowards and weaklings, they had smiled, trying to bribe the man. But Buddha was like neither, he was not angry nor in any way offended, nor in any way cowardly. But just matter-of-factly he said, "What next?". There was no reaction on his part.

But Buddha's disciples became angry, and they reacted. His closest disciple, Ananda, said, "*This is too much. We cannot tolerate it. He has to be punished for it, otherwise everybody will start doing things like this!*" .

Buddha said, "*You keep silent. He has not offended me, but you are offending me. He is new, a stranger. He must have heard from people something about me, that this man is an atheist, a dangerous man who is throwing people off their track, a revolutionary, a corrupter. And he may have formed some idea, a notion of me. He has not spit on me, he has spit on his notion. He has spit on his idea of me. Because he does not know me at all, so how can he spit on me?*".

" *If you think on it deeply,"* Buddha said, "*he has spit on his own mind. I am not part of it, and I can see that this poor man must have something else to say, and this is a way of saying something. Spitting is a way of saying something. There are moments when you feel that language is impotent: in deep moments when language is impotent, then you have to do something. When you are angry, intensely angry, you hit the person, you spit on him, you are saying something. I can understand him. He must have something more to say, that is why I am asking, "What next?"*.

The man was even more puzzled! And Buddha said to his disciples, "*I am more offended by you because you know me, and you have lived for years with me, and still you react*".

Puzzled and confused, the man returned home. He could not sleep the whole night. When you see a Buddha, it is difficult, if not impossible, to sleep anymore the way you used to sleep before. Again and again he was haunted by the experience. He could not explain it to himself, what had happened. He was trembling all over, sweating and soaking the sheets. He had never come across such a man; the Buddha had shattered his whole mind and his whole pattern, his whole past.

The next morning, he went back. He threw himself at Buddha's feet. Buddha asked him again, "*What next? This, too, is a way of saying something that cannot be said in language. When you come and touch my feet, you are saying something that cannot be said ordinarily, for which all words are too narrow; it cannot be contained in them.*" Buddha said, "*Look, Ananda, this man is again here, he is saying something. This man is a man of deep emotions*".

The man looked at Buddha and said, "*Forgive me for what I did yesterday*".

Buddha said, "*Forgive? But I am not the same man to whom you did it. The Ganges goes on flowing, it is never the same Ganges again. Every man is a river. The man you spit upon is no longer here. I look just like him, but I am not the same, much has happened in these twenty-four hours! The river has flowed so much. So I cannot forgive you because I have no grudge against you.*

"*And you also are new. I can see you are not the same man who came yesterday because that man was angry and he spit, whereas you are bowing at my feet, touching my feet. How can you be the same man? You are not the same man, so let us forget about it. Those two people, the man who spit and the man on whom he spit, both are no more. Come closer. Let us talk of something else.*"

Few proverbs, stories or passages which I have read over the years, served to monumentally change my outlook or manner of thinking about the world. But this short story, which I have stumbled upon several years ago, left a remarkable impression on me. I am still aspiring to live by its philosophical standards.

There is a lot to learn from this allegory and said of it, but let us try to apply its logic to the matter at hand. Before the story, I was sharing with you the challenges of when either a student or a parent addresses us in a troubling, annoying or disrespectful manner. How can we be more like the Buddha is such scenarios, and resolve conflicts as win-win situations? The answer is: with attentiveness and empathy. Let us a examine a real-life case study, then.

I have a colleague whom we can call Brandon Sensei. You can say Brandon is 'oldschool', and quite traditional in his mannerisms. He grew up with the arts from way back when they were still obscure and unheard of in the 1970s; back when there might had been a single school catering for 2-3 cities. Brandon saw it all, and matured into a skilled, knowledgeable and successful practitioner and teacher. Tall, impressive yet unassuming and modest in his ways, he is a man of character and a pillar of his community. But even a character like Brandon, whom I like to take advice from, is not above being human.

One day Brandon Sensei was approached by his student, James (another pseudonym). A man in his 30s, James was your typical cubicle-bound all-conforming geek-fantasizing crowd-pleaser. He wanted more than he could chew, and aspired beyond what he could handle. As he walked over to his Sensei, James had a solemn and anxious look on his face. Brandon asked James what was up his mind, and James admitted that for a while now, he wanted to study another martial art (the name is not important). He came over to ask his Sensei for permission to do so.
Brandon was weary of this. Generally speaking, he was not at all against the notion of expanding one's martial horizons. But the particular circumstances with his student James, called for caution.

Brandon Sensei had known James for 6 years already, and was certain that he was a good man, well-intended in all respects. But James, like most people, considered his training to be no more than a fanciful hobby. Though showing promise, he never quite made the effort to transcend the mediocre. Appearing to class once, sometimes twice a week, and neglecting to practice enough at home, James had not amounted to much in his art of choice, even after 6 years at the dojo. Though Brandon Sensei sure did his best to inspire and support him, James was not eager to make any changes or meaningful sacrifices in order to get better. He was not technically or intellectually mature enough to pursue and understand another martial art, as he could hardly handle his current style of choice.

In light of these circumstances, Brandon bit his lip and forbade his student James from beginning to practice another martial art [51]. James naturally protested in a mixture of shame, angst and frustration. Having already rehearsed such a scenario in his mind before going to see his teacher, James immediately pulled the classic childish "why him and not me?" question.

A friend of James' from the dojo, had several years back easily received permission from Brandon Sensei to go and study the same martial art which James was coveting. However, that man was a decade older than James, with 20+ years of additional experience in their martial art, often aided Brandon Sensei in teaching classes, and was training every day. He was not an amateur, but a devote practitioner. Brandon could trust that, unlike James, the other student would not become confused by studying another art, but

---

51 Some of the readers may frown upon such a decision. "Who is he to decide for his student, an independent adult, where to go and what to do?!". There are certain countries and cultures in which people are intolerant to the idea, of allowing one person to have such power over another. It is a matter of personal taste and particular martial traditions. Though I personally refrain from forcing such commands upon students, I can also understand where Brandon was coming from. He is human, after all. My preference is to allow persistent students to go about their way, after having received my opinion of it (which may be positive, as I do support cross-training after the student has matured). When I to find their actions in this context distasteful, I will not outright forbid them from beginning to practice elsewhere. But I will let them understand later, through my teachings and in an **indirect fashion**, that this may not have been the wisest choice on their part.

rather benefit from it. As a matter of fact, the other student who was James' senior, was even encouraged by Brandon to teach some of what he had learned at their dojo from time to time, as means of supplementing and enriching the everyday classes.
Despite of Brandon Sensei's best efforts and polite explanations to James however, his decision was taken to be too bitter a pill to swallow, and an act too offensive and totalitarian to reconcile. His student James opted to leave his school, never to return.

Having heard this story directly from Brandon Sensei, and being acquainted with the other people involved as well, I meditated a bit on what had happened. I soon came to the realization, that this chain of events was an affair which could have been potentially resolved by drawing inspiration from the Buddhist allegory I have quoted for you earlier.

In the true story from that martial arts school, Brandon was in the position of the Buddha, with a person supposedly 'spitting in his face'. At least, that is what he had subjectively felt as a teacher. We would all feel a bit uneasy, if not emotionally hurt, were a student to come to us and ask to study from another teacher. Depending on the student and the circumstances, this may sometimes be experienced as an expression of mistrust, and an earthquake tearing through a relationship. While some students we may be happy to have asked because this was due time for them to 'spread their wings', others who raise the issue could rub us off as being offensive.

Branson Sensei, having been offended by the student, focused on the 'spitting'. Neglecting to consider alternatives, he forced his student James to make a choice: 'renounce your spiteful ways (the wish to learn another art at another school) and continue with us, or leave'. This was arguably not the best course of action. Here are James' options and thoughts, illustrated, from his possible point of view:

Staying at the dojo

His teacher supposedly 'belittled' him – shame that he cannot untangle. The relationship with his teacher is not as good as before, and who knows whether it will improve. He does not know when and if he might practice the other martial art which he coveted. He does not get to do what he wanted.

Leaving the dojo

While the relationship with his Sensei will probably not get any better than with the other option, at least by leaving the dojo, he has CERTAINTY and CHOICE (he knows that he can study the other art, and can choose to do so immediately).

It should not come as a surprise to anyone then, that James chose to leave the school. Probably, most students who are like him, would do the same under these circumstances. I believe it to be likely, that James even subconsciously realized that this is probably what he would end up doing, even before he asked his Sensei for permission. But could this have been avoided? Yes, most definitely.

To have had a chance at a win-win resolution, Brandon Sensei needed to think more like the Buddha. The student, by 'spitting in his face', was trying to tell him something deep, which he could not express in words. James was fond of his teacher, and his teacher appreciated him, too. Case in point, that James stuck by his teacher and the dojo for 6 years, while most people who frequent a school once a week, tend to quit much sooner. James also took part in many festivities, and was well-integrated in the school community. He was not asking to study another art for the sake of abandoning his teacher, looking to spit in his face. This was his way of conveying something else which troubled him, and transcended his ability to use words appropriately.

- James may have been questioning his ability to use his art in self-defense situations, and sought solutions elsewhere.
- He could have felt that elements from the other art were missing in his own style.

- Possibly, he thought that by taking up another style, this was a shortcut for improving his overall martial arts skill, which was lacking due to insufficient training.

- Or simply, James was bored as for the longest time, he did not feel he had studied something new and exciting.

Whatever James' reason – one of the above, some of them or something else entirely, he did not mean to spit in his teacher's face. By focusing on the 'spitting', Brandon missed the point. He should have sat down with James for a long, private talk; perhaps over lunch someplace. James obviously had a strong yearning for a certain something, and had his teacher found out what it was, most probably he could provide his veteran student with a satisfying resolution.
People are seldom masochists. James was not attempting to tell his teacher: "*I am bad, please restrain and punish me!*"; a sad tune which his teacher regrettably played to. Rather, what James was trying to say was: "*I am confused and distracted. I am lost as to how to achieve a goal here. Please guide me toward a satisfactory solution*".
Thinking like the Buddha, we can observe that a scenario like this is not an invitation to conflict, but a plea to be understood. Then we can be neither offensive nor submissive, and instead ask: "What next?". By so doing, a disastrous potential can at once be overturned, and a relationship be sustained.

Brandon Sensei then, in my opinion, could have talked this over with his student James. Suppose for a minute James would have provided one of the answers I have detailed above. What could Brandon have done then, to mitigate the situation? Let us examine some possible solutions.

<u>James feels incapable and unskilled in his art, which leads him to looking for answers in a different art</u>: Brandon may offer him a free private class, to solidify his skill and understanding. Through that class, Brandon can demonstrate to his student, that through hard work, more skill is gained, and remind him that this is actually what he is lacking. James need to be helped with taking responsibility with his own development, and once he does this, he would gain greater satisfaction from his current practice, and may choose to remain at the dojo.

<u>James is uneasy to discover a certain martial art has training elements "missing" from his current style</u>: In this scenario, James does not even know if he likes what he believes to be 'missing', and being a mediocre student, cannot accurately make such observations. A student like that may feel somewhat 'cheated', as he thought that he was getting a 'complete package', and suddenly realized, like a child growing up, that we are all different, each with strengths and weaknesses. Now he is entering his 'martial arts teenage period' and considers rebellion. The best way to tackle his doubts and anxieties is to allow him to see how his current art can hold up against what is 'missing' (counter-techniques and methods), or better yet - how his art can be used in a similar way to these 'missing skills'. Sometimes, something as simple as a 5-minute explanation and demonstration will suffice to shut down the rebellion. Other times, you may tell a student that you would be teaching such concepts in the coming three classes (or another time), so he better attend them.

This yields two birds with one stone - improving that student's attendance, and proving to him your point. Because like I explained earlier, James does not know any better, you do not have to go out of your way to make your case. Suffice he can believe that he is not 'missing' anything anymore, and he will cease to complain.

James mistakenly thinks that another martial art is a quicker way to greater skill: This is the typical escape of the lazy. 'The shortcut to riches'. For a student to believe such a thing after having been with you for several years, demonstrates a flaw in how you deliver education to your students – so consider whether you convey often enough the message, that hard work yields results – not shortcuts. Frankly though, he ought to know better. Ask the student: "As a **novice** musician, do you get better at playing a guitar by learning the piano?"; "Has anyone become skilled quicker in gardening by learning carpentry?"; "Can you understand Law better and faster if you read about linguistics?"; etc, etc. Surely, by studying an additional 'thing', another thing can improve, even dramatically. But this is only true once you have attained a certain level (which James did not).
After having told the student that, he needs to be shown that hard work does lead to results. The solution once more may be a free private class. Make the focus of that class 1-3 techniques or methods which the student is terrible at. Tell the student: "You yourself is the shortcut to excellence! Let me show you". Then proceed to go out of your way to make him come out of that class with a feeling of having improved dramatically his performance in lackluster areas. By the end of that class, affirm and support his progress. Make sure he understands, that by attending more classes at the school and training more at home, he can make such progress on a weekly basis.

James was bored with his art [52]: When a student is bored with his art, this usually points to one of two possibilities, or both together. Either the student cannot find novelty in his own practice, or he is in fact not being taught anything new for a long time. Whatever the reason, it is important to not have classes which are too repetitive. But sometimes, certain students are simply not mature enough to learn anything new. The

---

[52] Solutions to this type of problem are also discussed in a chapter in this book titled **'Still Waters Breed Disease'**.

simplest solution is to take what they already know, and play with its many variations. A given movement combination can be shown with several stepping methods, different speeds, at varying heights, with changes in tempo, etc. Such changes help in teaching students how to improvise, and keep the classes fresh and interesting. A good teacher can take 10 complex movements or methods, and find so many uses and variations for them, that they could stretch and fill for him the span of months' worth of classes, had he wanted to. Via such measures, students are never bored. Therefore, my argument would be, that if the student is bored, more likely than not is that his teacher is not creative enough, or has not successfully conveyed to him that sort of creativity.

A unifying theme for all of the solutions I have offered, is that they all involve the teacher taking action to resolve his student's dilemma. In dealing with his student James, Brandon Sensei's choice in real life was to pose a 'yes or no' ultimatum, technically forcing the student to make a decision on his own. My suggestions include the notion of leading the student to an accommodating resolution, with him feeling that it was his choice, made with the support of his teacher. That is a true win-win scenario, and a superior way to conserve our student population.

To Teach is Never Enough

How many times have you seen a martial arts school which has been running for many years, but is full of people who are incredibly ignorant of martial arts on the whole? People who have no idea about the history of their own style, let alone that of others. Heck, I have many a time encountered people who cannot even name their sub-style or lineage! All they know is that they study 'Kung Fu' or 'Karate', and they cannot tell you much beyond that. As for matters and subjects such as psychology, anatomy, physiology, kinesiology, philosophy and such – of course they have not a clue. Perhaps these descriptions even fit some of your own students.

Why is it that so many martial artists are ignorant, despite having studied for years and sometimes decades at a given martial arts school? It is because what they learn in class is never enough. Think about it – this makes sense. The average student spends anywhere between 1.5 – 4.5 hours a week with his teacher, usually in a group setting. How much information and knowledge could possibly be transmitted to a person with such low exposure? It is a miracle that such people even manage to progress in their martial arts practice, let alone expand their horizons. With other skills we would have expected a person to train several hours a day to excel, and then with the martial arts we ought to foolishly believe 3 weekly hours and maybe 1-2 additional ones at home will be sufficient? That the physical aspects of the art are enough? This is very unrealistic.

There cannot be excellence in the martial arts without the student gradually becoming committed to do more in and outside of class. It is absolutely the teacher's responsibility to make sure that happens. The students need to be constantly encouraged to read, watch, explore and ponder martial arts and related subjects beyond what they study in class. They should be directly told, without sugarcoating the situation, that simply attending classes will not get them anywhere in the long term. They have to take on martial arts as a serious subject of study, each to his ability and based on his time constraints.

Here too you should not expect that they would naturally know what to do. You have to guide them in the direction of excellence. Send them or provide them with quality materials to examine and delve into.

I have gone further than most teachers by writing an entire book (in Hebrew) for my students, titled **'The Analects of Tianjin'**. That book, I made free for downloading from my own computer via a link, and I kept updating the contents on a weekly basis. As I am writing these words, that book-in-progress had dozens of chapters and was over 450 pages long. In this book I included many chapters, articles and translated materials (from English and Chinese) which I felt were of value for my students to read and learn from. The book was a great success among students, and among many members of the Israeli martial arts community. [53]

In addition to it, I put a huge library of martial arts books and other interesting works in our academy. I made a rule that a student must either read something related to the martial arts or watch a long video about them between last class and the present one. Those who did not read or watch something about the martial arts between classes, had to clean the floor, wash the dishes or water the many plants. This too was very successful, and got all students reading. By the time students complete their first year at my academy, they usually have already gone through at least one of my own books and would go on to study from many other works as well. We would also commonly discuss what students have read after the class had ended. By these measures I managed to effectively combat student ignorance in my academy.

---

[53] Years later, **'The Analects of Tianjin'** became the template for my more extensive English-language book: **'The Martial Arts Student'** (to be published in the future).

Beyond that, you the teacher must make for them the connection between the martial arts you teach and the reality of everyday life. You must use your superior knowledge of the martial arts and other areas of study to impart upon the students the impression and understandings of how the martial arts encompass much more than simply fitness and self-defense, and how they hold the power to change their lives and the whole of society for the better. A teacher who can do this shall be rewarded with students he can be proud of, who will possess both the knowledge and instruments to make the martial arts into tools for improving mankind.

Finally, the last key component of learning, which is not taught by the teacher per-se, is what the students absorb from the teacher's behaviour. This is conveyed well by setting a personal example – a foremost quality to be found in the conduct of any real teacher or leader.

Every martial arts teacher is, by definition, a parent. It does not matter whether one sees oneself as such. The students who engage in the martial arts under you come willing to learn things they do not know, and often have not the slightest clue about. Most among the students who shall last (even older folks) will develop the tendency to consider you as a parent figure; that is – a trusted person guiding them through the unknown. In this process, the by-product of their mindset will be that they will look up to your personal example in many things, not only martial arts. You will not hear about this from most of them, but it is quite certain that you shall witness the consequences. The best and worst martial arts teachers are mirrored, on the personal level, by their students' behavior outside of class. Your students will take a mental note of every gesture, word, act or step you make and take, because they have opened up their thinking and emotional mind to you. The martial arts teacher therefore needs to be almost a saint in his daily dealings with other human beings, at least as much as his students can witness, because any less will negatively affect the lives of others. Not all of us are perfectly well-behaved, and some arrive at teaching with a shadier past, but once a teacher, one needs to aspire to be greater for the sake of his students.

"The Truth is generally seen; rarely heard" [54].

In order to achieve all that I have written of in this chapter, the language of a teacher should be clear, precise and honest. Too many teachers are busy scheming politically among their students, and using cunning speech to manipulate others. Confucius said: "*Human beings live with honesty. Those who are dishonest, live feeling their lives are fated*". The dishonest are unfit to be teachers. Dishonesty in the world of martial arts is a social disease, which causes great suffering to many. People often invest a lifetime in the training of an art, and such individuals are especially prone to damage from dishonest teachers. Every teacher should consider that one act of dishonesty on his behalf, one directed misinterpretation, can send a well-intended person to stroll the wrong path for a lifetime (more about this in the chapter **'The Crime of Creating Ignorance'**, p. 531). Such acts are beyond cruel. Vagueness is not much better than dishonesty, for it allows the naïve and uninformed to come up with wrong interpretations. Though some answers should be found by the student without guidance, it needs be clear for him or her where they should be headed. Without knowing what to expect, most will be lost.

---

[54] Attributed to Baltasar Gracian (1601 - 1658 AD).

Better Get It Written

Do you have some written documentation, either physical or digital, of the many things you teach? You need it. Earlier in the book I have already suggested you do this with the curriculum, but frankly you should make an effort to document everything. There is simply too much to learn in a lifetime of martial arts practice and teaching to be able to remember it all. You are guaranteed to forget many of the most important lessons, details and anecdotes that ever came your way, and without documentation they may be lost forever.

Do extend this approach to other things pertaining to your teachings. Billing and a student database, as well as commentary on specific students which may prove important, and the likes of these – all are worthy for you to take note of.

I am very serious about preserving such information. Everything I ever wanted to document and keep (not just about the martial arts), I care to store as 3-4 copies in different locations. No theft, accident or natural disaster are likely to make my information disappear. Knowledge is something an insurance company can never pay you back for. Keep it safe.

Then encourage your students to do the same. It really helps. My colleague, Professor Stephen Jackowicz, told me of his first martial arts teacher in Korea. The teacher said to him early on: "***You must keep your own diary in which you will write down everything which is important to you about what you have learned from me. This diary of yours will be the only book in the world to answer the questions which you personally need answered most***". Master Di Guoyong of Beijing, whom I interviewed, told me he also wrote such a diary and encouraged his students to do the same.

Still Waters Breed Disease

My father had a very successful career as an attorney. The firm which he set up became one of the top 50 law offices in the country. Later he merged his group with an even bigger firm, becoming one of their leading partners. Suffice to say, the man knows how to conduct business and run a business.
My father always told me: "***A business either changes, or it stops growing. Your business should always be evolving, otherwise it tends to shrivel and whither***". This is true for martial arts practice. This is true for operating a martial arts school.

Look around your school. Observe the items decorating the floor, walls, corners, ceiling and windows. Is anything taken for granted? When last did you change the position of any item in this hall or these rooms? When last have you replaced or add such an item? Without the addition, subtraction or change in the position of things within the compound, the physical environment begins to be taken for granted. These my friend are still waters, and they breed disease.

Likewise, how do students react to what is in the school's physical environment? It is likely you have things like a printed curriculum, a calendar, images of people important to you, various training equipment, diplomas, etc. Hopefully these items are there because they are meaning to the school and to what you teach. When last have the students interacted with these items? When last have you made them stand in front of such items and explained their meaning and importance? Chances are that at least a few such things in your school are unused and taken for granted. Make sure this does not happen too often.

The school also needs innovation and change in terms of the curriculum taught from time to time, and in making social gatherings happen. This is discussed thoroughly in other chapters.

The Unifying Symbol

On the surface, the Mascot appears to be among the silliest things ever created by human beings. In sporting events we see grown men and women bounce about in absurd and ridiculous costumes, often of animals like lions, dolphins, dogs or even forces of nature or non-living objects. These animals, or other animated symbols, tend to additionally be placed upon the official uniform of one group or another. Seeing these weird symbols, one is prompted to ask: "What can an eagle possibly have in common with American football?!", or "How can an ice-hockey team be associated with an aquatic rodent such as a beaver?!". These are legitimate questions. The answer is almost always, that these symbols have nothing to do with the people who associate with them, or with the activity in question.

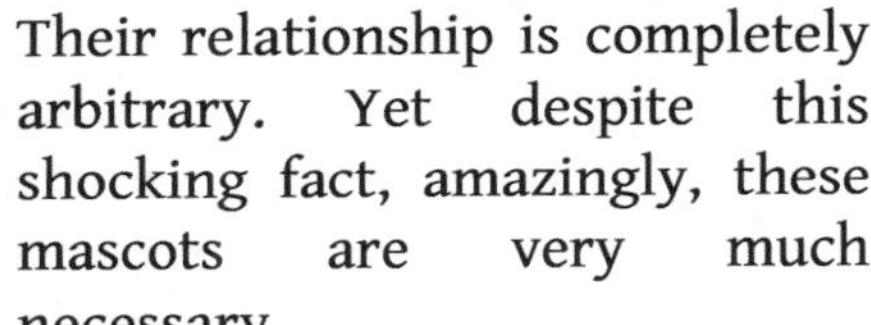
Their relationship is completely arbitrary. Yet despite this shocking fact, amazingly, these mascots are very much necessary.

You see, people feel a strong urge to band together behind a unifying symbol. The flag, the emblem, the mascot and the likes of these – they go back millennia. The unifying symbol is the embodiment of the joint sense of the community. The feeling of belonging to a group, is very abstract. Therefore, people create themselves visual and tactile representations in order to express and solidify such feelings.

I once visited a very large and successful martial arts school. They had the goofiest mascot. In the dojo was placed a plush doll of a moose, dressed in a Karate gi. The object was groomed, cleaned and taken care of. Whenever official photographs were taken, the moose would be included, held by one of the students. One could hardly believe that this wacky behaviour had been undertaken by people who were often 40-70 years of age, but it did. The animal known as a moose had nothing to do with that dojo, nor the martial art they taught. But it was a 'private joke' of sorts, and more importantly – a unifying symbol. Though silly and peculiar, it provided a sense of shared culture and communal belonging, as only members of the school understood the meaning of it all, and took care of the mascot.

Likewise, you see that in the Orient, nearly all traditional schools which operated in an enclosed facility, had at least one unifying symbol. Most commonly, it was the school shrine or altar. This object functioned as a vessel for ancestral worship and remembrance, with many ceremonial rites attached to it, but also served as a 'mascot' – a unifying symbol. This tradition is maintained in many schools to this day, and as teachers you are probably familiar with it.
Religious and spiritual connotations put aside, the shrine or altar is an instrument of communal harmony. It provides the students with a visual and kinesthetic representation of their feelings of belonging to a group. Like the moose, the altar or shrine is groomed, cleaned and looked after, and tends to appear in official photographs.

You too would be wise, to include a mascot in your school. When absent, feel free to invent one! Though it is more honorable and dignified to have a symbol which relates to the school's philosophy and teachings, practically almost anything will do. As long as it is respectable and not offensive, the shape or design of the unifying symbol matters less than its function as bonding substance for communities.

Creating temporary or playful mascots can often also work, as in the example of the moose. At my school, when we went to train at the park, we were often visited by a very friendly female cat, whom we named Señorita. She would go and rub against all students equally, seeking love and attention. She quickly became "the academy's cat", and part of the park-visiting experience was to expect the cheerful arrival of Señorita. She too was groomed, cleaned, taken care of, and appeared in official photographs.
A mascot can also be: document containing the moral philosophy of the school, a book written for or by the students, a flag, an emblem, a song (anthem), an heirloom object, or even a person. The mascot can furthermore be a transcendent belief or agenda. At my academy for instance, one such unifying symbol is the idea that our martial arts enable us to become the best version of ourselves.

Commonly, the teacher is one of the school's mascots, or even its chief unifying symbol. The problem here is, that other mascots are neutral (have no personality and opinions), while the teacher is human. Therefore, if a student's relationship with the teacher takes a turn for the worse, then at the same time, so does he become disillusioned with the community. That is different to when the mascot (the community) and the teacher have greater separation between them. Then, even if the student develops some resentment towards the teacher, he may still feel a connection to the community, and would not necessarily be so quick to consider leaving.

The best strategy in general, is to make the school and the community to be more than just about YOU and what YOU have to teach. When a school is YOU-centric, then this encourages false worship, a blind following, and a weak sense of loyalty in the long-term. When the unifying symbols are beyond the personal, then people can wholeheartedly unite behind them. The physical presentation of the symbol is not the most important, but rather what it represents to each given member of the community.

That being said, do consider solemnly the appearance of what you make into a unifying symbol, as at times it may be perceived as being too unusual, and put off outsiders who might consider joining the school. A famous example is of a notable and respectable lineage of Okinawan Karate, which opted to have a mermaid as their emblem (technically, an ocean-goddess that looks like a mermaid). The mermaid, or an ocean-goddess, symbolized something to the Okinawans, who live on islands. But it means other things entirely in Western culture, especially in light of the famous Disney animated feature: 'The Little Mermaid', which is the main association and exposure the common Westerner has to the concept of mermaids in our time. I have no doubt in my mind, that this particular lineage of Karate would have been able to amass a much bigger following, had they been using a mascot which is not a mermaid. Regardless of the validity of their craft and skills, it is not easy to find male adults in modern Western culture who would pride themselves wearing an image of a mermaid on their martial arts uniform, as it is considered overtly feminine, and even childish and naïve. This once more demonstrates the importance of carefully choosing a unifying symbol that could be well-integrated into the society and culture one lives in.

The Younglings

I have been working with children for longer than I have been teaching the martial arts - since I was 14 years old, so I have a lot of experience with this sort of endeavor and mission [55]. Teaching children is one of the most challenging aspects of our profession, and some teachers also consider it to be the most important. For no matter how much you have pushed forward an adult, a child always holds greater potential, relative to himself. You see, with an adult you can know what the person was, and marvel at what he is becoming. With children however, the achievement is primarily rooted in what the child has yet to become. Suffice that you have been able to prevent a child from becoming sad, depressed, evil, nasty, unruly, criminal or worse adult than he could have been, and you have done a great service for them and for society as a whole. You will never be able to witness the horrors of what a person may have turned into, but in saving children from such fate, that alone was worth many years of hard work for you and them, even if they did not manage to learn much or forgot all about what you taught them 10 years later. By saving a child from his or her potential disastrous fate, you are literally saving the world.

But there is also a positive side to it, of course. A child is a relatively clean slate to work with, a purer form of human material. Through your teachings, a child can also discover what he or she can become. This again might be something you will never be around to see, as most children do not stick around until their 20s and 30s. But it will be an influence for sure, if you can to help them with that. Consider every child a very long-term investment, and curb your expectations. As some of them will return to tell you of how much of a positive influence you have been in their lives some 5, 10 or 15

---

[55] Originally, I taught children the use of computers and programming in afterschool classes and summer camps.

years later, this would be enough 'emotional payment' to sustain you for a lifetime.

Concerning children and the martial arts, I will be honest with you in sharing a controversial point of view here: I am of the opinion that nearly all children below the ages of 6-7 should not be taught the martial arts, even if they can. Ours are specialized skills. Young children need a diverse and non-specialized skillset to deal with the world. This is true even when a child is willing and showing promise, talent and physical capacity to practice the arts. The fact that one is able to do something does not mean it is the right thing for them to do. Consider that many children are also able to reproduce by the age of 12, and we still prefer that they mature physically and psychologically before they do so. A growing person's body tends to precede in capacity the actual activities he ought to try and undertake.
Please note that I write of not teaching martial arts before the ages of 6 or 7. There is nothing wrong with diverse physical activities and games partly inspired by martial arts, which are not overly specialized. Indeed, this is what many schools choose to teach young children.

Children can seldom learn well privately or in groups of 2-3 individuals. They tend to thrive in bigger groups, but anything over 10 can get chaotic and is not conductive to learning. Group hype is a strong and important motivator for a child's cooperation and progress in class. Do not assume children are as independent as adults. Most of them need to be followers in a herd. It is a survival strategy – they rely more on the 'wisdom of the crowd' because their life experience is quite limited. They are also keener to try and prove themselves to others as part of their growth process. It is OK to tell a child that he needs to prove something, while with adults I would actually usually say the opposite: "*You do not need to prove anything to anyone but to yourself*".

As opposed to casual afternoon practice, **real traditional martial arts** cannot be taught to children below roughly the age of 9; being that their bodies are seldom strong or stable enough prior to that age, and they also lack proper judgement for using such skills. In modern culture, many children cannot even learn the arts well until they reach puberty, due to delayed cognitive maturity and being spoiled by technology and bad education. Remember that children are generally not allowed to cross a busy street by themselves until the age of 9, because in modern cultures it takes them 9 years on average to develop proper depth-perception and enough responsibility for their own bodies in order to not get themselves killed (let alone, keep the safety of others). You should not expect any child below the age of 9 years to be able to grasp anything serious, beyond the most rudimentary basics. Then rejoice if you win that student lottery, and along comes the exception and proves otherwise. This is not common. But it does not mean that children between the ages of 6 and 9 should not be taught – they can be, but what they learn would have little martial value. It needs to be a sort of play which is aimed at creating foundations for later martial arts training. Be honest with yourselves and parents, and avoid presenting classes to children ages 6-9 as 'martially-oriented' or 'self-defense'. Make the distinction. At best, they may be able to prevent a child their size from harassing them, but generally seldom stand a chance against a teenager or an adult. Proper education, physical and behavioural, would yield better results, and the focus should be on how to avoid trouble rather than how to get out of it on one's own.

Between the ages of 9-13 is when real traditional martial art training can begin. Progress will be slow with most children that age. What takes a child as much as six *months* to learn to do well at age 9, would take the same child six *weeks* or less to learn at age 14. But time is not wasted, for although much of the learning and teaching can be frustrating, the principles and thinking ingrained at the ages of 9-13 could serve a child quite well in the martial arts if he continues to train later in life. One of my own teachers, Sifu Sapir Tal, has had a long teaching career, spanning several decades. He always noted how these students who started very young were displaying a crooked and ugly version of his martial art during the first few years; yet as they grew older, they embodied and displayed an understanding and manifestation of the art which was often deeper than others who began training as adults.

Personally, when teaching kids ages 9-13, I place a strong emphasis on transforming the students from tender children to hardened adults. Notice I omitted the 'teenager' stage here, and this is the message they receive as well. More on that soon. I convey the idea that although I accept them as children and that some things we can work out and learn through play, I am now standing with them on the bridge to adulthood, and that they are training to successfully meet the real challenges which are ahead.

By the time children reach puberty and are past the age of 13, then whether male or female, they enter adult territory, get out of their sheltered 'safe spaces', and have to deal with people much bigger, stronger and more experienced than them, on a more frequent

basis. These teens need to be confronted with reality. This is why as soon as a child is past the age of 13 and is physically and mentally developed enough, I will move him or her to an adult's class – where they belong. The adults are expected to understand and keep their best behaviour, and they usually do. Proper introduction will result not in frustration on part of the adults, but in pride that they have a new responsibility of helping educate the younger generation.
When finding yourself in a situation where you have too many youngsters in an adult class, you may open a 'teenager class' for them or attempt to scatter them among several adult groups. But as soon as possible, get them back in line with the adults to challenge them properly. The best scenario is that of 2-3 teenagers in a group which includes at least 7 more adults in total. Less than 2 teenagers, and the only one there may feel a bit lonely and estranged (depending on his character, of course). More than 3 teenagers in such a group, and the adults will naturally protest and develop resentment for having to put up with too much silliness. To be clear – a teenager in this context I consider to be someone between the ages of 13-18.

Whatever you do, make sure to not mix between kids below the age of 13 and those above that age, especially not when larger yearly gaps between them are present. Such a combination is disastrous. Tensions arise very easily due to the great divide puberty creates between the wants, needs, likes and aspirations of children and teens. This comes especially from the direction of the teenagers, who are torn between their wishes to connect and play with the younger kids, and their strong urge to detach themselves from that world and environment in order to reach adult domain. The teens may begin to discuss among themselves things of more mature natures which are inadequate for the younger folks to be engaged in, and when the children ask about such topics they are frowned upon and scolded for their 'childish ways' and inability to fathom 'adult matters'. I write of this in mature language of course – they may not be as eloquent in representing such thoughts and feelings when they express and experience them.

A child, up to a certain point in his development (which can vary), cannot concentrate on any one thing well for over 15-20 minutes. This means that optimally, you need to change the subject of the activity or learning every 15-20 minutes. Their focus is also limited with regard to the class as a whole. In our modern and degenerated society, children up to the age of 9 can barely manage 45 minute of any given specific continuous activity – such as a martial arts class. Between the age of 9 and puberty, a child may increase this general attention span to the upward of 75 minutes, though many can only take an hour or so. But fear not, as there are solutions. You can increase the duration of each class with at least 10 minutes of stretching [56] (which does not require a lot of attention), and another 5-10 minutes of storytelling, discussion or relevant athletic play. By adding these segments of stretching, discussion or play, 45-75 minute classes can become 60-90 minute long, if you are dedicated and willing.

Storytelling is important in my opinion to the teaching of any martial arts student, but for children is it absolutely essential. Kids love stories, and these can be used to provide them with a sense of belonging, a history and connection to what they do, and most of all - to impart morals, ethics and good behaviour. Use stories which relate to the martial arts you teach and their histories, but feel free to borrow from other cultures and lore or even invent your own.

Adults are judgmental, but children are far more forgiving, and forgetful also. Teaching children is a great outlet for testing things you would like to tell or teach your adult students later. Often 'testing' such things through the reactions of the younger students provides ample opportunity for useful experimentation. Feel free to go wacky and wild, as long as it does not put anyone in risk. The crazier and more original the idea, the more the kids are likely to

---

[56] In my classes, each stretch is held for at least 2 minutes, and if the stretch is two-sided, then it is 2 minutes for each side. Anything less than that is ineffective in the long term for most people. Therefore our stretching sessions are usually 10-15 minutes long.

fall in love with it. In this book's chapter titled **'Latecomers'** (p. 234), there is a funny story of how a playful suggestion by a child led me to develop a decent solution for a problem I had in the adults' classes.

Control of the students' body language is an important asset in the hands of the competent teacher. Of this I have also written in the chapter titled **'Change and Cooperation'** (p. 91). With children, this skill of being able to recognize and control the body language of students is several times more important and crucial for their learning and development, than it is with adults. Because children are less formed and shaped by social norms, their body language more accurately and readily reflects their inner being. Always be watchful of how children move, for much can be deduced from this. There are two major harmful movement patterns among children which I have found to be both common and destructive, and therefore require close examination in this chapter. These are the 'unruly tongue' and the 'geisha syndrome'. I shall first delve into the nature of these problems, and then explain how to best deal with them.

In the traditional Chinese martial arts, the tongue is sometimes referred to as "the extremity of the flesh", and by flesh what is meant in this context is the muscular system of the body. The ancient Chinese intended to say by this, that the movement of the tongue has foremost influence over the function of the muscles. That observation is correct. When the tongue is unstable, the muscular control is poor and the entire body is unstable. The opposite is also true – refined control over the tongue and knowledge of how to use it in training and fighting, a very mature skill, can enhance muscular usage and control.
Humans have an inborn tendency to use the tongue to symbolize and signal mischievous and naughty intentions to others. Among adults, this inclination is more commonly seen in games pertaining to sexual temptations. Among children, the tongue is used in an overt and teasing manner for self-expression and drawing attention

to themselves. Children intuitively understand that by manipulating the tongue in the social sphere, they can lure others into various 'games' they subconsciously wish to be a part of. The problem here is that the unruly tongue habit of a child is also a source for chaotic and unstable movement, and prevents him or her from proper physical development. For as explained earlier, tongue stability is intrinsically related to refined muscular control.
Very rarely, one can encounter an adult who is still seen frequently rolling his tongue uncontrollably and popping it in and out of his mouth a lot. Such adults usually suffer from some childhood-related psychological inhibition.

To resolve the unruly tongue, simply make sure the mouth of all students is kept shut at all times, unless needing to gasp for air. This by itself will do, at least for their physical progression in class. The challenge here is to keep that mouth from re-opening, which happens often. A physical cue like a gentle slap on the hand or an encouraging friendly shout will work, but when correcting this issue with an individual you will need to remain vigilant and address the problem every few minutes. Usually within a few days or weeks, the problem will subside and disappear. In my experience, once a child's tongue has forfeited its rebellious tendencies, the child's overall behaviour, cooperation and learning greatly improve.

The other problem I mentioned, that of the 'Geisha Syndrome', has to do with overt feminine body language on part of the child. This is more of a problem for boys than it is for girls. What you will see is an inclination to fold the body towards its center, which can manifest in all sorts of ways. The hands and arms may come together, before or behind the body, with elbows straightened. In more severe cases, the arms and palms will attempt to actively 'coil' around one-another, like two snakes. The legs and feet will also have a tendency to come together and do the same. The feet will point inward. The knees will touch. He may look as if he is desperately needs to pee, but he does not. This can cause him to walk like an awkward penguin. The chin will tuck overtly. The back will hunch slightly. The shoulders will fold inward. The student will look confused and unfocused. His expression may also seem shy, even if that is inappropriate to the situation. The lips will come to a point, and the eyes will scatter randomly and may then focus on the nose. The body language will be so strange it would appear as if the student is acting on stage, but his movement is genuine. His voice will be weak and submissive and he is sometimes heard murmuring something to himself, but if asked about it will pretend he did not or will say 'it was nothing'.

What is going on here? The student is experiencing a disruption in his balance between his Yin and Yang, and has subconsciously adopted an extreme Yin, or very feminine behaviour. That sort of description would fit the historical Japanese geisha, who was expected to move and act in this manner, but is highly inappropriate for a male of any age. The syndrome is more common among boys, as children are more Yin by default, but can sometimes also be observed among younger men with a distorted self-image or possibly even hormonal issues.

There could be many psychological processes at work here. One child I taught, 11 years old, expressed this problem because his parents divorced. He took upon himself the burdens of his mother, felt responsible for what happened to her, and identified with her by becoming more feminine. He may have also been inclined to imitate her body language (which was exceedingly feminine) due to the disappearance of a dominant male figure from his daily life. Another kid who came to me at 15, experienced an even more severe expression of this syndrome. He was a young gay man who has yet to define for himself his role in relationships, and wishing to be the feminine side in romantic interactions with other men, he subconsciously imitated the body language of women to a ridiculous extreme.

In life, we are never purely Yin or Yang – each of us is supposed to feature a balance between masculinity and femininity. But when a person too strongly inclines to either extreme, or perhaps cannot lean in either direction and cannot decide what he or she is, then we have a problem. Of course in life and society, some of us would be more tolerant in that respect. However as explained in the second chapter in this book, a martial arts school is not a liberal democracy, but a meritocratic egalitarian dictatorship. There is no room within the martial arts school for playing either sexual or gender social games. As far as martial arts are concerned, this imbalance featured with the 'Geisha Syndrome' is a problem. The person with that problem:

- Cannot move well in class.

- Cannot really apply his martial arts.

- Lacks confidence to make the practice work for him.

- Cannot develop proper self-esteem due to poor body language (historically, geishas were meant to be kept down through control of their body language!).

- Sends others in his environment a message of weakness and fragility, which attracts negative and predatory behaviour outside of the martial arts school.

That last article is the biggest problem for these students suffering from said syndrome. Whether they be children, teens or adults – their body language is like a magnet for all sorts of bullies, sexual offenders, marketers of fraudulent schemes and other criminals. I have been a police investigator for 3 years of my life and worked with a whole lot of criminals, many kinds of them. Nearly all criminals I met operated on the same premise: like sly businessmen and sharks, they could 'smell blood' and would naturally hone unto and target the weakest, most vulnerable members of the flock, herd or school. Wherein your students are 'geisha-like', then they are prime targets for such vile individuals. Changing the way your students move and present themselves would be the first and most important self-defense method you could teach them. Better sooner, than later.

As with the unruly tongue, here also the key is controlling the body language through verbal and physical cues. Because of the nature of the problem though, you need to be gentler, kinder and more understanding, otherwise you will not earn decent cooperation and might even scare them. These gentle souls usually understand to some degree that 'they have a problem'. Therefore, if you can instill within them a sense of security and purpose, and explain to them the importance of looking erect, open and expressing confidence, then will gladly work with you on their personal growth.
For instance, tackling the issue with the young gay student, I explained to him that it is alright and acceptable in life to be more feminine than others. Because, frankly, that is what and who he is, and his inner nature I cannot and have no interest in changing. "However", I told him, "you may better express your feminine tendencies in a fearless and self-assured manner, which will not attract bad people into your life". This he could understand, and from that point it was possible for us to work together on redefining his Self, from a submissive shy shadow of a man to a bold and upbeat individual with a firm spine and a proud posture.

With children this tends to be easier, and often simply correcting their alignment would yield positive psychological improvement [57]. When possible though, the parents need to be involved in the process and be alerted that their child is expressing a certain difficulty.

---

[57] Chiropractors are very correct to point out that the body has an 'innate intelligence', which 'puts things in order' if the posture and joints are well-aligned. I agree with this observation wholeheartedly. Not only does one's body become more resilient and disease-resistant with proper alignment, but one's psychological constitution greatly improves as well. Even without expert spinal manipulation or similar modes of manual treatment, simply preventing people from exercising bad movement and postural habits can do wonders for them in class and daily living.

Now as for the most essential requirement for being able to teach children – you need their parents on your side. Without the parents' support, you have already lost the long-term game 99 of 100 times. To get the parents on your side, you need to remember their names, maintain a distant yet monthly connection, and uphold a high degree of political correctness in conversing with them, avoiding tensions at all costs (which is not the recommended way to deal with the students themselves).

The parents require constant reminders and examples of the following (which need to be honest):

- You positively affect their child's life.
- Their child has been improving on all accounts thanks to his or her martial arts practice. Compare the child to himself across the time frame of months and years to make that point clear.
- More practice on part of the child will yield better results. They need to make sure the child arrives at least twice a week, and optimally they need to make sure he or she are training at home.
- The parents cannot allow the child to give up.

Let us talk about that last one, shall we? In human societies, there is often a cycle of generations that alternates between 'harshness' and 'hedonism'. Characteristically, you will see a person having a difficult life, and then if that person is a good parent they will try to give their children an easy life. Then their children will become spoiled bastards and will not wish for their own children to be like them, so they will seek to make things more difficult for their offspring. These children in turn, having suffered at the hands of their parents, will then once more be more inclined to take it easy on their children, and so forth – the cycle continues.
This has been going on and on endlessly probably since humans existed. Sometimes you have two, three or more generations emphasizing either harshness or hedonism, but eventually the coin

tends to flip in the other direction. Now during the early 21st century we complain of the last two generations being spoiled, lazy, hedonistic, self-centered and incredibly stupid overall. These are correct observations, if we were to generalize. This is part of a growing trend towards hedonism which has its roots following the end of World War II, and is now reaching its peak. Sooner or later Western society will return to it harsher mode of living and education, but for the meanwhile we are stuck with this silliness.

Given this reality, what we martial arts teachers have to face during this time in history are hordes of younglings who reflect this hedonistic ideal, being protected by the overly aggressive umbrella of their sheltering parents. What a pitiful period indeed. These parents are all too eager to allow the child to give up on whatever is too difficult. In their shallow minds, their money can buy the child countless 'options' and 'alternatives'. They and their children have been indoctrinated to believe that diversity is a key for success. They confuse the approach often seen with toddlers, who need broad exposure to learn of the world, and the one more appropriate to older children, and especially teenagers and adults, who gradually require narrower specializations in order to develop a high level of skill and efficiency.

To prevent the parent from making the all too common mistake of thinking you to be like an expendable product, you need:

- To help them understand you and your school are one-of- a-kind.
- To make them believe that this is the RIGHT place for their child (if that indeed is).
- To aid them in seeing that their child needs discipline and continuity.

Children are fickle-minded, and prone to random thoughts and emotions taking control of their lives. Left solely to their own devices and judgment, most modern children would get themselves killed within hours to weeks. You cannot allow a child's momentary wish of trying something new, to be a ruler over his parent. I will tell you now honestly and outright – sometimes there is nothing you can do about it. Some of the so-called 'drone parents' who constantly hover above their children and monitor them, are so emotionally unstable themselves, that they and their children are doomed no matter how hard you try. They are exactly the kind of human material being discussed in this book's chapter **'Cannot Save Them All'** (p. 341). But damn you if you do not try! Forget about these parents and their faults. Do your best to ignore their often-terrible ideas and horrendous attempts at 'education'. As I have stated earlier – the parents do not matter. It is the children's lives and their future you are trying to save here, so when you speak with parents, in your mind always focus on that greater goal.

There is more to parent-oriented trouble which may befall you, and this can happen in unexpected ways. Here is such a story:
I recall once having taught a 16 year old kid, who looked quite promising and had good character. One night after the adult class was over, we all went out to eat at a Japanese restaurant. A few of the adults ordered sake (Japanese rice wine) to drink along with their sushi. I saw the kid constantly glancing over the sake, obviously wishing he could have some. I gave him my cup and let him have a small sip, and told him he could keep this between us. To me, this was a 'good uncle act', of helping the kid feel his way into the adult territory. Socially, that type of thing is also acceptable in Israel, for although the legal drinking age is 18, kids get to drink a little bit of wine on holiday celebrations even when relatively young. The kid was happy of course, and thanked me for the courtesy.
Well, can you guess what happened? A week later I get a call from his father, looking to make excuses to pull him out of the academy. Having heard it all before and not being fooled, upon inquiring and digging for a few minutes, I managed to get the father to admit the kid spilled out the 'secret'. Apparently, the father took no issue with the kid having a sip of alcohol. However, in that household the parents educated their children that they are not to hold any secrets from them whatsoever (something which naturally I was not aware

of). The father felt that I had been 'spoiling his child' by encouraging him to keep secrets from his parents. While I was able to ease the situation, make peace with the father and bring the kid back to class, things were not the same since. Eventually, the kid dropped out on his own a year later.

In light of this story, consider that there is a very delicate game to be played during the ages at which children begin to seek independence from their parents. Typically, that happens around puberty, though sometimes earlier or later than that. Many parents would pose demands that you keep them updated on every single step their little chick has taken. But that chick may be already wearing a flashy red comb and courting some hens by that time! Much of the child's growth happens beyond the watchful eyes of the parents. They often miss this, but you can see what is really going on. Then you have to navigate gently, because you want to respect the maturity and autonomy of the student as appropriate to his age, and also develop in him a sense of adulthood and independence. On the other hand, you do not wish the parent to become resentful when you cause the child to make a stand in his personal life as part of that growth. My suggestion: the student needs to get one message, and the parents – another. Each as fits them at that point in time. You should do your best to never pit a child against his or her parents of course. Whilst helping a child grow, you cannot allow yourself therefore to demand of him directly to be his own fully-independent person. Trust me that this will quickly reach the parents, and they do not like non-family members taking control of the process or interfering in it. So instead, simply provide the child or teenager with the opportunities and methods for growth, and allow him to do the work and discover life's greater mysteries on his own, for the most part. Likewise, do not become a parent's 'buddy' and share with her too much of her child's inner universe. The child will learn of this eventually, and this will form a chasm between you. The student needs to understand that there is a sacred space in your relationship with him that only you two will share, and that if he wants to, this sacred space can become quite meaningful.

Praise, and Its Downfalls

My own teachers have always been tough on me, seldom giving compliments or saying praise of my improvements and efforts. Despite dedicated daily training and a lot of personal investment on my part, I would never feel appreciated on the technical level (although, my interpersonal relations with them were always excellent and full of mutual recognition and gratitude). At times, especially during my first few years with each of them, this was emotionally burdensome for me. I could never tell whether they were pleased with my progress, and how they judged my skill. Mostly, I would be on the receiving end of lots of criticism, which was well-intended, correct, but also cold as ice.
Like a child sworn to remedy the harsh upbringing of his parents, I sought the opposite approach in my teachings, and usually opted to express boundless positivity towards my own students. To this day, there is hardly a class during which I do not provide each and every student with kind appraisal of some sort, appropriate to and corresponding with sincere effort. This approach of mine resulted in problems as well, and I shall explain why later.

Did you ever meet a teacher of the traditional martial arts, who has a balanced approached for complimenting and praising others? Such professionals are few and in-between. We tend to either give too much or too little praise to our students, and often the wrong amount of it to those who require the opposite. We allow our emotional whims to dictate the amount of praise we share with our students, and this is a dangerous thing. For praise, more often than not, is a crucial component in determining whether a student remains by your side for years, or leaves prematurely.
Do not get me wrong – praise and Ego-grooming is not really what our teachings are about. Rather, it is that 'final straw which breaks the camel's back'; the last measure by which many people decide, whether their 'investment' in your school is worthy of their time. They seek appreciation and confirmation, and without enough praise for their efforts, they will not find these, and leave.

They may feel lazy; or perhaps experience displeasure with the curriculum; possibly not get along well with other students; maybe they are dealing with a stressful time in their personal lives; anything could be troubling them. But one thing is certain: as long as they feel unappreciated by their teacher, and add that to their list of worries, they will have a solid excuse to give up on everything they have worked to achieve in the martial arts, and escape. In such a scenario, they may not even bother to let you know, and simply vanish from sight, at best sending an 'emissary' to deliver their formal apologies to you. That is, because without your expressed verbal empathy, over time they become detached from a sense of commitment and loyalty, or even fundamental etiquette.
Or otherwise, the complete opposite scenario may transpire. At a time of distress or great personal change, a student who has been experiencing a great deal of appreciation, may look down upon the teacher, the school or fellow students, and use that sort of arrogance to be his excuse for leaving.

This of course is more of a problem for the 'martial arts professional'. That is, the teacher who depends on students to make a living. He who teaches martial arts only to those he personally chooses, can at times afford to praise very little, if at all. That is because, in that sort of relationship, the students chosen ought to have a very strong motivation for study. But even he who does not teach in exchange for money or gain, needs to adequately address the human condition if he wishes to have students at all.

There are thus two ends to the spectrum of sharing praise: Over-empowerment and Intimidation.

Over-Empowerment

I would presume that you understand, especially having read this far into the book, that a major part of our line of work has to do with character-building. Praise is essential for that. Well-timed words of appraisal can within a few short months or years uplift an individual from the darkest pits of miserable depression and low self-esteem to even an 'alpha-male' status among friends and peers. My teachers

and I have seen this happen, many a time.
But then we often make the mistake, of providing that level of praise to someone who may not be lacking in character. We give such a person praise because we like him, but he already possesses a firm spirit and a determined will. Such people can easily and quickly become overpowered elements within the school.

My teacher Sifu Sapir Tal once had a student like this. He liked that student a lot, for the man was loyal, hard-working, talented and carried a promise for the future. My Sifu allowed that student to teach classes from time to time, and help him run the school. He shared much praise of him and gave him more credit than he deserved. This approach took a terrible turn.
Within a few years, the promising student began to boss himself around the school. My Sifu discovered that he would go about and tell other students what to do, and even whether they should or should not come to specific classes. My teacher warned him, but to no avail. Eventually, Sifu caught that student threatening another student outside the school, using verbal and physical violence. At that point, the formerly promising student was kicked out of the school for his unruly behaviour. The praise, responsibilities and honour bestowed upon him allowed his arrogance to develop, which led to disastrous consequences.

Intimidation

While I have personally never experienced a student becoming overpowered through praise, I have several times witnessed the opposite trend taking shape and causing damage. It is possible for individuals of weak character and low self-esteem, especially younger people or those without a strong social position outside the school, to be intimidated by praise. To them, a lot of praise and appreciation mean that they now have a bigger role to play at the school, but its lines and scope were drawn by the teacher, and not by them. They imagine themselves then as having to abide by standards and ideals which they consider too challenging. This frightens them, and they react accordingly. Even if your appreciation of them was sincere, in their mind this does not matter – what they see is the threat embodied in a more prominent social role or position, rather than its advantages. They also fear the perceived 'consequences' of failing to meet such expectations of others. They therefore develop the urge to be out of the spotlight by all means, even if your friendly intent positioned them on best stage possible.

I once saw Shifu Jerry Alan Johnson explain this to an interviewer in the following manner: "***...Some people self-sabotage, because they have the underlying agenda that they do no deserve everything they have built... If they have extremely low self-esteem, the way to approach them has to be correct and supportive. For a person who believes they are worthless, you can't tell them that they're good. You start off with: "You're not bad". They can relate to that and accept that. But if you tell them they're really good, they will reject everything that you have said, because their self-esteem is so bad. Slowly, in stages, you work them through so they can accept who they are*"**.

I once had a teenager who studied with me since he was a child. He was a bright kid, whom I liked a lot. After a number of years in the children's group, when he turned 14 I moved him up to one of the adults' group. This is a challenging transition to all teenagers, but one which I deem very important and necessary for them to grow, as it reflects the trials they face in their lives outside of the school, having to deal with adults and people bigger and more experienced than them. In any case, the kid did alright in the beginning.
To help build up his character and support him a little, I used to praise him a lot in class. It was honest, and he deserved it. He was very hard-working, never complained about anything, always cooperated nicely with others, and had an exceptional pain tolerance which allowed him to easily stand up to people more than twice his size. I was proud of him, and let him know of it. I would tell the other students in class, that they should aspire to have his various specific virtues, without saving him from criticism of course when due.

Long story made short – the kid quit. One day after three years, he decided to quit. He sent his father to talk to me. He returned two weeks later, and eventually quit for good a few weeks after that. He was experiencing some incredible challenges in his personal life, which I was well aware of and actually helped him with. He was happy that I did that. However, he was terrified from what went on in class. While next to me, he was all smiles and laughter. Then, his father told me, the last couple of times he came, when he would get out of class and get in the car, he had began crying uncontrollably. Apparently, according to his own testimony, he felt that my positive praise for him, which he in fact appreciated, was pressuring him to be more than he wanted to. I said so many good things of him, that he began to imagine himself as an ideal he could never live up to. That 'final straw', for a 'camel' already burdened by some harsh realities outside the school, broke him. He could not handle being so high, when he took himself to be so low. He had to escape, and there was nothing I could do about the situation. It was already too late.

My teacher Sifu Sapir, also told me of instances when he experienced similar, albeit milder reacts from young students. He had over the years several teenagers who asked him not to be tested for various ranks, because they felt this was too much of a responsibility for them. That is, despite the fact that by the time he asked them to test, they were by all accounts already over-qualified for the task.

The Guidelines for Praise

Is this not the curse of all parents, then? One way or the other, whatever we do, our children will forever be hurt by our actions somehow, and will likely also blame us for it, too. Such is also the problem with praise. However, if we were to make a mistake, I argue that at least we ought to err on the side of good. That is, it is better to indeed show praise and appreciation whenever possible and appropriate, than to avoid demonstrating them when we should. This we ought to do with some good and reasonable guidelines.

Honesty: If you are going to say it, make sure you mean it, and do not say it simply to manipulate a student to become something.

Timing: When in front of the student in question, attempt to say it only immediately after the praiseworthy act was done, or during the summary of that class. Praise people more behind their backs than in front of them, do so in a more overt fashion than you would speaking with them personally, and allow the other students to share with them that praise of yours as positive gossip.

Separate praise and entitlement: When praise and entitlement are not separated, people think that you praising them means that they now become something greater by mere show of kind appreciation. Some are over-empowered by this, while other cower from the responsibility this may entail. Make sure they understand that your praise is not means by which they suddenly become qualified or gain a social position.

Offer praise, then offer a broad perspective: Make certain that after showing praise to people, you care to mention the long way which is still ahead of them. Then they get a better perspective and can comprehend, that although they did well in present time, this does not mean you approve of their entire journey, most of which they still need to undertake.

Dale Carnegie, in his all-time classic book **'How to Win Friends and Influence People'**, suggests that we ought to praise everyone honestly as much as possible, almost without bounds. Sometimes in life, this is true, and a surefire way to be more effective in one's endeavors in the social sphere. But the brilliant Mr. Carnegie and the many wise and successful men he mentions, none of them ever had to teach the martial arts. In the context of a teacher-student relationship, especially in the traditional martial arts, praise has its limitations, as I have thus far demonstrated.

Through perseverance and bitter experience, along with empathy and some strategic skills, it is more than possible to use praise to our advantage. It can be turned from a nuisance and a sort of problems into an instrument for strengthening an entire student community. Follow the tips I have suggested above, pay close attention to people's reactions, and you will surely be on the right way to success.

The Checkup Routine

Consider your martial school as an ever-changing arena of information. You are like an army general. What happens when in war time, the general loses touch with a single battalion in the field? Disaster can occur. The battalion, going without guidance for too long, may lead itself into disarray. It could take up independent leadership and do as it pleases. It may even defect to enemy lines or simply withdraw from the scene entirely. Students are like that, especially during their first few years of study. They are akin to children, behaving like a sponge, as I had described in a previous chapter, '***The Younglings***' (p. 285). They are quick to get the message and go along with the program, and also quick to lose sight of their goals and forget about their commitments to the school and to themselves.

Once the school passes the threshold of about 15-20 students, it becomes increasingly difficult to keep track of students, their development, their status and their issues. This can lead to the problems I have mentioned above. But there is a very simple habit which can be of aid to you in mitigating this problem. It is the habit of routinely checking up on your students, every day.

We all have some 'dead time' to kill. We wait in lines. We water the garden. We mow the lawn. We drive the car. We take the dog on a walk. We do shopping. We watch silly things on a screen. Etc. There are a lot of hours in the human lifetime in which we do nothing. Sometimes this is good for the mind and the soul, to just 'do'. Other times, it is a waste. Make that time count. Call your students on the phone, or at least send them a recorded message (your voice counts, not plain text!). Ask how they have been doing recently. Show interest in their **families, careers** and **health** (some of the things that matter most to people). Be a good listener. Offer advice. Be willing to say you will physically help them, and be proactive about it.

It is not always immediately clear whom to call at a given moment. That is not a problem. In your mind or on your digital device, go over the list of students. Consider those students you have not had a good conversation with in a long time. Contact these individuals. Spend at least 10 minutes talking with them if possible, and if not, schedule another conversation for the near future. Even an hour-long conversation is acceptable if undertaken for a good cause. This is unlike a conversation with a potential student calling for the first time, which should be a short ordeal.

This habit of having a routine checkup with students bears significant consequences for the future of the school. It ensures that you and the students develop a closer and more meaningful relationship, based on trust. The students then will tend to remain by your side longer. Even if they leave the school one day, they would likely remain messengers of good will and would speak highly of their former school and teacher in the ears of others. Additionally, those among them who sought to find 'better alternatives' by 'grazing in foreign pastures', will quickly discover that other teachers may not be as empathetic and understanding.

Do pay attention to the fact, that in our time (early 21st century) we suffer much from alienation and loss of mutual grooming in society. We literally do not groom each-other physically as much as before in our history, and most of us do not invest enough time in developing and supporting meaningful relationships (unless romantic or short-term). For a student, the martial arts school can be a place of social grooming [58], both physical and inter-personal. You can bestow upon a student, within reasonable limits, the warmth and care that he or she will seldom experience from other people. This can mean a lot to an individual. That sort of behaviour and social support, for the majority of people is more important than fancy kicks or bulging muscles. It is therefore one of your strongest 'selling points'. Even though one could hardly 'market' this idea, its ripple grow to make powerful waves in peoples hearts and minds.

---

[58] The concept of 'social grooming' is discussed more thoroughly in the chapters: **'Not a Business, But a Community'** and **'The Personal Touch'**.

Set A Schedule

Related to routine check-ups on students, is the notion of a school monthly and yearly schedule. By that I mean, to set up in advance various dates, for special occasions and events, to take place in at the school or in relation to school activities. Things like rank tests, birthday parties, watching a film together, a training camp, a joint hike in the woods, a volunteer project for those in needs, and the likes of these.
Scheduling such events in advance, is more powerful than you imagine. With a single message sent to all students, setting a single date on their calendar, you can transform the manner in which students interact with the school.

Consider the example of a seminar. Suppose you were to declare a special seminar during the first week of August, scheduled to last 3 consecutive days, over a long weekend. The seminar requires a good incentive. So in order to enlist as many people as possible, the incentive being used is that you are going to teach a rare weapon's form and its many applications. This causes excitement and 40 students sign up in advance[59]. Now, here is what happens next.

Each and every one of the participants, assuming they truly and honestly intend to keep their obligation, will have to realign their entire life around this event you have created. Their families, friends, work, leisure, culinary choices and otherwise, are all going

---

[59] It is a good idea always, when organizing events, to place an ultimatum and have everyone sign up for participation a long time in advance – at least 2-3 weeks prior to the event itself, unless circumstances are unusual. I was never as successful as I was hoping for at organizing events, either in my martial arts school or my private life, when people were allowed to decide up to the last minute. Upon taking a leadership position, pursue it to the utmost – do not allow others to dictate the terms beyond advice and consultation. Also, as soon as possible and reasonable, delegate authority to trusted individuals to take care of the logistical aspects of organization. A leader makes the macro-level decisions and delivers the main act – he ought not be doing the work associated with the secretary.

to be affected. Due to the gravity of it all, the event and its contents naturally rise to a very high point of significance for the individual. Then the more they give up on in order to participate, the more powerful and important that event and the school become.

This requires much strategizing. Such an event has to feature content which you have been teasing for quite a while. I for instance have taught a series of workshops on Jungian Personality Psychology to my students. These workshops, given over weekends 1-2 months apart, were in total over 56 hours long! This I could not have achieved, without strategic 'teasing'. For more than two years, I have been dropping sentences about my "secret wish to teach this knowledge", or "how I might one day teach it to a student or two". I would only comment on this every few months. Then by the time these workshops were organized, people were willing to put anything aside to take part. It was indeed an incredible and enriching experience for everyone who attended.

But what I am here describing, also demands a great deal of responsibility on your part. Were you to manipulate people in such a manner, and cause them to invest so much for the sake of what you believe in and ask for, you must guarantee that it would be worth it for them. The event in question has to be truly meaningful and useful to everybody, and the choice of date and time ought to take into account people's needs and personal schedules. This is why the best of events are planned months in advance, and have trusted student working behind the scenes to find out the time frame that works best for most people.

Do not be deterred by the notion of setting up an event so long in advance. It works in the opposite manner to what you might expect. When an event is months in the making, the crescendo is all the more effective, and the culmination much sweeter and more satisfying. There would be the feeling of: "Finally, we have arrived! This is happening!!". As opposed to a casual weekend meeting, which was planned 4 days earlier and only attended by a few students. A long-awaited event is like an up-and-coming feature film, and your reminders for students can serve as the advertisement trailers.

The longer the event itself, the more commitment is required on part of the students, and the more time they need to 'prepare' themselves in advance. A 2-hour one-time meeting is nothing to fret about, and can be scheduled a week earlier. But a whole-weekend seminar begs at least a month ahead of time, and a training camp in a remote location cannot be organized efficiently unless arranged several months before it is to take place.

The major theme for success here is, as always, that the event is meant to be made **of** the student community, **for** the student community, and **by** the student community. This means:

- That the vast majority or all of participants are the students, and not guests. You do not want the students to feel like they are strangers in their own event.

- That the main goal of any school event is to benefit the students – not earning more money or recruiting new students. No shame in charging money for some events, but it ought not be the main motivation. The students need to know and believe that you have their best interest in mind.

- That the event is to be organized fully, or almost completely, by the students themselves. No rental catering services or professional aids of any kind ought to be used, unless the event is on a grand scale (like a big wedding) or entails visiting a commercial business (like going to a restaurant).

Yes, the teacher is the facilitator, the main attraction and the key ingredient for this recipe to take shape. But, the event ought to be about what the students want, covet and that will, in either the short or long term, make them happy and content. While in teaching the traditional martial arts I believe in 'eating bitter', special pre-scheduled events are about the cake, not the healthy vegetables (unless the event in question is a special training camp). They have to be desired; they need to be memorable; and having already given up some or many things to attend – they cannot be too taxing or extreme upon the students' lives.

Be wise about organization. Rather than being a 'chore', make the work done for the event a 'social promotion'. Delegate authority to those willing and eager to take part and contribute. Allocate responsibilities based on people's financial capacity and time constraints. Those who are low on funds ought to offer manual hands-on support instead of buying food. Those who are very busy with their careers, can help by giving fellow students a ride on the way, rather than make phone calls.

Events have the habit of escalating the potential of those which follow them, if they had been successful. I recall in the beginning of my journey as a martial arts teacher, it was difficult to get people to meet for pizza and entertainment at a student's house for 3 hours, or even attempt to arrange such a thing two weeks in advance. With the passing of time and the growth of our school and community, I could with ease schedule 6 months in advance, for a large group of students to attend a three-day-long seminar, training 6 hours every day. Some teachers I know could, by the power of their will and charisma, take with them groups of 10-20 students to a foreign country for a long training trip, and do so repeatedly every year or two. A truly inspiring teacher could literally have his students follow him to the ends of the Earth. But this long evolution of trust and leadership, begins with setting a schedule. Minor meaningful events, over time, will lead to great things.

Weapons Keep Students

Weapons are an extremely popular attraction for mankind. These are tools. We are tool-using animals. We were born to manipulate various instruments which we create and fit our hands well. A weapon, even a firearm, is commonly an 'instrument of play'. The weapons are to us like magical objects, which by their mere handling engage us within a 'parallel universe' of imagination. It is somewhat challenging, and takes experience, to be able to see the possible 'combative scenarios' when practicing empty-handed. With weapons, even beginner can relate. They want to relate. It is as in the words of my mentor and colleague, professor Stephen Jackowicz: ***"Put a Dao (Chinese broadsword) in the hands of the meek and the meager, and watch them being transformed by this object, which suddenly imbues them with courage and a will to do"*** [60]. Observe the phenomenon of historical re-enactments and live-action role-play, and you will evidently come to agree that humans use weapons to strengthen social bonds, and even self-medicate their bodies and minds.

Therefore a student, when he or she are finally allowed by their teacher to practice with a certain weapon, is usually elated. That moment is sometimes akin to a parent bestowing a child with a new toy. Their eyes light up, their spirit is high, and they are more eager than ever to learn. It is also more likely that with this weapon they shall sustain more practice at home, as opposed to solely having their empty hands or the occasional training partner. The weapon is more available, and to a degree more inviting. It is a partner which does your bidding with question, and thus can always be augmented and moderated to the level at which you feel most comfortable with. The majority of people have more fun training with weapons than they do with weights or by themselves.

---

[60] Not every weapon has that sort of quality and effect upon the psyche. The Dao happens to be so by the means of its shape, weight and handling characteristics.

A weapon is not an item meant for solitude, either. It is the instrument of the hero, and all of us are the heroes of our own personal story and journey. This means that this tool beckons to feel itself being rubbed against another weapon, by an almost subconscious urge that most people possess. That characteristic, though originally ingrained through warfare, is in our time community-building, as it encourages people to flock together to have their weapons collide.

You would be surprised to find out sometimes, that weapons also carry a novel value for some of the students which you did not anticipate. I have had a few students who sought to study weapons to enhance their practical skills in historical re-enactments or live-action role-play. Others who, having watched an impressive film actor in their early days using a weapon, held a secret wish to one day learn skills similar to his. Then there were people who felt safer carrying a weapon around in dangerous environments they worked at, or simply in their cars or homes. I even have a student who is a film director and editor, and for him, that sort of training contributed to his everyday job. Motivations for studying weaponry can be varied and diverse indeed.

Being that for the student, the weapon is a treat, and for the community it is a catalyzer and a bonding substance, we ought to use its teachings wisely.

I recall that in the beginning of my journey as a martial arts teacher, I held a very traditional view, that students ought to gain a very solid foundation in empty-handed practice before they could advance to weaponry training. But as they say, "***only a fool never changes his mind***". Back then, I did not appreciate enough the empowering qualities weapons could have over a martial arts school.

As the years went by, I became more lenient. I took the weapons out of the general structure of the curriculum. Though some knowledge of them was required for passing this or that rank and stage, I allowed myself to teach the weaponry skills more sporadically, and literally 'medicate' students with them as I saw fit.

One time for instance, I conducted a two-day workshop, 12 hours long in total, about the usage of the short stick. Surely, the students could not have gained an intimate knowledge of any weapon within that short amount of time. That would have been ridiculous of me to consider. But that was not the purpose of the workshop. Rather, these two days were a tease. I allowed many of my students to have a taste of something sweet, only to immediately withdraw it from them. I told them: "***You may continue to practice with your sticks, bring them to class and receive corrections. Some time in the near future, I will teach you more***".

Then came about the second phase of the plan. Two months later I declared, that I was willing to teach the complete usage of the short stick. The caveat: students who wanted to do so had to attended classes at least three times a week, and the new weapons class would be three hours long. That weapons class would be taught for no extra charge. Four of my students complied. This yielded many benefits:

- These students now attended more classes – sometimes even more than 3 times a week.

- These students became more invested in the school and loyal to it. They felt they were treated better, fairly, and earned their status.
- These students became more knowledgeable and skilled, and eventually learned the complete usage of the short stick of my traditions.

- These students also became role models for others, due to their choices and actions. Over time, they attracted additionally students to the weapons class, and contributed to others being willing to train more.

Such positive changes can do a lot for transforming the social atmosphere in a school, and significantly contribute to student retention in the long-term. Granted, at least in my school and a few others which I had observed, the retention rate was higher among students who graduated to the practice of weapons and have done so for a while, as compared with those who did not.

Then by all means, try to find ways to teach more weaponry skills. This will be worth your while. Though I seldom teach such things to novice students, they make for a big difference among the intermediate and advanced practitioners. Use the event-scheduling strategies discussed in the previous chapter, and make the study of weapons a celebration and an excuse to bring many students together. Your community will never be the same.

The Third Place

My colleague, Shifu Alex Richter, is a very successful teacher of Wing Chun. In his home town of New York City, Shifu Richter has a chain of schools with over 400 students, where he charges and receives a premium for his great classes. Shifu Richter was able to achieve this measure of success at a relatively young age, because he is a good teacher, charismatic and business-savvy.

Alex told me that he had once read of the marketing strategy employed by the coffee-shop company Starbucks. What the advertising department at Starbucks realized, was there existed what is called the 'Third Place'. People most often have their time at home, and their time at work. What is the third place, then? Simple enough – when they are neither at home nor at work. Then arises the question: "Where are people going to physically reside during that third time and place, assuming they are not commuting in a transportation vehicle?". The answer Starbucks came up with, was to make their shops home-like and cozy, providing sought-after free and paid services, so that their business locations would gradually become people's favourite 'third-time hangout spot'.
Seeking to imitate Starbucks, Shifu Richter also turned his schools into third-time niches – homey and welcoming 'social clubs' where students could both interact and have fun, or be by themselves and relax. These places were full of martial arts related magazines, books, and films, and featured lovely pieces of furniture. In drawing the students in to spend more time at the school physically, he made them more attached to his academies, and hence less likely to stop coming to classes. This approached worked brilliantly for him.

Yet the so-called 'third-time' is not solely about where one spends these free minutes, but also concerns what a person does with them. Here is the greater challenge. Since the onset of the television and mass-media, countless businesses and people of interest have come to compete for the attention of the public. In the 19th century, you may have lived in a village, where you may be bothered by a person seeking to sell something perhaps once or twice a month, at most, if anyone even got near you. In this day and age, millions of businesses worldwide are urging to knock on your physical or virtual door, every single day. As one's attention span is limited and a day has only 24 hours, this makes the challenges of a martial arts teacher living in the 21st century unique, and arguably more technically complex, than those of his counterparts from earlier periods in history. He has competition, and these other folks may even come from other industries, or even other nations.

I have long held a theory about information, which is relevant to mention here. Today humans have access to more knowledge than ever before. Yet, this has not made humans, on average, any wiser. One reason is that the fact that information exists and is available, does not mean people innately have an interest in acquiring it. A second and even more prominent reason, is that within that abundance of information and knowledge, a great portion of it is garbage and lies. The average person has little skill in discerning truths from falsehoods, and things meant for his benefit as opposed to things conceived to take advantage of him. People are aware of this. Part of the angst and frustration plaguing 21st century societies stems from this exactly – that there is so much abundance, and at the same time, so little meaning to it all. In this kind of existence, a man of wealth and influence can be he who knows useful truths, has access to them, can find them, and is able to teach them. Across the globe, people desperately seek such a person. You can be what they are looking for. Moreover, you can use this understanding to better your strategies during that third time I discussed earlier.

The idea is, that the quest for finding truth, especially in modern times, preoccupies countless individuals during their 'third time'. It is during the third time, that people engage in looking for what is real, sifting arduously through the mirage of illusions that the world

presents them. Even when they watch films, attend the theatre or frequent a stand-up comedy show, the quest for the truth and meaning is contained therein.
As stated elsewhere in this book, what people covet most, behind the masks and facades, are **Happiness**, **Meaning** and **Continuity**. Often though, they cannot obtain a complete Happiness until they have found Meaning, and therefore the search for Meaning is a prerequisite for a stable psyche. This, people understand intuitively, and they will flock to those who offer them Meaning, which they can discern is both truthful and useful. Meaning they can have, only when substantial truths about the world are understood.

The bottom line is this: If you can offer truths and meaning to people, they shall allot more of their third time to what you have to say.

How can this be achieved? By creating copies of yourself, to engage with the students during their third time. How are copies of yourself created in order to engage students during their third time? By writing articles and books, or by recording yourself in audio and video. I use all of these methods.

It was early in my martial arts teaching career that I came to realize, the classes did not provide me with enough time to convey everything I had and needed to teach. The average student spends 3 weekly hours with me, in a group setting. This is hardly enough for an education. Consider how parents may spend as many as 10-100 hours with their children weekly, and still by the time their offspring are adults, they have usually not learned everything their parents could teach them. So how are we, martial arts teachers, supposed to pass on our traditions, with an educational exposure less than a tenth of the weekly one the average parent has?...
It was obvious therefore, way back then, that my students needed greater exposure. In the beginning, I used to add minor lectures at

the end of a class. Five minutes here, ten minutes there. Many teachers do that. This is silly and ineffective in the long term. Despite such lectures being common, I still find that people may spend 30-50 years studying the martial arts, and are still relatively ignorant of them and of the world in general, knowing little of what was not explicitly stated in class. Something more radical needs to be done.

I initiated the change by writing articles for my students, which eventually became books. Later, seeing that not everyone reads, and even those who do are not studious enough in their learning, I understood that more initiative was required. The end-of-class lectures were not a good solution. Though I continued with them, they were delivered to a tired audience, who sought to go home and continue with their other business and pleasures. I therefore began recording lectures for my students, lasting anywhere between 5-30 minutes, several times a week, and sending them these audio files. My students were never obligated to listen to such lectures, but they all do, sometimes skipping a few here and there. Surprisingly, there had been created some mild peer-pressure to listen to these lectures of mine, since those who missed them were not in on the latest information I shared, as the others discussed it. Since the recordings could be accessed at any time, it was a convenient arrangement for the students, as everyone has got some time they could spare for passive listening – while cleaning, washing, gardening, showering, driving, etc. My students are always encouraged to use such portions of their third time to listen to my lectures and those of other people.

<u>This initiative had been very successful on several fronts:</u>

1. It created a more harmonious community in which people were commonly like-minded and discussed the same topics.

2. It occupied much of my student's third time, thus allowing the influence of the teaching to pervade beyond the classes.

3. It seemed to contribute much to student retention.

4. It reinforced things and ideas which were already stated or taught in the classes prior.

5. It encouraged the students to pursue further education.

This venue of action I would not recommend to everyone, as it bears with it great responsibilities. The teacher must be an excellent orator, with refined language and an ability to carry a narrative in an interesting way. The teacher must also be highly educated, and bring forth to the students' third time a quality of information which they would otherwise be hard-pressed to find elsewhere. The information itself can be martial arts related or different, but **needs to always be focused on helping people positively find Happiness, Meaning and Continuity via USEFUL and APPLICABLE methods**. Only by these means and measures can the recording of lectures for students be effective. When the students realize that their teacher provides them with access to information and knowledge which can hardly be found elsewhere, they would become devote listeners, and will also be more eager to follow your instructions in class.

In a world of fake diamonds, offer them a genuine gem – their being, which they would yearn to polish themselves. Your lectures and classes, should be the guide for unraveling that inner shine. As for the actual contents of what you say or write, I cannot prescribe an accurate formula. It is highly variable with accordance to one's personality, martial arts and the culture in which the teacher and students live.

Be honest about what you distribute to your students. You dislike advertisers who waste your time. So do they! Share with them only premium content, which bears significance to their personal development and your school's community. What is a type of filler rubbish or a cry for attention, would invite contempt. When uncertain about what can be said, consider important lessons you have learned in life, which are not easily found in books and articles, and discuss their relationship to the practice of martial arts. You are allowed to sound cliché at least once every few months – not all students are familiar with the typical martial arts folklore tales, in the likes of 'climbing up the mountain' and 'emptying one's cup'. Even such generic subjects can be enlivened with new plot twists, enlighten the newcomers and rekindle the passions of veterans.

Remember that in pursuing lectures or writing for your students, you are nowadays competing with some of the largest, most powerful conglomerates the world has ever seen, who also demand their attention, for financial gain. But you have the distinct advantage, of being a person of meaning in the students' lives, someone they trust, and a figure of authority who cares for their well-being; as opposed to the opportunist character or greedy company, who are only after their money. In drawing them near you, when you represent something authentic and meaningful, you are also pulling them away from the deceit of the mass-media and politicians. In this, you would also be doing a great service to mankind at large.

The Side-Quest

We martial arts teachers like to boast of how our beloved traditions are such exceptional methods for personal growth. This is what we tell people, do we not? Even the most sports-driven and competition-oriented schools will claim that the martial arts have the power to make you a better person. But in reality, this is no always the case. Martial arts are an instrument of empowerment. Trained correctly and diligently, they make people into more of what they are. The good can become virtuous, and the nasty can become villainous. This all depends to a great degree on the education one receives at the school by the hands of his teacher. When this education is lacking, a very skilled and capable practitioner can turn into a negative person, even a criminal.
I for instance have known a man who stole money from his students. Another who went into semi-retirement while retaining the monthly study fees and having their top students work for them, paying these people below minimum wage. Others, who used their power and influence to sexually take advantage of young students [61]. Then there is of course no shortage of 'high-ranking' martial artists who behave like hoodlums and bullies in public. We have all known or heard of such people. The martial arts did not make them into finer human beings, but rather more effective felons.

To prevent such disasters, the school's educational framework should therefore be strongly based upon the foundations of etiquette and morals (which are discussed in many other chapters in this book). But there is also the aspect of personal development, and that can and should be addressed through the school's curriculum.

One of the beautiful things we can do as martial arts teachers, is to create positive change in the people and world around us. An

---

[61] This particular problem is discussed in a later chapter titled '**The Alpha Male**'.

efficient way of achieving such a worthy goal, is to integrate it into the curriculum taught at the school. This is something which many martial arts teachers and organizations do, and I call it 'the side-quest'.
Usually when students are required to pass certain benchmarks to attain a higher rank, these pertain to martial methods and techniques, or demonstration of martial ability. But the requirements for rank can also be ones which have to do with personal development, and this is what a so-called 'side-quest' is all about. The gist of the idea, is to demand that a student undergo a personal transformation through performing a task, which for him can be a quest of sorts, either minor or major, technical or spiritual.

What is common as a form of a side-quest, is to ask students to write essays, usually as one of the requirements for a test relating to a higher rank (like a 3rd dan black belt or higher, or equivalent senior teaching positions). The idea itself is fantastic! I employ it in my school as well. There are nonetheless several flaws with this concept:

- The writing of essays, books or articles depends on many years of former intellectual training, outside of the school. The majority of martial artists come up with less than impressive literary achievements.

- The process of writing, while educational, is not necessarily so transformative for a student, especially for shorter works. Knowledge-wise, yes – there is some contribution. But a major personal development? That does not take place in most cases.

A superior approach, which needs not override the former but join with it, is to tailor a side-quest specifically to the needs, personality and life of each student. This of course also stands for inequality at the school, for some side-quests as such would naturally be more challenging than others. But it is nonetheless necessary, as people are different, and also feature differing levels of development in their personal lives as they pass through each ranks.

What I like to do, is to avoid side-quests altogether with novice students. As they begin to climb the ranks, I initially set them up with very small technical goals, to make them more agreeable with the idea of being tasked with a special assignment. So for example, for a student during his first 1-2 years of practice, I might tell him: "***when you undergo the test a month from now, you should strive to be able to practice this drill continuously for 5 minutes***"; or - "***while demonstrating this form, I would like you to show power, and be able to execute it in less than a minute***". Such things can be a small challenges, which are outside of the ordinary curriculum, that this student needs specifically, to improve some of his or her weaknesses.

With time, following several months and years of training, the side-quests can begin to drift away from martial arts, and towards the building of character. With the student seeking to attain higher, more meaningful ranks, he will also have greater motivation and agreement in dealing with bigger challenges.

One could start perhaps by suggesting things of this ilk: "***I feel you are ready for your next test. But you ought to know, that the next rank is more demanding it terms of the techniques and drills being taught. Lately you have been giving up on yourself too much when things get tough in training. Let me help you with that. We would focus on this mental conditioning for the next month or so, and once you have pushed through, I promise we would schedule the test as soon as possible***". Or possibly for a more experienced student: "***I really wish to test you for that higher rank three months from now. But as you know, with power comes responsibility. I want you to show me that you are worthy. You can do this, for instance, by helping more with beginner students. This and that student require encouragement and additional instruction. Please take some time during the next few months to provide them with appropriate inspiration***".

Eventually, the side-quests need to ascend to a plain dealing with the higher and nobler. The greatest of quests, I have issued for students who were facing the test following which they could become my disciples. Being one's disciple in the traditional Chinese martial arts means a great deal to both teacher and student [62]. That test, for a certain rank in our system, anyone can pass with sufficient technical proficiency and enough time spent training. However, the discipleship ceremony will only take place, if the student had proven himself to be a good person, and had prior established stable and positive relationship with his teacher. Despite bearing with it

---

[62] This is discussed at length in a later chapter in this book, called 'Shifu – The Chinese Teacher' (p. 361). It is important to stress that the notion of 'discipleship' is based on the strength of relationship and commitment one has with the teacher, the school and the lineage. Discipleship does not necessarily equal a level of a 'black belt' in terms of skill or knowledge. Most people are accepted as disciples in traditional schools within the first few months or years of their practice. At our school, it often takes the upwards of 2 – 4 years, depending on personal progress.

many responsibilities, naturally most students do wish to become disciples. Hence, testing for the rank following which discipleship becomes possible, has a similar psychological appeal to a 'black belt test' in other traditional schools [63].
This psychological appeal needs to be taken advantage of, for the benefit of the student. It is seldom the case that you can convince a beginner to undergo major life changes. But with enough time spent at the school, trust in one's teacher, and the right incentive, great things are possible.

My student **Noam** was the youngest member to attain such position at our academy. He was 18 years old as he approached the necessary test, following which he could have undergone the ceremony. Being of that age and of our era in history, like most of his friends he was lacking in Willpower. He needed to cultivate an inner drive, to lead him fully into adulthood. I had therefore tasked Noam with this challenge: Train 6 hours a day, for a whole month. He bitterly though bravely accepted and accomplished this, and later became my first disciple. This experience forged within him an inner resilience which served well his personal life and career for years to come.
My student **Yaniv** was nearing his discipleship at about 34 years of age. A lifelong professional musician, he was no stranger to vice. Over the years he managed to shed the majority of his corruptions, but one still remained – the smoking of cigarettes. I told Yaniv plain and simple: "***There will be no smokers in our martial arts family***" [64].

---

[63] There is little psychological appeal for 'becoming a black belt', if such a rank or title is awarded casually and can be attained rather easily. Rarity, scarcity and difficulty – a real challenge – are what elicits greater temptation and motivation on part of most people.

[64] I am well aware that there are many martial artists, worthy teachers among them, who smoke cigarettes. The choice to enforce this standard of healthy living is mine along, and does not reflect elements from the martial traditions which I teach and represent. The guiding principle here being, that a healthy martial arts school is made easier from a healthy community of students. Furthermore, since I preach on matters pertaining to a healthy lifestyle, I cannot be caught embracing into my family, individuals who feature behaviours which contrast my teachings.

He quit smoking within two months, putting an end to a disastrous habit he kept for two decades. He later became my second disciple, and his health improved dramatically.

Side-Quests are meant to help the students avoid the **Peter Principle**. For the benefit of those unfamiliar with the term, I will first explain this pervading sickness of modern human society, and its relevance to the martial arts.

The **Peter Principle** and tells us the following: "***In a hierarchy, every employee tends to rise to their level of incompetence***". What is meant here, is that there is a tendency in modern societies, for a person to continue to be promoted, until he arrives at a position or rank which he is no good at anymore. Then, he cannot be promoted further, but at the same time, he is not good at the level at which he had arrived.

Classically, this describes the politically-savvy manager, who climbs the ranks, arrives at a job position with a lot of power, but proves to be utterly incapable of handling such a responsibility well. Or, suppose you began working for a company as a secretary. Two years later you are head of all secretaries. Five years later you are tasked with managing the entire sales department, because you did well as a minor manager prior. But you know nothing about sales, and do not understand the company's products. Congratulations – you have just been promoted into your level of incompetence.
This is how the Peter Principle explains the existence of so many incompetent people at higher work and social positions. These people did some things well, and based on these, were eventually elevated to the position or rank at which they could no longer perform as decently as before. Once having arrived at such positions, they damage both themselves and their environment.

Now think about it. Nearly all commercial martial arts schools nowadays have some form of a ranking system. As teachers we are also aware, that in each of these schools tends to be a rank which predicts student dropout. Following arrival at that rank, many

students opt to leave the school. Often, this is the 1st rank of black belt, or equivalent. Why is it so?
A lot of teachers have pointed to the fact, that people mistake the coveted black belt to be a mountain peak, and once having arrived, feel they can move on to something else. This much is true many a time. Yet what is also commonly in the works here, is the **Peter Principle**, which I have described earlier. Past that higher rank, practice is always more demanding. Past that higher rank, one's performance is judged compared more with the higher-ranking students, than the lower-ranking ones. Past this rank therefore, many students cannot perform as well as before, unless they work harder. In other words, the students "have been promoted to their level of incompetence"!

Three measures are important for preventing the negative results of such rank promotions:

1. Educating the students to understand that there is always more room for improvement and growth, and that the study of martial arts never ends. To make them realize that a rank equivalent of a 'black belt', or a teaching rank, is 'only the beginning of one's true study'. These philosophical notions, while worthy and correct, unfortunately do not sway most students in this situation on their own. But alongside other measures, it is an effective psychological coping mechanism which does help retain students.

2. Avoiding the promotion of students to a higher rank until they are ready for it. Being ready means not solely being capable of passing a test, but also having the physical and mental capacity to deal with the material which the next phase entails.

3. To use side-quests for the sake of generating greater interest in the entire learning process. To achieve a higher rank as a technical triumph is one thing. To attain greater self-awareness, personal growth and enlightenment in the process – is another.

You see, the people described by the Peter Principle become 'stuck' at their position or rank, because they are relatively incompetent at it, **but more so because they do not change**. The majority of people, when they arrive at this so-called incompetence, simply lack the means of transforming their body and mind to fit more challenging requirements and circumstances. Remaining at a job in which you are incompetent and unhappy, is also a mark of an inability to change. In other words, the Peter Principle reflects both the improper promotion of people, and the difficulty these people experience in making change happen.

But the martial arts school is unlike a factory or a company. It should be a supportive community. As the leader of that community, you have the responsibility to empower your students so that the Peter Principle would not apply to them. You can provide each of them with fitting side-quests, to allow for their continued growth within a rank and beyond it. Consider what had been already discussed in the chapters '***What do they really want?***' and '***How to be happy?***'. The students almost always say they come for the martial arts, but most of the time, they attend your classes for other reasons entirely. Even the bouncer, the law enforcement officer or the soldier, do not seek the fighting in order that they could live in a perpetual state of conflict. Each of us is on a quest of self-discovery and individuation, and your side-quests allow everyone to keep themselves focused on the true path. They are not distractions from the main curriculum, but rather the bridges which allow the students to transcend it.

From Customer to Friend

1	Stranger
2	Stranger with common grounds
3	Acquaintance
4	Distant Friend
5	Friend
6	Close Friend
7	Family or friend who is like family
8	Best Friend or Life Partner
9	Soulmate

In martial arts and life, we can talk of a grading of relationships.

One of your goals as a martial arts teacher is to gradually and eventually bring most students from category 1 all the way to at least category 4 or 5. Beyond making life nicer for both you and the student, this will also help in ensuring the student remains with you for a long time.

You may be tempted to think that you can bypass this befriending process with tricks. For example, some think they can bring people who are already their friends to study at their school. This is a bad idea, and a waste of time. One is nearly never successful teaching his own friends well, especially in a group setting. A persistent and annoying fact in human society is that once you have established a strong personal relationship with someone, it is challenging to impossible to change the innate nature of it. So when you are already someone's friend, you cannot suddenly become that person's teacher or superior. The other party will not be able to change their alignment towards you and consider you differently, and so they cannot learn well at all and will give up quickly because they will sense the new arrangement is ruining the relationship. You should admit that it is very difficult to teach those who were already close to you, in all respects. The best-case scenario would have you capable of teaching them privately and partially.

When the student comes at your doorstep for the first time he is usually at category 1, and thinks of himself as a customer. This means that there is nothing personal to your interaction. He is going to invest money and time, and you will provide a service. This is a hole you want him to climb out of. As long as a student sees himself as a customer, he owes you nothing and is not truly a part of the school – he can leave at any time, even without notice.

Time naturally tends to create a closer bond between the student and the teacher and school, but this has to be actively encouraged. Most students who stick around will gradually gravitate from category 1 (Stranger - Customer) to category 3 (Student - Acquaintance). But without effort and intervention on your part, they may never go further.

There are two parts to this. One is the communal aspect, which is discussed in other chapters in this book. The other is the personal aspect. You need to get close to your student, to the extent which is appropriate and which the student allows you to and feels comfortable with. Granted, some students will naturally wish to open their hearts to you on their own. But a lot of students also view the martial arts teacher as a distant authority figure who is harsh and intimidating, given the physical nature of the profession. They will not know you can have a softer side if you do not show it to them.

You need to take the time and make the time to connect with the students, and that time resides outside of the class. This can be either before or after the class, or even via a phone call or a personal meeting. You begin the process by asking all students personally how they are doing, as a show of interest. Make this a habit, and make the question genuine. When they answer, do not just nod – respond and elaborate. Try to create a conversation. Then over time as the student will come to trust you more, the questions and inquiries can become more intimate. You should always ask from a place of true empathy and caring. Even if the student annoys you,

overcome your bias and attempt to be empathetic to the best of your ability.
Never ask personal questions directly – only in a roundabout way. Turn “is your wife cheating on you?” **to** “I notice you are upset... May I ask if I can perhaps help with some issues you may be experiencing at home?”. Transform “were you fired from your job” **to** “Hey, are you doing alright financially nowadays? We can talk about it and sort it out so you will not have to worry”. Change “I see that you are depressed” **to** “You know, I want to do something fun today in class. Tell me about some part of the teachings you really like – we will do that today”.

Through this the students will come to understand that you genuinely care, and will gradually open up to you – each to his or her capacity. This will, over the course of the first several years of study with you, move them from category 1 to category 4 or 5. You should continue to pursue your interest in their personal lives but be vigilant for any signs of resistance on part of the student to let you in further. Also, be very careful to avoid issues which are too personal (such as the sexual lives and habits of students) and issues which you are not knowledgeable enough to help and deal with (for which you should direct them to the right professional). On the latter, refer to the chapter titled ‘**The Part-Time Psychologist**’ (p. 532).

Categories 4 or 5, those of a ‘distant friend’ and ‘friend’, is where you want most students to stop and remain. Contrary to our intuition, greater intimacy can be a problem. A famous idiom proclaims: “Familiarity breeds contempt”. It means that becoming more intimate with someone causes him or her to consider you as equal or lesser to them, and enables them to disrespect you at will, having come to know or find the flaws in your character. Although I resent this proverb somewhat, it holds true for any relationship where a power difference needs to be maintained. As a martial arts teacher, you need to forever be the student’s superior, because the day you are no longer his or her superior they cannot learn from you anymore. Then you cease to be their teacher – emotionally and technically. When you allow the student go past category 5 – that of a 'friend', then this becomes a classic scenario of 'familiarity breeds contempt'. The moment this happens the relationship is forever altered, and you can seldom remedy the situation.

What to do in order to prevent this, then? Several things:

- Avoid revealing to students too much of your personal life. You can share some, but do not get into the fine details about anything unless the student has been with you for many years.
- Hold back your personal emotional self from students, apart from the use of empathy to help them in their personal lives.
- Do not invite regular students (non-disciples) to personal events or celebrations or to 'hang out with your friends'. Create separate social gatherings for the students.
- Do not speak to your students of your financial situation unless absolutely necessary, and if you do avoid revealing much details.
- Do not share important personal future plans with regular students, even if said plans are relevant to the school.
- Do not engage in any romantic relationships with students! Of this read more in the chapter titled **'The Alpha Male'** (p. 444).
- Do not converse with your students of politics or religion – at least not within the school.

All that considered, there are a few people whom we should over time let in what is often called 'the inner circle'. Every long-standing martial arts school has such an inner circle, and sometimes several circles. Traditional Chinese martial arts schools tend to have regular student circle, enter-the-gate student circle, disciple circle and then that of disciples who teach. Sometimes the enter-the-gate students and the disciples are merged and form the same inner circle. In traditional Japanese and Okinawan martial arts, you usually see the color-belts circle, the black belts circle, and a circle for those among the black belts above a certain grade (often beyond 3rd or 4th Dan). In other martial arts schools the division between circles might be somewhat blurry, but they still exist. In every martial arts school, the teacher should be at the very center of all circles.

Regular students are kept at the limit of category 5 – a friend at most. Inner-circle students can go beyond that. What is the criteria for allowing someone into an inner circle? In many schools this is based on rank or seniority. But I urge you to base this decision also, and more profoundly, on Trust. Your ability to trust a student should determine, beyond rank and seniority, whether he should enter an inner circle. This has to do with what I wrote of earlier – familiarity breeds contempt. You should be able to trust, that when the student crosses the line and becomes closer, he will not begin to look down on you or even betray you. The student should demonstrate fierce loyalty and good character in all respects to ensure that. Furthermore, an inner-circle student can potentially cause you the most harm. He will have better knowledge of the art which he can use to his advantage. He can expose details about your personal life that would wreak havoc within the school community and could potentially destroy your hard-earned reputation. "With great power comes great responsibility", says uncle Ben, and he was right. Once ordained into an inner circle, your relationship with the student changes forever – there is no way back. Make sure therefore you promote the best people to such positions.

One way to test students as they become closer to you, before advancing them inwards and towards the center, is to task them with various reasonable jobs and chores, and examine their reactions and dealings with the situation. Of this you can read more in the chapters titled **"Barter Glues Better Than Money"** (p. 238) and **"You Need Help – Ask For It"** (p. 524).

But even with inner-circle students, you need to set some limits. They may only advance up to category 6 (close friend) or category 7 (friend who is like family). A student should never become your 'best friend', 'life-partner' or 'soulmate'. Or perhaps put another way – a person who fulfills these roles in your life should not be your student. Beyond what I wrote earlier, of the difficulty to teach such people, they are terrible to keep around other students as their 'equals', because they are by definition not equal to them, and give rise to feelings of discrimination.
Consider for example a situation in which your girlfriend or wife attends some of your classes. Supposedly you are being very professional and not showing her any special treatment, but you will still find yourself in trouble. On her part, she will be upset as you are one person with her while you are alone, and another while you teach her in class, and she loves you for being the first you and not the second you. Then the students also, even if you do your best, their imagination will find ways to bend reality and see somehow that you were kinder, more helpful, more attentive or more considerate of her than of other people. Students who have been with you for many years may understand, but a lot of newcomers will unconsciously feel uncomfortable with the situation.

Now the inner circle itself can give rise to issues, too. Inner circles have a natural tendency to form in the shape of closed cliques, and when this happens they become a separate entity from the rest of the school. They tend to congregate among themselves, developing their own narrative, shared history, speech, lore and private jokes. They also train more amongst one-another and become less inclined to choose to train with other students who are outside of their circle. The other students see this and feel discouraged.
I remember that back when I was training in Okinawan Karate many years ago, the six black belts at the dojo (beside the teacher) formed such a clique. Being older and more experienced than myself, they often ignored me in class or even when I tried to speak to them, and made no attempt to help me join in practice or conversation. Overall

their rank and status turned some of them into vain and pompous individuals, and that reflected upon the entire dojo. I remember bitterly these experiences with them to this day.
I was astounded years later when I saw in another Karate school, that they have established a separate dressing and shower room for 'black belts only'. This, I thought, was only encouraging the type of problematic behaviour I have encountered earlier. So does the habit of allowing more veteran students 'better positioning' in the teaching room, as in distinct sitting locations or areas where only they reside. Keep in mind that any special treatment causes social turmoil, and you need to balance between your wish to reward some people and the need to prevent them from becoming estranged from their fellow students.

Fortunately, this last issue I mentioned, of the hostile cliques, can and should be remedied by the teacher. What it takes is for the teacher to be involved in assimilating and involving all inner-circle students in the training and activities of all others. In class, all students should work in pairs with all others at one time or another, regardless of status and rank. Outside of class you should pair 'unequal' students in other ways, also. Have them sit next to each other in social gatherings. Demand and veteran student to help a new student with this or that problem. Point out in class when a more novice student managed to understand something which even the more advanced students are struggling with. Make sure you maintain and sustain an egalitarian spirit (more on that in the chapter titled **'Merit, Equality and Leadership'**, p. 26). These and similar actions will keep people's egos in check and prevent the inner-circle cliques from overacting their purpose;

And what purpose is that? Of creating a sense of belonging and achievement. To provide an additional 'thing' for the students to strive for. Understand that for a lot of people, in the long term, the social benefits provided by the martial arts community outweigh the good things attained from the practice itself. Becoming a member of an inner circle is a part of it.

Cannot Save Them All

Learn to let go of people. You need it. First of all, let go of many of the callers. After a few hundred calls of interest and a similar number of casual visits to classes, you will naturally and intuitively learn who are those types who seem hyped but are obviously never going to join the school, or even get to a trial class. Do not let these people waste your time. Each such phone call can be a few minutes long. A trial lesson often means much more time lost, plus these folks drawing away well-deserved attention from your more veteran students. Over the course of an entire teaching career, we are talking about days if not weeks of wasted time on people you will never see again. Learn how to make them not want to come, or leave right away, if they are of a bad character or have serious issues which will only interfere with your teachings. Do make an effort to remain objective here, and only rule out those who are truly a problem and not people whom you simply did not like as much at first glance.

It is of utmost importance you do this with those who are mentally ill. The martial arts unfortunately attract many people with mental illness, commonly Bipolar Disorder, Schizophrenia and similar. I do not know the exact mechanism at work here, but having discussed this with many martial arts teachers, I know they have all experienced this phenomenon. You are not a professional psychologist or a psychiatrist. At best, people with serious mental illness can be taught in a one on one setting, alongside other forms of treatment. But the group classes are not the right place for them. Here you need to be honest, acknowledging what you can and cannot do. Trust me, it is for the better.

Show compassion, but also professionalism, and do not confuse the two. I remember once being contacted by a person over the phone, who suffered from mental illness, whom upon speaking with me sounded quite odd and problematic. He wanted to come to my

class. I politely inquired whether he has any medical condition that I should be aware of before he comes to practice with us. He frankly revealed to me that he suffered from a severe mental illness and was in fact forcefully hospitalized due to his condition in the past. At the time I had less experience, and felt the right thing to do was to attempt to be politically correct and not offend him by cutting him off at once. I reasoned that this type of person must have felt rejection by many people in his life, and that I should not be too blunt with him. See the error here? I was playing psychologist instead of being the martial arts teacher I should have been.

Tell you what happened. I asked him to bring me a letter from his psychiatrist which states he could practice martial arts and that it is safe, both to him and to other people. I thought this would resolve the problem. A few months went by. One day the man arrives at my academy for a trial lesson, without prior arrangements. Unfortunately, I could not tell that it was him at the time, as too much time has passed since our first conversation, and earlier we only spoke over the phone. Though during his trial class he had a very strange aura to him, like many people with severe mental illness he was able to hide his problem for the duration of the class. The next day I receive a phone call from him, in which he revealed that he was in fact the person who called several months ago and that he managed to 'trick' me into letting him in the class without the paper I asked for. Then he added: "*Thank you for the class. It was wonderful. You made my wish come true. I will never see you again. Goodbye!!!*". Then he hung up. This was about when I learned that

lesson I told you about earlier: **Show compassion, but also professionalism, and do not confuse the two**.

The second type of people whom you need to let go are those who behave like a virus in your school, spreading negative vibes and making students more hostile to one-another. This decision, of letting these types of people go, can never be financial – it must be community-based. Let us consider an extreme example for the sake of making a point. Say you have only five students. One of these students is unruly, impolite and unkind to the other four. You may be cautious in giving up on that particular student, because this means you lose 20% of your people, and that is a lot indeed. However, you should understand that a problem student is going to leave sooner or later, and that by that time more people will leave because of him. For this reason, he needs to go, and this cannot be postponed.

You should however aspire to never have to tell people to leave. This is the worst-case scenario. Instead, create the conditions in which they either change for the better or feel uncomfortable enough being their ugly selves that they see they do not fit in and choose to leave of their own volition. This is done by creating a connection in their mind between success in the martial art being taught and change in their attitude. You begin to repeat the message, in every class, that this or that method or technique will only work if they become more cooperative, less tense, perhaps friendlier, etc. You point to other people in the class who have made advances through undergoing personal changes. Then you further stress the point that you cannot technically convey this or that information if the student does not allow you to, through cooperation with you and with their partners. Students who really want to learn get the clue and make changes, while others who are not so decent tend to naturally excuse themselves and quit at that point.

Other students may require the opposite approach, using positivity instead. Have you considered inviting the student for a free private class [65], because you want to help them get better? You may not be keen on 'offering a prize' to a misbehaving student, but you should give it some thought. Many people, suddenly receiving such special attention, understand that something is up, and that they should become alert of the reason for them receiving a sudden benefit. Then, you can use the opportunity of that private class to have a long, friendly and in-depth chat with the problem student. Adults in martial arts classes often act like big children. He may have simply been misbehaving because he coveted your attention, feeling underappreciated compared with other students. Now you can prove that you value him no less than others.

I remember reading once of a tribe in Africa, in which they use positivity to deal with crime. Whenever a tribe member does something bad, even as horrific as murder, they do not incarcerate him or physically punish. Instead, the tribe surrounds that person in a circle, and for hours or days they feast, dance, sing, talk and mainly say good things of the 'offender', discussing his many good qualities and positive past actions. They believe that by doing this, they can reconnect a wrongdoer with his inner sense of goodness. We can learn from this and imitate that approach.

Mimicking the example above, in your private class with the

---

[65] For men who teach the martial arts, I suggest not offering free private classes to women. This can easily be misunderstood as an attempt to generate inappropriate physical intimacy, even if you are being very professional from your own point of view. Women should only receive private classes upon their request, and it is preferable to have at least one other person present in the vicinity if your student feels comfortable with it.

problem student, go out of your way to praise and encourage him, while of course remaining objective and sticking to facts without becoming too enthusiastic. Then once you feel you have elevated the self-worth of that student and that he has adopted a cheerful and cooperative mood, you can gently mention 'that one difficult aspect you have been observing in his behaviour which prevents him from being all of that he could be'. Following this generous gesture of the private class and having been as kind to him as you have, the student will likely feel discomfort and will more readily admit his faults and the need to correct them. In the event that he still offers much resistance at this point and refuses to admit mistakes, than you are truly unfortunately in view of an infantile mind in an adult's body, and you are not the type of expert that this student requires.

When things come to the brink, do not be afraid to kick a problem student out the door. By all means though, try to be polite about it, avoiding cursing, swearing, shouting or anything vulgar. Explain well the reasons for your actions and express your willingness to provide a second chance if the student returns a changed man in the future (do not provide a second chance at that exact moment though).

Then there are also cases so severe, that they actually require you to be vulgar. I was fortunately never a witness to such events in my own school, but I can give you some examples. Wherein you see a student performing an act of sexual harassment, an outright unprovoked violent assault, stealing from another student [66], bullying other people, and things of that nature – then this may call for public yelling and denunciation, perhaps even a forceful physical

---

[66] Be careful when dealing with thieves. Whenever someone steals for the sake of unjust enrichment, this is worthy of your wrath. But sometimes people may steal because they really are very poor and desperate. Do not condemn such people immediately. Try to keep their crime a secret and do your best to help them out. You may offer them to not pay for classes for a while. I have had students who, due to hard financial times, did not pay for months on end, at my encouragement. You can use the student community to help them find a job, or support them via other means such as donations of food, furniture or even by offering temporary or cheap housing. But have a one-strike rule. Steal again, and you are excommunicated for a lifetime.

removal from the premises. This is done because you need to make a point, loud and clear, for all to know and see. Failing to do this when due will tremendously weaken your image in the eyes of your students, and this damage will in turn be difficult and sometimes impossible to mend.

Then the last type of student whom you need to let go are those who choose to leave the school of their own volition. This does not mean you should not initially inquire for their reasons. The students in general need to know that part of the school etiquette requires a leaving party to come and speak with the teacher before they make their final decision. Many a time it is then possible to save the situation by being empathetic, and encouraging the student to reveal an underlying cause for his or her wish to leave, and solving their problem. But when the student's decision becomes final, you ought not chase him further. There are two possible scenarios here, if the student leaves and you do choose to chase him, and both are problematic.

Either you chase the student and then he feels disrespect or even contempt for you as this behaviour shows you are desperate to have him. This will forever undermine any possibility for a healthy relationship between you in the future, and will possibly damage your professional reputation.

Or alternatively, the student is actually hoping for you to chase him and beg for him to not leave, in which case that student is playing a childish emotional game with you. Under these circumstances, even if the student returns, he will likely continue to play such games, and teaching him will forever be a hindrance. You will have a very difficult time restoring the balance of power and putting an end to these games. For these reasons, you ought to avoid a chase following the initial 'breakup conversation'. I would even avoid more than three decent attempts to make contact with a missing student, wherein the student does not wish to answer.

A student leaving can become quite an emotional experience for a teacher. Sometimes we feel students to be like our children or family members. Other times perhaps we feel that the student 'owes us', and maybe we are right. But unless the background for the leave was some kind of personal treachery or betrayal, there is one more thing we should avoid, and that is burning our bridges.

Oh my, you would not believe how many times I wanted to tell a student to scatter, using more honest language perhaps, and that I never want to see him again. Some people I even felt really deserved a good slap or two. Take a deep breath. They are probably being more irrational at the moment than you are.

As long as you feel they might still be worthy of your teachings one day, do the opposite of your natural instinct. Instead of burning that bridge, bid farewell with a smile. Say something positive. Express a hope that you would see them again in the future, and tell them they are always welcome. Were they previously very positive members of the school community, you may even keep having them invited to school social gatherings, during which they would be under constant exposure to the school atmosphere, tempting them to eventually return.

You would be amazed at how, when following this advice, a lot of people whom you had no hopes for would suddenly pop up once more within months or years, sometimes after over a decade, and tell you they have been missing the classes, the people and your teachings, and want to come back. They might even apologize for their former behaviour, at which point you should shrug it off, give them a hug and pretend like nothing happened. But to be able to do this, they need to have a bridge to walk back on to you. Do not burn that bridge – one day some of them will want to use it again.

Return From Exile

People who make a sudden, dramatic return into our lives are often like a mid-summer thunderstorm. You are torn between this nice surprise bringing with it some well-needed breath of fresh air, and being caught totally off-guard. When these 'newcomers from way back' are former students, it is useful to know to how best handle them, as they reach out and ask to be welcomed once more. Among them with find the Good, the Bad, and the Confused.

The Good: These are past students whom you liked, and the feelings were probably mutual. Whatever led them astray, it can be forgotten. You know you want them because they are good students, and functional, positive members of the community. They will train hard in class and at home. Their good name and reputation precedes them. Unless their ancient deeds were horrendous or truly unacceptable, they are worth forgiving. Such people's positive impact on one's classes is more important than old grudges and disagreements. Additionally, they will value and cherish your willingness to forgive and accept them. Chances are, this time around they will do even better, and you can even openly discuss with them strategies to make sure this happens.

The Bad: These students have not been with you for a while, due to a very justifiable reason. They may have even been kicked out the school. In this group, we may observe those who performed sexual or physical harassments, bullying, theft, or other vile acts towards other people within the student community or outside of it. I would urge you to immediately reject such individual's return in 99.99% of cases. They may only be reinstated and reacclimated if many years have passed, they can prove without a shadow of a doubt that they have changed their ways, and it is possible to assign them to a group of students in which no one is familiar with them.

You must be aware of the fact that when you choose to allow such people back in the school, then their negative reputation can stick to you like a plague, even within the student community. People who fear them or are weary of them will come to question your choices and authority. The very act of allowing them back in a single class can lead to a rift in the community and a crisis of trust. Thus, as I have suggested, one ought to reject most of these people at the onset, and be very cautious in allowing any of them to have a second chance.

And the Confused: The great majority of returning students are made of people who are unsure of what they want. They usually took the training to be a minor pastime, which led to them quitting it at some point, as they failed to pursue their study seriously. Later they came to regret leaving, and seek redemption and a second chance. But their hesitant and indecisive nature can also be a serious waste of time for you, and the rest of your school. Returning students need to relearn much, if not all of the curriculum they have studied prior. They require extra attention, like beginners, at the expense of other students. Their ephemeral sense of commitment and short-lived focus, can easily once more become a black hole at the center of the school, drawing everyone's energy and attention before collapsing unto itself and disappearing.

Those who are confused then, sure pose a big challenge! They are not promising enough to let by casually like the good students. But neither is it simple to send them off immediately, like one ought to do with bad students. Over the years though, I have developed a simple strategy for dealing with such people.

When a confused student yearns to return, I almost always welcome him or her with open arms. There would be a cheerful talk, in which I will attempt to speak of a bright future together, and the positive virtues of the returning student. But, at the end of the conversation, there would also be presented a caveat. I will tell that person something along these lines:

"You have been away for quite a while, and we have been missing you. When someone leaves the academy though, this is not an easy experience for the community. I will welcome you to our family again, but I would like you to also demonstrate a committed act, to prove that you are serious. After all, if myself and other members of the school are

going to make the effort to help you get back in shape as soon as possible, then you need to affirm the sincerity of your intentions, too. My one and only requirement of you as a returning student is then, that during your first year here again with us, you pay for every 3 months in advance [67], and that this sum would be non-refundable. Accept this one and only term, and you can start again today".

That is fair to ask of them. They have been training at the school before. They are not being requested to pay for something which they are not familiar with; nor to pay more than other students. They need to demonstrate 'good faith' to earn the same from you.

This simple requirement makes things easier for all parties involved. There would likely be no wasting of your time, once this has been uttered. The overly indecisive, who would have quit after a class or two anyhow, would make a polite excuse and vacate the area immediately. As they are not willing to make even this modest commitment, you know they would have likely failed you once more.

---

[67] Make three months pay in advance your minimal demand, for everyday people of average or modest financial ability. When dealing with those who are wealthy, feel free to raise this demand to the upwards of a year's payment in advance (but no more). Consider that any payment demand of over three months can be a gamble, as a lot of people, even the wealthy, may consider this outright greedy and dishonest. But for some, it can also be taken the right way, to be meant as a show of sincerity in one's actions. Remember that the money is not the goal here, but rather placing the right type of ultimatum in order to yield the result you desire. Requiring someone to pay up front for an entire year in advance, can actually also be a way to politely decline the wishes of a person, who is truly not a right fit for your school. Though somewhat manipulative, it is still more polite than telling a person something like: "You do not have what it takes" or "I do not like you and thus unwilling to give you a second chance". This all is very much culture-bound, and depends on the local environment. In China for example, raising absurd financial demands or other unusual requirements is considered a polite way to convince a person to quit his dealings with you and stop nagging.

There are of course those who will make the payment, and still drop out later. This method of mine cannot prevent such occurrences entirely, though it does 'weed out' considerable percentages of problems-to-be. The other upside is, that even if the student had not lasted as you had hoped, then at least there was some minor financial reimbursement involved.

But one thing I should still stress above all:

The notion of financial gain should never, EVER be a consideration in either accepting or rejecting a student from becoming a student once more.

This, in my opinion, would go against everything the Oriental traditional arts represent, and is opposed to all that I wish to convey in this book. There are people whom I would have almost paid to be my students – so much I enjoy their company and their contribution to my teachings. Whilst others, I would not have as students again even if they bought me a house. You may think: "yeah right – who in their right mind would offer to buy you a house in exchange for status in a martial arts school?!". Well, have I got a story for you.

It was during the later portion of the 20th century that my Shigong, late master **Henry Poo Yee (1939-2018CE)**, was finally making his 'big break' into the martial arts scene. Although a highly skilled practitioner and teacher, who was training since the age of five, few have heard about him until his schools began to gather momentum, when he was in his 40s. As everybody knows, fame also attracts shady characters who seek to feed upon it from one's veins like vampires. Late master Henry was also a victim of at least one such person. So goes the tale which I have heard recounted from several veteran students of Henry Poo Yee, who in turn heard it from him on many occasions. Some of them were also first-hand witnesses to the events which I shall now be describing.

Igor Dowell (a pseudonym) was a successful businessman who had also been practicing the martial arts for many years. Sly, cunning,

manipulative and sophisticated in his ways, Igor was skilled at getting what he wanted, from whoever he wanted. His abilities as a martial artist and a smooth-talker made him notorious, and aided him in acquiring much coveted and often secretive knowledge from various masters. Being quite wealthy and fond of violence, perhaps in his mind, Igor imagined himself to be some type of a 'Batman' character, minus the vigilantism.
At one point in time, it came to Igor's attention that master Henry Poo Yee was not only teaching openly a very enigmatic and sought-after martial art, but was also likely to be among very few who had gotten a full transmission of its mysteries from the famous master Lam Sang, of New York City's Chinatown. Igor decided to make this knowledge his, and yearned to one day be acknowledged as a true inheritor to this style.

Having already been versed in other arts and groomed by other masters, Igor thought and demanded that Henry give him 'special attention'. To his disappointment, Henry had him enroll with the beginners' class. But that did not dissuade Igor. Being persistent and a hard worker, he came by many classes and paid for countless private sessions. Gradually, he eased Henry into considering him a pleasant companion. Beyond the various financial 'donations' and gifts, Igor took care to support Henry with greater exposure to the martial arts community through his business connections, drove him places and fed him well. He was a good student, and knew the perks of how to cater for a Chinese master and make a decent show of filial piety. His knowledge of Chinese philosophy and language were powerful assets in his arsenal. His understanding of them shone more brightly due to the fact that most of Henry's American students, were not versed in the Chinese cultural traditions to the degree that he was. The relationship developed to the point, that Igor escorted Henry on some trips and visits to China and elsewhere which other students were not invited to. Though this of course was due to the fact that all planning of said trips and visit was orchestrated by Igor, who was not keen on sharing his teacher's attention with other members of the school. He was never a part of that community, but an outsider who had infiltrated it, with his own agendas.

Despite Igor's wishes to gain exclusive status though, he was not granted such a thing by master Henry. He had spent less than 3 years studying with him after all, and Henry was a staunch traditionalist, who would usually not accept a person as an enter-the-gate student before a decade or so of practice within his organization.

Eventually, Igor grew impatient, and his inner businessman got a hold of him. He was following all the traditional requirements and codes of conduct and etiquette when dealing with his teacher, but was too anxious to wait any longer. He wanted the long-coveted status of being top-dog, as he considered himself to be from the beginning. That was about when he revealed his true nature to Henry for the first time.
Igor Dowell thus approached Henry with a business offer. He would have Henry retire to a lovely estate. Henry would be gifted with a nice house and a fancy car. He even went on to claim that he would provide Henry a 'limitless credit card' (a luxury at the time), and be responsible for paying all of his expenses. In return, he asked Henry to declare Igor as his 'number 1 student and inheritor', and hand him over his martial arts school and all of his secrets. Igor even offered to have it all finalized in a formal contract.

Late master Henry, being a man of upright moral character, was appalled by the offer. He immediately banished Igor from his school, never to be seen there again. No amount of money or assets was to Henry worth lying to others, or handing over his beloved and sacred tradition to a man who was not worthy of it. Henry knew the repercussions. He did lose a dedicated, albeit corrupt student. He was aware that Igor would now wage a long political 'war' to tarnish his reputation, in order to protect his own. But nonetheless, master Henry did not allow financial greed to cloud his sound judgement. When push came to shove, the wicked went flying out the front door.

In Business, Have No Doubts

In Hebrew there exists a proverb: "**When there is a doubt, then there is no doubt**"... that you know what needs to be done. Meaning, that if you doubt something too much, you should avoid undertaking it. This proverb points to one's gut feelings; to our intuition. I have come to live by this proverb. I seldom do business, or even speak with a person, when I feel there is something about him or her which oozes bad vibes. I take care to remind myself, that this does not necessarily mean that these are bad people or ill-intended individuals, but rather, that at this particular moment in time, they are not the right characters for me to interact with. It is vital in my opinion that we martial arts teachers, with our strong and well-developed intuitions, follow this principle to the utmost. Do not do business with people who rub you the wrong way. Do not accept students whose personality or actions seem inappropriate or ill-fitting to you.

Once a student brought to class a 70 year old man, who was a professor of Western medicine. The visiting newcomer was cheerful, friendly, cooperative and very wise. I enjoyed teaching him during that single class he attended, in which his training was very light and modified for his age and needs. But this lovely man, as wonderful as he was, did not come across as being in the right place for him. I listened to his voice, and he sounded overly tired, and with a tinge of desperation in his tonal expressions. I glanced at his gait, and he seemed struggling. I touched his torso, and he felt stiff and sick. I took many good, prolonged looks at his body. His nose had the scars which I could recognize as post-surgical for removal of cancerous tumors, which he shrugged off as being 'outdated', refusing to admit the existence of any other medical issues. He was obviously overweight and not in a good condition. His feet were pinkish, swollen and with rough skin, like I had seen those of late-stage chronic diabetes patients. In the beginning and the end of class, he required assistance for sitting and rising from the floor. I had doubts – and therefore, no doubts. The following day I called that man and regrettably told him that I think his medical condition makes him ill-fitting for our class. The man protested, and was not easy in argumentation, for as mentioned earlier, he was a professor of medicine. Nonetheless it was my school, and I had to politely dissuade him, with great pains to the both of us, for he was truly a nice person, whom under different circumstances I may have been able to help tremendously. Had he only come 10 years earlier...

The student who brought the professor to class, called me some three days later, sounding worried. "What happened?", I asked. The student told me: **"Oh, I am just concerned about my friend, the professor. He had dislocated his knee today, which is a bad omen at the age of 70".** I knew right then and there that I was correct with my gut feelings, but this was not surprising to me, having learned to rely on my intuition by that time. Yet this was not the end of it! Three weeks later, and the same student calls me, now sounding frantic. "What happened?!", I asked. The student told me: **"Oh, you will not believe what happened to my friend, the professor! He caught on to some nasty illness, and now he is in a coma!!".**

WHEN THERE IS DOUBT, THEN THERE IS NO DOUBT.

Just imagine the career-destroying implications there could have been had, if such a student was to suffer these types of medical pitfalls in class. As a Bachelor of Laws (L.L.B) whose entire family is full of lawyers, I can guarantee you that a casual 'letter from the doctor' about one's ability to practice, would probably not have been sufficient to save me in court from a medical professor who fell into a coma in my class (or more accurately – his grieving family which could have sued me).

In this day and age though, some people do not appreciate having to take a "no" for an answer, especially when 'doing business'. When you refuse to admit a student, he or she may protest. Even if they do not sue you because of it (which is an exceedingly rare occurrence), still they may end up becoming bearers of bad publicity and negative marketing for your school, possibly for many years to come. It is therefore important that when you make the case as to why a student cannot attend the classes, it sounds both polite and relevant.

Prevention begins, for me at least, even before people come to class. When I speak with someone on the phone or on the street, sometimes they simply look to be too mismatched for my school. A tactic I use then, is to make the ordeal seem too challenging for them, either physically, financially, or both. I could name a price which seems absurd, which often works, but this requires care, for some crazy folks may end up taking you on your offer, and then a morally upright teacher would feel an inconvenience in having to charge them an exceptional sum, different to what everybody else pays. It is easier to get rid of the misfits by sharing stories of the hardships to come. Often when I converse with such people, I tell them something along these lines:
"You sound like a really nice person. Our school could use good people, but naturally the training is not for everybody. Let me ask you something. We have a training method in our school, a type of standing meditation. You will have to stand in one place without moving for 40 minutes. It is quite painful and challenging. Here, this is how it looks. Can you really do such a thing? Because I will ask that of you, and it is not easy. Furthermore, we expect people to attend classes a few times a week, and if you plan on arriving to class sporadically, there would be no significant benefits to your training... So are you up to such challenges?". I guarantee you that this short description (and demonstration if the person was in front of me) weeds out 99% of the misfits immediately. The description is exaggerated, of course. That practice, of Hun Yuan Zhuang, is not very painful or completely immobile, and beginner students are not required to stand in that posture for 40 minutes. Neither is a complete beginner expected to arrive in class more than twice a week. But there is enough of the truth in there to both maintain a decent level of honesty and achieve the goal. Re-read the script above, and you

would notice I began the explanation on a positive note, and then ended it by allowing the person himself to make the decision of whether the practice suits him. Then if the decision is negative, he will know you appreciate him, and will not blame you for forbidding him from coming to class.

The same tactics should be used with students who have already attended your classes, but they require a more personalized treatment. Greater care should be taken so that such people would not be offended. As in medicine, prevention is superior to treatment following the onset of an illness.
First the students need to hear some moderate praise of him, focusing on his good qualities as a person. Then, he needs to be told a relevant reason, or preferably several, as to why the classes are likely not the right choice for him. With students who have already attended an introductory class though, you must be somewhat more decisive in your phrasing and tone of voice, for mistakes cannot be had. You have already decided they should not come to your classes – all that remains is to make them realize this without resenting you too much. Once they attend a second or third class, doing away with them in a courteous manner, is going to become far more challenging.

You should not worry about 'losing potential business' with students like that. A single misfit can easily repel the participation or enlistment of many other students over time. By following your time-honed intuition and working only with those people whom you wholeheartedly believe should be in your life, your moral compass will guide your on to greater success. Do not be swayed by those who say 'yes' to everybody. A traditional martial arts school is not a fitness club. A community is a privilege to join, a social luxury – not a humans-for-rent type of establishment. Having standards elevates your status and dignity. Knowing how to have standards without offending people, reveals finesse and wisdom.

The Soul of the Teacher

Shifu – The Chinese Teacher

Shifu, pronounced 'sshirr-fu', is one of the words used in Chinese when referring to a person who is a teacher. A regular school teacher however, would be called 'Laoshi', and not 'Shifu'. In comparison with 'Laoshi', the word 'Shifu' has a deeper meaning in Chinese language and culture. [68]

In daily life, the word Shifu is used as a title for skilled professionals with notable expertise. For example, a bicycle mechanic at the margins of a road (a common sight in Chinese cities) would be called the 'Bike Shifu'. A car mechanic would be called a 'Vehicle Shifu'. These people are experts in their respective fields (relative to other people), and so from their nicknames arose the common mistranslation of the word Shifu into the English language as 'Master'. This translation however strays much from the original meaning of the word, and unfortunately brought about the situation in which today we refer to many teachers of the Chinese martial arts as 'masters'. A 'master' implies having a 'mastery' of a certain skillset – attaining the highest levels of it, while in Chinese cultural and lingual perception, a trade-Shifu is simply a nickname for a professional – someone with specific expertise, who is not necessarily a master.

Then in the context of a teacher-student relationship, the word 'Shifu' has a different meaning entirely, far more complex and unique. In order for me to explain it, let us break down the

---

[68] In China today are spoken dozens of common dialects. The most notable ones are Mandarin Chinese and Cantonese Chinese. Mandarin is a dialect which originated from Northern China. Cantonese is a dominant dialect in Southern China. Though these dialects use mostly the same characters for writing, their pronunciations and sometimes grammar can differ significantly.

The Chinese government has for decades been heavily invested in creating a unified vision of Chinese culture. As part of this, Mandarin is being promoted and taught as the main dialect everyone ought to speak and write in (Pu Tong Hua – the Common Tongue). Cantonese on the other hand is being de-emphasized and suppressed.

The terms 'Shifu' and 'Laoshi' are in Mandarin, and their Cantonese equivalents would be 'Sifu' and 'Laosi'. The former are commonly used in Northern-Chinese martial arts, while the latter are spoken in Southern-Chinese martial arts.

'drawings' which make it the Chinese characters that spell 'Shi Fu'. First let us begin with the characters that make the term 'Lao Shi' (ordinary teacher). This term is made up of two characters:

Lǎo 老 – meaning 'old'. But in traditional Chinese culture, which pays a lot of respect for the elderly, the word Lao (old) also means 'Wise', 'Experienced' and 'Dignified'.

Shī 師 – meaning teacher or expert.

Therefore, Laoshi literally translates as 'Old Teacher', and understood as 'Respectable Teacher' or 'Dignified Teacher'.

The term Shifu, when describing a professional, is written as 師傅 . It begins with the character Shī 師, for teacher, and the second character is Fù 傅, meaning instructor. Hence, an 'instructor teacher'. Someone who merely solves problems, who can teach or shows you how to do something.

The term Shifu is slightly different when used in the context of traditional apprenticeship and martial arts training. It is then written as 師父. This term begins with the same character for 'teacher', Shī 師, but then the second character is Fù 父, meaning 'father'. Together, written like this, the characters in Shifu refer to a 'Fatherly Teacher'.

When ought a person be called Laoshi as opposed to Shifu? In China it is custom to use Laoshi for teachers with whom a social distance is maintained. A school teacher, driving instructor, someone teaching you a hobby craft, etc. Shifu would be the appropriate title for a teacher who maintains a family-like relationship with his students. Having defined this now, what can truly make someone 'a Shifu'? What are the requirements of such a person? I shall answer this from my own personal point of view, and in order to do so, will provide you first with a brief introduction to Chinese social norms.

The world of Chinese martial arts, like all of Chinese culture, is heavily influenced by the ideas and values of Confucius. The Chinese Confucian world view requires society to be orderly and well-structured.

In the West we speak of notions such as "to love thy neighbor", "thou shalt not do unto others what you do not wish to be done unto you", and similar concepts. The Chinese Confucian view also considers these principles sacred and vital. However, the ordinary Chinese person does not tend to apply them to everyone. Rather, the Chinese would be more inclined to exercise such ideas only among people with whom they have already established a relationship. This type of traditional relationship is called **Guānxì** 關係. By that I mean, the oftentimes, moral idioms such as "love thy neighbor" and "thou shalt not do unto others what you do not wish to be done unto you", are not universal from the Chinese point of view, and are commonly reserved to people with whom one has established

Guanxi. Once two people have Guanxi, they become more amiable and accommodating towards each other. Guanxi is also a 'system of social favours', and people who have it between them will indulge in an unspoken social game of 'I help you with this now, and you will, if the opportunity arises, help me with something else on the same scale of importance later'. Entering a Guanxi is most often done therefore by exchanging favours (such as gifts, discounts and services), and gradually over weeks, months or years, strong bonds are formed. Because people in traditional Chinese culture are not automatically giving and forthcoming towards others, the Chinese are inclined to create and nurture relationships with others as soon as possible, in order to guarantee the establishment of Guanxi and assure mutual aid and support. This is a very strong social ritual in Chinese culture, which is still tremendously relevant in our time.

As an extension of Guanxi, there is also another popular idea in Chinese culture, of one person adopting another as his kin – accepting someone as a 'family member' – most commonly as a brother or son. This idea has been demonstrated in China since ancient times. In famous novels such as the Romance of the Three Kingdoms we can read of adult men welcoming others as their brothers in ritualistic ceremonies, forming a blood bond which is not biological, promising to keep each-other safe and secure to the end of their days. This is a supreme social bond which everybody are expected to honour. Hence, adopted family is another meaningful form of Guanxi in Chinese society.

One of the common ways to become someone's family is via the relationship of a master and an apprentice. Apprenticeship under an expert used to be the favourable and preferable manner for acquiring professional skills worldwide – in China, Japan, Europe and the Middle-East alike. This was true even for professions which today are considered 'academic', such as Law and Medicine. Martial Arts were no different in this respect, and since time-immemorial great teachers would take disciples to work and study under them so they could learn the depth of their art and the secrets to their skills.

A student of traditional Chinese martial arts, would normally refer to his teacher as Laoshi (Dignified Tutor). But once such a student had been accepted as a disciple of the teacher – meaning he had established a Guanxi with the teacher and was deemed family, he shall henceforth refer to his teacher as Shifu (Fatherly Tutor). This is a reminder of the humane bond struck between the two in a public or semi-public ceremony, called **Bàishī** 拜師, which means: Respecting the Teacher.

The rules for that ceremony change among various schools and traditions, but there are a few common norms. The student will bow down on both knees at least three times, touching the floor with his forehead, while the teacher sits on a chair in front of him. The student will offer the teacher a gift, which will be either fruit, money in a red envelope, these two things together, or something else. Usually the gift is symbolic and modest, but some teachers require the students to hand over large sums of money. Then some words are said. I like to tell the student the following when conducting my ceremonies: "We are not the same blood, but now we are one. You arrived as a student, and now you are family". We end the ceremony with a loving hug, and afterwards have a feast with the other members of the academy and guests.
In our time, the Bai Shi ceremony is usually conducted at the request of the teacher. It may be done before the person begins his formal studies with the teacher, or after a few months or years. Traditionally it was frowned upon to accept a student as a disciple very quickly, and a teacher who did this was considered as someone who "did not guard well the gates of his house". At my school it takes someone about 3-6 years to become a disciple, while some other teachers may wait up to 10 years, wishing to test the student's character even more thoroughly before adopting him. Myself and other teachers also make technical requirements in terms of knowledge and skill before a person can undergo a Bai Shi ceremony, in terms of familiarity with the curriculum and proficiency in it. There are teachers who may never accept a given student, or any student, as their disciple, and their arts are sometimes lost as a consequence of such choices.

While for some teachers the notion of discipleship is purely symbolic, many consider it to be a major stepping stone in their relationship with their student, which appropriately yields a major change in the nature of that relationship. Often, only students who have underwent the Bai Shi ceremony and 'passed through the gates of the school' would earn the right to learn the more advanced training methods and techniques of their teacher's martial art.

But why ought a teacher adopt a student in this manner anyway? There are a number of good and important reasons:

1. In order to form a strong relationship of trust, based on commitment and understanding, which is like that of a father and son.

2. As good knowledge of the martial arts is akin to having a weapon and knowing how to use it. It is important to make sure that deadlier weapons are only given to those without extreme tendencies or overtly negative character [69].

3. So to encourage stricter obedience on part of the student and greater supervision of him, ensuring he would make proper use of the knowledge and traditions of the system, especially if and when he is to instruct others in these.

4. To guarantee that the more veteran students represent the system truthfully and honourably in public and shall avoid shaming their tradition, teacher or other members of their gongfu family.

5. For establishing a pleasant communal atmosphere and a genuine sense of friendship among the serious students and with their teacher.

---

[69] In our time, a popular saying is that if you want to kill someone there is no need for martial arts – one can simply buy a knife or a gun. However, this view is very simplistic and misunderstands basic notions of human psychology. When someone constantly wields a hammer, then everything looks like a nail. For a person who is deep in the martial arts, he can easily begin looking for opportunities to put them to use. A disciple ought to be someone whom the teacher believes can put the hammer down, only picking it up when truly necessary.

6. That the quality of teaching could transcend to the highest level - from the teacher's mouth directly into the student's heart (Kǒu chuán xīn shòu 口傳心授). Only by this sort of transference of knowledge, a heart-to-heart transmission, can a person fully comprehend and embody the deepest capacity of traditional martial arts. It requires hands-on touch and a personal connection to be maintained.

7. Ensuring the official creation of extra 'authority figures' within the school for others to look up to, whose status is based on merit rather than rank or seniority.

There exists, as stated before, a period of time between a person's entrance to the school as a student and being accepted as a disciple – Tudi (徒弟). This waiting period is called 'teacher seeking the apprentice' (师寻徒). In China originally, the student would usually be the one to ask to become a disciple, as the notion of apprenticeship was common and known to all. That is unlike in our time, when people are usually unaware of the social norms in this respect, so most often the teacher has to be the one to ask to establish such a relationship, if the student has not asked for it prior.

Why then was it once common for teachers in the Orient to wait for the student to ask to be accepted as disciples? The reason is that they wanted the students to consider such a responsibility solemnly and approach of their own accord and free will, not feeling coerced to do so or acting on a whim. From a modern, and perhaps more Occidental point of view, there are also logic and reason in having the teacher approach the student about this. Many people can simply be shy, timid and fearful of asking their teacher of a monumental thing as joining his family. Or, the student may misunderstand this is something expected of him. By passively waiting for a student to initiate, the teacher will likely miss many wonderful potential disciples, when a simple conversation could have made a difference.

At my academy, I made things easier by setting a specific technical benchmark for my student to become disciples. First they have to reach a certain threshold of the curriculum – level 10 (of 18), in order to qualify. By this I guarantee that their practice has matured to a degree, as is their familiarity with the art. Also, by the time they reach levels 5 or 6, they would have spent some 2-4 years at my academy, and so we should have gotten to know each other. These levels and their requirements are known to all and specified on the walls of the academy. Then once a student has passed these technical requirements, I shall allow him or her to become disciples if indeed by that time we have been able to establish a relationship of trust and mutual respect. Wherein this is not the case, the student will have to wait some more and modify his behaviour and attitude before he can go further. More important parameters for discipleship, I shall discuss in the next chapter.

In wishing to undergo the Bai Shi ceremony, I do not demand of my students to bring forth precious gifts or expect them to prove themselves in a competition of any sort. My only wish is for them to demonstrate apt knowledge, perseverance, willingness and a good heart, as well as a few additional elements of good character (see next chapter). I have set the technical demands for the Bai Shi qualifications so that nearly anyone who attends the academy could eventually reach that stage, if they try hard enough. The speed at which this becomes possible depends of course on how much they train. Those who practice only twice a week, but keep coming, may take up to 6 years. Others who make an effort to practice almost every single day, could get there in 3 years perhaps.

Due to the inherent immense responsibility, not every teacher would agree to take any student as his disciple. Some teachers also take issue with someone becoming their disciple if he is already another teacher's disciple. Their line of thinking is this: "How can I trust someone who already considers another as his father in the martial arts? Can that person truly be loyal to two fathers?". Such things change based on individual preferences of teachers. Commonly though, a person who is already experienced in the martial arts might actually be tested longer than others before attaining the teacher's full trust [70].

The duties for a person accepted as Tudi (徒弟) are not towards the teacher alone. Being accepted into the gates of the system means becoming a part of an extended family, which includes the teacher's wife, his children, as well as other disciples past, present and future. All disciples ought to treat one-another as brothers and sisters. Some schools use a hierarchy between older brothers (became disciples earlier) and younger ones, but this type of approach is more appropriate for Oriental societies, and I have not implemented it in my school. Because the disciple is akin to the teacher's son, he must also look after him when the teacher grows old and requires aid. This responsibility is greater for those whom the teacher has declared as successors, if there are any. Such a duty can prove essential and even life-saving wherein the teacher does not have a supportive biological family. Two prominent examples: The creator of Bagua Zhang, Dong Haichuan, and the famous teacher of Jook Lum Southern Mantis, Lam Sang, both spent years living with their disciples, and were nurtured by them in old age.

It is further expected of the disciple to be especially morally upright, make a sincere effort to inherit whatever he can from his teacher's system, and act consciously and actively to increase the school's reputation and legacy. It is important therefore that the teacher clarifies to the student wishing to undergo the Bai Shi ceremony, that the status of Tudi bears with it serious responsibilities, which

---

[70] Another social norm in traditional martial culture is for a student to ask permission of his teacher before going to study at another school. Wherein his relationship with his teacher are decent, then his teacher may equip him with a recommendation letter to ease his acceptance into the new school. Becoming a member of a new school without letting all teachers involve know one's full personal history in the arts, is considered taboo, and can result in a student being shunned from many establishments. There is a measure of reason in this, as acting in such a manner indicates that the student attempts to hide things and is willing to lie. Without honesty there cannot be established any healthy human relationship. In the words of Confucius: "*Human beings live with honesty. Those who are dishonest, live feeling their lives are fated*".

cannot be evaded. That is, unlike a regular student, who has no special responsibilities as such and may only volunteer.

For the teacher too, his responsibility as Shifu is a heavy burden to bear. Some would argue, greater than that of all of his disciples together. Students who passed through the gates, though they take care of each other and the school, usually they only have to look after the teacher. But the teacher has to look after many as his own children, oftentimes adding to his already extant biological children and grand-children.

The teacher is by default he who has arrived further than his students in the martial arts. His body and mind are more resilient than most. For these reasons, the ideal Shifu is akin to an incorruptible supporting column for his students, and this is how they ought to see him. This brings about the known phenomenon among traditionalist teachers with established schools, of not a single day passing without a student requesting the teacher for some advice or assistance. The Shifu will take responsibility for the physical and mental well-being of all of his <u>devoted</u> students, and especially his disciples. This includes not only the teachings of the martial skills, which ought to be excellent of course. There is also the medical perspective. The teacher should educate himself thoroughly so to make sure his teachings would not bring about injury, and also so that he could treat, at least to a minor degree, the injuries of students, be them physical or emotional, even if he is not a doctor.

In accepting people as his disciples, the Shifu also now has a commitment towards them to allocate the utmost time and attention to provide them from his knowledge in the most detailed and intimate manner possible; something which ought to require many resources and a lot of time. This very chapter, originally written alongside many others for my own students in Hebrew, is a testimony to this commitment of mine, to provide them with broad education.

As for my personal case – at my academy all call me 'Shifu' (rather than Laoshi). There is a reason for this. As a teacher, I consider it my obligation to also be a 'father' to my students. My school is neither

a 'pastime' nor a 'hobby' – it is an Academy, in the ancient Greek sense of the word – a dignified social institution. The students at my academy are not 'customers' or 'visiting tourists', but friends and family. All of my students know that they can approach me at any time or day, with any problem or concern. I tend to be involved in the personal lives of my students (when they wish to let me in), and aid them to the best of my ability. A person who chooses to become a member of our academy is for me a 'project'. It is someone whom it is my duty, even obligation, to help improve his or her life, and aid them in becoming the best version of themselves.
I do this by going beyond the martial arts; utilizing the teachings to convey knowledge about physiology, anatomy, biology, practice theory, Eastern and Western philosophy, morals, psychology, history, nutrition and more. Through this, the students are quick to realize by being provided with practical examples, how the lessons taught by the martial arts are readily applicable in their everyday lives. A student who despite my and his best efforts is unsuccessful on his journey, is for me a personal failure as a teacher.

It is my personal responsibility to be a Shifu for the students, and that responsibility is heavy and worthy. I am proud to be a part of martial lineages spanning hundreds of years, and my mark upon that collective history I shall leave first and foremost as a decent human being, and then as a martial artist. This is the message which I convey to my students, and that is the essence of our academy.

The Family You Choose

"The student searches two years to find a worthy teacher, but the teacher searches ten years to find a worthy student." – Chinese Proverb

I often tell my students, that your martial arts family, unlike your biological relatives, is the family you choose. Therefore, it is important for one to choose wisely. All the more, when it is the teacher choosing his disciples. The question of why ought a teacher appoint disciples, has been discussed in the previous chapter. In this chapter, I would like to survey the technicalities of choosing such people to be appointed.

When considering new people for discipleship, first one should think it over for a few weeks or months. Then, it is important to consult extant disciples on the question of whether this or that person is worthy. Though the final decision is entirely yours, the action itself is akin to adopting a 'child' into your family, and therefore it is significant to discuss such matters with the other 'children'. That is not solely meant to provide the disciples with a sense of participation in important decision-making. These people are hopefully one's circle of trust, with rich life experience, and have known you for quite a while. They can provide very good opinions and analysis on such matters. Though I would not cast a vote, as a martial arts school is not a democracy, it would be wise to avoid appointment of disciples whom the other disciples clearly cannot get along with.

Over the years arose a need for me, to make the disciple-appointing process and deliberation more precise. Otherwise, the risk of bias can be great. Years may pass between the appointment of one disciple and the next, and in the meanwhile one could easily shift and alter his standards. This is why I have written down the following rules, to aid with the process. The first 10 rules deal with requirements for discipleship. Albeit not being a secret, I do not intentionally publish these requirements to students either. It is better that the student comes to meet such requirements naturally, without prior knowledge or coercion. Then the next 8 rules concern expectations from disciples. These are provided to people before undergoing discipleship, to make sure they understand what they are getting into. That being said, the prospective disciples are not made to sign any document or swear by such regulations, as the relationship to begin with ought to be based on trust.

Requirements for Discipleship

1. Has a good heart. In Yiddish this is called being a 'Mensch'. Confucius thought of it as having Humaneness (Rén 仁) and being a 'Virtuous Person' (Jūnzǐ 君子). This first and foremost requirement, of having a good heard, is for the most part very difficult to teach. One is partly born with it, and in part learns it early in life. Having a major change of heart as an adult is uncommon. Some people simply do not have a good heart. They should not be a part of your family. Having a good heart means someone mostly has good intentions and follows through with them. Now granted, all people believe they have good intentions. I guarantee you that Adolf Hitler, Joseph Stalin and Mao Zedong all believed they had good intentions. But there is a gap between believing you have good intentions, and actually carry forth actions which are objectively good. Choose as disciples only those who think they mean well, but also prove it in their actions.

2. Has a good name. Reputation is very important. The reputation of the potential disciple will merge with that of the martial arts family as a whole, and each one of its members. Thus, one cannot afford to choose someone of ill reputation. It can be challenging to change, but a person can positively affect his reputation and alter his perception by society, though that normally takes several years. It light of this, some people can 'amend for their sins or misgivings'. Having a good name also means, of course, being capable of demonstrating proper etiquette and decent behaviour inside and outside the school; that is, possessing the ability to sustain a good name.

3. Has proven his loyalty to his teacher on several different occasions. Tests of loyalty, unlike the character trials (see next article), should be undertaken without the student knowing that he is being observed. One type of loyalty test is simply providing a student with chores from time to time, and watching how he handles them. Other tests of loyalty can be more manipulative, if you may. For example: you can have a colleague of yours try and tempt the prospective disciple to come to his class, and even to join his school. The student must not know that the colleague is a friend of yours. You may then take note whether the student cooperates with him in any way, and if he later went and reported you of what had transpired. A proper, loyal student ought to ask for your permission to even attend a class at another school, and surely not join another school without having discussed things with you in advance. The latter, manipulative variety of a loyalty test, should be reserved only for special 'borderline' cases.

4. Has withstood a specific character-trial given to him by his teacher. I have previously provided such examples in the previous chapter titled **'The Side-Quest'** (p. 325). Testing the student with a character trial before discipleship is more important than the technical rank test, for it reveals who that person truly is. It also proves to the student himself in an honest manner, whether he is ready or not to become a disciple.

5. Is financially independent and not in any serious debt (with the exception of a house mortgage). This is the only controversial rule I have for discipleship. Being a part of a family means we support each other financially and otherwise in times of need, each to his best ability under the circumstances. It cannot be allowed that a person who is already a known 'financial liability' would enter the family, for it would immediately place an economic burden on everyone else. What would I consider a 'serious debt'? That definition will probably change depending on the person. But you can aim for something like: "not owing more than the sum of what he normally earns in three months".

6. Is over the age of 21 and has been consistently training for at least 3 years at the school. People too young tend to be immature. Generally speaking, most people under the age of 21 have not yet experienced a meaningful, deep and mature romantic relationship, with all of its adult intricacies and commitments. Many also still carry the silly belief that "they know things better than everyone else". Until young people understand fully the meaning of being a part of a family, they are not fit for discipleship. A student made disciple who is too young, will end up shaming the gongfu family by misbehavior towards superiors in public, and failing to fulfill some of the duties allotted to him.

Awaiting 3 years at the least before discipleship is due to the fact that, on average in human relationships, you need at least 3 years of close familiarity to get to know someone well. Some teachers test students for 10 years or more before allowing them to become disciples. Personally, I find that excessive. Remember that the best way to make people trust you, is to put trust in them.

7. Is diligent in his study and practice of martial arts. This includes having passed technical rank tests and having shown improvement in skill over the years. Also, minimal expected attendance in classes, and willingness to train more and work harder in the future.

8. Is intelligent and makes an effort to acquire further education. I believe that truly stupid people are rare. The majority of those whom we consider 'dumb' simply lost track of education at an early age, and have not learned to use their minds properly. As a martial arts teacher, we and our art can make them more intelligent. But until they become so, they should not be made family. Additionally, they need to want to acquire further education, which needs not necessarily be formal. Diplomas are not that important, as much as the learning itself. Uninquisitive people make for poor family members. Make sure therefore that the candidate is not ignorant, and is eager to learn.

9. Is free of addictions. This includes alcohol, drugs, cigarettes, and whatever may resemble them in habit. The destruction of the body will eventually make a person dumber, less able, and worse yet – a financial liability on his martial arts family. The addictions take precedent over family, and therefore must be eliminated.

10. Maintains good relationships with his peers at the school. A person who is considered problematic by several people in the school cannot be made into a disciple. This would set up a bad personal example and breed bad politics and resentments. Even if the person is upright and worthy in your opinion, he needs to first correct at least some of his relationships within the school before he can become family. Take the initiative and help him achieve this by mending old wounds and unnecessary rivalries.

The requirements for discipleship should not be thought of as a point-based test. It is an 'either all or nothing' situation. A person who cannot abide by all 10 requirements, should not be a disciple.

Expectations from Disciples

1. Set a moral personal example in the Wu Guan[71] and outside of it. People are not perfect. This expectation would need to be later further encouraged and enforced for most people. A wise Shifu would know how to use the right disciples to sway another in the right direction.

2. Retain your good name, and work toward making a good name for your teacher and Wu Guan. A person's reputation is like an invisible shadow which forever stalks him, and is constantly expanding in all directions. A school's reputation is the same. Student recruitment, financial success and the future of the teachings on depend on such reputation.

3. Aid fellow members of your gongfu family to the best of your ability. The model should be a happy, functional and moral biological family. Mutual aid makes this privileged 'social club' into a lifeline in times of crisis, and can also aid by making connections in personal and business matters alike. The concept of Guanxi needs to be made clear to disciples from the time before they were chosen. One for all, and all for one.

4. Show preference in friendship and favours to members of your gongfu family over most other people, and regard them as equal or superior to your biological family. I have no shame in professing that a good gongfu family should be supportive of nepotism, as long as it is applied within reasonable and legal guidelines. It helps to have a member of the gongfu family who is an attorney, to aid with that. A gongfu family is, in part, a sort of little 'secret society', and such was always the nature of these establishments.

---

71 Wǔ Guǎn 武館, meaning 'Martial Hall', is the traditional name given to a martial arts academy in China. It is the equivalent to the term Dōjō 道場 .

5. Refrain from abusing the support of fellow members of your gongfu family. As the Shifu, you have the obligation to enforce this expectation to the utmost. Make sure that when major resources are allocated, it underwent prior deliberations and received your approval.

6. Commit to excellence in your training more so than casual practitioners. The disciples need to set a personal example for others. Doing is by showing commitment to training is one important way to make it manifest.

7. In respect for your teacher and your ancestors in the martial arts, commit to teaching at least one person in your lifetime, to the best of your ability, what you have been taught, to the fullest extent possible. This expectation, a disciple may sometimes carry forth only years or decades after having joined the gongfu family. To help ensure this would happen, always tell the disciples that teaching is the venue through which one learns best, of himself and his martial art. That much is true, and will hopefully motivate them.

8. Continue your positive association, affiliation and commitment towards your gongfu family, even if by accident, disaster or other unfortunate circumstances, your cease training. A family is forever. A person who does not understand that, should not have been chosen as a disciple to begin with. The only circumstances under which I can conceive of a disciple leaving a family, are by means of being expelled due to extremely inappropriate behaviour.

While I see the requirements for discipleship as being absolutely essential and irreplaceable for any gongfu family, the expectations from disciples can naturally vary a lot between schools.

A young teacher should be eager to have his first 1-2 disciples, but choose them more carefully than those who would follow. The first 1-2 disciples would often serve as the main supporting pillars of the school, aside from the Shifu himself. They set a personal example which comes from the student body itself, thus making it easier for the other students to relate to their upright behaviour. When I appointed my first disciple, Noam, he was only 20 years old. While worthy in terms of skill and character, he was still too immature at the time to bear the family responsibilities pertaining to things like logistics and leadership. He caught on to those gradually in the years to follow. Though I had not other options at the time, a person over the age of 25 would have made for a better first disciple. My second disciple, Yaniv, became family at the age of 35. His vast life experience served to counter-balanced his gongfu brother Noam and bring him into the fold.

For the middle-aged or senior teacher, the opposite is true. He should not at all be eager to accept new disciples, and rather than preferring the older folks, the younger lads pose an advantage.
The veteran teacher ought to already have some disciples in the family. Then these questions arise: how many should there be, really? Is there even a final limit to such a number?

Well, consider this akin to having a biological family. A young adult, under normal circumstances of the human condition, usually wants to have children as soon as has the time, career-allowance and financial capacity afford it. That is similar to the situation with the young teacher hoping to have disciples. The children and disciples are important to the father and the Shifu not just emotionally, but also as they quickly become a helping hand in the family business and in the business of running of family. But as the years go by, 4 children can yield 2-4 grand-children each, who may each yield several grand-children of their own; not to mention the spouses they married and their relatives, who also become family members. With biological families, within several **decades**, we could be looking at group of 20-50 people, and more. But in martial arts families, what may take the upwards of 80-90 years in terms of multiplying biological family members, can manifest within a third of that time! For a new disciple may enter the martial arts family every 2-10 years (sometime several together), and student who is a Shifu himself could begin taking in disciples, too. Then how many people can one really deal with in a reasonable way? That would depend on the emotional and organizational capacity of the head of the martial arts family.

I have a colleague in the martial arts who is a very famous teacher. Let us call him master Dong. When master Dong was a younger man, he had very few disciples – perhaps only 3 of them. But further into his career when he was middle-aged , master Dong sought to expand his school, and later organization, all over the world. To achieve this, he appointed many disciples, and eventually gave a lot of them a teaching license. Trouble was, master Dong went a tad overboard with his attitude towards discipleship... Within a decade, he had over 200 disciples! This, I gather, must have backfired. For how can any man truly operate a group of 200 people like a singular, biological family? Such a task is impossible. Beyond the ridiculous logistics required, people could never relate to, or even come to know, all of their gongfu family. [72] The disciples facing such a scenario can also become resentful, for having been allotted a 'special status' which is no longer a rarity. As in the famous law of markets: when there is excess in supply, there tends to be less of a demand. When discipleship appointments become too common, then the value of what it means to be a disciple, sadly diminishes.

There is also the opposite example. There was in the 20th century a very famous teacher of Bagua Zhang called Xie Peiqi. The lineage of the art taught by master Xie was Yin style Bagua Zhang. This lineage includes a vast amount of material. Most practitioners would require over a decade to study and embody all of the curriculum even if they practiced with their teacher for several hours a day, and few can manage to learn even a third of that complex system.

---

[72] You may remember 'Dunbar's Number' from the chapter titled '**Not a Business, But a Community**'. Please refer to that chapter. In short, Dunbar's Number suggests that there is anthropological and sociological evidence to show, humans thrive in social groups of up to about 150 people. In groups greater than that, social coherence and harmony are disrupted.

Because the transmission of that tradition requires the teacher to invest over a decade in essentially living with a disciple in order that he could become its inheritor, master Xie took it upon himself to invest much time and effort to pass it on to the next generation. Unfortunately due to sad circumstances, his top disciple and contender for inheriting the style died prematurely at a relatively young age. Master Xie was at loss, but eventually found another person who was trained well and become the successor, whose name is He Jinbao. But master Xie was already old (though still strong and vigorous) when he taught He Jinbao. Had he not found He Jinbao in time, or was something to happen to He Jinbao, that particular tradition could have died with master Xie, and lost forever. That is what can happen, when the teacher takes too few disciples, or teaches only a few disciples the full curriculum.

Therefore we see, that having too many or too few disciples, can both pose problems and challenges. What then should or could be the golden number? I personally believe that a good number to strive for would be between 10-50 disciples, spread across one's martial arts teaching career. Consider also, that each of them may end teaching and having their own disciples, meaning that if they were also to have 10-50 disciples each, the size of the family at the generation of the grand-disciples, could reach some 100-2500 people (10 disciples with 10 grand-disciples each being the minimum = 100 people, and 50 disciples with 50 grand-disciples each being the maximum = 2500 people). A martial arts gongfu family with 100 – 2500 people is a force to be reckoned with. Even the minimum number is formidable. It makes for a small army. These the economic power, connections, favours and communal strength of such a group is tremendous. When such a family was build based on strong moral foundations, amazing things can be achieved. It is both a guild and a paternal fraternity, and as such should strive for high standards of conduct, else politics can make it disintegrate.

Consider that even if the number 2500 sounds a bit excessive, it is not terrible given the conditions. The Shifu only needs to know well and be in close contact with his own disciples (of which I have suggested, it is best to have no more than 50). The Shifu and the grand-disciples are more distant from one-another, though still

committed to the same solid bond which is the lineage. In any case, for most schools, reaching 50 disciples who are up to standard and having them appoint 2500 disciples altogether, would be a measure of outstanding and unheard of success. More likely for most that the numbers shall be much lower, if indeed the rules, regulations and expectations are upheld as I have previously explained and recommended.
The Shifu also has the right and authority to decide to 'close his hands'. One may opt to stop teachings, or simply choose to not accept disciples anymore, and send discipleship candidates to study under his own disciples. Such are good ways to avoid an overt surplus of disciples.

Earlier I have written, but have yet to explain why, for veteran teachers, young people ought to be targeted and preferred for discipleship. The reason is that the older the teacher becomes, the more fossilized the mindset of the school turns with him. I have seen many teachers past the age of 55, whose approach reflects the world they were living when they were teenagers and young adults. They were alienated and blinded from the wishes and culture of the younger generation, because most of their students were past the age of 40. This is a treacherous swamp which a long-lived martial arts schools can easily slide into. The teachers can feel comfortable in the waters they have grown accustomed to, without realizing these had long-since turned stale. As with a biological family, the arrival of a newborn when the other children have already matured, can positively transform the extended clan, and drive new and exciting energies into the household. Such can be also some promising younger disciples, who are added to a well-established gongfu family. They themselves can be made to feel honoured by the opportunity, whilst the elders can be honoured by them as their seniors. A careful and dignified introduction of the newcomers into the fold can thus be a blessing to all.

The Colleagues You Choose

Apart from our martial arts family, what commonly defines us in the public's eye is the professional company we keep – our colleagues. One ought to be extremely careful in his choice of colleagues. In any professional sphere, people actively search for allies. You will likely seek such people, and you would be surprised to find that, if your name is out there, they will also be finding you. Then, offers are made.

"How about we have a joint class with our students?"

"Let us organize a seminar together!"

"I think it would be fantastic to join our organizations."

I would be extremely thrifty, cautious and prudent in agreeing to any such suggestions or similar. Likewise, I would be very careful in considering someone's offer to read or watch his book or video, with him expecting me to later promote them. These are often, though not always, traps. You can effortlessly find yourself in a deep hole that you cannot get out of without becoming dirtied in the process. Here is what happens:

You spot an opportunity. You are trying to be a good person. You may also be flattered that a colleague has put faith in you. So you say "YES". Then sooner or later you find out, that there is a problem. The colleague is not who he seemed to be. Perhaps he has a terrible reputation; or he may be corrupt, even mentally unstable. We have our fair share of problematic characters in the martial arts, you know. But then, you are stuck. For once you got in the game, there are only two options – either you play along, or you get out abruptly. Playing along causes you one type of trouble, and getting out, another. For people with whom 'you agreed to play' do not see to kindly that you choose to abandon them, and they tend to remember and tell others of what a terrible person you are.

Moreover, once the public knows you have been associated with that colleague, it is not easy to shake off that association. I recall for instance, there was a friend of mine many years back who was a very successful and skilled Karate Sensei. I liked the man. He was genuine, fun to be around, and overall a good guy. I knew him from before I was a teacher myself. He was educated, respected among his peers and his future seemed promising. Then one day, he flipped.

Well... This was not really a 1-second process, of course. Due to some private circumstances and life changes, his dojo's etiquette and community deteriorated, in terms of their values. A cult-of-personality sort of setting emerged, which though mild, was

disturbing. Eventually, the Sensei opted to join a television show of the 'Reality-TV' genre, notorious for its provocative contents. That decision led to the breaking down of his dojo over time. Following these events, he began to associate with questionable 'celebrities' and adopted a persona much unlike that he had before. Though I was always convinced that deep inside must have still lurked the same lovely guy I knew before, his public image was now very different.
I broke off my ties with the man as soon as his natural charisma began sweeping his school in a direction which was not to my liking. However, I knew that our mutual association was by then too strong. For a long time, people kept pestering me with questions about him, and why we were related, even though we were not. It had taken years for this association to fade among the public, and there was hardly anything I could do about it.

My main advice to you would be, that one ought to choose wisely and carefully. One should pick as his associates those who share the same values as he does, are of a similar or higher social standing, and hopefully a similar or higher level of education. When professional reputation is concerned, one could not afford 'charity cases'. To uplift those who have a problematic public image, one has to already possess an incredibly powerful social standing. Only then could a teacher risk to support those whom others look upon as troublesome or unworthy, without too much damage inflicted to oneself.

Remember Your Origins

Our journey through intimate interpersonal relationships, be them romantic or otherwise, takes us through three main stages.

1. In the beginning, we fall in love with the other person and what he or she represent. We create a glorified image of the human in front of us, which is more positive and flattering than that person actually is (naturally, we do not become close with those whose vices stand out more than their virtues).

2. Later if the relationship persists, as we come to know these people, we are gradually disillusioned with their mannerisms, and their aura diminishes in our eyes. Still, we find a balance between their flaws of character and our wish to keep them in our lives. Otherwise, we move on.

3. Finally, after several years or decades of familiarity, we are able to see people for who they truly and honestly are. Their drawbacks, defects, blemishes and weaknesses are as evident and obvious to us as black cat in a white room. Still, we may nonetheless accept them as they are, for what they are, and continue to cherish and perhaps even love them, despite of and perhaps in light of, our understanding of their complexities.

It can be argued that in the martial arts, our relationships with our teachers pass through the same three stages. At first we are 'in love' and at awe of them. Later they become multifaceted individuals with many layers to their being. Finally, with enough time, as we all grow and mature, we arrive at the somewhat shocking realization that they are, most often, like us - simply ordinary human beings, albeit perhaps with exceptional skills, abilities, talents and knowledge.
In a sense, unless the martial arts school operates like a sort of cult, the students do eventually comprehend the humanity of their teachers. However, in my experience, if does take people a very long

time, often years or decades, to completely depart from their overwhelmingly positive bias of such authority figures.

The three stages of disillusionment are for us a test of character. Can we continue and appreciate our teachers, even as their constitution and disposition are not as glorious to us as before? That is a difficult question and challenge we face as teachers ourselves, especially as we set out to establish our own schools, organizations, curriculums and legacies. There is a clash between our yearning to transcend past generations, and our need to respect them. For how can one sustain a healthy measure of deference, whilst venturing to exceed his own ancestors and superiors? All the more pertinent, when this is accompanied by a teacher of ours who had over time revealed himself to be depraved or otherwise sinful and wicked.

Many a time, this bothersome dilemma leads people, even those who are otherwise morally upright, to begin to belittle and deride their own teachers, in their own mind and possibly even in speech, in front of students and other spectators. In our modern tongue, we refer to this phenomenon as: "Spitting into the well from which you drink". Unless one's teacher is of an utmost righteous and honorable demeanor, a real saint, then by all means, one is quite likely to slander or stain his good name in some way at least a few times, either intentionally or accidentally, as the years go by. This is similar to an adolescent lad attempting to come in grips with his parents and upbringing. He feels almost compelled to rebel and 'attack' them, on his quest to find balance and self-definition. Their blunders and failings require illumination, in our foolish thinking, so that growth can occur.

As we thus arrive at the point during which our being is compelled to be critical towards our own teachers, we should abandon the present moment, and instead remember the past and consider the future. On the professional front, everything we are today was made possible by our teachers in the martial arts. They likely worked tirelessly and sacrificed a lot, to be capable of handing over to us their knowledge and insights. Such is the past, with its culmination of an interpersonal relationship which is far heftier and more substantial, much of the time, than any imperfections our teacher may manifest. Then future-wise, we ought to take into account our own image and heritage. The personal example we set forth, is the one usually adopted by our students. As we present our teachers, so shall we be scrutinized in the passing of time.

"***When a student reaches a level at which he is qualified to teach, he often truly recognizes, for the first time, how talented his teacher is***" – Sang H. Kim [73]

---

[73] Sang H. Kim, ***Teaching Martial Arts***, Turtle Press, Chapter 2: The Essence of Teaching, page 37; Second edition, 1999CE.

Who Needs Traditions, Anyway?

When I was younger, I thought that the main reason traditional martial arts require Structure, is that they cannot exist otherwise. But then one day, I discovered I was wrong. Along came a Russian martial art called 'Systema', and proved me otherwise. After having had exposure to this martial art, I needed to reconsider the whole notion of why we hold our own martial traditions as so sacred. This text I have written as means of dealing with this dilemma.

The term 'Systema' simply means 'System', and refers to a number of martial arts lineages originating from Russia, featuring mostly original materials. These schools of martial arts have been on the receiving end of a lot of criticism throughout the early 21st century. That was because a number of teachers from said schools presented themselves publicly with magic tricks and charlatanism, which were considered ridiculous to experienced martial artists of other styles. But allow me to assure you, that among the jokers are also a good number of excellent teachers, who engage in authentic and effective combative teachings. One of these people is my friend and colleague, Sharon Friedman.

Playing pretend is all nice and dandy in a seminar setting with an audience of blind worshipers, which is the preferred mode of engagement for Systema charlatans. But it is a whole other ball-game when a man like Sharon Friedman, who has been infantry for decades, gets a call and is told that his service is once again needed across the border. For Israelis like Sharon, that border can be as little as 30-120km away. One day you are playing with your young child; then eight hours later, you can find yourself in a war zone. Sharon has been living that reality for a very long time. He cannot afford playing pretend. When something is not martially viable, that means he may not see his family again the next day. Not many martial artists can say this in our day and age! Therefore, Sharon's Systema reflects the need to effective combative methods.

Sharon's Systema is also really a spit in the face of countless things which the traditional martial arts take for granted. Ranks, rules, lineages, dress codes, hierarchies, ceremonies and other traditions are, for the most part, non-existent. Even martial applications do not really exist in the form of a curriculum. Only principles of movement are taught. Hardly any exercises are routine. Techniques and other movements are never repeated more than once in succession, since Systema encourages the free-flow of energy, and since every single movement in combat is different, the energy cannot be 'forced' to go the same route as immediately before - it always changes. The body is seldom propelled with forced effort, but rather by allowing momentum from one lever to affect the next, moving almost is if one were a 'perpetual motion machine'. This sort of movement pattern can look odd and even clumsy, but with the right intent can prove deadly effective. The art encourages one to move the opponent not by coercion but rather through 'agreeing' with his pressure, and leaning into his weakest point in order to destroy his balance. Because of these unique attributes, the traditional martial arts which Systema ends up being most similar to, in my opinion, are Zui Quan (Drunken Boxing), and to a lesser extent Bagua Zhang.

Yet despite some surface similarities, because of the first set of unusual traits I have detailed above, Systema has a philosophy which stands in strong opposition to that of traditional martial arts, especially of the Chinese variety, which covet structure, cherish order, and abide by the Confucian world view. The name 'Systema' is somewhat ironic in this respect, as it is likely the most unsystematic martial arts system ever devised. It is as if a bunch of crazy Russian radicals decided to make a martial art based on the combined precepts of Libertarianism and Anarchism with a touch of drunken wisdom, and somehow succeeded. The practitioner of the traditional arts is then forced to contend with the fact that this very absurd-sounding and seemingly-unreasonable idea actually works. It is as if a hardcore Capitalist had found a large, thriving community of happy Communists, or a Catholic priest discovering surprising wisdom in Hindu sacred polytheistic scripture. That is to say, that when a seasoned practitioner of the traditional martial arts acknowledges the value in Systema, this means one has to inspect deeply and confront his innermost beliefs as to what he considered a foundation for his entire practice, in order to live in peace with the fact that something so radically different can be convincing and legitimate.

Fortunately, it appears that Sharon and I speak the same language. In fact, I have found more commonalities with his general approach to combat than I do with a few traditional Chinese martial arts I know. His Systema talks about the same general principles which all of the internal arts share. Things like moving from the Kua and Dan Tian, being soft but not flaccid, yielding without losing, rotating with circles and spirals at all times, allowing the energy of the opponent and the moment decide the right course of action, basing movement on one's internal sense of balance rather than trying to outdo the other person, freeing to area where the opponent does not put pressure, etc. In terms of movement principles then, indeed, we are quite similar. The main differences appear in terms of the interpretation of how best to resolve the opportunities which arise, and how to teach this thing to begin with. The greatest difference then being, what we consider 'traditional'.

From Sharon's point of view, Systema is a philosophy of life. It is a statement about personal freedom. His art is something which can only be embodied or helped in finding within oneself. Learning it cannot be coerced in any way, and he has no wishes to do such things, or for a matter of fact to force anyone to do anything whatsoever, unless he himself is forced to make something happen. His Systema does not differ much from his own personality; though I have found myself mocking him for orderly cutting up his schnitzel before eating it, with a structure and procedure befitting a real authoritarian and not the free spirit which he usually is. He laughed. He is a really funny guy. I doubt someone could hurt his ego with a schnitzel joke. He does not not put much of an Ego out there to be shot at, and whatever is presented yields effortlessly.

So why do I practice and teach traditional Chinese martial arts, and not Systema? Or otherwise, why not adopt a Systema-like approach to teaching? This is an important question to ask. My answer was found, surprisingly enough, in thinking of Anthropology.

What Systema represents, in my opinion, is the ancient method of teaching among humans, based on patterns rather than repetition. The transmission of knowledge is undertaken in a raw format, with little theory or structure. The focus is laid upon highly individualistic development; like a bushman instructing his son on the capture and killing of animals. Only the natural principles are preserved. Much as in our hunter-gatherer days, before civilization. Although some lineages of Systema affiliate themselves with Christianity, the method itself has a very Pagan vibe to it. Not in the religious sense of the term, but in the manner of conceiving the teachings. The movement patterns, exercises and thinking are quite primordial, but in no sense 'primitive'. It is advanced technology of survival, encapsulated in an organic form.

The story of the Garden of Eden tells of the descent of humans from 'Paradise'. In the metaphorical sense it is also a tale of the transition of humans from natural habitats into settlements, and their choice of leaving behind the law of the jungle in favour of laws we ourselves created. When we invented modern societies, we paid a heavy price for distancing ourselves from Nature and our connection to it. Systema is, as I see it, a rare breed of martial art which connects people to their inner animal in a very deep way. That is unlike the Internal martial arts of China, which although aspiring to embody naturalness and natural principles, still assume movement patterns and teaching curriculums which are innately complex and cultured.

The burden of tradition and civilization alike, is that they bind you to a path, and often to an occupation as well. Even a master is not truly liberated, for he operates within the world of human concepts. So for example, the farmer cannot leave his field for too long; The shopkeeper cannot abandon his business without special arrangements; he craftsman requires a market to sell his goods and needs to keep manufacturing what people desire; and so forth. Likewise, the traditional martial artist has exercises, forms and movements, which amount to a curriculum, that he needs to practice regularly to sustain. It is the collector's dilemma – you want to have many things, but having them requires that you constantly cater for them, too. Eventually you become endlessly occupied with 'stuff'. Preservation becomes a chore. That is the point at which great masters, like many of those who created the traditional Chinese martial arts, condensed their methods and principles, to prevent their systems from becoming too overwhelming and difficult to learn and maintain.

My argument nonetheless is that despite the failings and challenges of tradition, it is worthwhile. The Old Testament arrives at the same conclusion, irrespective of religion. Despite the allegory of the fall of man from heaven, the Bible still spends the greater portion of the rest of the story justifying human existence in the framework of traditions. It is a philosophical statement about human society, asserting that although it is flawed, there is merit to its mechanism.

Repetitions is frowned upon in most drills in Systema. But as traditional martial artists, we understand the value of repetition. What we get from repetition is an enlightenment of a method or a principle. We do not simply do it – we can understand it. That is the essence of being a modern human. Our primal ancestors survived brilliantly for hundreds of thousands of years, with natural grace. But they could never rise much above their inherent nature, until they had become civilized. Yet civilization was not attained by coincidence, but rather through intentful creation.
Repetition! The ape who repeated the construction of a stone knife,

until he had it right. **Repetition!** The farmer who repeated the sowing of seeds season after season, until he could finally yield a proper crop. **Repetition!** The physicist who repeated simple equations, until his skill became sufficient to help build a spaceship.

Repetition, with intent. Repetition, with structure. Repetition, that gradually transforms into a tradition. What are the traditional martial arts, if not the sum of such repetitions? Each generation is the repetition of the previous one, hoping to improve upon previous attempts. To teach repetition, and to teach the lessons of the many past repetitions, is to be the human who stepped out the jungle or the savanna.

We might be tempted to idolize the supposed nobility of Systema's approach, of not holding unto anything or anyone. But that would be throwing ourselves in the direction of one extreme. The other extreme would be a total dictatorship, cloning people like robots, as some countries and martial arts organizations nowadays yearn to do with their citizens and students.

Tradition is neither of these extremes. The concept of Tradition in the martial arts is to balance between the need for personal freedom of expression, and a binding structure we inherit from past generations. Though I have earlier suggested that civilizations and traditions supposedly enslave us, that is only half the truth. They also liberate us from animalism and provide us with a venue through which, we can become something more.

What are the most important things to any human? They are arguably: Happiness, Meaning and Continuity. Nearly everyone wants to be happy, to have a meaningful life, and to feel that their essence, either biological or philosophical, continues to live after they have passed away. These three treasures – Happiness, Meaning and Continuity – are offered to us via the concept of Tradition. **Happiness**, we find through the joy of the practice, and especially when repetition provides us with a sense of security and accomplishment. **Meaning**, we attain because traditions allow greater understanding of what we do, building on the accumulated wisdom of past generations. **Continuity**, we establish by including a part of ourselves in that which is passed on to our students, and do so in a very intentful manner. We also have Meaning in allowing the continuity of past generations to flow through us.

Thus, the Structure which is a house, is to the bushman perhaps a four-walled prison, but to the modern man a shelter, and a glorious invention full of potential. Surely, the house has it challenges and limitations, but nonetheless, few today would cherish and choose the 'freedom' which can be derived from living in an arbitrary tent. Yet it is not a bad idea, for the landlord to go about the occasional hikes in the wilderness, and for the aboriginal to find comfort in a fortress once in a while. Both can learn a lot from the experience.

Examine Yourself

It is relatively easy being sincere with others.
It is more difficult to be honest with yourself.

Confucius said: "*When you see the Junzi*[74]*, aspire to be like him. When you see a person who is not a Junzi – examine yourself.*"

This proverb by Confucius is interesting , because it does not follow typical 'Western' logic, which considers the negative to be the opposite of the positive. Most people would expect, that since Confucius recommend we imitate the virtuous man, he would also likely wish for us to not be like that person whom we consider unvirtuous and immoral. Yet Confucius thought otherwise. He does not call upon us to reject outright those people whom we might consider problematic. His message is far more humane and complex.

Why then does Confucius suggest that we "examine ourselves"? This is because inside us there are prejudice and bias which lead us to view someone as "negative" or "morally flawed". We must surpass our sense of self-worth and seriously consider the following questions: What makes he who stands in front of me, a person with whom I disagree? Would I not have acted the same or similarly to him had I been in his condition and under the same circumstances? If not, how would have I acted? These are perhaps the most important questions to ask.

Then, we may investigate deeper: What are the motivations of said person to act in the manner in which he did? Is my way necessarily superior or more appropriate than his? Few are those

---

[74] Junzi 君子 – a term meaning 'A Gentleman'; a virtuous man; a person with worthy moral virtues and behaviour. Someone who is both educated and humane. Often referred to as 'the superior man'. Becoming such a person is the Confucian ideal.

who can overcome their automatic reactions towards the people different to them, and succeed with an intentional and continuous effort, during their daily lives, in finding the spiritual fortitude to remain logically and emotionally objective. Here therefore Confucius reveals to us a profound life philosophy – instead of using the 'problem-person' we meet as an excuse for anger, rejection and the fortifying of our pre-existing opinions, we can make that person into a vessel for our self-improvement – just as we should do with those whom we consider virtuous.

Of this Confucius additionally said: "*When I walk in the company of two men, each of them will be my teacher. I shall pick the good points from one of them and imitate these, while the bad points of the other – I shall correct within myself*".

Later, the Confucian scholar Mencius added his own interpretation: "*Whenever you take care of others, yet they still do not return you affection, examine yourself – were you truly good? Whenever you give advice to others, but they refuse to accept it, examine yourself – was your advice truly wise? Whenever you are polite towards others, but they still do not return in kind, examine yourself – were you sincere?*".

Real Time

In martial arts there is real practice time and perceived practiced time. Some people say they practice for 2 hours. All fine and dandy, but when you come to watch them train you seen it is actually 90% chatting with friends and 10% training. This was not two hours – that was a total of 12 minutes!

But you play the same game as a martial arts teacher. You also like telling yourself you are doing more than you really are doing. Do you count these hours teaching students as genuine practice time? I do not. I have my own practice time, by myself or with veteran students, gongfu brothers or colleagues, and then I have the lessons I teach, which I consider to be just extra. For a lot of teachers though, they consider their classes to an integral part of their practice time, or even all of it. Well, this is just you kidding yourself. You may be getting some practice, and more than likely a decent workout, but this is not **REAL TIME**. This is not the time that matters, and not the way to really push forward and stay ahead. Be honest about it. Make the effort. Get real practice time. This is what sets you apart from the amateurs. They get to some of the classes. You attend 99.9% of the classes and then spend more time practicing on your own. This is partly why you are worthy of being called a martial arts teacher. Prove yourself worthy of the title.

The Most Genuine Question

John Taylor Gatto (1935 – 2018CE) was a famous American educator and pubic speaker. He spent three decades in the United States' public school system, thrice earning the title of 'New York City's Teacher of the Year', and once the title of 'New York State Teacher of the Year'. It is obvious then, that this exceptional individual, John Taylor Gatto, used to not only work for the 'system', but was also highly appreciated for his work.
But having grown wiser over the years, Gatto finally decided to quit his job as a school teacher, having become fed up with what he considered to be the physical and psychological mass-torture of young people. He spent the latter half of his adult life lecturing and preaching against the system he once used to diligently serve.

There is much wisdom to gain by listening to John Taylor Gatto, and as he frequently appealed to teachers, a lot of it is relevant to us as well. Once thing Gatto said in particular, struck a chord with me. He proclaimed the following of his role as a teacher:
"I believe that it is the right of every child to ask, in a polite way... Taking into account that I am only human... What is it that we are doing here (in the classroom), and why are we doing it? And if I cannot answer that question well, then I think that child is entitled to leave the premises and do as he pleases, as long as he does not go wild and brings the house down". Such is the most genuine and fundamental question that a student may pose to a teacher – including he who instructs the martial arts.

This is a very controversial statement to make in the context of public schools, but in my opinion, less so for our own establishments. This is where we must cultivate honesty and humility. Can we say such a thing to our students? Are we truly knowledgeable enough of our skills and methods, to be able to come up with a reasonable answer to most things they might ask? And if not – how could we work hard to remedy the situation?

Case in point, would be the novel and often strange ideas on how to interpret movement forms in the traditional martial arts (Kata or Taulu). We have all been there. Having learned a movement or two from our teachers, we are confronted by a situation wherein a student asks us about the martial usage of said movements. We then realize, that we have never had the opportunity to ask our teachers about the meaning of these movements, of which our student now inquires. Worse yet, we have discounted our ignorance over the years, and never bothered to have a decent reality-check of these movements. Now, we are stuck.
You know what the most common scenario is then, right? The teacher, being embarrassed and wishing to avoid losing face, makes up a vague explanation and attempts to sweep the question under the rug; or opting for the inferior option – makes up some interpretation on-the-fly, which would not likely work in real life, or even in class for that matter.

There are two corrections to be made here, on part of the teacher. The first would be in the immediate proximity to the embarrassment. A true professional should possess the spine and integrity to tell a student that he does not know; which does not mean that he could not add, that he would pursue and come back with an answer some time later!
The second proper correction would be for the teacher to sincerely seek explanations and clarifications for those holes present in his curriculum and understanding of it. This includes going back to one's teacher and bowing down once more, or sometimes asking colleagues humbly for instruction with respect to a particular dilemma as such.

By knowing well not only our techniques and methods, but also the reasons for why we teach, why we do things and why we ask others to imitate us, we then become upright and worthy role models. With a genuine spirit and a striving for authenticity, this can be made possible. Then, when students ask us why a certain thing is there, we would have the answers which they deserve.

No Apologies

I grew up in a culture which does not believe in needlessly apologizing to other people. It is considered a sign a weakness to do so, and attracts negative attention from abusers and wrongdoers, who immediately spot a potential victim. Trust me when I say this as a former policeman – when your apologies are overdone, the most vile of creatures are drawn to you like a moth to a flame. Needlessly apologizing is also the mark of the submissive – it is not befitting of a person such as a martial arts teacher, who ought to be in a position of leadership.

In everyday life, I do apologize frequently, and also do my best to admit my mistakes when due. But I do not take a proactive approach about it. Rather, it happens only when necessary. Etiquette is essential – being overly accommodating, is not.

In martial arts we have a very strange phenomenon in that respect. Some of us have adopted a mode of 'apologetics'. I am talking of martial artists, especially teachers, who blubber endlessly about why their martial art should be THIS, but it is actually THAT.

You know what I am talking about. Those teachers who say: "***Oh back in the days, a few hundred years ago, our martial art could have been used for real fighting. Nowadays we are more at ease, less confrontational***"; or the others who proclaim: "***Well of course what I teach you cannot be at its most effective. We are not like the sports fighters who train 6 hours every day. We simply lack that level of fitness and professionalism. But otherwise, we could have been more combatively viable***"; then there is also the likes of: "***We could be deadly but we prefer to focus on health***"; and even: "***This technique is too dangerous to be taught in full***".

Such words, although common, are of no sense to me personally. But we ought to ask: why do teachers express such things in the first place? The answers are:

1. To sell something – they feel that apologetics would better present the material to people who are interested in studying it, whether new or veteran students.

2. To justify themselves to others – for whatever reason.

My beliefs are as follows. Whether your martial arts are more combative or decidedly peaceful – all is good as long as you deliver decent instruction. Apple and Oranges – to each his own. Whom am I to judge something which I do not understand?
But, that being said, I do not buy into the notion that anyone should be apologetic in order to convince others to have interest in their 'product'. You can arouse interest without resorting to the negative. I also do not believe in the need for expressing any form of an 'inferiority complex'. A teacher who feels inferior, should consider perhaps whether he ought to teach to begin with.

Let us assume that you feel somewhat unconfident or incompetent to a degree with you martial art, even as a teacher. Alright, it happens to all of us at least a few times in our career. The question remains – why ought you share such feelings with students? What benefit could possibly be derived from it?
The students look up to the teacher as an authority figure. The teacher may be wrong or insecure. Granted, we are often wrong and sometimes insecure. But this cannot be too frequently shown to the students or shared with them in any way!
The students who step into your school are looking to 'purchase' a 'vehicle' for success and happiness. Imagine yourself going to purchase a car at a dealership. The car salesman tells you, that he is not sure whether the emergency safety mechanisms will engage during an accident. You are likely to not buy a car from him, and in fact will probably never walk into that dealership again. Possibly, you may share this awkward story about the car saleseman with friends, too. Even if you were naïve enough to still purchase the car from that salesman, you will always remember his insecure statement, and it would haunt you for years. That is the sort of damage, that apologetic statements can do with students.

Additionally, why ought a student follow a person who is not decided and resolute in his ways? People can detect insecurities from a mile away, especially if you post them on a giant billboard.

So what ought you do instead? Well for starters, correct yourself. In the event that you believe that something is 'wrong' or 'off' about what you teach – change it! Or otherwise, perhaps look for another martial art to provide better answers. Self-doubt is seldom an empty statement. It points to a problem inside of you that needs solving [75].

Then in class, rather than focusing on the negative, stress the positive. You do not have to blubber on and on about what the art is not. Instead, speak of its strengths and positive aspects. There is **no need to apologize** for what is 'missing'. The students are present in the class because they think they can gain something, and not because they believe that the teaching is 'lacking'. The notion of something which is missing, is most often a fabrication of the teacher's own mind, and would not have occurred to most students if it was not said. The teacher's own inferiority complex, can through apologetics spread self-doubt like a disease. It is a plague of

---

[75] A good example is the ever-controversial topic of ground-grappling. It is an element which was historically 'missing' in most traditional martial arts. But there are solutions. Some teachers resort to studying martial arts focused on ground-grappling, such as Brazilian Jujutsu, Pankration or Penchak Silat, and teach them alongside their original style. Others have, through the studies of other arts, developed an approach to ground-grappling based on their own style. Either way, such people acted to resolve the problem of self-doubt they may have had with regard to ground-grappling, rather than complain about it.

Another decent example is that of one's inability to use a traditional martial art combatively, or to make one's techniques and principals manifest in a live combative environment. This is usually the result of lack of certain training methods, rather an innate flaw in the art. But teachers and students commonly prefer to complain and apologize, claiming that 'the art is somewhat anachronistic'. In so doing they spit in the face of their martial ancestors and call them stupid, which they likely were not. A martial art which is 200 years old but fails to work combatively in modern times, is usually the fault of the modern practitioner and not of the art itself or past teachers. It is easy to blame your predecessors or apologize for their 'inadequacies' in creating something 'flawed'. It is more difficult to work on changing yourself and work hard to make what you have work, or admit that perhaps you should be practicing something else.

your own making, and its main symptoms are lower student retention and a less overall confidence and ability among those who remain.

Therefore, my teaching ideology includes **NO APOLOGIES.** When I compare my martial arts to anything, then it would be for purely technical reasons. I refrain from initiating a discussion in which the mode of express is: "Our art should be THIS, but is instead THAT". This is passive-aggressive and I do not like it. Wherein you believe that your martial art should be something, then make it so, or alternatively, change the way in which you think of it and teach it to other people. But do not make excuses or express apologetics for "what it should be".

The bottom line is, that it does not matter what your art looks, feels or operates like, as compared with other martial arts. You owe nobody any apologies for doing what you love and believe in. Flaws in your practice or teachings, can and should be corrected. But the students need not be exposed to any of the inner insecurities of their teacher. Rather than talking about what your martial art is not, speak of what it can do for people in their personal life. When questioned about the 'downsides' of the teachings, talk frankly and honestly, but do not apologize, and attempt to do so privately rather than in front of a group.

Teacher Identity Crisis

There is a famous psychological problem which plagues successful people, which is called the **'Imposter Syndrome'**. You have probably heard that term before. An imposter's syndrome tends to manifest, when someone reaches a certain measure of success, compared to oneself, but was not ready for it. Then, psychological problems develop. Good examples I shall summarize in the following fictional tales, which nonetheless describe real-life events which transpire every day:

Moses, a rough middle-aged man who lives on a farm, won the lottery and became a multi-millionaire overnight. Initially he is thrilled and was constantly celebrating. Two-three months down the road, he may begin a drug addiction and develop an existential crisis. Within a few years, he loses his fortune.

Laura, a lovely lady from a poor neighbourhood in a big city, received a major film role at the age of 22. Her life seemed to turn around in the best of ways. But media attention and loss of privacy took a toll. Laura, being unable to cope with having become a 'someone special', eventually spiraled into depression, and after a decade of acting eventually committed suicide.

Such examples are so common, that you have probably read about them many a time throughout your life. But why do such things happen? Well, to a great extent, they occur because the people who suffer were not prepared for the kind of status, fame or notoriety which they quickly earned. There was a major gap between their private image of themselves, and the image the public now had of them. In other words, their **Shadow** (true Ego) and **Persona** (the cultivated Ego their wear as a mask). Or otherwise, they wanted to project to others a certain Persona, but because of their circumstances they ended up appearing and thought of in a different way than they would have liked. This can all be explained very simply: when you do not want to live up to what you have become, there is suffering. To prevent suffering, you must either revert back to what you were before, or learn to embody your new

Self. Otherwise you suffer what is called the 'Imposter Syndrome' – feeling that you are 'unworthy of your position, title or status', and that there is inadequacy between who you are and what you have become.

Martial arts teachers, being human, suffer for the same imposter syndrome, albeit in ways which match their profession. What I commonly see happening to martial arts instructors, is that they often refuse to live peacefully with the idea that they are now both teachers and leaders. Age and experience do not necessarily play a role. I have seen many people in their 50s and 60s, some with decades-long experience, often with good skill as well, who are not at ease with being martial arts teachers, despite having been so for a very long time. When such a phenomenon takes place, we see it primarily in two different ways:

1. Aversion to Money: A teacher who is unwilling to charge money for instruction because he feels uncomfortable about it (not due to other reasons). This often masquerades as benevolence or charity, but stems from a person feeling ashamed of his position. I have already dealt with money-related issues in other chapters in this book, so I do not wish to repeat the topic here.

2. Aversion to Status: Here we see a man or woman who ask others to not call them by any official title related to teaching, often not even Mr. or Mrs. this or that. In the traditional martial arts [76], this type of behaviour pretends to be modesty, but is actually internal cowardice and lack of willpower to be what one functions as.

---

[76] I should stress that in non-traditional martial arts, the idea of teaching titles is often non-existent, though even in a boxing or MMA gym one may be called 'Coach' and not referred to by his real name. I therefore solely pass judgement here on those people who operate in a sphere of martial arts instruction which claims to be traditional, for otherwise article number 2 above may not be relevant.

In both types of aversion, to money and to status, there exists the false sense of 'being unworthy of what one receives'. That is a bad place to be. A responsible person ought to either give up his status altogether if he takes issue with it, or learn to live with it and accept it fully. The passive-aggressive attitude of manifesting a status and then denouncing it, is inappropriate and disreputable to any profession.

The issue of Aversion to Status yields an interesting social phenomenon. I recall when I first started teaching, that I have encountered a number of colleagues who publicly criticized me for using the title 'Shifu'. Their supposed rationale had been, that traditionally a 'Shifu' is a sort of title that should only be used by students referring to their own teacher. It was not, in their opinion, a title that one could use when referring to himself. I assume you could already see, how their own Aversion to Status brought about a situation wherein they were willing to publicly admonish another teacher for the sake of not having to deal with their own inner conflicts. For if they were to recognize me as a 'Shifu', that would mean in turn that they would also be expected to call themselves a 'Shifu', which is something that they were not willing to accept. These teachers are of course the minority, for the vast majority teachers of traditional Chinese martial arts living outside of China, take no issue in using the titles of 'Shifu' or 'Sifu'.

Now, I have already explained fully the meaning of the term 'Shifu' in the earlier chapter: **'Shifu – The Chinese Teacher'** (p. 361). There is truth in the claim that because 'Shifu' is a personal title which reflects the relationship of someone with his own students, then that sort of relationship is private and not public. This is reasonable rationalization. That being said, nowadays the word Shifu is also a professional and educational title; much like that of a Doctor (Dr.), a Professor (Prof.), a CEO, a Bachelor of Laws (L.L.B), a Master of Business Administration (M.B.A) or even the President of a country. I see nothing wrong in presenting yourself as the professional you are, and a confident man without an imposter syndrome should not see a problem here, either.

As a teacher of traditional Chinese martial arts, what am I to answer when people ask of my professional title or education in my field of practice? Should I just tell them: "I am Jonathan"? Of course not! I ought to say: "I am a Shifu", and then provide the names of my arts and teachers, as well as a brief overview of my experience. That is what the general public expects and anticipates. Remember an important idiom I have shared with you in an earlier chapter: **All speak highly of the virtues of Modesty, but nobody wants to buy her products.** I know some martial arts teachers who are so saintly modest, that their income gradually disappeared, and hardly anyone had ever heard of them. You cannot expect to make a living out of teaching the martial arts, if you are not willing to tell people who you are, what you are worth and what your professional experience is. This includes your professional title!

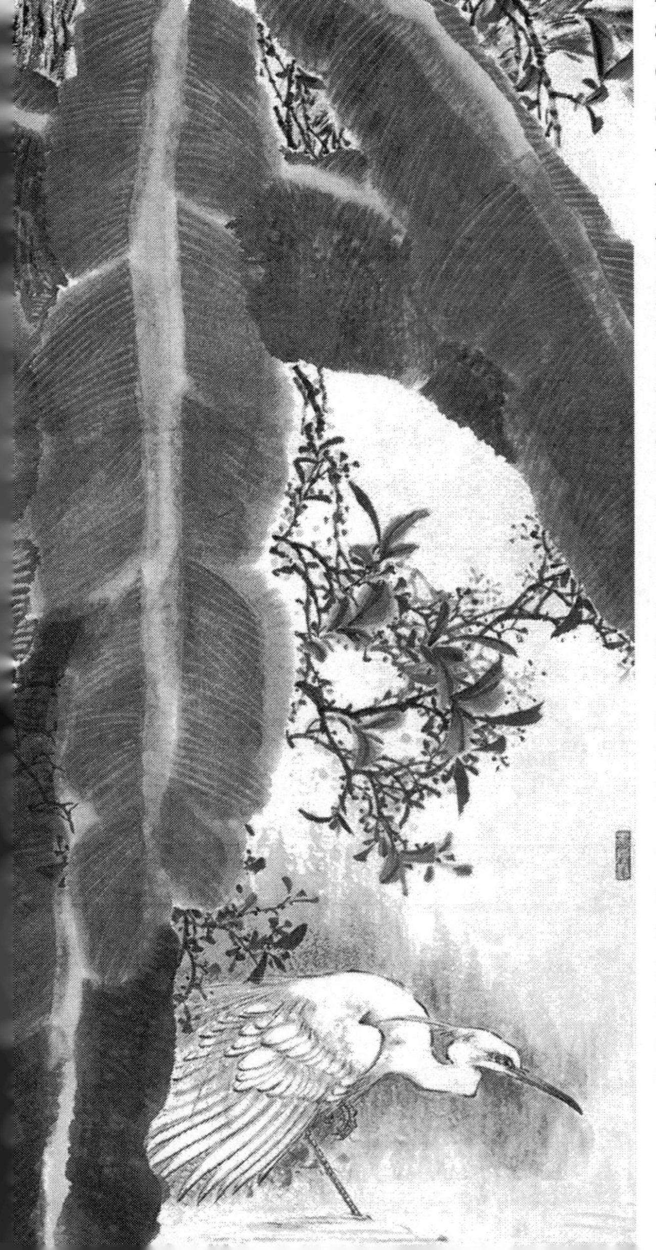

When someone calls me on the phone and I can tell that it is a person who is interested in classes, my first words usually are: "Hello! Who do I have the pleasure of speaking with?" [Then I get a name] Continued: "Good day Mr. NAME ! You are speaking with Shifu Jonathan Bluestein, head of Blue Jade Martial Arts Academy. How may I be of assistance to you today?". Were I to say: "you are speaking with Jonathan", that person might mistake me to be a secretary, or may even think they have called the wrong number! The potential student expects and even demands an authority figure. He or she did not call in order that they study with a "Jonathan", but with a Shifu. Most potential students could not care less that you have an identity crisis with your professional title. They want to know that the person whom they might study under is qualified or certified, and the first measure of assessing such a thing, their point of view, is hearing or seeing that you are a relevant and appropriate professional title. It is exactly for this reason that doctors and lawyers place their university diplomas on the walls of their clinics and offices. This provides an initial level of legitimacy and assurance to all newcomers, and such a thing is very important. So why ought a Shifu, who often studied longer and harder than a doctor or a lawyer, not use his professional title? **HE SHOULD**.

The irony is, that this use of the word 'Shifu' which is controversial to some in traditional Chinese martial arts, is commonplace with the equivalent 'Sensei' in traditional Japanese martial arts. Teachers of traditional Japanese martial arts refer to themselves by a myriad of professional titles, including but not limited to: "Sensei, O-Sensei, Renshi, Kyoshi, Shihan, Hanshi, Shidoshi, Soke" and more. Though some of these titles are considered more extravagant and less modest than others, they are all nonetheless used, by dozens of thousands of people worldwide. Such teachers often also place their dan ranking next to their title. None of this is considered out of the ordinary. The only controversies arise when a teacher of the Japanese arts assumes a title he was not given or is unworthy of. But otherwise, it is the acceptable custom to use professional titles in presenting yourself publicly, as it should be.

You want modesty? Fine. You do not have to mention your professional title everywhere. To most people I am simply Jonathan, and not 'Shifu' or 'Shifu Jonathan'. That is unlike say medical

doctors, who commonly expect nearly everyone to call them by their professional title. But when conversing about my profession, dealing with a person who has a potential of becoming a student, or presenting myself in an official capacity, then I understand the importance of not omitting my title and education.
All the more when students are speaking with me – they should call me Shifu. Older readers may remember that once, elementary-school and high-school students called the man or woman in charge by their professional title – 'Teacher' – rather than by their personal names. Many point out to what I consider to be factual, that many problems with modern education began when the process of teaching became overly 'democratized', and the distance between teachers and students was reduced.

The roots of the imposter syndrome are in improper cultivation of Self-image. Earlier I brought on the examples of those who became rich and famous overnight. Such people often never considered themselves to be rich or famous before. Because it did not occur to them, they did not imagine and rehearse such a scenario in their mind. Therefore, they were not prepared for it. Martial arts teachers are the same. Those who never imagined themselves to be teachers, commonly end up with an imposter syndrome.

I know a man, let us call him **Shifu Samuel**, who has been teaching traditional Chinese martial arts for several decades. Samuel's school is very successful and he is a good teacher. Throughout the years, his demanding tutelage produced over 20 individuals who were granted a rank at which they were permitted to open a school on their own. Alas, none of Samuel's top students wanted to! They all felt much more comfortable sticking to their everyday jobs and frequenting classes once in a while, than becoming teachers. They were not even interested in engaging in teaching part-time. Their teacher Samuel, a really good man, complained to me often of how he kept his chicks inside the nest for too long, which caused them to get too comfortable and prevented them from aspiring to become independent and spread their wings. That sort of problem interfered with the Samuel's wishes for his

school to expand.
The mistake which **Shifu Samuel** made and had told me of, primarily had to do with him not encouraging his students to envision themselves as teachers. His veteran students often helped him with teaching classes or even substituted in his absence, but that did not mean they possessed a teacher's mindset. They always considered themselves as 'sidekicks' to Samuel – never leaders like him. Because they have not been engaged throughout the years in the fantasy of commanding their own ranks, even when they were given permission and encouragement to go ahead and accomplish this, they were unwilling to manifest a vision which was not theirs.

To avoid Samuel's mistake, I make sure to embed within the students' minds the idea, that one day they might be teachers. This I plant in their heads by using both direct and indirect measures. I would hint at this many a time in classes. Once in a long while I might also tell students, that the true debt a practitioner owes the lineage if he is to practice for a long time, is to one day teach the art to at least one other person. It can be a student, a friend, a colleague of a family member, but this is a debt which should be repaid. Additionally, I speak of the virtues of teaching, and the importance of it for personal growth and development of skill. I repeat such things often enough so students never lose touch of the idea that they will probably teach something to someone at some point in the future. That much is sufficient to entice those who are inclined to begin a fantastical journey in the land of imagination, and if they are capable of repeating this script for a while, having cultivated this sort of idea, they would not suffer from an imposter's syndrome when they arrive at a teaching position. It all depends on the proper mental setup, and the latter depends on you – the teacher – for leading the subconscious mind of the students towards the right path during their first few years of practice. Paying close attention to such a delicate aspect of the teaching, can over the span of decades determine the destiny of the entire school or organization.

The Eternal Student

My friend, grand-master Keith R. Kernspecht, is one of the most commercially successful martial arts teachers to have ever lived. His organization, the EWTO, had over a thousand schools when these words were written. Keith told me in 2017CE: "***I am an eternal student of the martial arts***". He really meant that. When I first met him, at the age of 72, he was still spending up to 6 hours a day practicing, and was meeting regularly with teachers equal to him or sometimes more skilled and knowledgeable than himself in order to study from them.

It has been a personal observation of mine that people begin to die from old age when they can no longer learn new things. This is also the way in which martial artists begin to wane and whither. Beyond pushing your own limits and exploring in depth what you already know, you must keep on learning from others in some way or another – for your own sake and so that you can set the right example for your students. Do not ignore this need, for it is a type of essential nutrition you must consume in order to survive as a teacher and a human being.

Though new teachers can be difficult to come by, especially as you grow older and more experienced, learning does not have to be something of a long-term commitment. Consulting with colleagues and mentors, admitting to them what you do not know and asking for answers and guidance – that is also learning.

Remember the words of Confucius:

"True knowledge is knowing the extent of one's ignorance".

The Young Teacher

I began teaching the martial arts at a relatively young age. Many people feel that it is inappropriate to begin teaching the art when one is young, as they relate scholastic and spiritual maturity with the appropriate age to begin instruction. In agree. Indeed in the world of martial arts, hardly anyone becomes notable, well-known or universally respected before the age of 35, and commonly only past the age of 40. Gongfu requires decades to be cultivated to a prominent degree. There are nonetheless several things to be said of on the issue of teaching the martial arts at a younger age.

It is for a good reason, that most consider the age of 16 to be the bare minimum for allowing one to initiate any sort of teaching whatsoever. The majority of practitioners though, cannot do so prior to the age of 18. This age-limit rule, extant in many traditional schools, of refusing to bestow a teaching rank to a person younger than 18 years of age, is reasonable and grounded in reality. Perhaps among the ancients, living under natural human conditions, one could have been readied sooner [77]. But alas, in our modern society, even the ripe age of 18 years seems to be plagued with a multitude of infantile tendencies.

For a person between the ages of 16 and 18, if they were to teach anyone, it would be more appropriate for them to instruct those among their age group or younger. I have in the past witnessed vile instructors allow teenagers as young as 13 to teach the art to students of their age group or younger, often with as little as 2-3 years of experience in practice themselves. Such young people are

---

[77] Alexander the Great, a famous historical prodigy, was already taking part in active warfare at the age of 16. But he was also the son of a famous conqueror, and a student of Aristotle, one of history's greatest philosophers. By his example and that of others, we learn that unusually gifted individuals are capable of leadership even as young as 16. That being said, the vast majority of 16 year olds I encounter today could hardly defend themselves against their cat or lead their dog around the neighbourhood.

often taken advantage of by lazy teachers, who make them into their willful slaves, taking care of some of their classes for little or no pay.

An appropriate thing to consider here, is that although young people are sometimes quicker to learn physical skills, they are slower at intellectually comprehending them. Many are the teenagers who can perform the most fantastic physical feats. But they are almost always akin to trained monkeys – what they can do, they do not necessarily understand, and usually cannot teach. Therefore we need to establish separation between technical skill, and intellectual capacity, both of which are needed in a teacher's arsenal.

The conclusion should be, that for a person under the age of 18, it is required that they spend more time training before attaining a teaching license. Say that in one's system, the average number of years which take one to become a teacher is 5 (with daily training). Then for the young lad, that number should perhaps be 7 or 8. For during their formative years in the art, they are still immature, and also distracted by countless other things. Schooling, first-loves, clashes with family members, physically changing shape, emotional turmoil and much more – these are heavy burdens that they have to face whilst learning a martial art.

What else is crucial is that such people receive a surplus of mentorship on the teaching craft, and allowed more time than others to experiment with it within the confines of the school, before spreading their wings and seeking new venues.

But should these people teach to begin with? What are the virtues of allowing the younger folk to have claim among us teachers?

I recall late master Wan Laisheng[78] giving the following advice to people: "***I recommend that you go and study with people who are in their 20s. For it was when I was in my 20s, that I was most inspired***". What younger teachers lack in life experience and maturity, they make up for with energy, enthusiasm, creativity and

---

[78] Wan Laisheng (1903–1992CE) was a famous teacher of the traditional Chinese martial arts, and lineage holder of the Ziran Men tradition.

the need to prove themselves. A teacher in his 20s has some qualities which a master in his 60s will lack, and vice-versa [79]. Technically, the master is always the better option for any potential student. But masters are difficult to come by. Additionally, often the master is so sick and tired of instruction, having done it for so long, that the little one might get from his wisdom, is less than the great amount of information the younger and less experienced teacher will do the utmost to convey. With a master also, the students often witness and experience the 'end-product' of decades' worth of practice. That may be a very well-polished jewel, but the students might not necessarily be capable of discerning from it, how to make their rough diamond shine. The younger teachers, to a degree, develop alongside their students.

Finally, we should acknowledge that in order to learn how to teach, one has to engage in the actual deed, much like fighting is learned in part by facing actual violence. Are we then to expect, that one first attains mastery, or a high level of practice, before he or she attempt teaching? That would make most people 35 at the least before they have had the chance to teach their first class. That would be akin to spending a decade or two studying martial arts, before attempting to apply their techniques against a resisting opponent. I therefore beg to differ, with those scolding younger instructors. When qualified and sufficiently skilled, they <u>**must**</u> teach. It is through teaching that we have the potential to develop our arts and skill the most.

All this is encapsulated in two Hebrew proverbs:

"***A man cannot buy himself wisdom with his bread***" – Meaning, wisdom is earned through hands-on experience; and –

---

[79] It is a common belief throughout diverse fields of study and practice, ranging from Soccer to Physics, that the greatest potential for creative expression in most people, is usually during their 20s. While not true for everyone, modern research has shown that the brain seems to 'lock-in' into more predictable and structured patterns by around the age of 25. Note that this refers to the greatest outbursts of creativity, relative to one's potential, and not to overall achievement or ability.

"***Better be the tail of the lion than the head of the fox***" – Meaning, that it is preferable to be the lesser among a group of superior individuals, than the leader among a group of inferior people.

The young martial arts teacher ought to be provided with the opportunity to practice what he is destined to do; and, it is better for him to be at the position of a novice teacher among more experienced ones, than be considered an exceptional practitioner among those who cannot teach and do not understand what teaching entails. This will allow him the opportunity to gain wisdom through hands-on experience.

More Fearsome Than the Tiger

I would like to tell you a short story. This historical allegory, which comes from ancient China, is astonishing enough as a standalone piece. But this story I bring to you, is even more fascinating. For as you would discover momentarily, it is very much relevant to the global martial arts community of our time. Here is then, a tale worth repeating.

One day, the Chinese sage Confucius was passing by Mount Tai, escorted by his loyal disciples. As Confucius and his followers were crossing the mountain range, they heard sounds of anguish from a distance. Approaching to ensuing drama, the group came upon a woman who was bitterly crying in front of a grave. Confucius sent forth one of his disciples to inquire. The disciple said to the woman: "***Having perceived your lamentations from afar, we could sense that they expressed a misery rooted in great sorrow***". The woman replied: "***Indeed! A tiger has killed and eaten my father-in-law, and later my husband suffered the same fate. Now, my son has been swallowed by another tiger***". Upon hearing this, Confucius stepped forward and told the woman: "***If so, why do you remain in such a place?***". The woman replied: "***Because here at least, I am not persecuted by the local government***". Confucius then turned to his disciples and told them: "***Remember this lesson young men – that an oppressive government is more fearsome than the tiger***".

Confucius seemed to have believed, then, that personal safety, while of utmost importance, is only secondary to being free. A person, like the woman in this story, would rather take significant physical risks, than be subjected to limitation upon his or her independence. I gather, that whenever a martial artist is practicing a dangerous technique, that he is making this exact statement – that it is better to be alive and at some risk, than being secure and in a prison.

Nonetheless, what else can this story mean for us, martial artists who live over two millennia past the age of Confucius?

The traditional martial arts have done quite well for themselves for the past few thousand years, and especially in the preceding century. Yet today, we face a new idea about the traditional martial arts – that they should be regulated. This is an incredibly preposterous and unusual suggestion, for outside of the context of military and police, the greater portion of martial arts teachers for all of human history, operated outside of the big and slimy claws of politicians and governments. Now, this is changing.

All over the world, during the past several decades, there have been people calling for the regulation of martial arts. This makes more sense for sports-oriented styles, of course. Whenever competitions

are involved, rules and logistics become complex and specific, and then regulation is welcome, though it frequently turns greedy and excessive. Since sports martial arts are inclined to represent cities and nations, whilst appealing to receive public funding, then in so doing they enter an unholy marriage with 'The System'.
The situation with traditional martial arts is different. The argument for regulating them usually stems from fear. Proponents claim that without regulation of the traditional martial arts, charlatanism would ruthlessly wreak havoc, and that poorly-trained individuals would end up causing physical harm, even deaths, among their students.

I am here to suggest and point out to you, that this line of thinking is utterly ridiculous. Let me begin by reminding the reader, that there is overall a far greater number of people being injured and killed yearly in sports martial arts, than in traditional martial arts. That is despite the fact that sports martial arts are heavily regulated, often by several organizations and the government combined. That is albeit sports martial arts more commonly using protective rules and equipment, while in traditional martial arts the greater portion of combative training is without such things, or with their inclusion to a more limited degree. Therefore, it can be stated with absolute statistical certainty, that rules and regulations do not prevent injury and death in the practice of martial arts and, if anything, may only increase their prevalence.

Likewise, weapons placed in the hands of qualified martial artists, seldom lead to serious injury or death, and that is well-known. All the while, whenever weapons of any type are placed in the hands of governments, death is imminent and inevitable. Not that governments should be without weaponry, but as you know, they are unfortunately irresponsible with its handling and instruction.
Furthermore, do try to remember the historical precedents with weaponry and its regulation. The Okinawans lost much of their armed traditions when the invading Japanese forbade them from wielding and even owning such items. The Nazi Party also, in its unscrupulous takeover of Germany, ventured early and made haste

to eliminate private ownership of weaponry across the land, as preparation for the terrors to come.

Worst yet, is that the entire argument for regulation is rooted in falsehood and deceit. Suppose a man was to undergo a state-certified instructors' course to be able to legally teach the martial arts. I underwent such a course, quite professionally constructed and taught, lasting over 250 hours. In my home country of Israel, there is indeed such regulation, though moderate still in our time. This supposedly important course – does it truly tackle the important issues pertaining to safety and professionalism in the teaching of the martial arts? Hardly so, in my experience, even when taught well.

Consider for example, this pressing matter of preventing injury. What is the cause of injury in martial arts classes? Most often, negligence or accidents. But by what manner of behaviour or occurrence do negligence and accidents lead to injuries? This happens when people are involved.

Bad students, who should not be taught the martial arts, injure others. Poorly taught students, who cannot apply techniques well, often end up in accidents. Students who are emotionally unstable, or unable to leave their egos at the door – they cause such troubles. Ill-minded people. Bad tempered individuals. Immoral characters of various types. Those who lack mindfulness... and so forth. Their vices and faults have in common, that no regulation or 'special course' taught by outsiders are going to correct them. Only one's parents and direct teachers in the martial arts, may have substantial sway in that respect, affecting morality, character and attitude. Indeed, government regulation has never in history corrected human relationships in deep and meaningful ways. At best, it may incline some to be more polite and less extreme in public. But when punches come flying, in the heat of the moment, people resort and fall back into their habitual nature. So whichever was not dealt with appropriately by us as parents and teachers, the government surely could not fix.

The question remains though, of what can be done in light of the existence of another problem - the 'elephant in the room' – the real infestation of the martial arts scene by countless bad instructors and charlatans. Or otherwise, the fact that some individuals are simply not very well qualified. That is an additional argument used in the advocacy of regulation – that these people must be stopped somehow. We martial arts teachers bemoan the fact that cynical and rapscallious bozos take advantage of naïve students. We ask – what could be done to prevent this?

One approach is that of administrative regulation, by which we make the statement, that we would like the government to come in, and order everyone around as if it were a kindergarten teacher – which makes us infantile, too. This approach assumes also, that the students are akin to mindless children, who cannot possibly make good decisions, and are always disposed towards becoming 'easy prey' for the martial con-men. It places immense power in the hands of clueless bureaucrats, most of whom are not martial artists, to make edcisions and control things which they do not understand.

Others still, strongly favour the approach of vigilantism. That is, to encourage martial bullies to go an 'shut down' charlatan teachers and their schools. The martial bullies receive publicity and attention, while the community is said to benefit from these actions. One such man in China, Xu Xiaodong, went on a crusade against 'fake masters', beating up a few of them and gaining national exposure, eventually causing the Chinese government to persecute him.

Another form of martial bullying common today, is making a public mockery of the charlatans, by caricaturing, insulting and deriding them with a special 'rally of shame', perpetrated by dozens, sometimes hundreds of people.

There are inherent problems with martial bullies, though. Should a bully be made a hero? Who gets to choose the charlatans? Is that not political? How is this virtuous? What kind of message does bullying send to young people? Can bullying help correct the ways of the wicked, or does it merely further traumatize them? What happens to a mad dog once he is out of 'bad people' to bite?... and so forth. Appealing to martial bullies I should tell you, is not that different than appealing to the government. One act calls upon the forces of 'order', and the other summons the forces of 'chaos', yet in both instances there is reliance on an external entity to solve your own problems. Regulation, be it by a bureaucracy, a ruffian or the lynching of someone's reputation, is still oppression all the same.

Then we can think of another approach, which I endorse, saying that if we the worthier folk were to make good knowledge accessible to the general public about real martial arts, then potential and current students would be able to make better decisions about what is right for them and who to study under. This approach assumes that it is possible, and indeed of superior merit, to place faith in people's capacity to draw reasonable conclusions and choose well, when they are presented with truthful and clear information and explanations.
To be virtuous and responsible in this manner, is no quick solution. It bears neither the allure or power nor the imminent motivation of a threat to one's financial or physical well-being. But this approach has the capacity to transform people, rather then simply push them around to obtain technicalities.

The risk in choosing to let the government into our traditions, goes beyond merely considering other human beings to be inferior to their innate amplitude. It is in truth a strong statement about one's inner wish to hand over his arms to be shackled – a form of self-imposed enslavement. By what moral right can a politician or bureaucrat of any stature, interfere with the scared traditions of countless generations, when these are being exercised and taught in private, without public funding, and whilst benefitting communities and harming no one? The traditional martial arts are at their core the heritage of links and bonds across many generations of personal human relationship. To replace such priceless chains of human fulfillment and destiny with the manacles of the State – how can this be called righteous? How can it stand in the test of time, to be considered anything but an outrageous betrayal of the trust bestowed upon a Shifu, a Sensei or otherwise, by his ancestors and predecessors?

Neither will a regulator stop at the puny measures of extorting fees and enacting mild codification. For those who can, by your own request of them, determine what is fit for you to teach, can go down that slippery slope swiftly. Tomorrow they shall endeavor to proclaim that some are not fit to instruct at all due to arbitrary considerations, and the next day, that certain styles are inherently 'too dangerous' and should be abolished. Have they not already made similar statements and laws pertaining to specific dog breeds and types of people in society, having done so throughout all of recorded history? It is said that power corrupts, and that absolute power corrupts absolutely. But allow me to assure you, that the power which corrupts the quickest, is that which you ask another to have over you. Such is the fate of those who covet regulation.

Let he who fears, change himself for the better! The proper way shall not arise and be erected by the actions of strangers with foreign interests, but through introspection and a willingness to act from within the community which feels the burden of the times. For in sincere adulthood we fathom and embrace, the ability to resolve our challenges through self-correction, without becoming anxious to the point of rushing to seek an outsider to save us from our downfalls. Else, how can we call ourselves martial artists or mature individuals? What we teach is the defense of the Self – so that we do not have to rely on others in times of distress. In appealing to politicians and governments, I can only envision Self-defeat. Then as it stands, I would rather live among the tigers, then be operated by the bureaucrats; and you must be able to discern real felines, from those made of paper.

The Language of Martial Arts

A major disagreement exists in the world of martial arts concerning the question of whether it is of superior value to study just one art in great depth throughout one's lifetime (perhaps supplementing minor knowledge here and there along the way), or engaging in the study of several systems. It seems that both approaches have yielded exceptional masters, and that their usefulness depends on the individual. Nonetheless, discussions concerning this topic tend to focus on things like techniques, breadth of knowledge, time allocated to training, availability of teachers, etc. Nearly no one talks of the psychological value of learning several styles.

For a person such as myself, who always favours Quality over Quantity, it is peculiar that my circumstances have brought me to train in many styles. True, that as a matter of fact I have invested the majority of my time across the years in the practice and teaching of Xing Yi Quan and Southern Mantis, and to a slightly lesser degree Pigua Zhang. However, I have had reasonable experience training in Western Boxing and Shito-ryu Karate beforehand, and afterwards I have also experienced small bits and pieces of Baji Quan, Shaolin Jingang Bashi, Chen style Taiji and a few others. Why then did I choose to do this? Because every martial art is a language, and the language which is a martial art is a key to one's soul.

Observing the mannerisms of different nations, they all use the same words. We all have a 'mother' and 'father'. Only so big is the conceptual world of human beings. The same goes for the martial arts – among them, most techniques are shared, and found across a wide variety of styles. Surely, in many systems are also unique and distinct methods and pronunciations, just as in some languages we may find 30 words for 'green' or 20 notions of 'honey'. Yet overall, there is a limit set upon the technical diversity itself. What then makes it worth one's time to invest the countless moments required to study anew? It is the human element that makes that difference worthwhile.

For though a technique may be seemingly identical, the body mechanics and mindset driving it are not. Neither are the rulesets for usage, the order in which things are put to practice, the angles, the pace or even the sounds. Upon closer examination, a set number of techniques always yields an abundance of dialects. These in turn were not delivered from the heavens. They were created by human beings, who systematized their practice.

A martial arts system, like a language, is not merely a hollow construct. It is a philosophy of existing through the flesh, and a way of conceiving the world at large. Choosing ways in which to fight and train, and developing these further, mirror the hearts and minds of people. Strategies, Tactics and Techniques are beyond their application – they are a manifestation of the psyche of generations past.

Thus, to study a style of martial arts is to have an opportunity to listen the ghosts of your movement ancestors. Can you hear their words echo through your tendons? Are you aware of their sorrows and joys when your body adapts to their form in the present?

Unlike a computer, a human being is a universal entity. The cosmos is contained in your mind's eye, and you are it also. The machine, when presenting a picture on a screen, regenerates coordinates of various colours to present a picture; and that picture will be the same one forever, for the machine's memory is fixed rather than organic. But not so with the homo sapien, who embodies constant change. When your memory recalls a thing, it cannot manifest it as it was. Rather, the endless network of the psyche experiences once more the journey which led to the image you are seeking, and through that quest is revealed afresh the earlier experience, now also in a slightly different light. Therefore, to be able to remember is to again cross a path once traveled, and with each passage to engrave clearer the road you had taken in your mind. To this extent, by the virtue of every memory being a pilgrimage to the past, the teachings of the old masters – their methods, skills and techniques

– literally rewire your being in their footsteps. Once understood, this reality cannot be evaded. Once comprehended, by your presence they shall remain. How appropriate is thus the Chinese name for movement forms – Tào Lù 套路 – 'a set of roads', left for one to walk by those who came before.

As with anything else, to gain a perspective, you require a view which is not one-sided. You do not see your own faults to their fullest extent by only asking your closest friends and family members of them. Similarly, there is only so much that your own main art, and your teachers in it, can tell you from their vantage point. Over the horizon though, there are other families and languages – the reflections of different past lives. People who sought to understand the same human conflicts, but had existed in a sphere of their own. To tap into their parallel fountain of knowledge is a path to wisdom, but that can see only he who in his great fondness of the art was willing to once again be a child.

Frowned upon is the situation, in which relatively so little written information was left to us by those who came before. Yet keen were they in guiding us through their legacy in subtle ways, and one's forms and methods are full of their footprints and anecdotes. They prompt and tease you to ask: "Why?". Indeed, why did they create things in the manner in which they did? The majority of practitioners sadly dismiss the judgment of their predecessors, or make for simplistic answers in order that they could cover their ignorance rather than truly solving such riddles. My experience has taught me though that more often than not, the only way to answer the question of 'Why?' is to follow the example of the men who preceded us. In choosing to practice their traditions, to accept wholeheartedly their reality, and augment one's own to it. Then over the course of years, it is gradually revealed that the movements speak, and your body has a story to tell. A bicameral mind is reawakened, a collective consciousness evoked; a tale which surprisingly is not your own, but the accumulation of many other lifetimes; a greater truth for the careful listener. Then it occurs to me, once in a long while, to put in the effort to learn something new; for I never tire of listening.

The quarrels and choirs, shouts and desires
Mingle in the heated fires
Of past greats whispering
Through iron wires
In my ears
They talk

Be their presence ever witnessed
Through the breaths of men at war
Combat raging ever present
To resolve conflicted Self

Heed their speech oh my disciple
Bear their emblem in your heart
Keep their spirit shining lively
And let them guide you through the dark

For where you stand, where lays your shadow
There was once a man like you
In his senses keen, observant
He once sought this knowledge too

What he left is mere intention
Barely any shape or form
Yet his spirit, everlasting
Now his wisdom is reborn

Empathy is the Highest Skill

As I went on with my journey in the martial arts, eventually I came to realize that the highest skill a practitioner could manifest is that of Empathy. People misunderstand and misuse the word 'empathy' quite often. We tend to think that empathy is something to be associated with benevolent behaviour. In fact, empathy is neutral. It is simply the ability to resonate fully with the emotional being of another person. Whether this ability is used for good or bad purposes, is entirely up to you. Case in point – famous leaders who have used their empathic skills to control others and manipulate them into horrendous acts of violence, as was demonstrated in Nazi Germany and commonly seen in cults.

Observe great warriors of past and present, and note that many of them speak of empathy without necessarily naming it. They talk of the ability to connect to their opponent on a deep level, touching his innate psychology. From Miyamoto Musashi to Muhammad Ali and Mike Tyson, this has mentioned and utilized since time immemorial. Why Empathy? Because through empathy, the connection with the other becomes instantaneous and sincere. "Only I know the opponent, but he does not know me" (he only knows himself) [80].

The irony here, is that under normal circumstances, to cultivate empathy requires a person to invest in positive uses of it. Thus, the fighting man finds that on the path to martial excellence, for his own egocentric self-development, he needs to become emotionally attuned to other people. Which, for the sane person, means he would often end up being coerced to help them. This is one of the points where the ways of the warrior and the healer interconnect. Rising to a new capacity for destruction, relative to oneself, requires growth in the positive interpersonal sphere. Natural Yin and Yang interplay in human affairs.

---

[80] A famous verse from the Taiji Quan classics.

The observant teacher would be able to discern in daily endeavors with students, to what extent he has developed his empathic abilities. This is partly as furthering your empathic capacity helps you directly with student retention and recruitment. But there are also other, more subtle ways to notice this. To explain such notions, I will share with you a personal story. For the sake of privacy, I have altered the names of some of the people involved.

A few years ago I attended a workshop at my teacher's, Sifu Sapir Tal's school. Many students of mine and of my Sifu took part in that workshop. The event was hosted by a guest teacher from another style, a colleague of ours, Aaron Sensei (pseudonym). The guest teacher brought along with him to the workshop an acquaintance of his, whose name was Barry (pseudonym). So four main characters to this tale: **Sifu Sapir**, who hosted the seminar; **Aaron Sensei**, who taught there; **Barry**, the participant Aaron brought with him; and **myself**.

Barry had an inspiring story. About a decade before the workshop took place, he was involved in a head-on car collusion, and suffered terrible injuries. He was hospitalized and could hardly move a limb. The doctors told Barry he would never walk again, and his body was confined to a myriad of instruments and machines. Additionally, while Barry was a 'normal' person prior to the accident, the nerve and brain damage left his cognitive abilities impaired, making his speech slurred and thinking slower, although his mind was still as sharp as before. Barry fought a war against all odds, and after a decade of hard work became a self-sustaining individual, capable of walking, training in the martial arts, renting a house, having a job, and dating women. He was also working as a motivational speaker, sharing his inspiring life-story. All that considered, Barry's body never fully recovered, and he was suffering from various joints problems and physical challenges.

During one part of the seminar, a drill was set up with one person standing in the middle of the room, and all the other participants surrounding him. At Aaron Sensei's gesture, one participant would

come out of the circle and attack the person standing in the middle, attempting to take him down. When in was my turn to stand in the middle, I manage to thwart all attempts to take me down, except for the last one, which was Barry's.
Aaron signaled to Barry to jump me as my back was facing him, so by the time I managed to turn half-way towards him, I was already on my way to the floor. In the rolling process, I caught his neck in a rear-naked choke, and managed to land us together in a position very disadvantageous to him. I began to choke Barry as slowly as I possibly could, pausing momentarily in-between, and shouting at him to 'tap', as is customary in such cases to prevent him from suffering potential damage. But Barry, determined to prove himself as always, would not tap, and used all of his power to try and get away, as my grip tightened. After a while, I let him go despite his insistence on not tapping, but by then the poor man nearly lost his consciousness, took a minute to stand up, and was coughing for a while later. I felt bad for him, and ashamed of myself for not letting him go earlier. After all, he was not a 'normal' participant, and I ought not to have felt obliged to prove anything in front of the other students present.

Some time passed. Aaron Sensei was quite overzealous to make Barry 'the star of the show' and find ways to elevate his self-esteem and overall confidence. He knew Barry came from a full-contact fighting background in the martial arts, so he asked of some people directly to come and spar with Barry for a bit, without gloves or protective equipment. Two novice students of my Sifu did so as he asked this of them, sparring with Barry for a minute or two, each. Then Aaron Sensei asked for more volunteers to step forth. I very much wanted to help the situation, but would not bulge. I thought to myself: "Ought I do such a thing? He is not my student and I am not used to practicing fighting with him, let alone without protection. Wherein he tries to hard, I could really hurt him. I nearly killed him earlier!". Thus, I remained in place and did not volunteer.

All the while, I could see Sifu Sapir's face being uneasy with the situation. I could tell that he was not too enthusiastic about Aaron

Sensei's approach, but on the other hand did not wish to contradict him, and sought to show him respect as the guest instructor at the school. Sifu Sapir was likely just as hesitant at that moment as I had been. Yet, within a few seconds, Sifu said that he would spar with Barry. So he did.

When my Sifu came up to spar with this charming man, this was like empathic poetry in motion. Sifu, with his great deal of experience in teaching and also raising four children, knew exactly what kind of treatment Barry needed. He gave him some light butt-kicking, but also taunted him positively to hunt him down and strike, even allowing Barry to hit his belly, ribs and face. At all times, Sifu maintained a balanced atmosphere, with both of them being able to showcase fighting spirit and their relative skills. Never did one appear to dominate or humiliate the other, as they were in true and sincere harmony, giving and receiving, exchanging rather than clashing. This went on for several minutes, as the rest of the students and me were all watching in awe. After this sparring match, Barry was overjoyed, and had a big smile stretching across his face for hours. Sifu could have put him down with one strike, but rather he chose to use his hands to make him feel dignified and worthy, an equal among equals.

This event shook me to the core. It was then and there that I realized, how big was truly the gap between my skill and that of my teacher's. In part, this was shown through my teacher's tremendous capacity for empathy, with which I was lacking. The best I could do for a man in distress, was to overcome him without killing him. My Sifu, on the other hand, was capable of elevating that man's spirit and creating for him a positive memorable experience which may possibly last a lifetime. That day, I felt very proud being my Sifu's student. I took care to tell him as much, and why I felt this way.

Martial Arts Psychotherapy

People often make the mistake of thinking the martial arts were meant to be a vessel for turning people morally upright. This is not accurate. The martial arts were all originally created as means of teaching people how to defend themselves or kill. As I often tell my students, the martial arts themselves are without an agenda as to what type of person you should be. They are a tool, like a hammer; and as the proverb goes: "When one has a hammer, everything looks like a nail". Whoever wields the power of the martial arts, does not necessarily tend to become a good person. Rather, he becomes empowered to be more of Himself. A decent human being may thus turn into a most benevolent spirit, while an unworthy character may turn into a full-fledged scoundrel. One's potential is increased, either way. Without special guidance on part of a teacher, such is the nature of the martial arts – they empower, but without coercing one in any particular direction. The choice is up to the individual, but the process of psychic transformation unfortunately remains subconscious for the majority of practitioners.

I am of the opinion that it is possible, once again with proper guidance, to make martial arts into a form of solo psychotherapy, so that they do not solely empower, but also lead to positive personal development among all practitioners. This is an aspect of martial arts training which is seldom spoken of, and I wish to elucidate it in this article.

Why do people seek the aid of a psychologist? Often the reason is that the mechanisms behind their psychological problems remain dormant in their subconscious. They cannot access the roots of these problems or deal with them on their own, and therefore they require the assistance of a professional, or sometimes simply a friend or family member. But even a psychologist most commonly does not himself resolve the inner turmoil of the patient. Rather, he or she would help lead the person to a solution via means of conversation. We can therefore point out to the fact that what a person is actually seeking from a psychologist, most of the time, is not truly to be 'fixed' by him, but to be provided with the instruments and guidance for self-correction. My understanding is that Chiropractic is founded on a similar principle – that the professional merely adjusts, while the patient's body is itself the instrument of the actual healing.

Having understood this truth thousands of years ago, the Indian and Chinese traditions have developed methods of self-cultivation to serve, in part, as solo psychotherapy. Most types of meditation are such instruments, as is a great portion of Yoga and Qi Gong practices. Martial arts can function in the same manner, but this is often missed or forgotten, for it takes a great deal of skill to teach methods of this kind to people. Nonetheless, many individuals may develop such a capacity independently, as did I.

In practicing the martial arts, the body itself is the psychologist. But one has to slow down in order to listen to what he says. In moving quickly, the message is blurred; as in a music concert, where the noise obscures the lyrics. Only when training very slowly, or holding static or semi-static postures, can a person attune himself to what the body has to say. Then, the practice becomes simple, if one cares to listen.

The basic notion to work with is that every single emotion and thought finds expression in bodily function. This means that anything you think or feel, will manifest in the flesh in some way. Most commonly, thoughts and feelings express themselves in the form of muscular tension. In this I argue, that when people experience muscular tension in practicing the martial arts, nearly every single instance as such is related to a thought, a feeling, or a memory. The natural state of the human body is complete relaxation – as in deep sleep. When people imbue cannabis, their muscles tend to relax – not because cannabis causes a chemical reaction inducing muscular relaxation, but rather because it relaxes the mind, reduces worry, and thus the muscles do not tense up to contain thoughts, feelings and memories. Yet cannabis only resolves such challenges temporarily, and also features other side-effects which are not always appropriate; hence, not a complete cure for these particular types of afflictions.

Muscular tension is not the only bodily mechanism used for coping with thoughts, feelings and memories. Secretion of additional stomach acid, changes in one's heartbeat and blood flow, headaches, pains and many other things, also spontaneously appear in relation to something which bothers our minds.

It is important that we understand why this happens. At least while one is alive, the body and spirit are one. Whatever the mind conceives in abstraction, the body seeks to imitate in physical form. Especially with muscular tension, using such a mechanism allows us to physically feel something. I will give you an example you are familiar with. We have all experience many a time the annoyance of wishing to choke someone, but realizing that the person we despise in not in our vicinity, or is impossible to deal with under the circumstances. What do we naturally do, then? We make a choking gesture with one or two hands, and apply pressure as if we were choking that person. Consider that this exact mechanism, you are probably using every single day, often several times a day, whenever you need to deal with something difficult. This mechanism allows you to make the abstraction physical, and therefore someone attain a sense that it is under your control. From the brain, to the nerves, then back to the brain. But as with the example of the cannabis, this is false consciousness. One merely creates the illusion of a solution, but does not truly deal with the problem. It is a shortcut, allowing us to alleviate the stress of a thought, feeling or memory in the short-term, as this takes up far less resources and time than a long-term resolution. Sadly, this bears dire consequences.

When the many moments of denial add up, they actually waste far more of one's time than acting decidedly to achieve closure for a certain thought, feeling or memory. But even worse is the fact, that when we embed a thought, feeling or a memory in the flesh, we are also interfering with many bodily systems. When the habit becomes chronic, actual damage is being done, and the condition can develop into an illness. I would go as far as to argue that, apart from external pathogens, toxins and medical negligence, the greatest untold killer of human beings is their own faulty subconscious. However, its mechanisms are often too complex for science to comprehend or do serious research on at this time, at the onset of the 21st century.

Why are the martial arts a good psychologist? Because they point to exactly those bodily mechanisms where we hide our thoughts, feelings or memories. Nearly every single correction I make in the movements or postures of my students have to do with some part of their bodies being hindered by their own psychology to some extent. It is quite astounding to realize, that many years of effort in acquiring skill in the martial arts and other pursuits, are entirely wasted simply due to resistance generated by our own psyche. But the method for dealing with the challenge is in fact so simple, that it could be described in a single paragraph.

What the practitioner ought to do, is to move slowly, or not move at all, with any given martial arts method. When such condition is sustained for many minutes on end **without stoppage**, it becomes readily apparent where exactly in one's body is found the resistance. At times such a realization demands several hours of practice, over several days or weeks. I often tell my students, that the best approach is to take a single movement, combination or form, and practice them consecutively for 3 hours. This is a proven method to cause a significant change in both body and mind within the span of a day. In any case, eventually will be found the bodily part or mechanism responsible for hindering one's movement or posture. Then this bodily part or mechanism has to be released. Hidden psychological truths reveal themselves at two intersections – once at the exact moment when the problem first presents itself during practice, and once more when the problem is resolved.

The practitioner needs to ask himself consciously in every single practice session – what thoughts, feelings or memories arise when my body hinders me from doing something properly? By these means he can discover what is subconsciously haunting him. Then once greater accuracy and skill are acquired with the certain movement or posture in question, the very correction of that movement or posture will teach one how to release himself from the chains of the thought, feeling or memory which have been troubling him.

This is easier said than done, of course. Only those with a strong will to change who they are, can induce an intricate form of solo psychotherapy. Yet this is the supreme, ultimate method. It costs not a dime, and yields the most effective and long-lasting results. For whichever you can change with both your mind and body, tends to last.

As a teacher, once you have yourself attained a measure of excellence in such solo psychotherapy, it gradually becomes possible to extend your ability outwards and reach the hearts of your students. I was not born with a tremendous natural capacity for empathy. But commonly, I can see through a person's movements, the demons which lurk in his soul. At times this seems almost psychic. I have been able to discern from people's martial body language things like their parents being divorced, having had a fight with their spouse before coming to class, a project they have not told me about, and even things they have yet to become aware of themselves such a secret wish to change a career. Granted, I am not a mind-reader. But through experience, by teaching martial arts every day for many years, I became keen on observing signs of thoughts, feelings and memories as they express themselves in the flesh. This ability, which arose initially from my own solo psychotherapy, I have used in order to help my students cope with their challenges. I have the means of aiding them to gently bring the repressed to the surface, and find the physical means for both understanding it, and releasing themselves from the bondage.

Words That Are Stronger Than Punches

The emotion most destructive for one's Lungs, is that of Grief. We all intuitively know that. When a person is facing a grieving situation, even over the death of a hamster or the loss of a job opportunity, their capacity to breath diminishes. When grieving is more pronounced and painful, crying and weeping commonly ensue, and then the lungs weaken significantly. This is quite dangerous to one's health. Oxygen is more important than anything. With lowered oxygen levels over even a few hours, the body's defenses are fragile, and the internal organs do not function well. We then also cannot regulate the acidity levels of our blood. Many other troubles follow. This is why people who are grieving terribly, are far more prone to also becoming sick, and then grieve further. It is a vicious cycle. Some individuals grieve for a tremendous loss in life, such as the act of having been given to adoption as children, and can carry that burden inside them all their lives. That too affects their lungs and breathing patterns.

The opposite to the emotion of Grief, is the feeling of being Blessed. To be grieving, is to hold the belief that you do not have what needed to have been. To be blessed, is to believe that you have more than enough. By this logic I would like to point out to you, that it is possible to cure Grief by offering a Blessing [81].

Now this line of thinking, if you look into it, seems to prevail throughout all ancient cultures. A man of spiritual eminence in the eyes of the community, such as a priest, a shaman, a rabbi or similar, would frequently 'bless' the believers. There is of course, a strong

---

[81] In the monotheistic traditions of the West, this concept goes all the way back to the Book of Genesis from the Old Testament. There, the brothers Jacob and Esau are involved in familial politics, over the question of who would receive the blessing of the patriarch, their father Isaac. Since those times when that story was written, and probably before them, the notion of receiving a blessing became a core concept in the religions and traditions of Judaism, Christianity and Islam.

religious aspect to the work these people are doing. But the psychological effect is no less important. For if a man who receives a blessing can gain the belief that he has been filled with plenty, and be programmed into a state of an 'abundance mentality', it is then possible for him or her, in part or full, to transcend the grief which plagues them. This means that a blessing, correctly bestowed and timely applied, has the power to heal both the body and mind of a grieving person. That sort of knowledge, I did not appreciate fully until I have had the opportunity to put it to good use myself.

A number of years ago, I had a student who was a cheerful, pleasant academic. Let us call him **Jamie**. Like many other academics, Jamie was flexible in his thinking and stiff in his flesh. But he made steady progress through training, and was getting much better. Unfortunately, Jamie quit his practice after only six months, to concentrate on his Phd thesis. Some people cannot take the pressure of both thinking and moving at the same time. Jamie was nonetheless very polite and courteous in leaving, and we parted on good terms.

A short while later, I found out through another student, that Jamie had experienced a most awful tragedy right after he had left our academy. His young nephew, a little girl of 5 years, suddenly died overnight. In the afternoon of that dreadful day, she was happily playing with her mates in the sandbox. By evening, she had a mild fever. Some hours later, her parents found her struggling to breath. She died on the way to the hospital. It was ruled as a medical anomaly – "death by lethal unknown strain of bacteria". This was a silly way of saying they had not a clue why the child had died. My former student was childless himself, although married, and his nephew was the closest thing he had to a daughter. I knew that he must have been devastated no less than her parents were.

I made up my mind immediately to attend the shiv'ah[82]. I was there two days later, bearing material and spiritual nourishment. I entered a small apartment in a quiet suburban neighbourhood. Its insides looked like the Israel of olden times – mellow, cultured and full of art and books, hanging on the walls and laying on shelves everywhere. It was almost akin to a miniature North-European estate of the enlightenment age. I recognized these people to be of my kin, unlike some other, uncouth Israelis who put the reputation of Jewish intellect and virtues to shame. This was the spirit from before the country had been tainted by corruption and barbarism. Sitting in the living room were the grieving parents – a young couple in their 30s, the grandparents from both sides of the family, and another uncle with his wife. My student welcomed me inside and offered me beverage and appetizers, trying and failing to sustain a cheerful spirit. The deceased youngster had been the youngest member of the family, and the only grandchild to have thus far been produced, and prior to her untimely demise, was the whole family's center of attention. The atmosphere, as expected, was tense and depressed. But these people were civilized enough as to not make an overly needy or dramatic emotional scene, even in light of such tragedy. They bore their sadness with dignity, rather than capitalizing on victimhood with the loud calls of wild beasts, typical of some other inhabitants of the land. I respected that.

Taking my time and caring to not appear in a rush, I gently transitioned between the many chairs which filled the void, to align myself for some time next to one family member, before approaching another. My ears were open and my heart was patient to these people, before I endeavored to say something of my own

---

[82] The Shiv'ah (literally: Seven) is an ancient Jewish mourning tradition. Upon someone's passing, a family member or a close friend open their home to visitors, morning to night, for the duration of seven days. It is customary that all relatives and friends of the deceased would show up for at least an hour or two, especially if they did not attend the funeral. Commonly, even distant acquaintances come and show their respects. Attendees sometimes come more than once, and often bring food with them. The atmosphere tends to be sad but hopeful. The purpose of the shiv'ah is to help those who suffer deal with their grief via communal support. Stories are told of the deceased and his life, and the food offers additional comfort.

volition. It is crucial on such occasions, that one respects the need for others to express themselves, even if in silence on their part.

By the time when most children are put to bed, I was the only guest left who was not a family member. The noble folk surrounding me were tired, but anxious to break apart the gathering, though growing absent of things to say. Witnessing this emotional stagnation, I gathered my courage to act upon the circumstances and attempt to be of some support to these people, albeit being a complete stranger to most of them. By that time, they were huddled together like a wet flock warming one-another in a bitter storm. I then took a chair and placed it right in front of them, and politely

requested if they could kindly bestow upon me the opportunity to say a few friendly words. My wish was granted, with some surprised gazes of wonderment.

To be perfectly honest, I had not a plan for this – I improvised what came to mind. I began by thanking the family for allowing me to share their intimate moment with them. I described my positive impressions of each of the men and women present there, even if the most I could say was a single sentence. In so doing, I added charitable words of the honorable aspects of their character in their manner of dealing with what had transpired; choosing to highlight the affectionate bond they had for one another, and how even in dire circumstances they were able to find strength and nourish each-other. Rather than speaking of the tragedy of a girl who died young, I discussed and praised the many positive traits of the people whom she loved in her lifetime, and the joy they must have brought her with their boundless love. Carrying it further, I explained to them how, in my opinion, it was in the power of a person to sway the hearts and destinies of others by his or her existence, even if they happened to only live for a few years on this Earth. Surely, the little girl's life could never be considered 'a waste'. Up to a few days ago, her being was the golden thread which brought a whole family ever-closer – a social fabric which will never be undone. Then following her departure from us also, her memory will be alive within all those who knew her, affecting their existence positively for eternity. Though we cannot reason perhaps why things have happened, we can still see how her life was, and will continue to be, a blessing to us all. "Why should we bless the child and ourselves rather than grieve?", I asked; answering immediately: "Because to be blessed is the opposite of grieving, and it allows all of us to celebrate the endless beauty and supreme joy that life could provide us with – that which was, is now, and will continue to manifest in our presence, if we only so wish".
"Indeed then", I said in my finishing remarks: "***I would like to bless you all! This family is of distinguished and humane bearing. You are all wonderful people, who deserve the best in this world. Though you have been met with the utmost difficult challenge now, together you are strong. Though your***

gift has departed, there is still grace and a point to your life. Those who are gone, have not been in vein. Have faith in a better tomorrow, and know that you are blessed to have one-another. You were blessed before, and you shall continue to be. This is what I believe, and may my words bear substances for the years to come. I too, have been blessed by your presence".

That was the gist of a speech which probably lasted 10-15 minutes. Time stood still then, and I cannot remember all the details. The people who I was consoling were slowly nodding in solemn agreement, being too somber at the time to react in a more substantial manner. The most important aspect to my speech had been not its contents, but the fact that I meant what I said wholeheartedly, and therefore came across as genuine and made an impact.

About a week later, I received a phone call from my former student. He wanted to thank me for the great service I have done unto his family. He said that my speech had left a profound mark upon them, and completely changed the manner in which they were digesting their loss. They now had a brighter outlook, and renewed energies to act and continue with their lives. For years later, that student continued to tell people of that one night when his Shifu blessed his family. It was a special moment which he, and perhaps they also, will never forget.

Such is the power of a blessing well-placed and properly articulated. Such are words which can be stronger than punches. As authority figures in our students' lives, we have the capacity and responsibility, to bring about such positive influence. We can make the difference in the lives of grieving individuals, by applying our earned wisdom and spiritual prowess to difficult situations. Though no martial arts tradition has within it rules or guidelines for dealing with those in despair, in means not that we should omit to notice, that this ought to be a part of our calling. This is what is meant by Leadership. That you do not wait for the opportunity to come, or for someone to select you to fulfill a social role. Rather, that you rise to the occasion when others would not.

The Alpha Male

Men who teach the martial arts are naturally placed by others in the socially advantageous position of the 'Alpha Male'. The nature of the profession creates this scenario by itself, and even those who are in their everyday lives mild and timid often become the 'silverback gorilla' in the eyes of their students. What is going on?

The answer is simple. You are in charge. Other men pay you to be in charge. People do your physical bidding and take this to extremes. You usually have the final word. You physically put down other males as part of the teaching process. The surrounding males allow you to do much without objections and seldom challenge your authority publicly. All of this of course for a good purpose – to help people in a place of learning, and should never be taken advantage of in a negative manner. Still, the innate biology of the human species causes this type of situation to be interpreted in a very specific way.

The social rank of the Alpha Male carries with it some challenges and problems as well, which I shall discuss shortly. But we nonetheless need to preserve that position if we are to govern the martial arts school effectively. That is because unfortunately, if students cease to believe that we fulfill the role of an alpha male, they would become challenging to teach, or quit outright.

Dominance can be asserted by forcefully winning a position, but respect can not be taken – it is earned. In nature among primates, the successful alpha males, those who last in the long term, are usually not bullies, but benevolent rulers. As such, their status is earned and manifested gradually. Likewise, you cannot expect to be viewed or considered a leader immediately when you open a school. It can take several years to establish firmly your position as such, to the degree that people would follow you with true zeal.
The consolidation of your status is done in part by being generous,

empathetic, willing to work hard to resolve conflicts, and elevating those in need. These qualities were all observed in chimpanzees who are alpha males. Though all of these qualities are address in other chapters of this book as well, allow me to portray them from the chimpanzee point of view.

Generosity: The alpha male is eager to give more than he is eager to receive. In our hyper-alienated social sphere, in which money often precedes courtesy and kindness, being generous is more prized than ever before. Most if not all of your students are products of a mass-production system of education. They will tend to appreciate personal care and attentiveness by a teacher, when provided in moderation [83].

Empathy: Alpha males among chimpanzees show the greatest capacity for empathy, as compared with other males. This surprising fact illustrates the role of the alpha male as the main caretaker of the community. This is the reason politicians hold and kiss babies during their electoral campaigns. But I do not recommend their shallow deceitful mannerisms. Your empathy should be genuine, supportive and providing comfort. When you truly care about other students and their well-being, others will notice.

Resolving conflicts: A successful martial arts community is a peaceful one, and the alpha male is the main instigator of maintaining that peace. I have never had students who resorted to physical violence among themselves, which was not part of the training. Verbal violence is so rare, that I have perhaps heard it once

---

[83] One has to be careful here. Students always require just the right amount of support to put themselves back together and push forward on their own. Excess attention to a student often results, over time, in a sense of ungratefulness and taking the teacher for granted. Be both timely and moderate with your generosity. By providing people exactly what they needed, nothing more or less, you can instill in them a sense of a great contribution on your part, even when you have not given a lot.

every few years. In Israel where I live, verbal and physical violence are quite common. But not so within my school. The reason is that the roots of conflict are severed at the onset. I interfere in student disagreements and arguments and prevent escalation before it has time to mature. When students practice combatively, I would physically step in and cool things off if people step out of line. Sometimes this can be annoying to a teacher, as people behave like children in class, and often you feel like operating a kindergarten for adults, as people exhibit petty quarrels over the most trifle of matters. But by catering to these situations exactly, your position is strengthened, and the community is gradually harmonized.

Supporting those in need: In the chapter called **'The Benevolent Ruler'** (p. 34), I mentioned Confucius stating that a leader should show encouragement by teaching the incapable. But this goes beyond that. The alpha male is in nature often the first to support the underdog – the member of the group having most difficulty. It demonstrates to other members of the group that he has power, for he can allocate time, strength, patience and resources to aid another.

At our school was once an event that brought together all of these important elements I had just described. One of my students was injured in class through an accident, breaking his finger. The bone snapped at an odd angle and therefore required minor surgery. This was the only major injury we have had at the school up to that point. I organized for him a fundraiser among the other students, so he could pay for the surgery, and made sure I contributed the highest sum (even though at the time, I could barely afford it). I traveled some distance to get him a Chinese medical ointment to help reduce the swelling and support blood flow. I paid to have a special medicine for bone healing delivered to him from abroad. I visited him both before and after the surgery, and was in contact with him daily for support. In so doing I demonstrating all of the qualities expected of an alpha male, but did so not thinking of these, but rather because I truly cared for my student, who had been with me

for several years already at that point. This event turned from misfortune to an advantage, as it helped solidify communal kinship and amicability.
These qualities then, do more than simply help the teacher become popular among his students. They build up the school community, set an appropriate personal example, and guarantee that the teacher will always be supported by his students in times of need, with them repaying in kind.

All this considered, the alpha male paradigm also has potential for causing problems, for you and those around you, if you are not cautious.

Often an issue could arise in that the teacher forgets to turn off the overt 'alpha male mode' when interacting with people outside of his school. Check yourself on this and avoid it. Certainly, not all walks of life require you to behave similarly to how you do at the school.

By far however, the most dangerous and potentially disastrous situation is that of undesirable female attraction. It is quite well known in martial arts communities that teachers tend to attract some of their female students, either intentionally or unintentionally. This happens with a relatively small percentage of female students, yet is notable enough to be considered a 'widespread phenomenon' in the world of martial arts. Being the 'alpha male' in the room contributes much to this phenomenon. Men who may otherwise not be considered as attractive, can become magnets to some types of women. This is to be avoided at all costs.

I too experienced this first-hand. While in my personal life I had both successes and setbacks with women throughout the years, as a martial arts teacher too many unwanted opportunities were literally flocking in my direction.

I remember for instance that years ago I had a female student who began behaving strangely in class. I was fortunately the only one to notice that in the midst of joint demonstrations with me, she would start to play very subtle 'games', challenging me in a way she should not have done based on the demonstration, and compelling me to forcefully subdue her (by creating situations in which failing to do so will cause me harm or loss of face in front of other students). Eventually that woman, a most lovely, smart and beautiful lady, asked me on a date, and attempted to convince me that we would work out quite well together as a couple. Being as polite as possible, I refused, explaining that as a teacher I could not be dating my own students. That woman became occupied with a new relationship a few months later, and left the school soon thereafter. Though I will never know whether this was the reason, I assume that once the romantic option was completely off the table, she felt she had no reason to stay. With other women, this happened much faster. Those who showed interest would tend to leave within two months or less, as soon as no potential romance was gestured back in their direction.

One of my good friends, a Karate Sensei, actually married his long-time student and love, a wonderful woman of great character. I believe they had become romantically involved after several years of her studying under him. But this example is truly exceptional and had special circumstances attached. Sometimes a romantic relationship as such can be more reasonable if the teacher and student are both consenting adults and have known each other for a very long period of time. But usually, it would be immoral to date one's student, for one has an unfair influence over the entire relationship from the onset [84]. It is also a perilous adventure to undertake. In modern developed countries, it has become common for women to use the law to take revenge upon a man who let them down, or at times even for financial greed or extortion. A single police complaint has the power to completely destroy a martial arts teacher's career. This is not a chance worth taking.

Another troublesome aspect of such a relationship is that by dating a student, the teacher risks being impartial or being perceived as such by other students of his. Once the students become aware of such a relationship, then how can one later claim impartiality? This creates a need for the teacher to constantly 'prove' something to the students, which is in itself unhealthy. Then what kind of message does this present to the students, who are likely to not be intimately familiar with reasons and causes? They now understand that they can act in the same manner as their role model, which can manifest as a very negative influence.

There is also a physiological side to such social issues. Wherein your practice is vigorous and healthy, simply by going at it and leading many men, your testosterone and confidence levels are inclined to naturally rise - often to optimal levels. This tends to increase sexual

---

[84] In law this is known as taking advantage of one's 'position of trust' or as 'professional abuse', and in some countries and situations is considered illegal by default, or at least something which makes a student liable to sue the teacher (or the boss for that matter).

potency and also one's urge to fulfill it. This is felt like a craving which grabs the whole body; as an inner force attempting to subjugate your decisions to its will. It can be quite powerful and disorienting, leading one astray [85]. That sort of influence can physically draw a man in the direction of a woman he considers attractive like a magnet, and make him say things to her which his rational self would avoid. That is the root of many troubles which can befall those who do not exercise fierce self-restraint.

As martial arts teachers, we should admit that we live among 'colleagues' who criminally abuse their power against women (and men), performing vile acts, sometimes even with underage teens. We the teachers should by all means oppose such men and act to excommunicate those who have, without a doubt, hurt women.

I know of a certain instructor in my native homeland who was convicted of several sexual acts enacted against his students, who were minors at the time. His supporters argued for his innocence, but myself and many other respectable teachers knew that the man likely did what was attributed to him. He was convicted and sat in prison for several years, but after serving his time he went back to teaching martial arts, and has in fact become more successful than before.

A friend of mine is a famous Israeli teacher who likes mingling with a lot of colleagues. This friend of mine went at one time to a social gathering with several other teachers, and to his surprise and dismay that convicted felon I told you about, then recently released from jail, was there at the table with everybody. My friend, not wanting to make a fuss or be overly judgmental while not knowing

---

[85] Due to the natural differences in the physiology of males and females of the human species, women are not commonly haunted by the more radical influences of excess testosterone, and seldom experience such effects. But these are of frequent appearance in the lives of alpha male figures. This is partly why so many famous male actors, politicians, athletes and businessmen have a difficult time preserving the integrity of their marriage or long-term relationships.

all the details, initially ignored him. My friend felt uneasy however, since he (my friend) came to the event with his wife and son. Then after a while, my friend was shocked to see that the convicted felon put a female teenager on his lap, who was not his relative, and was petting her! My friend quickly left the scene with his family, utterly disgusted with what he saw, and cut all ties with those people who invited that man over.

Likewise, another friend of mine, a famous Shifu from Canada, tells of how he left his first martial arts teacher after he discovered the man was engaged in immoral acts with minors.

Consider therefore that as martial arts teachers, the great power of being perceived by others as alpha males also places us at a position of great responsibility. Make sure you and your colleagues hold this to be a sacred principle in your practice and community.

A Curious Mind
Memories of Master Zhou

It is a peculiar and somewhat surreal thing that, a Westerner belonging to a nation of people who are less than 15 million in number worldwide, who dwells in the Middle-East, would come to be a student of another man, half a world away – one of nation counting over 1.5 billion people. Some would call it Karma, Fate, or Divine Intervention. I, for one, attribute this to the power of Human Wills. For where two people search the same thing, its shape, nature or distance matter less than its essence. What one looks for, with unquestionable desire and an utmost thirst, will bring one to find the answers, in the existence of other human beings. So it came to be, that I have become a student of master Zhou Jingxuan; a man quite unlike myself, who nonetheless shared with me something transcendental and special. A connection to an ancient mindset, now long gone from the soul of the majority of humanity. This keen interest in the Martial Arts – a glue that

brings people together and bridges across cultures like no other; a gift that master Zhou was handing over to those eager to accept, passing it on as it had been passed to him.

Seeking truthful and serious traditional instruction, I came to study, many years ago, under master Zhou's student, Shifu Nitzan Oren – a fellow Israeli, and nowadays also a dear friend. Later, on several occasions, I have had the chance to study directly under Zhou Shifu for long periods of time. With both teachers I have studied Xing Yi Quan and Pigua Zhang. My last training period with Zhou had been for several months of daily training, during Summer and Autumn of 2014CE. Prior to that, I have also trained daily with Zhou Shifu for a month in summer 2010CE, when he had come to Israel to instruct his Israeli students and their students, and in summer of 2012CE in China.

To understand what Zhou was about, it is instrumental that I tell you of the place that molded his being. Master Zhou was born and had lived all of his life in Tianjin city, China. Today, Tianjin is a booming metropolis of 15 million people, with infrastructure and facilities no less impressive than those of famous European cities (albeit its pollution being quite terrible). But at its core, Tianjin is an ancient city, and up until the late 20th century, it was still quite primitive in its construction and accommodations, not to mention the living standards, which were fitting of a third-world country. While culture in some respects has always flourished, either above or below the surface, the mentality and mindset of most of this city's inhabitants was always that of the poor and struggling. Even today, it can be said that large portions of the city are one big 'rough neighborhood'. This is the environment engulfed Zhou’s existence throughout his life – a place which builds character, psychological endurance, and sharp survival instincts.

Tianjin, circa 1930CE:

Tianjin, 2012CE (when I visited there for the first time):

In 1931CE, the Empire of Japan had invaded Manchuria, with the goal of conquering all of China, marking the (true) beginning of World War II. The China that was invaded had been at its weakest point in many centuries, following 200~ years of economic conquest by Western powers, and a succession of terrible civil wars. The Chinese barely survived the great war, in which the Japanese Imperial Army was not only close to occupying all of China, but performed some of the worst atrocities and war crimes in recent memory, including mass murders and rapes of thousands and tens of thousands of women at a time. Tianjin suffered significantly from this occupation, and so had Zhou's family. His grandfather in turn, set out to fight the Japanese. The Chinese army was so scarce in resources, that it was frequent that the soldiers would run out of ammunition, or lack firearms altogether. The 29th army, which Zhou's grandfather joined, had therefore experimentally equipped their soldiers with additional weapons – Dao and Da Dao swords (standard and enlarged curved sabers), to fight the Japanese at close quarters, or when the ammunition would run out. It is almost unthought of that in the age of automatic and semi-automatic guns, that people would be fighting against such weapons with swords, but the 29th army did so quite successfully. Zhou's grandfather survived the war, at the cost of seeing all his friends being killed by the Japanese. It seems to me that this traumatic experience of the most brutal kind of fighting had undoubtedly affected young Zhou Shifu, who took to heart the lessons of war and violence. From his grandfather, he even learned the Dao form they used to train in order to kill the Japanese.

In the pictures: Left – A Chinese soldier, carrying a Da Dao sword on is back, waiting at the Tianjin railroad station. Bottom – Another soldier of the 29th army, carrying Dao swords on his back.

For Zhou, it was obvious from a young age that he was going to practice martial arts. The district he lived in, Hong Qiao (红桥), is one of two districts in the city of Tiajin famous for their martial artists (the other being Nankai 南开). He lived near Xigu park – an impressive island of greenery in the middle of gray Tianjin, which had over the years become an attraction point for many martial artists. The teaching atmosphere was very different from other places, especially compared to schools in modern times. People simply came to the park and practiced. You could have chosen between many teachers, and if you had the right connections, also be recommended by your own teachers to become a student of others. Because of these unique circumstances, Zhou had the opportunity to get to know hundreds of highly-skilled martial arts teachers in his lifetime, and study under quite a few of them.

Beginning at age 9, Zhou started his studies with the arts of Chuo Jiao, Fanzi Quan and Tan Tui. Later, he also learned Pigua Zhang (under two teachers), Xing Yi Quan (under four teachers), and Baji Quan and Jingang Bashi (under two teachers who are gongfu brothers) and Li style Taiji Quan. Additionally, all of Zhou's teachers taught him several weapon forms, each. Some of these weapons are related to the arts he had studied, while others such as the Six Harmonies Spear form or various joint-locking forms are interdependent from style. Overall, Zhou Shifu ended up having over 13 long-term teachers, out of which he became an official disciple (indoor student) of seven.

Zhou also had encounters and knowledge exchanges with several other martial arts teachers. Since he had over the years become such an enormous fountain of martial knowledge, there were always people who were interested in learning his skills – especially material from his rare art of Shaolin Jingang Bashi. It is not the custom in Chinese society, however, that two people of the same class (say two veteran teachers) would become each-others student. Because of this, Zhou exchanged knowledge with these teachers on a friendly basis, and gained insight into the use and theory of many other martial arts and weapons in that manner.

As a child, Zhou was mischievous and adventurous. This had probably been his way of coping with the harsh living conditions in Tianjin, past the Cultural Revolution (a time of great poverty and death throughout China). The country was difficult to survive in, and life was chaotic. People had to learn how to endure and manage, and teach these skills to their families as well. Thus, when Zhou began his martial arts learning at the age of 9, and through his teenage years and early 20s, he was involved in a lot of fights that were forced upon him by others. Initially, he was wary of violence.

But early on in his training, older gongfu brothers have ordered him to pick up fights with other children, while they watched his back. Unable to refuse, he learned how to fight in this manner at a young age.

Times have since changed, China and Tianjin have become relatively safer places, and Zhou the adult turned more peaceful in nature. Also in accordance with the times, Zhou has since been accepting students with all types of goals in training – not just martial; he eventually enjoyed teaching people who sought learning the arts for self-preservation and development as well. He himself had also begun to practice more health-oriented methods over the years, to balance his previous martial escapades. Zhou's previous martial experiences were still evident though; as he demonstrated the proper execution of movements and martial techniques, he did so with a fierceness and intimidation of a true fighting scenario.

In the picture: Members of Zhou's gongfu family – practitioners of Baji Quan and Jingang Bashi, some of them members of the Communist Party. Circa 1980s. Zhou is sitting in the front row, on the far left, wearing a white shirt. Behind Zhou stands his grand-teacher, Tian Jinzhong, wearing glasses. To Tian's left stands another grand-teacher of Zhou's – Zhao Fujiang (bald man with dark-blue shirt), who was master Tian's younger gongfu brother in their Baji lineage.

When Zhou was a young teenager, he recalls, there was a certain Taiji Quan teacher in the park. To Zhou and his friends, that old teacher was a target for ridicule, as he looked funny, and they did not think much of the slow movements he had been practicing. The old man, on his part, did not mind at all the children's behaviour, and completely ignored them. They used to come at him in the park when he was not training, and try to push him over. Zhou vividly remembered how, despite their best attempts, they could not do anything to him. Whenever they pushed on him, his body would collapse and absorb their energy with no apparent effort. Those who used too much force on him would be bounced back or into the ground by their own strength and momentum. Later as he became a teacher himself, Zhou was stricken by this silliness and his former disrespect towards the old man, when he was younger. He said: "I wish I was wiser, and would have gone to study under this man, as he had obviously possessed great skill in the martial arts".

Such experiences, as well as Zhou's tutelage by many teachers over the years, have made him garner much respect towards other arts and martial artists. It was difficult, and often impossible, to make Zhou Shifu speak badly of other people and their arts. He could go in-length for many minutes on end, on the wonderful skills of practitioners which he thought highly of. But ask him of someone who is not skilled or is not a good person, and Zhou would have rather said he did not know enough about this person or his martial art, than speak badly of them. He also regretted not having the chance or the time to practice under or with martial artists of styles he had not learned. While Zhou was very satisfied and enthusiastic about the styles he practiced and taught, this yearning for more knowledge was derived from his great appreciation of other practitioners and their arts. Having trained in Xigu park since childhood (and later started teaching there), Zhou was a very familiar figure in the park. It seems that most people who went there knew him somehow – if not by name, at least by recognizing his face and composure. Since his youth, he was also been famous

around his neighborhood for his excellent skills in Pigua Zhang.

In Chinese society, where one's name, Ego and 'Face' often play a huge role, it is rare that people publicly ask others, who are not their own teachers, to instruct them. Such an act would, in this traditional society, indicate that the person asking instruction is 'lesser' or even 'inferior' to the other. Nonetheless, I have myself seen many people in the park approach Zhou Shifu, asking him to teach them a little something here and there, or to correct their practice. I have also been witness to several parents who came to Zhou, and asked him to formally accept their children as his students. These parents were interested in the physical well-being of their children – their health and ability to protect themselves, and also in exposing their children to traditional Chinese culture, in an age in which most Chinese children were more interested in imitating American culture.

As stated earlier, China at large has suffered from two centuries of Economic and Military occupation by Western powers. The very center of this ugly takeover was the city of Tianjin, which still features several neighbourhoods with lots of beautiful Western-style architecture, reminiscent of 19th century Europe. These times were then followed by several decades of strict Communist rule, which was also anti-Western in ideology, and actively fought the West in the Korean War and during the Cold War. That said, it was to be expected that the older Chinese generations would not think highly of Westerners. Neither did Zhou think too positively of Westerners, when he was younger. Having never learned a foreign language or known a Westerner as a friend, like most of the Chinese of his generation, his opinion of Westerners was shaped by the bloody, turbulent history of China over the last few centuries. While one could hardly suggest that this social anti-Western mindset was stained by harsh things like Racism, one could say that suspicion, prejudice and bias were definitely common in this society towards foreigners. Which is perfectly understandable, by the way, considering their historical circumstances, and China's isolation from the Western world throughout most of the 20th century.

I believe that Zhou's ideas about foreigners must have taken their first shift once he began to teach Westerners in the 1990s. Slowly but surely, he came to understand that they were not at all as bad as they were always portrayed to be when he was younger. A major change of heart was in the years following Zhou's acquaintance with my teacher, Nitzan Oren. At the time, and throughout his life actually, Zhou had trouble with students leaving his side before they could learn a reasonable amount of martial material and skills. Most of the young Chinese tended to neglect serious martial arts practice, possibly because Zhou was more readily available to them (did not appreciate him enough because of that), and also because the pursuit of careers and finance was of a greater interest to them than training. Few of Zhou's Chinese students tended to stick around for over 2-3 years at most, and those who did, usually never trained as hard as Zhou had probably hoped for. One Chinese female student of Zhou had stayed with him for 11 years, and had reached a very good level. Unfortunately, she quit training altogether once she got married (as commonly happens in Chinese society, which is still very chauvinistic compared to the West).

Nitzan was the exception, remaining by Zhou's side for 7 years straight, and studying with him daily. It was the first time that Zhou had had such a serious-minded student. In the beginning, Zhou still carried some cultural biases and prejudices towards Westerners. Over time though, Nitzan's persistence and perseverance have made him change his mind about Westerners. Following Nitzan, more and more Westerners came to study with Zhou. He then noticed that, not only were these people willing to come all the way from another continent to train with him, some of them also invested more effort in their training than many of his Chinese students. He also figured that these Westerners were genuinely interested in traditional Chinese culture, which ironically, many of the younger Chinese were now throwing away, in favour of chasing fantasies related to the Consumerism and Hedonism of the globalized "American" culture. In an age in which the Chinese are quickly losing their own cultural roots, Zhou had found comfort in knowing that there are foreigners willing to put in the time and effort, to preserve what is dear to him. That is why, as a mature adult, he had a drastic change in some of the ideologies he had been indoctrinated into since early childhood, and have come to accept Westerners as equals, and decent people. To the extent that at such an age (when he was over 30), a person is willing to consciously have this big a change of heart, is in my opinion a wonderful testimony to Zhou's pragmatic, humble and down-to-earth character. In our time, many Chinese (in mainland China) treat foreigners nicely, but think and speak badly of them behind their backs, as a result of the education they had been receiving from youth (though the situation is improving, and there are also many Chinese who are most welcoming and kind towards foreigners). Zhou has transcended that nationalistic mentality, and had come to accept Westerners without prejudice or bias. That sort of attitude may 'go without saying' for a person educated in the safe confines of a Liberal Democracy, but for a person who has been brainwashed all his life as a citizen of a Totalitarian state, this is not at all obvious. During the last decade of his life, Zhou came to have many foreign students worldwide, and took great pride in many of them.

In general, it can be said that Zhou Shifu was very dedicated to his students. He treated everyone with equal care and attention, whether Indoor or Outdoor students, young or old, Chinese or Western, long-term or short-term. He garnered respect for any student with a sincere interest in martial arts, and would have gone out of his way to teach more if the student worked hard. Sometimes, one even had to ask Zhou to slow down, as he was so eager to teach more as soon as he thought the student was capable.

As mentioned earlier, in China many still have mixed or negative feelings towards non-Chinese. Therefore, in the park, rude people would sometimes pass by and mock or laugh at foreign practitioners. These acts are disgracing, especially since a Chinese would usually not dare to behave in that manner towards another Chinese in public (we should consider that sadly, this phenomenon also exists in the West). Zhou could become very upset with such people, and would have immediately shouted at them and scolded them for talking of or behaving badly towards his students; making sure they would leave the place at once. It is important that I stress in any case, that such people are an exception to the rule, and that most Chinese think positively of people who are sincere in their efforts to learn aspects of their culture. More commonly, I would encounter Chinese people who were very happy to see a Westerner practicing Chinese martial arts.

Martial arts were everything to Zhou – his hobby, his job, and his way of life. While educated to an extent in Calligraphy,

Chinese literature and Classics and even in Traditional Chinese Medicine, martial arts were always his focal point. In his lifetime, he had many jobs in commerce and trade, from book-salesmanship to gem-trade, but teaching martial arts have remained his only steady occupation. Like many other great teachers of the past, this kind of lifestyle is what had helped him reach a superb level of skill in his pursuit of choice.

There are some teachers who have had more influence over Zhou than others. One such teacher, which he held in high esteem, is master Li Guoliang (of Tianjin; there is another well-known teacher by the same name from Taigu, whose name is written with different Chinese characters). From master Li, Zhou had received much of his knowledge of Xing Yi Quan – a lot of which is rarely seen elsewhere nowadays, and have also gained the deep foundations in Zhan Zhuang (standing post) training. These teachings have deeply affected the way Zhou Shifu practiced and taught martial arts. Zhan Zhuang, and other skills taught by master Li, had become 'obligatory material' for any student who came to study under Zhou (with proper, specific adaptations being made for the particular martial art the student is practicing). Zhou considered the Zhan Zhuang training to be the most important, and have told his students that: "Even if one cannot practice at all on a certain day, it is still vital that one would somehow make time for practicing Zhan Zhuang for at least 20 minutes". Another skillset that Zhou would teach, to advanced students, are his Dan Tian development methods, which he had learned from several teachers, but in particular and most of all from Zhao Fujiang (one of his grand-teachers). To train these, one first needs a solid foundation in Zhan Zhuang, which requires prolonged daily practice. The Dan Tian methods can then be introduced, and later be implemented and embedded into any of the arts Zhou had taught, in most fighting movement.

In the picture: Zhou Shifu, with one of his top students, Ben Bario from Israel. HaYarkon Park, Tel-Aviv, Israel, August 2010CE.

Master Zhou was also a big exponent of the notion of Quality being more important than Quantity. Although he himself have studied many arts, he had dedicated several years, and many hours a day, for the practice of each of these arts. Therefore, it was important to him that students spend the time required to hone their ability with each method, drill or technique, before they move on to learn more material. Zhou was also pragmatic in his approach however, and did not force the students to abide by his wishes. Nor did he even coerce anyone to study a particular art or skill, and the final choice was up to the student. His words were a hearty recommendation –that is often better adopted, but is not strictly dictated or enforced. A student's free will and self-actualization were, eventually, the most important things to Zhou when he taught.

In the picture: Zhou Shifu demonstrating an application with his Israeli student, Etai. During this particular moment, Zhou was showing how proper alignment and structure, as developed through Zhan Zhuang training, can make it easy for a small person to resist a much larger individual. Zhou is roughly 5'6 in height, and Etai is 6'4.

Because many of the higher-level skills Zhou learned had originated from his Xing Yi Quan practice methods, and possibly because of his teacher's requests, Zhou refrained from allowing videos of his Xing Yi to be taken. It is a shame, as his Xing Yi was truly exceptional. I remember vividly how I watched Zhou demonstrate things with his Xing Yi that others only speak of.

For example – many people have written of the difference between 'Ming Jin' 明劲 (obvious power) and 'An Jin' 暗劲 (hidden power) in the art. Few teachers, though, can show the difference well. Zhou once demonstrated this difference to us students, using the same movement – Pi Quan – Xing Yi's most basic movement. The first variation, of 'obvious' power, had cut through the air like a baseball bat making a home-run. It was blunt, solid, sharp and defined. Then he delivered the 'hidden power' variation, which is of the higher level. It shot away like lightning tearing a gap in the air, lashing out with a true killing intent, which was at once both subtle and frightening. Myself, I could demonstrate this too nowadays, but it had taken me many years of practice to do so, and I still look up in my memory to Zhou Shifu's example. In his demonstration, even though he had not touched anyone, you could feel the differentiation of spirit and intent behind the movements in a very distinct fashion.

Another time, I have had the 'privilege' of Zhou asking me to try and use short-power striking (Cun Jin 寸劲) on him. This meant I needed to shock him with a strike from zero distance – my hand already on his chest. I was not skilled enough at the time, and Zhou was not satisfied with my power. I could not at all affect him. He then asked me to be his dummy. I was to stand in a strong stance, and flex my chest muscles as he was about to release his force to the side of them. As he did, I felt nothing on the surface of my skin, and he barely seemed to move at all. It was as if he had touched me with cotton. From roughly the middle of his striking palm, it felt as if a very thin needle had dug deep into my chest, and within it had carried an explosive charge, which was then detonated as it had reached the middle of my torso through the route set by the 'needle'. For a split of a second, I felt Death. Psychologically, the closest sensation I could think of is when one vomits badly when one is very ill, and momentarily feels like he is about to die. That is somewhat how I felt – for a moment, as if my game was over; there was not even enough time to fear what was going on – it was only the knowledge of impending doom that was quick enough to enter my consciousness. Luckily, master Zhou knew what he was doing, and did not shock me with his full capacity. Neither was there any damage or pain following the moment of the strike. Still, this was a humbling experience, which had made me realize some of the true potential of what Zhou was teaching.

In the picture: Zhou Shifu, demonstrating an application on Tom, one of his Israeli students. HaYarkon Park, Tel-Aviv, Israel, August 2010CE.

This all reflects Zhou's liking for the hands-on teaching approach. He rightfully believed that in order to truly understand martial arts, the student must ***feel*** them. This meant, beyond the obvious, that the student should have had free access to touching Zhou's body when he performed movements, to get a sense of how the body is supposed to move; also, that the student should have been able to execute the techniques on Zhou himself. These things are absolutely essential for learning Zhou's martial arts. They also expose the intimacy of the relationship between Zhou and his committed students – with both sides expected to openly ask any question, and not shy away from physical contact. This is the traditional manner in which many Chinese martial arts were taught, but this approach is becoming exceedingly rare in the teaching of traditional martial arts; especially in the West and in Japan, where because of cultural politeness and social norms, many prefer a more 'sterile' learning environment and a teacher that keeps his distance and plays the role of an 'authority figure'. Zhou would have none of that, and never claimed to be an authority on anything, or expect a better treatment by anyone because he was a teacher.

When I knew him, Zhou Shifu was closing in on his 50s, yet measuring by his skill and power, one could have never guessed. He would still casually perform splits, move faster than any of his students, exert a greater amount of force than them in his strikes, and easily toss people weighing twice his weight. Other things Zhou could do are, too, out of the ordinary. By the power of his mental intent alone, for example, he could make the hairs on his hand stand erect or fall (these are moved by tiny muscles under the skin, which in medical literature are said not be under one's conscious control). I have also seen Zhou using mere one or two fingers to strike people in demonstrations, making them collapse sideways or to the ground at a great velocity because of the shock.
It is not that Zhou was a Superman of sorts. He was nothing but an ordinary person who has taken his skills to a very high level, in a process lasting several decades. He was the first to admit, for instance, that he is not a strong man, and could not carry or lift exceedingly heavy weights. His skill with the martial arts, involving an attuned technical ability and a body built around this skillset, is what enabled him to handle other human beings, in fighting, much better than people who are physically bigger and stronger than him but were not as well-trained as he was. Some of the arts his taught, such as Baji Quan, lend themselves well to people of a greater mass and height. Still, Zhou had proven that with dedication and perseverance, one can reach a level in which is the skill itself matters much more than other attributes.

To have had the opportunity to learn with Zhou and his student Nitzan is something I shall always cherish. I feel that such a privilege, of finding a true traditional teacher of the Chinese fighting arts, who is both capable and a good person, is rare, even in the age of globalization and access to Internet resources. One of the biggest regrets I have in life is, that my own personal circumstances have not allowed me to spend more time with Zhou Shifu, and take from him what he so willingly aspired to give to those interested.

In the picture: Zhou Shifu, teaching Baji Quan to a group of Chinese students. All of them are bigger and heavier than him. The Chinese guy standing directly behind Zhou is Xiao Hei 小黑 – a national Western-Boxing champion, who is 6'4 and is twice Zhou's weight.

It was August 2010CE when I first met master Zhou. We invited Zhou over for a month-long training camp in Israel. I had the privilege of studying twice a day with him for a month, and even hosting him in my house for a week. Since Zhou had never travelled outside of China, and myself having never met him or had a Chinese person as a friend or spoken much Chinese, this was obviously a fertile ground for cultural discovery and comedy.

Zhou was a man of great skill, though this skill was hidden beneath a very simple-looking surface. I was initially perplexed as to how I was to behave around such a man, but my fears were soon gone as I

realized Zhou was one of the most down-to-earth people I had ever known.
During my first lesson with him, he was keen on testing my Xing Yi Quan. Being such a hands-on guy, he wanted me to apply a technique on him. His "faster, stronger!" yells got the better of me, and I accidently hit him in the face. He did not block the blow because I was not actually supposed to hit him, and his hands were down. I was, of course, terrified of what happened. I just hit my teacher's teacher in the face, during our first-ever class together! To my surprise, Zhou was smiling, laughed for a second, and shrugged it off. That is the kind of person he was. Since that incident, I have come to see that this was Zhou's way of doing things. He would go about checking stuff himself, setting a personal example.

A few days afterwards, we drove Zhou to conduct a street-fighting workshop at my friend's Karate school. Though the people there were complete strangers to him, some of them teachers, he frequently asked that they manage to apply techniques on **him**. [86] He also went about to invest a lot of time in personally explaining things to a young 10 year-old boy who attended the workshop, though it was unlikely that he would even see that child again.

When teaching Zhou was very serious, and was fond of yelling instead of just talking when martial arts were the topic at hand. I figure that he was not actually shouting because he was angry – he did so because he cared so much about the students, and wanted his teachings to be clear and taken seriously. Underneath this mantle of seriousness though, he was humorous and fun-loving person. One could not dislike him, as he was constantly in a semi-serious semi-mischievous state of mind.
When I was around him, Zhou was always very humble. He insisted on carrying his luggage and our equipment on his own, and was

---

[86] One should understand that in the context of the Chinese customary habits of "saving face", which are nowadays have also unfortunately become spread among many teachers in the west, this kind of behavior is uncommon.

embarrassed when people did things for him which he could do by himself. I always had to fight with him over letting me do things for him. He even wanted to make the meals for me and wash the dishes at my house after we were finished eating. He was particularly shocked to discover that at the price of one meal at an Israeli restaurant, he could have bought weeks-worth of food in China!

While living in my house, we obviously had a hard time communicating. What could have led to frustration, often resulted in laughter. Zhou always made fun of my muscles, since he believed weight-training was bad for my development in martial arts. As I came back from the weight-gym one evening, all "pumped-up", he took off his shirt and began bodybuilding style posing in front of the mirror, hilariously mocking how I looked. Zhou's muscles were soft as cotton.

The "hands on" thing had a few quite literal implications. One day, briefly after waking up and getting to the park, Zhou asked me for an arm-wrestling contest. Although I was working with weights for a few years by then and considered myself quite strong, I could not move his arm (at the time I could easily do pull-ups with 40kg attached to my waist, and Dips with 60kg attached to my waist. Zhou never trained with weights). At another time, Zhou asked me to move him, while he was just standing regularly. Though I could lift over 160kg of dead-weight off the floor, I could not move him an inch. More disturbingly – I could not even lift him upwards, while he was only weighing about 60kg. His control over his and my center of gravity was so refined, that I could not do anything, yet could not even feel how he was manipulating my strength to his advantage.

Zhou was especially fond of one type of movies – the kind where people kill each other violently, with as many bloody casualties as possible. When watching these movies, he would ask me to rewind some scenes, so he could analyze how the men fought. He would later usually go on lecturing on how they did this or that incorrectly (no matter that I could not understand back then), and ask me to stand up in the middle of the room so he could demonstrate "how to do it right". At one time he took up two large magazines and rolled them into "swords", reenacting an entire scene from ***Gladiator*** with me, doing it "right" this time (I was always playing the guy who got killed with a rolled-up magazine-sword).

The Chinese people are notorious for "eating anything on four legs that is not a table, anything that flies that is not a plane, and anything that is in the water that is not a boat". Zhou's eating habits proved that phrase to be (almost) correct. He happily ate all the different meals I have made for him, and only resented cheese (which was surprisingly still very unpopular in China during the early 21st century). He had some interesting culinary innovations. He liked the Salami Sausage I offered him, but since he thought it to be "raw meat", he suggested we put it in the microwave. Another time I made him some pasta with tomato sauce. I afterwards gave

him some chocolate waffles for dessert. Verifying they were indeed tasty, he went on to dip them in the remaining tomato sauce.
As an effort to help Zhou feel 'at home', we took him to a restaurant ran by Chinese-Jews. He did not think much of the food. A pretty dog with blue tinted fur that a couple had brought with them (to the restaurant) caught his attention. He then told us of how he and other children used to hunt and eat stray dogs (reader, do remember these were poor and harsh times in China, in which many millions were starving to death, and he was living in a very poor neighbourhood). He continued by commenting that unlike "those people from southern China", people from his province do not eat things like rats and snakes (dogs were OK, though). His childhood dog-eating experiences made him somewhat suspicious of dogs, but he did like Cats. My teacher had a few earlier horror stories of Zhou sending cats flying through the air after they have made the mistake of touching his leg as he was giving lessons. My experiences proved that there were at least some cats he did like. My gongfu uncle Ben had two nearly-identical cats (both called "Snooze"), and while living at Ben's, Zhou was always playing around with the cats; frequently yelling "sloooos, slooos!!" at them and bursting out laughing from their reactions ("sloooos" is apparently "Snooze" in Chinese). He also had an (culinary?) interest in my cat, but the cat did not stick around to find out what Zhou wanted to do with it...

A true martial artist in heart, his subject of study occupied Zhou all day long. When he was talking about anything, the conversation would return to the topic of martial arts in a matter of minutes. When doing anything not related to martial arts, his thoughts would wonder back to fighting in no-time. Driving him around in my car, he was constantly throwing all kinds of martial movements in the air; his face showing in-depth analysis of this or that technique. I almost got myself into several car accidents because of this. His sudden hand gestures would often look like he was warning me from imminent danger, which took my attention away in the direction he was pointing at, and almost got us both killed.

In the picture: The author with master Zhou, at the entrance of the Chinese restaurant in Israel, which fortunately did not serve dog meat!

People often wonder what makes one a "master". When Zhou was asked that question, he plainly answered that one should train a lot, and listen to his teacher. Having lived with such a man, I could account for another important trait – curiosity. A child-like curiosity. Zhou was curious about anything new he saw, and could not wait to get his hands on it and his mind wrapped-around it; mixing things up and creating new ideas out of the existing matter. It seemed that whenever shown something new, he got it right every time from the second he learned how to do it. This curiosity was at its strongest in relation to martial arts. Zhou was a fountain of knowledge, and he always wanted to know more. He had a lot of teachers, with whom he studied for many years, and he continueed his research into the martial arts to his last day with the enthusiasm of someone who started it yesterday.

People think a child acting like an adult is special, but what is even more special, in my opinion, is an adult that can think like a child. Were we to take one lesson from Zhou, it should be to always maintain the curiosity and playfulness of a child, and bear thought with the weight and experience of an old man.

"A master in the art of Living draws no sharp distinction between work and play" – L. P. Jacks

<u>In the picture:</u> Master Zhou, with the backdrop of Tel-Aviv's shoreline. Year 2010CE.

In early January of 2015CE, master Zhou suffered a stroke. I knew this was coming. I had a premonition. I have been trying to tell people for a while at that point, that I believed Zhou was not feeling well. I could see his light dwindling. He himself shrugged it off, and did not even consider he was in danger. But then in a moment, some months later, his brain became swollen with blood, and he collapsed. When he had woken up 24 hours later at the hospital, half his body was paralyzed. He gradually retained consciousness and was able to utter some words, understood everything and recognized everyone. His condition was stable, and he was taken out the emergency room. The doctors believed he would survive and get better. In the meanwhile, over 20 people in our gongfu family worldwide, in the West and China, collected money to pay for his hospital bills and care. We managed to transfer the money in time. It was touching to see how everyone cooperated together as a big loving family to take care of him, even though we live so far apart and many did not even know each-other. Shifu received the money and was happy and moved.

A while later though, on the 27th of January, Zhou suddenly had issues with high blood pressure, his condition deteriorated very rapidly, and his lost consciousness again. Within a very short time the doctors declared him in a vegetative state. The family chose to let him off life-support so he could die with dignity. His two sons were by his side when he passed, in his sleep.

I have spent a few months of my life studying privately and semi-privately with master Zhou, in Israel and China. He was a good man. Better than most. Not once he uttered a bad word of other martial artists or martial arts. Not once did I hear him curse or swear. He loved his close students like family. They were his sons. Though few have lived up to his expectations, he always gave every student his all. He smiled big and lived big, to the best of his ability. A true carnivore and a heavy drinker (never an alcoholic). He did not smoke. I know that he lived his life to the utmost, and most of the time, to me at least, he seemed happy. He cherished his little fortune and the people who loved him, though his life was tough, and he constantly struggled to make a living. A true people-person, he was seldom alone apart from his personal training. Everywhere he went, there were others to enjoy sharing his company. Many of his students kept coming to classes for years after they have already stopped actual serious training, just to be around him. He never asked anything of me but dedication, and felt uneasy to be receiving any sort of favour or fancy gesture of respect. He strove to give his students more than they gave him, and went out of his way to try and pass on his knowledge to the next generation.

Zhou was a great master of the martial arts. I have always said that videos did not do him justice. The people who saw him for real in his full glory all knew he was a true killer, and that his level of skill was extremely uncommon. When demonstrating seriously, he had an aura of Sha Qi that cut through the air like a knife. He was a martial genius. In 41 years of practice he had studied in great depth over 6 complete systems under more than 13 teachers, and learned minor amounts of martial skills from countless others. Many of Zhou's teachers were still alive when he passed, and I cannot fathom how they must have felt, burying a disciple... burying their child. His knowledge was enormous. There was hardly any weapon one could think of he could not play with: jian, dao, miao dao, guan dao, sticks, staffs and spears of all sizes and of countless forms, meteor hammer, rope dart, double clubs, iron whip, nine-section whip, large farmers fork, halberd, and many more... he knew them all and taught them too. He was also very knowledgeable of meditation practices, and had decent knowledge of traditional Chinese medicine, able to treat well with acupuncture and converse with TCM doctors on the classic texts. Having grown up during the Cultural Revolution, master Zhou was self-taught on many such matters and subjects, and others he had studied strictly through oldschool discipleship and eating bitter. He worked hard, trained hard, and to his last day none of his students exceeded his skill.

Master Zhou was the best student of quite a few teachers, who chose to pass unto him their most complete transmission and most vital skills. Much of what he knew was highly esoteric, not seen anywhere on videos, neither discussed anywhere in writing. I am afraid that many of these things we, his students, shall never even know of, because he did not have the opportunity to teach them. Zhou Shifu was highly respected in the martial arts community of his home city of Tianjin, and many teachers came to study with him or asked him to exchange knowledge with them. Due to his status, he was able to make his arts more complete, by filling-in skills, methods, drills and forms from many different lineages. He was a walking encyclopedia of all of his arts, and remembered by heart hundreds of forms, which he could perform instantly - sometimes after not having practiced them for decades. It is said that when an old man dies, a library burns to the ground. Master Zhou was not even old, but what had been lost with his disappearance from our world is the sum of not a single library, but of knowledge spanning many generations. May he rest in peace.

In the picture: Master Zhou visiting the grave of his beloved Shigong, late master Tian Jinzhong. He was very attached to master Tian. Once when I showed Zhou Shifu a video of his Shigong, he began crying while marveling his gongfu and good character.

A Stranger Would Not Understand

People die, but ideas live on. The workings of trillions of billions of neurons, all bent on the creation of something better. A mass-gathering of thought, pronounced physically, verbally, and sometimes written. The anthology of life-works of souls long-gone, but who are still very much alive in their essence. The legacies of these people, as passed down through rough touch, from one person to another. The burden of a thousand generations thus lies on the shoulders of one middle-aged Chinese man. He alone, the sole inheritor of a complete system of martial arts. Once upon a time, a common property among many. Now, a memory contained within the minds and hearts of one man and his elderly teacher, and embodied in their gong fu.

A stranger would not understand how heavy an intangible burden can be. Another human could not begin to realize the implications of carrying such weight; day in and day out, holding unto it, not knowing if in the distance, there shall be another who may take upon himself this load. The road is long, and tedious, but the work is gratifying and profound. The job of carrying a large chest full of treasures is a privilege. Yet, no one appears to be eager for such gifts. That which is free demands responsibility, and people would rather pay for those things with no requirements attached. The tragedy of modern times – the fall of culture. A loss so great, for which tears will not be shed. How can something be mourned, if it was not cared for to begin with? None will attend the funeral of a martial art, and neither there shall be a grave. A language of the body, a landmark in history; alas, eventually only a droplet which fell into the river of the cosmos. May its ripples continue to silently flow with the stream of endless human creativity.

In Retrospective

By Nitzan Oren

***"Sometimes you will never know the value of something, until it becomes a memory"* – Dr. Seuss**

On one of those freezing-cold mornings of a casual Tianjin winter, I woke up to the sound of a phone call. On the line was my teacher, Zhou: "Get dressed and arrive as quickly as possible at Xigu park; Li Guoliang is arriving for a visit!!". Grandmaster Li was the first indoor student of Lu Zhongren, the originator of "Lu Structure theory" (a training system devised from Lu's life-long experience with Xing Yi Quan and Yin-Yang Ba Pan Zhang). Li became Lu's personal student although the age difference between them was only 12 years. Years later grandmaster Li accepted my teacher Zhou as his personal student, and taught him both Xing Yi Quan and Lu's structure theory.

I dressed hastily, skipped breakfast, and ran straight to the train station. An opportunity to meet a teacher of that caliber was too rare to miss. The long wait and the slow ride to the park had increased my tension as I anxiously expected meeting teacher Li. The calls from my teacher while on the bus did not help much either: "What's going on? Where are you??".

I entered the park, and at a remote distant corner I saw my teacher. Master Zhou waved at me and pulled me towards a friendly "grandpa" of a short stature. "Meet your gongfu grand-teacher – Li Guoliang". Li was sparse with words, and after a short introduction got right to the point: "Show me your Zhan Zhuang". I chose the offensive "Nine Defenses" stance, and started practicing. He circled around me, inspecting my stance, and fixing various angles in my posture. After half an hour he asked me to stop. "Not bad, not bad... Now show me how you release cùn fā jìn 寸发劲(explosive short-force). I had a few years of Xing Yi practice behind me by then, and was no stranger to this type of force. This time though, Li wasn't so pleased. "Not fast enough". I asked him to demonstrate on me how to release such a force. He then put his forearm on my solar plexus area, and delivered a "light" blow with

a short, sudden movement. I felt as all the air from my lungs was blown out, and it took me a while to recover. It was incredible; Nice to find out there was still much to be aspired for, and be reminded that the climb up the mountain is far from being finished.

After the ordeal, Li gave me a few emphases on movement and the way in which power should be issued. "There is a sort of circular grinding movement in the hip", he said, and demonstrated. He could see that I did not understand what he had meant, so he asked me to put my palm on his hip. At the time, I did not know how to define the movement I felt; Something moved in there. I told him: "OK, I can see and feel the movement, but how should I go about practicing in order to be capable of executing it?". "Practice", Li answered, and smiled.

The next week I tried practicing the same slippery circular movement, but all of my efforts were in vain. At our daily practice session, I told Shifu Zhou about the frustration I felt for failing to do that movement. Zhou giggled. He then told me of one of the times when he had learned a movement, but could not exactly copy his teacher, of which case his teacher commented: "You will understand the movement after I am dead". "What does it mean?", I asked. What a horrible answer, I thought to myself. Zhou explained: "An imitation of an External movement is a limited way to teach it. There are movements which cannot be learned just by copying them. As long as we learn under the guidance of a teacher, we try to copy his movement – to watch him do it and imitate him. The meaning behind that proverb is that after our teacher is no longer with us, and we try to recall that same image of our teacher demonstrating, we are actually recreating a feeling. That feeling is the missing element, which enables our body to move as we wish it to". After he finished explaining, Shifu Zhou asked me to try and recreate that lesson at the park. I began reconstructing within my imagination that moment when grandmaster Li demonstrated the movement for me, and found myself executing a similar movement.

It was only months later that I managed to put into words the insight I gained from grandmaster Li's lesson. I understood that trying to imitate a movement by watching the performer directs our intention outwards. On the other hand, when we imitate a movement by recreating it with our memories, while trying to "feel" that movement as it had occurred in our past, we direct our intention inwards, towards the center of our body. Because the center of the body is the source of movement in Xing Yi, when intention is kept at the center of the body, we gain more control over the origin of the movement. The change begins by transitioning from looking outwards, to looking inwards; and it all happens thanks to our view of things in retrospective.

Shifu Nitzan Oren is one of the teachers of Shifu Jonathan Bluestein. He is a notable scholar and author of Traditional Chinese Medicine. He conducts teaching and treats patients in his native country of Israel. Shifu Oren is a disciple of late master Zhou Jingxuan.

Toes That Cast a Shadow

Once upon a time there was a very skilled and knowledgeable teacher of a certain martial art. That teacher invested decades in training under the finest masters. Unfortunately, with his abilities arose also his sense of self-worth, and his Ego was inflated to an alarming degree. Thus was created an unsightly combination, between a person whose body was more capable than others, but whose mind was vile and corrupted. This is a common story in the martial arts.

But having known this man, I realized that there was much to learn from him, despite his personal downfalls. Alas, we were not of the same style, and I did not feel comfortable sharing a learning experience with him due to his offensive personality. Still, we had in common many practice methods and approaches to body mechanics and training. I had therefore decided to do my best to deduce from my modest exposure to his teachings little nuggets of wisdom and inspiration. As I had previously done with many fine practitioners whom I thought highly of, I sat down and spent many hours in front of his video demonstrations, to analyze and examine the similarities and differences between how he and I do things. In doing so, I sought not to learn his art of course or to imitate his form, but simply to explore new ideas for my own practice and teachings. The experience, as always, was fruitful and successful. I recommend readers to do the same. Dedicated, prolong and concentrated viewing of a serious practitioner's videos, for many hours on end, often repeating the same segments over and over again, is a surefire method for attaining higher realizations in the martial arts. It does however require that one would already be a seasoned practitioner and preferably a teacher himself, of a similar art or style, to be capable of deducing and generating a positive outcome.

One of the fascinating aspects of reviewing any given video many times over, is the amount and resolution of detail that the viewer can come to comprehend. The viewing process quickly becomes boring and tiresome, no matter how 'interesting' the material. This leads the eyes to shift the focus to many different things.
As I was watching that teacher working his way through explanations and demonstrations for the 3rd or 4th time, my gaze was already hovering to other people in the picture, strange sounds in the background, what people were wearing and facial expressions. By the 5th or 6th viewing, you seem to remember better than the teacher himself what he is about to say or do. Slowly but surely though, many small and important details rise to the surface. Gradually the mirror neurons in your brain begin to seize the rhythm, tempo, flow, angles, directions and alignment of everything the teacher does. Following a few consecutive days of this self-afflicted reprogramming torture, you seem to come to some personal 'understanding' of the man seen in a video like that. You may not know his art, but you really 'get him', subjectively speaking of course. Once you try, with honest dedication, zeal and empathy, you will know what this means.

Some time into this particular experience, a peculiar realization came to me. I caught myself looking at that teacher's shoes. I recall thinking: "How odd! His toes cast a shadow". Wait a moment here... What?! This did not make sense. But there it was. This is what happened:
The teacher was wearing flat-soled shoes. The design of the shoes was such, that the front of the shoe was naturally curved upwards. This meant in turn, that when the teacher was standing flat on the ground, even with supposedly 'perfect' posture, all very erect and 'correct', his toes cast a shadow; the entire part of his foot from the middle of the ball of the foot to the tip of the toes, was above ground, inside the shoe. For him though, it likely felt as if the feet where touching the ground, as they pressed against the shoe from the

inside. Nonetheless, the front part of the shoe was hovering slightly above the floor. In Chinese martial arts terms, he was constantly 'uprooted', and this was obviously bad for his balance and had negatively affected his personal practice for much of the time. Incredibly, this was a major flaw in this man's martial practice, and although he was a more skilled and seasoned practitioner than I, he likely was not aware of the problem. Shoes are simply central to most people's lives from a very young age. They are taken for granted. It took a barefoot-walking outsider from a different martial art, watching with care, to notice this problem.
As the years went by, gradually I was also capable of discerning additional small flaws and imperfections in that teacher's movement. Sometimes he would unnecessarily gaze at the floor. His back was not always as straight as it should have been, perhaps. That did not negate from the fact, that I have managed to learn a lot from him. A great practitioner's skill and understanding is not the sum of his few physical faults.

I take this story and experience to deliver us two important lessons about martial arts and life:

1. We all have 'toes that cast a shadow'. There are flaws and problems in the personal practice of all martial artists, teachers and masters included. Often, it takes an outsider to find these out. Someone who is neither your teacher, nor your student. There is much valuable information to gain from such people, if we can locate them, trust their judgement and ask of their opinion.

2. By watching a person for long enough, under many types of circumstances, it is possible to learn things about a man, which even he does not know about himself. One needs not be another's equal, to be an efficient observer. But it is required of one to have passed a certain threshold of understanding and life experience, to be a valid and accurate observer as such.

The Extent of Your Knowledge

For your own sake and that of your students, it is a good thing to be honest about how much you really know. Teachers tend to sway in the direction of one extreme or another when they speak of their knowledge. The modest ones say they know very little. But then, how can a person who knows very little be trusted by others as their teacher? Then there are those, usually who do know very little, who say they know a whole lot – much more than they were ever taught. These folks who are prone to exaggeration in that respect are fooling themselves and will also eventually be caught by their lie.

But, giving you the benefit of the doubt that you are more likely to belong with the first extreme rather than the second, here is the problem with being too modest – it is not necessarily more trustworthy than making big claims.

One of the greatest human faults is making up an answer for a question one does not know the answer for. The largest amount of human misery throughout history was inflicted by this mechanism. The pursuit of sanctifying and endlessly interpreting false answers is a menace upon our existence. The antidote is Humility - the ability to admit one does not know. For sometimes, a lack of reason and cause can be more powerful than knowledge itself.

I will give you an example from my own life and experience, with the appropriate usage of pseudonyms.

Say we have a martial arts lineage: **Dave** >>> **Matt** >>> **Ken**. In this lineage, Dave learned a martial art in China. Then

Dave taught the art to Matt. Then Matt taught the art to Ken. Three generations. Ken, who is 3rd generation, is a most excellent teacher, very skilled in his craft in all respects and by all accounts. But Ken wants to respect his teacher Matt, 2nd generation.

So what does Ken do? Ken tells his students: "You know, I only ever learned no more than 30% of what Matt had to teach". This already has the students shaken. On one hand they see Ken is highly capable, and they have yet to reach his level. On the other hand, he speaks of his knowledge as being merely 30% of the whole – so what does it make them, the students? Are they really THAT ignorant?

Then it gets worse. One day the students attend a seminar by Ken's teacher, Matt. Seeking to honour his teacher, Dave, they hear Matt say: "Oh, Dave was so incredible, I could never aspire to be as great as he. I only ever managed to learn 30% of what Dave wanted to teach us". Now, this really gets the students thinking hard of what they are learning. How does it even make sense? If Dave only got 30% from his teacher, and then Ken only managed to scrape 30% from Matt, then are we supposedly

learning an inferior product of an inferior product?! A negligible amount of what could have been?
These are the sad and true consequences of overt modesty – because it is an extreme, it also leads to dishonesty and interpersonal issues, despite the good intentions. The right way to showcase what you have is neither by putting yourself down, or putting others down, in order to make a point. It is by embodying a character and teachings which are unique yours, and that people like to listen to and learn from. When you put this to practice, it is possible to tell people exactly what is the extent of your knowledge, and it will matter little to them, as they will care about your personality more than the technicalities. But make an effort to claim you are greater or smaller, and you have shifted the focus and made the students occupied and haunted by things which are vague and confusing.

Indeed, there is no value in being too modest, even though this quality seems to be over-emphasized in martial arts lore. The problem with modesty is that while everyone appreciates her virtues, no one wants to buy her products. Immodesty however is frowned upon, but its ways are the source of much envy. The good is valued but not sought, the bad is dismissed and yet coveted. Such is the moral double-standard of society.

The sage is therefore he whose deeds are glorified, but not by his own word, and his skills cherished, without having to advertise them. Paved is the path before that man, and though the bricks are his, he had not placed them. Where his leg reaches, a foothold aligns. To the place his thought wanders, another completes the vision. His will be done thus, not by forcing, but by the others wishing to become its extension.

The Usefulness of Things

One of Bruce Lee's most famous quotes had always been: "**Absorb what is useful, reject what is useless, and add what is specifically your own**". There is a far more ancient quote by Zhuang Zi (dating over 2300 years ago), which I felt was somewhat of an answer to Lee's advice. Zhuang Zi said the following: "***What is "uselessness"? In order to understand it, we must think about "usefulness" first. For example, the earth is limitless but the earth that human beings step on is but of the size of our feet. Hence we dig the surrounding ground and only leave out the ground underneath our feet. Is the ground underneath our feet to be considered "useful"? In sum, things that might seem to be "useless" are actually "useful"...***".

The usefulness of a thing is thus not defined by the appearance of it, but by the circumstances and times. In Zhuang Zi's example, the ground which surrounds us appears useless, because we do not stand on it, and therefore it supposedly "has no use". So we dig the entire ground beneath and around us, with the exception of the small patch of ground that we use to stand on – the stuff that is supposedly "useful". Only then, it is suddenly revealed that what we dug out the ground had potential usefulness (for further walking and standing), which at the time prior and during the digging went unnoticed. Essentially, by "<u>rejecting the useless</u>", what we have done was to "<u>cut off opportunity</u>".

Lee's advice had been sound, but in my opinion, it requires modification and caution on part of those who wish to apply it. To reject something, to call it useless, more commonly has to do with not wishing to understand a thing, rather than using a "functional philosophy". Everything has a use, when put to use in the right time, under the right circumstances, and by the right person or entity. Uselessness does not objectively exist – it is a highly subjective definition. A useless technique for you is a winning technique for your colleague or student. A badly executed movement in sparring might be excellent for self-defense on the street. A training method not understood today can be the best training method 10 years from now. A stance which is very uncomfortable for your body structure can prove effective for dealing with your opponent.

In the uselessness of things
|Limitation is defined|
When no use can be found
One blocks both body and mind

Rejection of ideas
Is denial of oneself
To reject is easy
Understanding requires strength

Then learn to deal with what's different
From your innate being
And accept possibilities
Without adding your thing

Your Precious Underlings

Just as most adults in romantic union yearn for children, so do most martial arts teachers have the wish that one day, they would have beloved offspring to carry forth their martial genes. Eventually if you have persevered and worked things right, you too would reach the stage of having veteran students, disciples or instructors who had studied from you and work with you. As a leader, a martial arts teacher - what would be the best course of behaviour with such underlings?

Mencius gave us the following advice[87] : "***When the prince regards his ministers as his hands and feet, his ministers regard their prince as their belly and heart; when he regards them as his dogs and horses, they regard him as another man; when he regards them as the ground or as grass, they regard him as a robber and an enemy***". What is meant by these wise words Mencius had spoken?

I shall start with the worst of situations Mencius described. When you consider and behave towards the people who serve under you as if they were the ground or grass, means that you disrespect them; that you have no qualms about tramping over their dignity and considerations. Your behaviour thus humiliates them, for you treat them like dirt. Those who experience this type of attitude, would come to regard their teacher as someone who had robbed them, or as an enemy. A robber – because in you they saw a promise which went unfulfilled, and an opportunity which was stolen from them. An enemy – because you are 'putting and keeping them down', hence limiting their growth, which would be a mode of action befitting an opponent.

It is very important to understand in this context, that such an inauspicious interpretation of the relationship may arise, even if

---

[87] Mencius, Chapter 8: Li Lou, Verse 31. Mencius was an intellectual descendent of Confucius who extrapolated on the teachings of his forebearer.

you were objectively well-behaved towards your underlings. As you know well, a simple misunderstanding can cause a person to feel as if you trampled their pride or honour, without you intending it to be so. Therefore, any event bearing hurt feelings between you and an underling must be resolved quickly, else he or she could develop a grudge befitting an adversary rather than a teacher.

To be thinking or acting towards one's underlings as "dogs and horses" (in the context of physical labour), means that you consider them to be nothing but vessels to get a job done[88]. Much like a lot of people think and act towards their employees. The dogs and horses, being beloved and cherished friends to mankind, are surely better treated than the grass beneath one's feet. But the relationship here is nonetheless utilitarian, and can still come off as offensive. Every person would like to be acknowledged as an individual, not merely as a utensil or an instrument. Though dogs and horses may be given chores and are of importance, they have traditionally been considered to be 'below' their owner and of significantly lesser status. Neither are they entitled to an opinion. When people are treated as such, they may still take orders and do one's bidding, but they will come to think of their teacher as any other man they know. In other words – because they are being talked to and commanded as if they were merely the vessels of a work force – like employees, they will establish the attitude of thinking of their teacher as their employer; and, within such terms and conditions, they could leave at any moment without regret or remorse, as the relationship is non-binding, due to an employer being a person with which agreements can be made and broken at will. This model then, of 'dogs and horses', nears resemblance to the modern Capitalist job-market, and likewise does not excel at sustaining long-term work relationships, which last many years or decades.

---

[88] Mencius writes this in the context of the agricultural society which China was thousands of years ago. His 'dogs and horses' then are farm animals – not the child-like pets many have come to consider them as during the 20th and 21st centuries.

The most suitable and appropriate attitude recommended by Mencius is that of regarding the underlings as one's "hands and feet". There are several layers of meaning to this.
Firstly, that the hands and feet are very important to your everyday function. So should the underlings be given positions and powers of importance to the everyday function of one's school or organization, if they are indeed worthy. Secondly, that the hands and feet are the soldiers of the mind. Your thoughts and wishes should be manifested smoothly and fluently through the actions of your underlings. Lastly, that the hands and feet 'get all the action', and are the first probes in testing new things and dealing with them, though guided by the mind at all times. So should the underlings approach new people and situations on your behalf, reserving your direct interjection for when you are truly needed, and leaving the casual operations to the people you trust.

Mencius notes that when you act in this manner, your underlings would come to view you as their belly and heart. A person (teacher) may be able to survive without his hands or feet (underlings), but the appendages (underlings) cannot survive without the belly or the heart. In this is implied, that the correct manner of behaviour and attitude towards one's underlings, yields an awe on their behalf, which causes them to consider you as invaluable and irreplaceable. This is achieved by treating the underlings respectfully and humanely, giving them ample opportunity to prove themselves, putting trust in them to do so, and considering them as part of one's own constitution.

Mencius further said on another occasion[89], on something related to what I have discussed earlier. He said: ***"Kindly words do not enter so deeply into men as a reputation for kindness. Good government does not lay hold of the people so much as good instructions. Good government is feared by the people, while***

[89] Mencius, Chapter 13: Jin Xin, Verse 14.

***good instructions are loved by them. Good government gets the people's wealth, while good instructions get their hearts*".**

By this he meant, that in leading other people, mere actions cannot compare in their impact with setting good personal example through one's instruction (teachings). Once more here, using the words of Mencius, the 'Government' may be likened to the martial arts teacher.

Good governance, Mencius explained, is effective in obtaining the wealth of the people. But that does not, by itself, form a strong dominion over the citizens. For the people would be willing to neglect their duties under the law, as soon as the governance becomes weaker. They do not feel obliged towards what the government asks of them, because their behaviour is motivated by the effective actions of the sovereign – not by appreciation of it.

Alluding to martial arts teachers, that is the sort of situation when a headmaster manages to get the underlings to do his bidding, but only by the strength of his fists, character and status can he enforce his rule. In so being, the martial arts teacher is a good manager – but not a worthy leader.

In comparison, there is also the government which hands out 'good instructions'. That means, that its laws are virtuous, clear and concise, and that the people can understand what is expected of them. Then, suggests Mencius, the citizens would naturally develop affection towards the sovereign.

It is the same with presiding over one's underlings in a martial arts school or organization. Shouting orders and demanding obedience to rules, can be effective and attain results. But far superior to it, is allowing one's underlings to naturally absorb the vibe of correct operation, by setting a personal example, providing excellent instruction, and using kindness as a measure rather than one's ability to enforce everything with precision. Through such actions and mindset, the underlings would come to better appreciate their teacher, and would stick by him with loyalty and devotion, regardless of the circumstances.

The Crime of Creating Ignorance

Like human beings growing old, martial arts also have the sad tendency of deteriorating in their quality over the decades. As a martial art is handed down through the generations, knowledge is always lost. A teacher cannot transmit every single thing he knows to his students, and those in turn are often not always willing or wise enough to try and grasp it all. Still, one can compensate. Lost understandings can be recovered, techniques can be reinvented, and principles rediscovered. We can also learn from other teachers, to complete that which we are missing. With enough effort put forth, we still prevail. There is still hope for the traditional martial arts if we have enough people who care for them, and are willing to make the efforts and sacrifices to preserve these traditions. Trouble begins, as in human relationships, with keeping secrets.

The habit of keeping secrets dates back to eras in human civilization when martial arts were used daily in life or death situations – either on the battlefield, or to protect oneself, one's family or one's property. At those turbulent times, the martial arts were the equivalent of secret military technology. Had you needed to cause someone serious harm, you would use this technology for that purpose. Because of this, keeping the martial arts secretive was justified and understandable, and this approach became wide spread in many nations. At those times, knowing the insides of other martial arts was a matter of gaining the upper hand on a potential enemy[116] – like having a video of a future contender is crucial for a boxing champion to prepare himself for competition in modern times. Outdoor fights would gather many spectators; some of which wouldn't just come for the entertainment – they were there for literally collecting counter-intelligence. You also would not want anyone learning the unique abilities developed within your martial art, only to have them used against you at some point.

Survival could also bear financial or honourary overtones. In not-so-ancient China, people from one martial arts school would often challenge people from other schools. The outcome could bring about life-changing consequences for the loser. Firstly, physically losing would mean "losing face", which is of great insult and stigma in Chinese traditional culture. Secondly, the impact of losing face in this scenario usually had the following implications – Had the challenger lost, he would be expected to beg to become a student of the school that had beaten him, or leave in great shame. Had the school representatives lost, the school's headmaster would often leave in shame, with the winner having the option to take over the school and all of the students.

Today, we live in an era when there is no more need for sacred secrets. Over the course of the 19th, 20th and 21st centuries, the traditional martial arts became almost completely obsolete as daily martial weapons. One no longer needs to train for decades to be able to kill someone with a wooden weapon, or empty handed, in an instant. Anyone interested in killing for any purpose could just purchase a gun at a local store. Anyone wishing to invest in self-defense could buy a taser. As these arts were no longer secrets that needed to be kept to stay alive, and with the gradual rise of globalization, every single "secret" in the martial arts world became available to anyone dedicated enough to practice to the point he would be able to learn and utilize it. Some knowledge is still rare compared to others, but none is a true secret any more because many people have it. Things that were once passed to a single person within a generation are nowadays known to thousands (and sometimes dozens of thousands) of serious teachers. In an age where people no longer dedicate their entire lives to the research of martial arts, keeping secrets only serves to hurt the conservational effort of traditional arts, of which their higher levels of practice are rapidly disappearing. Although this practice (of keeping secrets) is becoming extinct, there are still teachers, mostly in the Orient, who insist on keeping secrets in the traditional manner.

One aspect of this line of thought can be justified – you would not want to teach deadly techniques to some hoodlum or potential murderer. Those types, however, do not tend to stick with martial arts long enough to learn such skills – purchasing a gun or a knife is much easier. Moreover, they could always find an alternative to learning such skills if they wanted to. Another reason for some teachers keeping secrets is the fear for their trademark skills. With the onset of widespread video, there were many known cases of deceitful individuals who copied fancy or impressive movements from the videos of great masters, subsequently claiming they were those masters' students, or belonged to their martial lineage. Fearful this might happen to them, some teachers refrain from showing aspects of their arts when filmed. They can even go as far as to alter their filmed performance, with movements done wrong on purpose and segments omitted, so anyone trying to copy them would reveal himself and his fraud had he tried to show his skills in public.

There is, though, a darker side to some teacher's habit of keeping secrets, which I call "***The Crime of Creating Ignorance***". Traditionally, in China, there are two types of martial arts students – those who are considered "regular students", and those who are private disciples – formally accepted into the lineage of the martial tradition through a ceremony called "Bai Shi" or "Bai Men" ("pay respect to your teacher" or “bow at the door” in Mandarin Chinese). These students are in turn called "indoor students", or "those who have entered the door" – meaning they are accepted within the doors of the (martial art's) family's home – they become part of the family. Once a person is a formal disciple, he is usually given instruction on everything within his martial art of choice – no secrets. That is not the case for those who are not accepted as such. These people are omitted from learning the essence of the martial arts, and are only allowed to "scratch the surface", so to speak. At other instances, being a formal or informal disciple wouldn't matter – if a teacher did not like student for any reason, he would just

refrain from teaching him important points, keeping him from attaining a good level of expertise.
All of this has grounding in reality, at least in the short term. Why teach someone "outside of your family", who you don't necessarily trust, your "secret stuff"? Why bother teaching a lazy student the "good stuff"? It is all understandable. What has come about from those attitudes towards teaching in the long-term, though, is horrendous (and as with anything horrendous, it has to do with mathematics!).

Let's pause for a minute, and observe a short **fictional** allegory:

Master Jerry was famous worldwide as a great teacher of the martial arts. Jerry was not an old-school kind of guy – he did not think much of "initiation ceremonies", and taught in modern-day America. Unbeknownst to his students, Jerry had a clear policy he kept to himself. He would not teach his whole art to lazy students who thought they were smarter than him. In fact, he hated lazy students so much, that he would purposely teach them some wrong principles and inaccurate techniques, so "they will never get it". Two students stuck with Jerry for 30 years – Kramer and Newman. While Jerry liked Kramer a lot and taught him all he could, Newman was a lazy bastard who always thought he knew better, and thus Jerry made sure he did not fully understand the art, and had it the wrong way. After thirty years, Jerry passed away from illness, and the two veteran students started teaching separately. Kramer had named his martial art Jerry-dō ("The Way of Jerry"), after his beloved teacher. Newman, who did not really like Jerry and was just in for "stealing" his art, called what he taught "Newman Kung Fu".

Kramer always emphasized quality in his teachings, so he would only allow for two students to carry on and teach the tradition of Jerry- dō, and made sure this continued in the same fashion with their students, and so forth. There were 2 teachers of the second generation of Jerry-dō (Kramer's students). Four students in the third generation (Kramer's grand-students). It grew with each

generation in the power of 2, so the fifth generation had 32 people teaching Jerry-dō (not including past teachers).
Newman, on the other hand, was into making money, and allowed for 15 of his students to teach his crooked kung fu, and made sure each of them also qualified some 15 teachers on average, and so forth. Second generation of Newman Kung Fu included 15 teachers (Newman's students). **By the time Newman's Kung Fu had reached its fifth generation of teachers, over <u>750 thousand</u> people were cluelessly teaching a martial art which a man named Jerry intentionally taught wrong.**

This is the destructive nature of exponential growth. A poor judgment on a teacher's behalf that may have even been justified in the short term turned out a complete disaster, which has affected the lives of many people that that teacher would never even come to know. The teacher would have been much better off not teaching such a student anything at all, preventing him from a chance to spread ignorance. A teacher is liable for what he or she passes on to future generations. You choose who you teach, and what you teach those individuals. Unfortunately, many throughout history have put their own immediate desires for taking revenge on some students (or just keeping them as income when not intending to teach them seriously), before the horrible consequences such actions could bring to others (who might spend decades studying an intentionally-deformed style of martial arts). While the blame for spreading ignorance is first and foremost of the student himself, the teacher is guilty with the crime of creating that ignorance on purpose.

Fakes and Charlatans

Someone once asked: "How many martial artists does it take to change a light bulb?". The answer was: "5". One to change the light bulb; one to say this was not the right technique for changing the light bulb; one to claim this method of changing the light bulb would not work on the street; one to suggest that this lineage is no good at changing light bulbs; and one to insist only he knows the secret way to change light bulbs properly, so the person who supposedly did it must have faked it somehow... By all means - among the five, be the one who actually changes the light bulb, rather than the other four.

Within the world of martial arts there are many people who present themselves as something which they are not. We martial arts teachers are all too aware of such shady and ill-intended characters. They use deceit and lies to steal people's time and money. Very dishonorable.

However, as martial arts teacher, it is absolutely crucial that we avoid engaging in crusades against these men. Remember – we have chosen the profession of teaching, not **persecuting**. The world of martial arts is not a police interrogation chamber or the court of law. When you feel the uncontrollable urge to lash out at such a fool, always remember three things:

1. "*Never argue with stupid people. They drag you down to their level and then beat you with experience*" [90]. Though it is commonly claimed that "no publicity is bad publicity", let me assure you – publicity gained through picking up fights with the unworthy is, in fact, very bad publicity.

2. Whenever you take on a crusade, people are watching. The public is watching. Potential students are watching. Current students are watching. Your friends and competitors are watching. All of these people expect you to be a martial arts teacher – not a crusader. Assuming that 'additional profession' is disharmonious to one's reputation. Socrates said: "*Regard your good name as the richest jewel you can possibly be possessed of – for credit is like fire; when once you have kindled it you may easily preserve it, but if you once extinguish it, you will find it an arduous task to rekindle it again. The way to a good reputation is to endeavor to be what you desire to appear*".

3. It is a known fact that you should acknowledge, that the most successful martial arts teachers, of any style and in any place, seldom engage in either the persecution of others or in arguments with those lesser to them. Think about that.

---

[90] Spoken by Mark Twain.

The Naysayers

Winston Churchill is credited with saying the following: "**You have enemies? Good. That means you have stood up for something, sometime in your life**". How true! Since the moment I began to openly talk and write of the martial arts, I have always had negative figures lurking around and looking to make me into their enemy. Over the years, I have been told everything bad imaginable of my martial arts and my knowledge of them. But I have done better to deal with it than simply be pulled into a vortex of endless argumentation. Here is then, a healthier approach.

The curse which accompanies nearly all martial arts teachers is that of the nasty naysayers. They stick to us like mosquitos to warm blood in a humid rainforest. You try squashing one, and then more blood spills and within a short time you are having a war with hundreds.
There is frankly no way to prevent the existence of naysayers, same as mosquitos (though some modern laser devices look really promising!). You should learn to live with them, and this is better done by either ignoring them outright, or if you cannot resist the urge, answer them only politely and positively (only if the matter has become public, as a private discussion with such people is a waste of time).

You see, these people who look to bring you down because they need that blood to survive. But you need not be a part of that war. You can, in replying to them publicly, be so kind and well-mannered, as to drive them mad with hunger. Pretend as if no offense was taken, and be a foremost gentleman in your interactions. This is likely to cause them to infuriate even more, at which point you opt to simply stop that sort of correspondence, which was a silly affair to take part in to begin with. Were you up to your best behaviour, you need not worry, as those who have witnessed what had transpired would usually be able to discern who is worthier among you.

But the absolutely superior counter-warfare to the threat of naysayers, and some would argue the best form of revenge, is simply becoming the finest version of yourself that you can be. Focus on working hard and becoming successful. This is the ultimate. Sometimes when I feel a need for a little bit of motivation, I think of these countless people who throughout my life tried to put me down, in some way or another. Oh, I would have loved to see their faces as I turn into something far greater than they or myself could have ever imagined. This is a lovely thing to think about, and though it should not be the main motivation for you to succeed in life, it certainly helps.

Therefore, do not consider these naysayers as enemies. Rather, use them as fuel – to motivate you to push harder, and to show the world that you possess self-control and character in dealing with difficult people. This is one of the hallmarks of a mature personality and of an accomplished martial artist – to be able to transform a difficult situation into an advantageous one, and use the opponent's power against him. Those who can do this in a confrontation are skilled. Those who never have to do this are wise.

Assume the Best

Get used to assuming the best about people by default, yourself included, as much as you can. Otherwise, your life on this planet, especially as a martial arts teacher, can get quite miserable.

A student left you? **<u>Assume the best.</u>** Never attack him or her for doing so. Always try to maintain a good, or at least neutral relationship. Do not play silly games with such people. Be courteous. For your own sake, try to think of their lives outside of martial arts and come up with the many reasons which may have driven them on that path. Of this you can read more in the chapter titled **'Cannot Save Them All'** (p. 341).

Do you see a nasty critic online, making vicious remarks of either your teachings or those of a person you care about? **<u>Assume the best.</u>** That person must be suffering, for he needs to say bad things of others to make himself feel better. Choose your actions wisely. Often it is best to ignore. Sometimes it can be a good opportunity to reply with humour. People can often tell when someone is being very rude. Being able to make fun of the situation in a respectable manner will earn you points among those who saw what had transpired. Otherwise you may reply very politely and explain something a person was criticizing, if it pertained to your teachings. It is quite common that people criticize what they genuinely cannot understand. Being able to explain it to them coherently without the explanation sounding like an excuse may even make them change their minds. This is the ultimate victory. This is made possible only if you began the interaction by assuming the best.

Having a difficult time with your martial arts school? **<u>Assume the best.</u>** People usually do not dislike you personally. No one is conspiring against you. Do not make failure personal. Failure is not a punishment – it is a teacher, like yourself. When your language or tone of voice become harsh at times towards a student, you often mean to make him focus or quit doing silly things he is not supposed to be engaged in. Now failure is the teacher, and you are the student! Do not be intimidated by the rugged demeanor. Rather, listen to what failure says. He is trying to tell you: “You need to change, because things are not working well this way”. He is your teacher. Assume the best about its intentions – they are neutral, and you can learn and grow from them. Make the necessary changes, and do it TODAY.

The One Thing Everyone Dislikes

Is called Greed. A teacher may be the a most fantastic, successful, cheerful, skilled or qualified professional – you name it. When he is greedy however, everyone will know. The Greed will be that 'BUT' factor in people's descriptions of him. "Oh, so and so has such impressive techniques! BUT, you know, he is greedy with money..."; "Have you heard of this guy? He is a terrific teacher, for sure! BUT, well... He really does charge too much, and is always on the lookout to get more cash out of you".

I am not a believer in the age-old harmful idea, that a martial arts teacher should be poor, or should be expected to teach for free. To each his own, yes? But I think those who devote a great deal of their working hours, perhaps the majority of their time, to training and teaching, should be appropriately compensated by those who express an interest. That being said, a line can be crossed, depending on the local culture and community and their standards. When is the line crossed? It is when you see the person standing in front of you, every single time, as first a customer, and a student – only second. When this line is crossed, and students become clients who pay for a service rather than members of a community and parts to a relationship, then you have stepped out of the realm of TRADITIONAL martial arts, and into the realm of pure business.

The difference? A business has as its main agenda, to make as much profit as possible. For a traditional martial arts school, earning more money is just one among many other agendas, and while important, it is never **the most important**.

Again – to each his own. I would not judge. Martial arts and their teaching can be great for society in a variety of models, be them more business-oriented or community-driven. But the one thing you can be certain of is, that you cannot cross that line I have described, and expect there would not be repercussions. People will know, sooner or later, and they would be talking about it. Also, the people being attracted to a business and remaining with it, are those more inclined to seek a business-oriented relationship; and such a relationship, does not work well with the traditional model of instruction – at least in my opinion. For a person cannot be, at the same time, a teacher-mentor or a father-teacher, and a 'deliverer of paid services'. There exists a tension between such personas, which cannot be completely mitigated.

Here is a personal example of the negative effects of greed, and its affects on a professional relationship:

Here in Israel, an infamous 'sports institution' lobbied parliament members to enact an amendment to our sports laws during the early 21st century. The amendment declared that henceforth to the end of time, all Israeli martial arts teachers would be required to undergo a universal certification course, approved by the State, to be allowed to legally teach. That vile sports institution lobbied the Israeli parliament to enact such a ridiculous thing, because they were the only local organization at the time offering general instructors courses for martial artists, and were also the only ones granted the permission by the State to grant the now legally-binding diplomas. How convenient.
Some years later, the headmaster of the martial arts program at said institution, quit his job there, and decided to open a competing instructor certification program in his own dojo. Silly as this country is, that man had to get all the way to the supreme court to received a ruling, that the State should also allow him to deliver those certification diplomas. This goes to show the level of moral and legal corruption which manifests when martial arts meet with state-level politics.

A few years before I opened my first martial arts school, I went to undergo that certification course at that headmaster's dojo. I had to do this, for unless you obtain such a tdiploma, you cannot get any insurance in Israel.
The course itself was bearable, at times even interesting, and expensive of course. No one pretended that this course was meant

to change the lives of the participants. The headmaster himself admitted his understanding, that all who were present there chose to give him their hard-earned money only because the State forced them to get this certification. Though the experience was pleasant enough, the business side of things, and the politics, tainted the nature of the relationship, and the participants felt like fish out of water. Though everyone respected the senior headmaster, it was difficult to consider him as one's teacher, especially in light of the financial and political circumstances.

For some years following the course, I continued to recommend potential teachers to attend it at the headmaster's dojo. But an unfortunate incident changed my mind.
One day I sought to obtain a copy of my certification diploma in the English language. The alternative was to pay much to a notary to have it translated, as the original had only been provided in Hebrew. I called the headmaster, and to my surprise he demanded that for this single sheet of paper, which required him but a single click of a button to send to his printer, a sum worthy of a fancy meal. I was shocked that this man, who had already gained a substantial amount from me originally, and was a colleague who knew of my help in promoting him, would raise such a demand. It was greedy and distasteful, abruptly ended our relationship, and saw an end to my recommendations of his course. On his part though, this was simply a business transaction. But that one transaction, cost him many more.

To take from this, is the lesson that what may appear casual and commonsensical to you, may come across as too business-like or even greedy to another, under various circumstances. It is wise then, to avoid a scenario, in which colleagues or students consider your motivations to be too overtly financial in nature. This is ill-serving to one's reputation.

Opportunities Skip a Locked Garden

The world is full of people who wonder: "Why is it that I never got my opportunities to do great things in my life and career?". Honestly speaking, the answer is nearly always that such a person is himself to blame. How many people are in your neighbourhood? In your city? In your country? Even a tiny fraction of these people, associated with you as martial arts students or partners in business, could have made you rich, successful and perhaps even happier. But of these countless possibilities for action and interaction, one often manifests an amazingly small number of useful relationships. Why is that?

Well theoretically, if you could appeal to more people, that would be a good start. This is where things get complicated. We want to remain authentic, so there is only so much we are willing to change in who we are in order to look and sound like what other people want. Indeed, at the extremes, those martial artists who sell their soul for a profit, are lowly and unworthy. But there is another way, a simpler way, to attract other people and opportunities. This can way can be pursued by means of changing one's attitude, rather than one's personality or behaviour. Changing our attitude can attract people to us on all walks of life. One proven technique for changing one's attitude and attracting more people and possibilities, is adopting **a mentality of abundance.** Let us see how a good argument for this mentality of abundance was made in an ancient allegory, from the **Book of Mencius** [91].

This scholar **Mencius** whom I mentioned just now, was a successor to Confucius, lived several generations after that great sage-scholar,

---

[91] Mencius, Chapter 2: Liang Hui Wang (King Hui of Liang).

and studied with his grandson. Like his forerunner, Mencius also traveled between the old Chinese kingdoms, and sought to teach and inspire morality among their rulers and citizens. His exploits and teachings are in part recorded in the **Book of Mencius**. The first two chapters of that book tell stories of the conversations Mencius had with various kings. In their conversations, the sovereigns look to make their kingdoms more efficient and profitable, and encounter novel and unusual suggestions from Mencius which they did not expect.

One king whose name is Xuan, is baffled as Mencius confirms to him, that another Ancient King by the name of Wen, had a park the size of 35 square kilometers. King Xuan finds something confusing about ancient King Wen's garden. Mencius tells King Xuan, that albeit king Wen's park being this large, no less than 35 square kilometers, the citizens of king Wen's nation still thought of their king's park as being 'small'. King Xuan points out, that his own park is only 20 square kilometers, and still his people think it is 'large' – despite his park being smaller than that king Wen owned. King Xuan then inquires with Mencius, what could be the reason for this – that king Wen's people considered their sovereign's park as 'small' though it was large, while his (king Xuan's) park was talked of as being 'large' while it was relatively smaller? After all, king Xuan would like his people to view him as a benevolent ruler, and not someone who lives too lavishly.

Mencius has a simple and clear explanation for this. He tells king Xuan, that the park of king Wen was indeed large in size, but entry was allowed for those citizens who wanted to cut grass or gather fuel wood for their own use. Also hosted there openly were those who sought to catch pheasants and hares. Because king Wen willingly shared his park with the people, they thought of it as 'small' – as many were permitted entry and rights to its resources, or at least had the opportunity to claim such benefits.

But what about king Xuan's park? When Mencius entered king Xuan's kingdom, he was careful to find out what were the local customs, and what was forbidden. He learned that if someone was to hunt a deer in king Xuan's park, that person would have been treated and punished like someone who had murdered a human being. Because king Xuan kept the park for himself, the people thought of it as 'large' – as it was reserved for the benefit of only a single individual and his family.

Thus far was the extended answer of Mencius to king Xuan. Now I shall elaborate more on this important message.

What King Xuan was lacking in, was the **mentality of abundance**. Instead of feeling that he has abundance, king Xuan suffered from a **scarcity mindset**. He felt as though, despite having this extensive green terrain under his control, that he did not possess enough, or that somehow by sharing the park he could lose it. He therefore acted like a miser with his resources. The result had been, that the people psychologically felt that his park was 'large', though it was physically smaller than that of a previous sovereign. It was also a lose-lose strategy, as he was left both anxious of the negative image of him this created among others, and unable to use the park he had for further growth. What is not stated but is hinted, is that this generated enemies and challenges for king Xuan, as the people must have been displeased by his miserly mannerisms. This is why he sought the advice of Mencius – for he knew that this was a sign of troubles to come. Further we should not neglect the observation, that had he shared his park in a similar fashion to king Wen [92], then not only that area would have been thought of as 'small', but the people also would naturally have been more inclined to wish that their King's territory be expanded and for his power to grow, for it benefitted them as well.

As martial arts teachers and modern day individuals, we suffer from the exact same flaw which was the bane of king Xuan and others in his time, thousands of years ago. All too often, we feel we have to keep too much of our resources to ourselves. Here I wish for you to consider all of those things which are not material resources like money and real-estate, the latter perhaps more relevant for the wealthy. You have many other resources that you could share, like social connections, knowledge, love, food and ideas. You are probably are a miser with these, too, compared with your potential for sharing. One of my most beneficial changes in life had come about, when I began to more openly share my social connections,

---

[92] Be mindful that I am not here suggesting that everyone should open up their gardens to strangers under all circumstances. I am not a Communist. Be mindful of the details. Consider the people in this story were kings. They had massive areas of land at their disposal, with these parks being just parts of their overall territories. Furthermore, their citizens paid them taxes. Under these conditions, sharing in the spirit of king Wen makes a whole lot of sense. One ought to share when he or she objectively have some abundance – in land, food, resources, money, love, connections or otherwise. Though it is often observed, that those most poor sometimes are more generous than others, which can result from greater empathy and understanding, or sometimes in subconsciously understanding there are strength and wisdom contained in the idea of 'investing in loss'.

knowledge and ideas with others, without fearing they may use them to undermine or supersede me.

Research has shown that among social mammals, the beta males constantly compete, while the alpha males are more generous and benevolent, on average and relative to the circumstances. Why? Because they have an abundance mentality. The majority of martial arts teachers whom I have encountered, who were both successful and worthy, displayed this alpha male quality of benevolence and generosity.

A truly enlightened sovereign of his kingdom – one who has rulership not only in name but also in spirit, can find it in his power to allow others into his park, without fear of loss. When this is undertaken, and you are truly and genuinely set out to offer from your resources to the appropriate people in a thoughtful and appropriate manner, then suddenly the opportunities will present themselves. The right people will, in the process of months and years, discover that your park is open and inviting. Many of them will by these actions, appeal to you, and it would seem as if you have gone on an ever-growing 'lucky streak' in your life and career. But for this to happen, a park must be both cultivated, inviting and without unnecessary boundaries.

The Sound of Success

Many people imagine the sound of success to be that of cash banknotes rubbing against one-another, or that of coins amassing as a nice mound. For others yet, the sound of success is the loud engine-thunder of their favourite expensive vehicle, or the bustling metropolis rushing beneath their luxurious apartment. Such are some people's likings. For me, by the way, it is the crunchy consumption of homegrown fruits and vegetables. But within the martial arts school, the sound of success is the tone of your voice!

Your voice tells extant and prospective students who you are, what you are about, what is your constitution, and what intentions you may have. It is of utmost importance to learn how to use your voice well.

I recall my late Shigong, master Zhou Jingxuan, having mastered that skill to a high degree. A native Chinese man with very few English words at his disposal, he had meager linguistic means for explaining his martial arts to people who did not understand his own language. Fortunately, master Zhou had developed a capacity to use his tone of voice in radical and surprising ways, to convey meaning in his teachings. He would invent sounds and non-verbal bodily expressions, to channel every single intent and idea he had. It was in his capacity to lead a student to performing a movement correctly or understand a concept, by the virtue of issuing many small, sharp and loud 'sound-cues', accompanied by a dynamism and articulation of an expert theater actor. He used such cues as means of 'controlling' and 'guiding' a student from afar, and also included them in his own demonstration to make a point about the intensity, effort, emphasis or thinking required for the particular exercise, form or technique. It was to the uneducated foreigner like watching a silent film – the soundtrack was absent, but the meaning was there. Master Zhou was therefore capable of achieving the most remarkable results when instructing even those people who could otherwise not understand him.

Chiefly expressed through tone of voice is one's energy level. Do you recall the first chapter in this book? In it I set up the presupposition, that a martial arts teacher is a performer on a stage. The performer's tone of voice should deliver to the audience his inner energetic state, and those viewing 'the show' are attuned and listening. Furthermore, the audience is there, in our case, to **raise** their energy level. No one walks into a martial arts school to sob or have a laugh, at least not as a main agenda. We have books, movies and the theater as outlets for these. The martial arts school is a venue for gaining Vitality. It is therefore crucial, that vitality is expressed in your voice, at all times.

When I say "all the time", I mean it. For there are times when we, being human, are perhaps sick, depressed, worried, anxious or otherwise unwell. But this matters not to our 'audience'. For them, we are a 'myth'. As martial arts teachers, we represent a world beyond their own. A world in which 'magic' takes place. A world which is out of the ordinary. A world to which they can retreat from theirs, to attain a momentary relief from the pressures of their daily lives. In that imagined world the sovereign, which is you, is in possession of a fountain of vitality; and the extent to which that fountain is full, is initially judged and assessed by your voice. Leave the fountain dwindling or dry for too long, and members of the audience will seek to refill their reservoirs elsewhere.
Due to this situation, when our energetic resources are low, we have to pretend, and do it well. This is a lie, but it matters not. For the fountain which the students seek, is not found within us, but within them. By our words, actions and tone of voice, we merely enable them to access their own potential and energetic resources, even when they feel and think that this came from us. Therefore, pretending is good enough, when one cannot do better. As long as the students benefit, there is nothing wrong with that.

The chief properties for maintaining a high level of energy in tone of voice, is to be loud (not screaming), clear, coherent, positive, driven, confident, speaking at a moderate speed but without stops, flowing, courteous, polite, genuine and welcoming. When all of these combine, the listener feels that you have something great to offer, and even if they decide that this is not meant for them, they know that you honestly believe in it. People can usually discern whether you are genuine in the message you convey. They may not know whether someone is factually lying to them or not, but they can commonly tell whether or not the man talking has personal conviction and belief in the cause. For this reason, it is important to have faith in what you say, and when you lack faith – examine why and change accordingly. All this is true whether speaking to one's own students or to strangers for the first time.

What many fails to realize though, that tone of voice and usage thereof, are skills to be practiced like a musical instrument. Even now, many years into teaching, I still find myself honing and improving this skillset. It requires daily work, training and attention. Some may even benefit practicing in front or a mirror, or speaking with their spouse. Commonly, when we examine the great success of various people, in the martial arts or elsewhere, we fail to take into account this particular skillset of theirs, and how far it had gotten them. Mastery of this art, can truly yield incredible results.
My mother for instance, had mastered the 'dark side' to this skill. She is a shrewd and aggressive lawyer. Since I was a young boy, I remember her speaking with various customer service representatives and company managers for hours on the phone at a time. She spoke with such people for so many thousands of hours, that she became capable of manipulating them to do anything. Ordinarily, most of us would be unable to reach beyond 2nd or 3rd tier of customer support personnel via means of a phone conversation. Not my mother. I saw her, dozens and possibly hundreds of times, manage to have her call transferred directly to a top manager or even a CEO of a company, sometimes within 15-20 minutes. She did so by effectively and viciously oppressing and stressing the

representatives to such a degree, psychologically intimidating them with slight cues and suggestions, that they could not possibly handle her presence, and felt compelled to abide by her wishes. It was not a pretty or a positive sight to behold. However, by these means my mother was capable of overcoming many injustices done unto our family or friends of ours, often bringing about a major change in the manner in which a big company treated its customers. She did all this, by intuitively honing her tone or voice and choice of words like master craftsman hammering a sword into shape.

Despite having gained much exposure to my mother's conversational exploits, I could never come to imitate her style or gain her effectiveness with these types of daily challenges. Nonetheless, her bitter lessons taught me that proper speech can make the difference between having or lacking food on the table. Much due to the influence of both my parents being educated lawyers, having earned a degree as such myself (L.L.B), and having been a police investigator for a number of years, I too achieved decent competence and ability with the spoken and written word, even before I was a martial arts teacher.

But this changes not the fact that such skills, especially the oral variety, require daily maintenance and exercise. In the martial we tend to say that "everybody has got only two arms and two legs". By this we mean, that in sparring and fighting, eventually a limit to what can be done. But in verbal interactions, this does not hold. Every day brings forth a new challenge and a new adventure. Every student and every relationship is a whole new world in its own right. This is why the usage of our voice and language can always be improved. There is not doubt in my mind that those who shall invest in their mastery, would see their martial arts schools thrive.

Enthusiasm and Its Limits

Enthusiasm is the number one motivator for your students' training. It takes most people a long time, anywhere between several months to several years, to become highly and strongly enthusiastic and self-motivated about their martial arts practice in a meaningful and long-lasting manner. Until they reach that point, and past that stage also, your personal enthusiasm in class is the greatest motivator for their willingness to train – in and outside the school. Overall, when around people and especially students, be enthusiastic about your martial arts about 200% of the time (that is, 100% in the school, and then 100% outside the school!). On those days when you do not feel extra-cheerful, do your best to fake it. You would be surprised how much your own 'act' can eventually lift you up also from a groggy state of being to feeling wonderful, in a matter of minutes. Nothing gets me energized like beginning to lecture with passion about the martial arts and demonstrating them along with that sort of speech. Within 5 minutes, I feel as like a changed man. The more hyped I become, the more attentive and impressed the students are. Bear this in mind.

Here is a caveat though: Enthusiasm is for those already sold on what you do. The general public requires milder treatment. Ordinary everyday conversations with people about the martial arts cannot be carried with the same zeal as talking to students – they would quickly tune out, overwhelmed. Speaking with those interested in coming to class, too much enthusiasm can turn them off just as it happens on romantic dates. The person showing interest in your classes usually wants to play a social game, and in this game there is going to be a 'transaction' of sorts: he or she want to be convinced, you need to convince them, and then their coming to your class and perhaps staying is the making of the 'deal'. Imagine then, given this is a 'deal', what happens when you want to buy a car or a house from someone, and they are all too keen to get rid of it. You become suspicious. You do not feel comfortable making a deal with someone who is overly enthusiastic. The same works with telling people about your martial arts or trying to have them come to class. For this reason it is also important to try and keep conversations short, and then 'cut to the chase'. Five minutes is already a lot! Strive for moderate enthusiasm only, and gently pressing the person to make a statement about his or her interest within that time frame, setting up the details of when and where.

You Need Help – Ask for It

Once a good friend of mine, a karate Sensei, went to visit a class held by a colleague of his, a Shifu of traditional Chinese martial arts. Following the end of the class, my Sensei friend was surprised to see his Shifu colleague was sweeping the floor all by himself, while the students were chatting elsewhere, packing their things and leaving. My Sensei friend was saddened and disappointed when he witnessed the Shifu's students' behaviour. He was upset that the Shifu's students were not helping him with the cleaning. I heard that story many years ago and it resonated in my mind since. Why was it that this teacher had to clean by himself? Was he not respected by his students?
Nowadays knowing who that teacher is, I tend to believe he suffered from what we can call 'help shyness', or perhaps had an 'excessive sense of independence'. A lot of martial arts teachers have such traits.

What exactly is that 'help shyness' among martial artists? On the path of martial arts practice and teaching you meet and interact with a lot of people. But most of the walking there is to do on that path, you have to do on your own. Because of this, we martial arts teachers have the tendency to bear too much responsibility on our shoulders. We are used to being independent. But you do not have to carry all that weight by yourself. In fact, you should not! In running a martial arts school, it is crucial to assign duties and chores to students.

When I first began teaching martial arts I failed realize this. I sought perfection in operating my school, and thought that I could only attain it by managing everything on my own. What a glorious mistake! I was also cautious of asking students to do things for me, fearing they might consider this as their teacher taking advantage of them. Nothing could be further from the truth.

In any healthy relationship, there needs to be the proper balance. You are the teacher. You are THE authority figure in the school. You have to act like it. People expect you to command them, within reasonable limits. Get the students to do cleaning: of the floor, cups, plates, library, weapons, restroom, etc. Ask a student to go fetch everyone something to eat for a post-class feast (everyone share the expenses of course). Make a trusted student in charge of some advertising, under your directions. Have another trusted student arrange social gatherings. Be the boss – be the manager – of others, not just yourself. Then in the management of the school, engage more with the MACRO, not the Micro – the big picture, not the tiniest of details. All the while, you should lead by example. Be the first to grab that broom. [93] Have the students see you wash dishes once in a while. Be involved in the projects you issue, but let others take care of them. Also, be ready to make an effort and help students learn how to do this, at the school and also in their personal lives with their own challenges. [94]

Consider what I have already written of prior in this book: one of the best ways to build a relationship of trust with someone, is to put trust in them. Often when you might be thinking that you do not wish to burden a student, he is thinking the opposite: **"*Why isn't my teacher trusting me to do anything in this school? I have been here for a number of months or years already, and he still does everything by himself and does not allow me to take part*".**

At my school we have the 'Weekly Food Duty'. Each week I assign one student to bring food and drinks to class. These have to be

---

[93] Nowadays it is easy to purchase a robotic aid or hire someone to do the cleaning for you. Do not be tempted to do this. Cleaning is not a chore, but a key component in the training of traditional martial arts.

[94] I am always astounded how badly most people wash dishes or sweep floors. I have to teach those skills to many of my students, especially children. Be it with the broom or wipe, focus on economy, efficiency, speed, timing, rhythm, angles, strategy, tactics and technique. Relate these lessons from cleaning to their martial arts training.

healthy – not sweets, snacks or anything with refined sugar or preservatives, preferably organically-grown and appropriate to the season. Students like this duty. Each week one of them has an opportunity to contribute, and bring 'his vision of what we should all be eating'. Within months of beginning this tradition, people began to bring food even when not on duty. Also, many of them make a special effort to prepare tasty foods at home and not just purchase them somewhere. This is a wonderful thing which greatly aids in building a sense of communal effort and egalitarianism [95].

Beware though to never make the students feel like they are your employees. This can be very counter-productive. Only assign serious chores and duties to students who are mature enough, without an argumentative Ego, and those who have been with you for at least several months. Whenever a student is experiencing difficulties in his personal life or is not attending classes as much as before, that is not the right time to assign chores to him. Also make sure that what you ask of students is within the limits of something that directly or indirectly helps the school. That would be considered an acceptable duty or chore. Any specific help with your personal life is, alas, a <u>personal favour</u>. The latter you should only seldom ask of students, and when you do, such favours should only be asked of your most trusted and veteran ones. Such people you should have already educated to the point at which they understand you would have done the same for them (and you should indeed if they ever need you to).

Now that you have understood that you have an army of helpers, do not limit their aid for your goals only. Be on watch for personal problems plaguing the lives of any of your students. Many a time, they need all the help they can get. This could be with anything whatsoever. Maybe they are looking for a new job. Possibly their wife just divorced them and they need a place to stay for a while. Perhaps they require someone to help them with their studies. Or

---

[95] The usefulness and purpose of Egalitarianism are detailed in the second chapter in this book, titled '**Merit, Equality and Leadership**' (p. 26).

they may simply be new in town and would love to have someone show them around. All of these problems and countless others, your students will usually be shy of asking their fellow classmates to help them with. Here you can step in and make a difference. Attempt to politely and gently offer to have 'the school' help them out, and ask for their permission to present the problem to the other students. Then choose either a public or private way of presenting the issue, using amiable and respectful wording, and asking of others to volunteer to aid that student who needs help. Sometimes based on the severity of the issue at hand and your level of influence, you may even choose to outright make students into volunteers for a cause. For example, if a student is sick at the hospital and you know she would really appreciate company, then you go there yourself and make sure other students do the same – at least a few of them. This manner of humane behaviour and action is more important than martial arts techniques, and in the long term this is also crucial for keeping a school operating as a functional and healthy community.

Be Your Own Professional

Are you familiar with that scenario when a martial arts practitioner goes looking for solutions elsewhere, outside of his art and school? This is very common and popular. In our era, everyone seems to wish they could have a bit and a bite of everything. So you have that student who really was taught some excellent resistance-training methods by his teacher, but still feels he needs to go push more weights at the gym. The guy whose martial art is full of fantastic meditation practices, but nonetheless 'supplements' with two other 'spiritual' classes every week because, *obviously*, more is better. Or that person who is always gasping for air in class, but somehow comes to believe this is best solved by more cycling, running and swimming rather than simply practicing more of his martial arts. You know these people. Perhaps you may have even been, or are currently, one of these people.

This sort of thing happens when an insecurity exists. When someone simply cannot have enough, and is also confused about what he has and does not have.
A similar phenomenon occurs when we martial arts teachers need some professional aid. Then suddenly we can imagine ourselves to be helpless, and be tempted to call upon the expensive aid of various individuals supposedly more qualified to do the job.

Do you really need that lawyer? Accountant? [96] Secretary? Interior decorator? Website builder? Marketing advisor? Advertisement designer? Handyman? Let me tell you – I have managed just fine without a need for renting the services of all of these people! By doing so, I have saved incredible amounts of time and money. A great deal of what these professionals do you can teach yourself how to do just as well. Alternatively, use the student 'communal

---

[96] Sadly, most Americans and Brazilians do need accountants, due to their baffling and unreasonable tax codes. My condolences folks – it is easier in other countries.

inventory' – either as hired professionals or better yet, as volunteers. A school with as little as 30 students is one with at least 7-8 students who are seasoned professionals of some notable expertise. Other students may not be skilled professionals themselves, but certainly know a bunch of people with skills, possibly friends or relatives, who owe them a favour or two which can be directed into the school. This is the way to go. First observe and research objectively whether you can do without a professional, either on your own or with the support of those who are close to you. Then hire one if you cannot.

Be honest here. Time-wise, this job of teaching martial arts is not a bad deal. Assuming your sole occupation is teaching martial arts – how much do you teach? Likely 5 hours a day at most, if you are busy. Then how much time is put into your personal practice? I train at least 3-4 hours a day, all week, outside of my classes. You and I have a lot of spare time on our hands. What are you going to do with that spare time? I write books and articles, but I also invest in study.

Part of what I study is the work of those professionals I do not wish to ever have to pay for.
For example, I have a bachelor's degree in Law (and also in Government Studies), so I can write and manage my own contracts. I also have built my own websites, for my school, books and other projects. Would a professional lawyer or website builder have done a better job than I did? Possibly. But do remember: **If you want to get something done right, you have to do it yourself.**
The only exception I would take to this advice, is when one's school become a chain of establishments, or even a big organization. Then, the overbearing bureaucratic needs of management are indeed better met with professional assistance. A 'big firm' cannot be managed like a 'family shop'. But even then, it is better to draw upon the aid of long-time friends and your 'communal inventory' of students than rely on people you do not know.

In my experience with so-called 'professionals' of various fields of expertise, we martial arts teachers often encounter problems with them. The majority of experts in any field do not understand the special needs and requirements of the martial arts profession, so their aid is limited by their knowledge of what you do and how well they can understand your explanations. I have casually discussed my school with several 'marketing experts' over the years in order to learn of what they could offer, and what I heard was always the worst advice imaginable; each of them competing for 'silliest idea award'. Likewise, people such as website builders whom I spoke with, were often not at all in tune with what martial arts are about or what people are seeking in a martial arts school. A lot of these professionals are more strongly affected by movies they have seen of the martial arts, than what you explain to them.

Then there is one other type of professional businesses which you can and should do without – the publishing company. I remember when I sought to publish my first book, **Research of Martial Arts**, of having to chase around some publishing houses, practically

begging for them to talk to me. They were often very rude and condescending, and some did not even bother to reply to my letters and emails. Those who read my manuscript told me it would never sell. Eventually one publishing house, a famous name in martial arts publishing at the time, was keen on doing business. But to make it happen, they demanded I cut 30% of the content (!) and also rearrange many of the chapters.
At that point, it seemed hopeless. That publishing house was the only one who even offered me a 'deal' of sorts. You know what I told these people? That I have no intention of cutting or changing even a single word in my book based on their feedback. I politely declined their offer and self-published my book. I relied on fellow colleagues for some help with commentary, editing and spell-checking, and did most of the work on my own. With much effort and dedication, the book later became an international best-seller in its topics of interest, and my royalty earnings were much better than what I would have made working with a publishing company. That is, despite the countless professionals who told me it would never sell. There is no reason to compromise when you know for certain you have a good product, and as a martial arts teacher you definitely are more qualified to know than those who are at best martial arts hobbyists. Therefore, with book publishing too, feel free to do away with the 'professionals'. This book too is proudly self-published.

The people who actually provided me with good martial arts marketing advice, and in fact the finest advice for anything related to operating a martial arts school and teaching, were martial arts teachers themselves. Yes! Surprisingly enough, these are the best people to listen to and learn from. Thus, in short, the best professional to trust is the one with hands-on experience. Titles, degrees and diplomas are not nearly as important.

The Part-Time Psychologist

The martial arts teacher is never just *that* – a Sensei, a Shifu, a coach, an instructor, etc. As anyone who has been in this profession long enough knows, we are also forced to perform like part-time psychologists, medical doctors, language teachers, massage therapists, philosophers, marriage counselors, businessmen, authors and much more. The martial arts teacher is often one of the closest private trustees of any given student, and he may be bestowed upon the honor by such student to fulfill the demands and expert responsibilities of many such professions.

This naturally challenges us to become highly educated and skilled in countless fields of action and study. However, we should not make the glorious mistake of presenting ourselves and thinking of ourselves as true professionals in fields which are in fact beyond our expertise. As uncle Ben says: "We great power comes great responsibility". Consider this solemnly. Whatever you tell a student, he may end up taking more seriously than advice provided to him by another, perhaps more skilled and qualified professional. That can bear consequences, very serious consequences, for a person's health, life, relationships and financial situation. Be cautious with this. Whenever you feel that problems presented by a student are dragging you beyond your knowledge or intellectual capacity, be honest – tell the truth – admit when you are unsure or do not know, and do your best to send that student to the right person. Referring people to those who can change their lives for the better can be no-less important that doing the job yourself. Being a professional is also about knowing your limits, for your own sake and that of other people.

Hidden Transmission in the Martial Arts

There is a coach, and there is a teacher. A coach provides you with tools to success. A teacher passes unto you a system of thinking and doing for personal growth.

A teacher teaches, but his shadow also speaks. Have you ever heard the whisper of a teacher's shadow? It is thick, and resonates through your core with the might of an earthquake, though so elusive you may not notice.

A future You carries on a movement long ago taught, and then it strikes the unsuspecting onlooker, that your shadow is not truly yours. It fluctuates to the rhythm of another, and others that came before.

The Japanese call this Isshin Denshin 以心伝心– a heart-to-heart transmission. The Chinese call is Kǒuchuán Xīn Shòu 口傳心授 – Teachings verbally transmitted from the heart. A way shown without being described, a path drawn without being illustrated; a book of knowledge that contains not a single word.

Thus, the technique of martial teaching is Shamanic, unwieldy. Growing another's skin on top of yours. Such is the traditional method of apprenticeship.

It is often pondered why a lot may bend a knee to a master, yet few if any reach his status. Many a time, the answer is that skill is only absorbed by him who had been observant.

For how many a things can be verbally elucidated? There is a limit to what can be willfully given; and the rest, stolen property it ought to become, as had been noted the clever T.T. Liang.

Then it remains, that by being the thief of another's spirit, we can borrow a pair of eyes with a vision of a thousand things which are beyond the colour spectrum of most men.

Unbeknownst to us, our progress is also an evolution in the assimilation of the mindset, mannerisms and character of he who shares the wisdom. For an intangible presence is manifested in every moment, and our ability to contain it largely affects long-term understandings.

A tone of voice, an expression of one's face, a trait of gait or the calmness of bearing. These and others are more than mere aspects of the personality. They are seamless stitches in the fabric of martial expression. To give heed by these attributes is the making of an astute investment. To embody them, truthfully and sincerely, is to be able to accept a full transmission.

The Art in Martial Arts

There are many forms of publicly acknowledged arts in this world, such as painting, sculpting, music, theatre, poetry, etc. There are also those who claim their lifestyle or hobby to be a form of art, although it is evident that the mainstream will not deem theirs as acceptable as others.

Whether something is an art or not may be dependent on the person who is engaging in it. Professional sports are one example we can observe. These are activities where the main motivation is winning. This by itself is not an art. An athlete, however, may pursue his sport of choice in an artistic manner. Such is the case with great basketball players, whom in their symbolic movement patterns when reaching for the basket express themselves artistically in motion, also influencing the emotions of the audience. Bodybuilders can look upon their sport as a mere beauty contest, which happens to involve lifting weights as preparation. For many of them nonetheless, Bodybuilding is a lifestyle and an art-form. One might often hear or read about bodybuilders referring to their profession as "sculpting in their own flesh"; achieving total control over the development of their muscles' size and shape, they use resistance training, diet, and other methods to sculpt their inner-selves into their external appearance, and then expose their masterpieces for the world to see.

Traditional Martial Arts are a different animal. Instead of encouraging one to push-forth his Ego by curving its image externally, they celebrate the fall of that Ego, and promote the creation of an improved human being. It has been my observation that in sports, personality changes are often a by-product of training. Traits such as determination, fellowship, courage, patience and others may result from hard, prolonged training. In Traditional Martial Arts, one is not simply altered by practice – one constantly changes his life and personality, in a conscious endeavor, so he or she could become better martial artists. Changing oneself for the better is not merely an outcome, but a necessity posed by training in order to improve your skills physically – to attain more of one's inborn capacity and talent.

How does such a thing come about? Simply enough, the process is rather technical, even quite physical in the beginning. (Traditional) Martial Arts are a lifelong process where one has to constantly question himself. This starts on the physical level, but is inherently rooted in our minds. I will therefore give a glimpse as to the theoretical thinking process that may accompany a martial artist.

Nothing confronts us better with ourselves than being forced to be on our own, concentrating on a single task. Such is, for instance, the practice of Zhan Zhuang. When ordered by yourself or your teacher to stand in a fixed position for a long period of time, you initially make some effort to focus on your physical body, trying to align and engage all the technicalities that are part of the stance. Soon enough though, your mind drifts to faraway places, for it takes many years of practice to truly achieve lasting focus & concentration. As you carelessly allow yourself to contain thoughts and emotions, they immediately manifest in your physical being. You were angry at the woman who left you, which has now resulted in your breath being stuck in your chest. You find the kids that mock you on the sidewalk annoying and wish to hit them, causing your shoulders to become tense, stopping your blood from reaching the fingers and warming your palm. You are too bothered and anxious because of your tasks at work, which shifts your attention from dealing with the pain in your legs, to thinking about your boss. You recall a loved one who had passed away, causing your facial muscles to express your sadness, preventing them from relaxing.

"***Your vision will become clear only when you can look into your own heart. Who looks outside, dreams; who looks inside, awakes.***" - Carl G. Jung

All of those things which induce flaws in your posture are flaws in your own personality. Had you forgiven the woman who left you, cleared your heart and moved on, you could have breathed more easily, relaxing your chest and dropping your breath to the Dan Tian area. Were you more understanding towards the children who were mocking you when you were training at the park (with them doing what children tend to do), you could have loosened your shoulders, and allow for better blood-flow. Had you taken the difficulties in your professional life more lightly, you could have shifted your focus from your boss to your aching legs, and have enough concentration to loosen them up and avoid the pain. Finally making peace with the reality of your loved one having passed away would have expressed itself on your face, which could now be calm & tranquil, not revealing of your thoughts and intentions.

The only way to overcome your physical handicaps is therefore digging into the very essence of your psyche, and dealing with everything that is unpleasant. Only coming to terms with your true being can drive improvement on the physical front. In the martial arts a man can be naturally skilled to a great extent, but all possess the same limit to their natural capacity – the ability to deal with themselves. Given that one is healthy and capable, the main limiting factor for skill development will always remain the mind. For this reason, the sages of martial arts of old have realized this one truth ages ago – the art in martial arts is not found in physical confrontation – it is the art of cultivating oneself. Thus, real masters of the martial arts do not express *themselves* in motion, but rather their *achievement* of conquering that which they once were.

"When you see the Single Whip posture of an old Taiji master, what is inside of that movement? All of his life is inside..." – Master He Jinghan

<u>Epilogue:</u> Life and Virtue

One historical discussion turned on the question,

"What is the greatest misery?"

A Greek philosopher answered,

"An impoverished and imbecile old age".

A Hindu replied,

"A harassed mind in a diseased body".

Khosru's vizier won the dutiful acclaim of all, by saying:

"For my part, I think the extreme misery is for a man to see the end of life approaching, without having practiced virtue."

Will Durant, The Story of Civilization, The Age of Faith,
Book I: The Byzantine Zenith, Chapter VII: The Persians

Did you enjoy this book?

Then please, by all means – share word of its existence with family, friends and acquaintances.

Jonathan Bluestein has written additional best-selling titles, including:

Research of Martial Arts

An incredible body of knowledge about martial arts theory and usage, for all styles and practitioners. Considered a 'classic' in the community of traditional martial artists.

Chinese Medicine Can Heal You

Discover the true meaning of Traditional Chinese Medicine. How does it work? Can it help you become healthier? How to choose the right practitioner? These and hundreds more questions are answered in a coherent and fascinating manner.

Prosperism

A novel perspective on Capitalism, proposing a new and never before seen socio-economic theory on how it can be made better.

And more!

The Author would be happy to receive feedback, and answer any relevant questions. Seek him out.

Skill is acquired through continuous practice, sophistication
& depth (are achieved) by giving thought to it

功夫憑苦練 奧妙賴深思

Printed in Poland
by Amazon Fulfillment
Poland Sp. z o.o., Wrocław
06 September 2023

0eb1dca6-8bbd-4042-9f36-4197bf14889bR01